References for the Rest of Us!®

BESTSELLING BOOK SERIES

Are you intimidated and confused by computers? Do you find that traditional manuals are overloaded with technical details you'll never use? Do your friends and family always call you to fix simple problems on their PCs? Then the ...*For Dummies*® computer book series from IDG Books Worldwide is for you.

...*For Dummies* books are written for those frustrated computer users who know they aren't really dumb but find that PC hardware, software, and indeed the unique vocabulary of computing make them feel helpless. ...*For Dummies* books use a lighthearted approach, a down-to-earth style, and even cartoons and humorous icons to dispel computer novices' fears and build their confidence. Lighthearted but not lightweight, these books are a perfect survival guide for anyone forced to use a computer.

> "I like my copy so much I told friends; now they bought copies."
> — Irene C., Orwell, Ohio

> "Quick, concise, nontechnical, and humorous."
> — Jay A., Elburn, Illinois

> "Thanks, I needed this book. Now I can sleep at night."
> — Robin F., British Columbia, Canada

Already, millions of satisfied readers agree. They have made ...*For Dummies* books the #1 introductory level computer book series and have written asking for more. So, if you're looking for the most fun and easy way to learn about computers, look to ...*For Dummies* books to give you a helping hand.

Corel® Linux® FOR DUMMIES®

Corel® Linux® FOR DUMMIES®

by **Stephen E. Harris**
with Erwin Zijleman

Foreword by Mike Cowpland,
president and CEO, Corel Corporation

IDG Books Worldwide, Inc.
An International Data Group Company

Foster City, CA ◆ Chicago, IL ◆ Indianapolis, IN ◆ New York, NY

Corel® Linux® For Dummies®

Published by
IDG Books Worldwide, Inc.
An International Data Group Company
919 E. Hillsdale Blvd.
Suite 400
Foster City, CA 94404
www.idgbooks.com (IDG Books Worldwide Web site)
www.dummies.com (Dummies Press Web site)

Copyright © 2000 IDG Books Worldwide, Inc. All rights reserved. No part of this book, including interior design, cover design, and icons, may be reproduced or transmitted in any form, by any means (electronic, photocopying, recording, or otherwise) without the prior written permission of the publisher.

Library of Congress Catalog Card No.: 99-67171

ISBN: 0-7645-0667-6

Printed in the United States of America

10 9 8 7 6 5 4 3 2 1

1O/QR/QV/QQ/IN

Distributed in the United States by IDG Books Worldwide, Inc.

Distributed by CDG Books Canada Inc. for Canada; by Transworld Publishers Limited in the United Kingdom; by IDG Norge Books for Norway; by IDG Sweden Books for Sweden; by IDG Books Australia Publishing Corporation Pty. Ltd. for Australia and New Zealand; by TransQuest Publishers Pte Ltd. for Singapore, Malaysia, Thailand, Indonesia, and Hong Kong; by Gotop Information Inc. for Taiwan; by ICG Muse, Inc. for Japan; by Intersoft for South Africa; by Eyrolles for France; by International Thomson Publishing for Germany, Austria and Switzerland; by Distribuidora Cuspide for Argentina; by LR International for Brazil; by Galileo Libros for Chile; by Ediciones ZETA S.C.R. Ltda. for Peru; by WS Computer Publishing Corporation, Inc., for the Philippines; by Contemporanea de Ediciones for Venezuela; by Express Computer Distributors for the Caribbean and West Indies; by Micronesia Media Distributor, Inc. for Micronesia; by Chips Computadoras S.A. de C.V. for Mexico; by Editorial Norma de Panama S.A. for Panama; by American Bookshops for Finland.

For general information on IDG Books Worldwide's books in the U.S., please call our Consumer Customer Service department at 800-762-2974. For reseller information, including discounts and premium sales, please call our Reseller Customer Service department at 800-434-3422.

For information on where to purchase IDG Books Worldwide's books outside the U.S., please contact our International Sales department at 317-596-5530 or fax 317-572-4002.

For consumer information on foreign language translations, please contact our Customer Service department at 1-800-434-3422, fax 317-572-4002, or e-mail rights@idgbooks.com.

For information on licensing foreign or domestic rights, please phone +1-650-653-7098.

For sales inquiries and special prices for bulk quantities, please contact our Order Services department at 800-434-3422 or write to the address above.

For information on using IDG Books Worldwide's books in the classroom or for ordering examination copies, please contact our Educational Sales department at 800-434-2086 or fax 317-572-4005.

For press review copies, author interviews, or other publicity information, please contact our Public Relations department at 650-653-7000 or fax 650-653-7500.

For authorization to photocopy items for corporate, personal, or educational use, please contact Copyright Clearance Center, 222 Rosewood Drive, Danvers, MA 01923, or fax 978-750-4470.

LIMIT OF LIABILITY/DISCLAIMER OF WARRANTY: THE PUBLISHER AND AUTHOR HAVE USED THEIR BEST EFFORTS IN PREPARING THIS BOOK. THE PUBLISHER AND AUTHOR MAKE NO REPRESENTATIONS OR WARRANTIES WITH RESPECT TO THE ACCURACY OR COMPLETENESS OF THE CONTENTS OF THIS BOOK AND SPECIFICALLY DISCLAIM ANY IMPLIED WARRANTIES OF MERCHANTABILITY OR FITNESS FOR A PARTICULAR PURPOSE. THERE ARE NO WARRANTIES WHICH EXTEND BEYOND THE DESCRIPTIONS CONTAINED IN THIS PARAGRAPH. NO WARRANTY MAY BE CREATED OR EXTENDED BY SALES REPRESENTATIVES OR WRITTEN SALES MATERIALS. THE ACCURACY AND COMPLETENESS OF THE INFORMATION PROVIDED HEREIN AND THE OPINIONS STATED HEREIN ARE NOT GUARANTEED OR WARRANTED TO PRODUCE ANY PARTICULAR RESULTS, AND THE ADVICE AND STRATEGIES CONTAINED HEREIN MAY NOT BE SUITABLE FOR EVERY INDIVIDUAL. NEITHER THE PUBLISHER NOR AUTHOR SHALL BE LIABLE FOR ANY LOSS OF PROFIT OR ANY OTHER COMMERCIAL DAMAGES, INCLUDING BUT NOT LIMITED TO SPECIAL, INCIDENTAL, CONSEQUENTIAL, OR OTHER DAMAGES. FULFILLMENT OF EACH COUPON OFFER IS THE RESPONSIBILITY OF THE OFFEROR.

Trademarks: Corel is a registered trademark of Corel Corporation. Linux is a registered trademark of Linus Torvalds in the United States and other Countries. For Dummies, Dummies Man, A Reference for the Rest of Us!, The Dummies Way, Dummies Daily, and related trade dress are registered trademarks or trademarks of IDG Books Worldwide, Inc. in the United States and other countries, and may not be used without written permission. All other trademarks are the property of their respective owners. IDG Books Worldwide is not associated with any product or vendor mentioned in this book.

 is a registered trademark under exclusive license to IDG Books Worldwide, Inc. from International Data Group, Inc.

About the Authors

Stephen E. Harris is the founder and president of QwkScreen, a software development and consulting firm dedicated to making the computer screen a friendlier place. Author of the best-selling *WordPerfect for Linux* and *WordPerfect Office 2000* Bibles, Steve's a proud member of the Corel Beta Squad. He lives in the woods of western Massachusetts with his wife, Githa, three cats (Tiger, Becky and Chester), bears, deer, turkeys, and other assorted wildlife. You'll find Steve, plus WordPerfect solutions and links, at www.qwkscreen.com.

Erwin Zijleman started out as a development sociologist, specializing in urban sociology and education in third-world countries, particularly Southeast Asia. He now works as a software scientist, specializing in PC office applications. Erwin is an avid beta tester of Corel products, and has co-authored other WordPerfect titles with Steve. He lives near Amsterdam, in the historic center of Leiden. He enjoys the companionship of Anja as well as his cat, Bagu.

ABOUT IDG BOOKS WORLDWIDE

Welcome to the world of IDG Books Worldwide.

IDG Books Worldwide, Inc., is a subsidiary of International Data Group, the world's largest publisher of computer-related information and the leading global provider of information services on information technology. IDG was founded more than 30 years ago by Patrick J. McGovern and now employs more than 9,000 people worldwide. IDG publishes more than 290 computer publications in over 75 countries. More than 90 million people read one or more IDG publications each month.

Launched in 1990, IDG Books Worldwide is today the #1 publisher of best-selling computer books in the United States. We are proud to have received eight awards from the Computer Press Association in recognition of editorial excellence and three from Computer Currents' First Annual Readers' Choice Awards. Our best-selling ...*For Dummies*® series has more than 50 million copies in print with translations in 31 languages. IDG Books Worldwide, through a joint venture with IDG's Hi-Tech Beijing, became the first U.S. publisher to publish a computer book in the People's Republic of China. In record time, IDG Books Worldwide has become the first choice for millions of readers around the world who want to learn how to better manage their businesses.

Our mission is simple: Every one of our books is designed to bring extra value and skill-building instructions to the reader. Our books are written by experts who understand and care about our readers. The knowledge base of our editorial staff comes from years of experience in publishing, education, and journalism — experience we use to produce books to carry us into the new millennium. In short, we care about books, so we attract the best people. We devote special attention to details such as audience, interior design, use of icons, and illustrations. And because we use an efficient process of authoring, editing, and desktop publishing our books electronically, we can spend more time ensuring superior content and less time on the technicalities of making books.

You can count on our commitment to deliver high-quality books at competitive prices on topics you want to read about. At IDG Books Worldwide, we continue in the IDG tradition of delivering quality for more than 30 years. You'll find no better book on a subject than one from IDG Books Worldwide.

John Kilcullen
Chairman and CEO
IDG Books Worldwide, Inc.

Eighth Annual
Computer Press
Awards ≥1992

Ninth Annual
Computer Press
Awards ≥1993

Tenth Annual
Computer Press
Awards ≥1994

Eleventh Annual
Computer Press
Awards ≥1995

IDG is the world's leading IT media, research and exposition company. Founded in 1964, IDG had 1997 revenues of $2.05 billion and has more than 9,000 employees worldwide. IDG offers the widest range of media options that reach IT buyers in 75 countries representing 95% of worldwide IT spending. IDG's diverse product and services portfolio spans six key areas including print publishing, online publishing, expositions and conferences, market research, education and training, and global marketing services. More than 90 million people read one or more of IDG's 290 magazines and newspapers, including IDG's leading global brands — Computerworld, PC World, Network World, Macworld and the Channel World family of publications. IDG Books Worldwide is one of the fastest-growing computer book publishers in the world, with more than 700 titles in 36 languages. The "...For Dummies®" series alone has more than 50 million copies in print. IDG offers online users the largest network of technology-specific Web sites around the world through IDG.net (http://www.idg.net), which comprises more than 225 targeted Web sites in 55 countries worldwide. International Data Corporation (IDC) is the world's largest provider of information technology data, analysis and consulting, with research centers in over 41 countries and more than 400 research analysts worldwide. IDG World Expo is a leading producer of more than 168 globally branded conferences and expositions in 35 countries including E3 (Electronic Entertainment Expo), Macworld Expo, ComNet, Windows World Expo, ICE (Internet Commerce Expo), Agenda, DEMO, and Spotlight. IDG's training subsidiary, ExecuTrain, is the world's largest computer training company, with more than 230 locations worldwide and 785 training courses. IDG Marketing Services helps industry-leading IT companies build international brand recognition by developing global integrated marketing programs via IDG's print, online and exposition products worldwide. Further information about the company can be found at www.idg.com. 1/26/00

Dedication

To Mike Cowpland, for seeing further down the road.

Author's Acknowledgments

Although any shortcomings are my own, this massive work is necessarily a team product involving publishers, editors, designers, proofreaders, indexers, and typesetters, as well as the people in promotion and sales. Will the dedicated pros at IDG Books Worldwide please stand up, so that the audience can see you? Now shine the spotlight on Susan "the picky" Pink for the fabulous job she did in editing the book. What a pro! She can crack the whip, but you never feel the lash.

Special applause for David Mayhew, the champion of this project, and to Andy Cummings, captain of the acquisitions ship.

This project could never be a success without the generous and attentive support from many folks at Corel. Chip Maxwell, please come up to the stage and take a bow for your tireless support of authors and publishers (prolonged applause). A special hand for Phil C. Rackus and Jason Grenier, for lending us your technical expertise. Then there's Eric Forler, Nicholas Blommesteijn, Jon Riis, Ming Poon . . . the list goes on and on.

As always, I must thank my attorney/agent Joel L. Hecker, Esq., for his wise counsel and support. To Jan Westerman and René Nieuwenhuizen, thanks for your help on the networking intricacies. A very special acknowledgment to Githa (my wife), for reading drafts and enduring my crazy schedule.

To my co-author, Erwin Zijleman, my gratitude knows no bounds. I couldn't imaging doing the book without his intelligence, humor, and constant support. Please note that although the book is written in the first person, the *I* is a shared one.

Special thanks to Augrin Software ApS (www.augrin.com), for making great screen shot captures possible with their EasyCopy/X and EasyConvert software.

— Stephen E. Harris

Publisher's Acknowledgments

We're proud of this book; please register your comments through our IDG Books Worldwide Online Registration Form located at http://my2cents.dummies.com.

Some of the people who helped bring this book to market include the following:

Acquisitions, Editorial, and Media Development

Project Editor: Susan Pink

Acquisitions Editor: David Mayhew

Proof Editors: Teresa Artman, Dwight Ramsey

Technical Editors: Jason Grenier, Philip Rackus

Media Development Specialist: Megan Decraene

Permissions Editor: Carmen Krikorian

Senior Editor, Freelance: Constance Carlisle

Media Development Manager: Heather Heath Dismore

Editorial Assistant: Candace Nicholson

Production

Project Coordinators: Valery Bourke, E. Shawn Aylsworth

Layout and Graphics: Amy Adrian, Karl Brandt, Brian Drumm, Kristine Leonardo, Barry Offringa, Tracy K. Oliver, Mary Jo Richards, Brent Savage, Jacque Schneider, Brian Torwelle, Erin Zeltner

Proofreader: Corey Bowen, John Greenough, Marianne Santy, York Production Services, Inc.,

Indexer: York Production Services, Inc.

Special Help: Beth Parlon

General and Administrative

IDG Books Worldwide, Inc.: John Kilcullen, CEO

IDG Books Technology Publishing Group: Richard Swadley, Senior Vice President and Publisher; Walter R. Bruce III, Vice President and Publisher; Joseph Wikert, Vice President and Publisher; Mary Bednarek, Vice President and Director, Product Development; Andy Cummings, Publishing Director, General User Group; Mary C. Corder, Editorial Director; Barry Pruett, Publishing Director

IDG Books Consumer Publishing Group: Roland Elgey, Senior Vice President and Publisher; Kathleen A. Welton, Vice President and Publisher; Kevin Thornton, Acquisitions Manager; Kristin A. Cocks, Editorial Director

IDG Books Internet Publishing Group: Brenda McLaughlin, Senior Vice President and Publisher; Sofia Marchant, Online Marketing Manager

IDG Books Production for Branded Press: Debbie Stailey, Director of Production; Cindy L. Phipps, Manager of Project Coordination, Production Proofreading, and Indexing; Tony Augsburger, Manager of Prepress, Reprints, and Systems; Laura Carpenter, Production Control Manager; Shelley Lea, Supervisor of Graphics and Design; Debbie J. Gates, Production Systems Specialist; Robert Springer, Supervisor of Proofreading; Kathie Schutte, Production Supervisor

Packaging and Book Design: Patty Page, Manager, Promotions Marketing

◆

The publisher would like to give special thanks to Patrick J. McGovern, without whom this book would not have been possible.

◆

Contents at a Glance

Foreword ....*xxv*

Introduction *1*

Part I: Leaping to Linux *7*
Chapter 1: I Can't Believe It's Really Better! 9
Chapter 2: Up, Up, and Away! Installing Corel Linux 17
Chapter 3: Starting Up, Doing Things, and Shutting Down 35
Chapter 4: Post-Install Tweaking 45

Part II: Taking the Grand Tour *71*
Chapter 5: Dancin' on the Desktop 73
Chapter 6: Meet the Stars! 85
Chapter 7: Graphical Gizmos 97
Chapter 8: Window Wonders 111

Part III: Linux the Way You Want It *121*
Chapter 9: Desktop Dynamics 123
Chapter 10: Decorating Your Desktop 153

Part IV: Doin' Your Own Thing *171*
Chapter 11: Managing Your Files 173
Chapter 12: Finding Stuff and Opening Archives 195
Chapter 13: Putting In a Good Word 211
Chapter 14: Playing with Pictures and Sounds 223
Chapter 15: Cruising in Cyberspace 241
Chapter 16: You've Got Mail! 255
Chapter 17: Upgrade Madness 273

Part V: The Part of Tens *281*
Chapter 18: Ten Cool Desktop Tricks 283
Chapter 19: Ten Things I Circled in the Book 291
Chapter 20: Ten Places to Get Free Help 301
Chapter 21: Ten Places to Get Free Stuff 309

Part VI: Appendixes 315
Appendix A: Commands to the Rescue! 317
Appendix B: Glossary 329
Appendix C: About the CD 339

Index 347

IDG Books Worldwide End-User License Agreement......372

Installation Instructions..379

Book Registration Information.......................Back of Book

Cartoons at a Glance

By Rich Tennant

page 315

page 7

page 121

page 71

page 171

page 281

Fax: 978-546-7747
E-mail: richtennant@the5thwave.com
World Wide Web: www.the5thwave.com

Table of Contents

Foreword .... *xxv*

Introduction *1*
    About This Book 1
    Conventions Used in This Book 1
    What You're Not to Read 2
    Foolish Assumptions 2
    How This Book Is Organized 3
        Part I: Leaping to Linux 3
        Part II: Taking the Grand Tour 3
        Part III: Linux the Way You Want It 4
        Part IV: Doin' Your Own Thing 4
        Part V: The Part of Tens 4
        Part VI: Appendixes 4
    Icons Used in This Book 5
    Where to Go from Here 5

Part I: Leaping to Linux *7*

Chapter 1: I Can't Believe It's Really Better! 9
    All Right, What Is Linux? 9
        Born free 11
        No more software criminals 11
    Why Should I Use Linux? 12
    What's So Special about Corel Linux? 12
        Simple to use 12
        Smoother than Windows 12
        The Debian advantage 13
        Updates don't get easier than this! 13
    The Four Flavors of Corel Linux 13
    Corel Linux Is Less Powerful, Right? 15
    Can I Still Use Windows? 15
    Preparing for Takeoff 16

Chapter 2: Up, Up, and Away! Installing Corel Linux 17
    On Your Mark . . . (Considering Your Needs and Options) 17
        The essentials 18
        Hardware reality check 18
        Getting hardware help 19
        Don't engage in unprotected installs 19

Corel Linux For Dummies

        Can I remove Corel Linux after it's installed? 20
        What's automatic and what ain't? 20
    What Should I Install? 21
    Where Should I Put It? 21
        When free space isn't free 23
        Waddaya mean I can dual boot? 23
        Peace, brother OS! (Linux and Windows under one roof) 24
    Get Set . . . (Making Your Selections) 24
        Breaking the sacred seal 25
        Step 1: Booting the installation CD 25
        Step 2: Agree to the onerous terms 27
        Step 3: Who are you? 27
        Step 4: What do you want to install? 27
        Step 5: Where do you want to put it? 28
        Step 6: Reviewing your selections 30
    Go! 31
        Step 7: Off you go! 31
        Step 8: Entering the promised land 31
    Welcome to Corel Linux! 33

Chapter 3: Starting Up, Doing Things, and Shutting Down 35

    Starting Up and Logging In 35
    Starting Windows or Another OS 37
    Starting Corel Linux in a DOS/Windows Partition 37
    Launching WordPerfect and Other Programs 38
    Managing System and User Tasks 39
    Am I Running Out of Disk Space? 40
    My Kingdom for a Command Prompt! 41
    Logging Out of the Desktop and Shutting Down 42

Chapter 4: Post-Install Tweaking 45

    Welcome to Mission Control 45
    Using Other Languages in Corel Linux 46
        Changing your preferred language 47
        Using international keyboards 48
    Configuring Your Keyboard and Mouse 49
    Setting the Date and Time 50
    Setting Up Printers 51
    Connecting to the Internet 54
        Essential dial-up hardware 54
        Another essential: Your ISP 55
        Configuring your dial-up connection 56
        Connecting and disconnecting 60
    Hooking into a Local Network 60
        Two types of local network hookups 61
        Getting hooked up 61

Is Anyone Missing? 66
Changing Your Boot Defaults 68
Installing Acrobat Reader and Netscape Communicator 70

Part II: Taking the Grand Tour 71

Chapter 5: Dancin' on the Desktop 73

Wow! This Is Linux? 73
Panel Discussion 74
Launching Programs 75
Switching between Programs 76
Did Someone Say "Multiple Desktops"? 77
    Sticky windows 78
    Desktop Manager tricks 79
Your Keys to Success 79
    Global (desktop) keyboard shortcuts 81
    Standard (program) keyboard shortcuts 82
Getting Help 83

Chapter 6: Meet the Stars! 85

Stars on Stage 86
Costars on the Main Menu 88
Supporting Cast on the Submenus 89
Installed Extras Not on Your Menus 91
Good Old Command-Line Extras 94
Program Wannabes 95

Chapter 7: Graphical Gizmos 97

Jumping into Windows 97
    Opening and closing times 98
    A quick look in the title bar 99
    Big things from little buttons 99
    Dropping in at the menu bar 100
    Getting fast food from the toolbar 101
    Going for a scroll (bar) 101
    Grabbing the latest gossip at the status bar 102
The Incredible Right-Click 102
Conducting a Dialog 103
Working with Selected Stuff 107
    Selecting text and graphics 107
    Moving and copying selections 108
Deleting Information and Getting It Back 109

Chapter 8: Window Wonders 111
Window Diving 111
    Moving a window to the top of the pile 112
    Pushing the panel button 112
    Keyboard to the rescue 113
Cleaning Up the Place 113
    Close the window! 114
    Moving windows around 114
    Roll up the window 115
    Iconify, iconify! 115
    Making the window BIGGER (Or smaller) 116
    Going for the max 117
    Arranging and uncluttering windows 117
    Organizing the mess into multiple desktops 119

Part III: Linux the Way You Want It 121

Chapter 9: Desktop Dynamics 123
It's Your Desktop! 123
    Keeping your desktop from session to session 124
    Putting nicknames on your desktop 124
    Removing and editing nicknames 130
    Putting links on your desktop 130
    Customizing your menus 131
    Adding buttons to the panel (not) 137
It's Your Keyboard, Too! 137
    Creating a custom keyboard scheme 138
    Switching keyboard schemes 139
    Deleting a custom keyboard scheme 140
Fine-Tuning Desktop Operations 140
    Changing the location and size of the panel and taskbar 140
    Autohiding the panel 142
    Fine-tuning your menu display 143
    How many desktops did you say? 145
    Renaming your desktops 145
Customizing Window Operations 146
    Setting keyboard window controls 146
    Changing how your mouse behaves around windows 147
    Setting your window button display 150
    Making order out of window chaos 150

Chapter 10: Decorating Your Desktop 153
Customizing Your Desktop Backgrounds 154
    Painting your backgrounds 154
    Wallpapering your backgrounds 156

Table of Contents

A Few More Background Options 157
Changing Your Window Colors 158
Changing Your Screen Fonts 160
Customizing Your Desktop Icon Display 161
Putting on the Style 162
Throwing a Theme Party 163
    Satisfying your theme hunger 165
    Adding and removing themes 166
    Creating your own themes 166
Making a Joyful Noise 167
Putting on the Pixels 168

Part IV: Doin' Your Own Thing 171

Chapter 11: Managing Your Files 173

What Kinds of Files Are We Talking About? 173
Going Home 174
What's All This Other Stuff in the File Manager? 175
Poking around Your Folders 176
    The virtue of virtual neatness 176
    Field guide to folder trees 176
    Revealing the tree 176
    Climbing the branches 178
Checking Out Your Folders and Files 179
    I didn't want to see them anyway! (Granting permissions) 181
    Sorting your folder listing 184
    Retracing your steps 184
    Customizing your File Manager view 185
Working with Files and Folders 187
    Naming files and folders 188
    Creating folders 188
    Renaming a folder or a file 188
    Launching an application or viewing a file 189
    Selecting files and folders 190
    Moving files and folders to another folder 191
    Copying files and folders to another folder 191
    Moving and copying with drag and drop 192
    Dumping stuff in the trash 192
    Fishing stuff out of the trash 193
    Emptying the trash can 193
    Deleting files and folders 194

Chapter 12: Finding Stuff and Opening Archives 195

Finding Files and Folders 195
    Doing a basic search 196
    Stopping a search in its tracks 197
    Clearing your search results 198

Corel Linux For Dummies

What do I do with the stuff I found? 198
Sophisticated searching 199
Finding a Computer on Your Network 200
Getting into Files on a Network (Mounting a Network Share) 202
Disconnecting a Network Share 204
Creating and Managing File Archives 205
Creating an archive 206
Extracting an archive 208
Editing and viewing an archive 209
Setting Archive Administrator options 210

Chapter 13: Putting In a Good Word 211

The Premier Word Processor 211
Your Handy Little Text Editor 212
The programmer's delight 213
Creating a text file 213
Setting Word Wrap and Editing Options 214
Setting Text Selection Options 215
Jotting Down Notable Ideas 216
Once it starts, it never stops 216
Creating a note 217
Deleting a note 217
Renaming a note 218
Mouse dragging operations 218
Cutting, copying, and pasting text 218
Inserting the date or a calendar 218
Alarming notes! 218
Changing the appearance of notes 219
Printing a note 221
E-mailing a note 221
Exiting the Note utility 221

Chapter 14: Playing with Pictures and Sounds 223

GIMPing with Graphics 223
What GIMP can do 224
Launching GIMP 226
Creating an image 226
Toolbox tricks 228
Using the selection tools 229
Selecting foreground and background colors 229
Taking an art course 230
Working with PostScript and PDF Files 231
Opening and viewing a PostScript file 232
Printing a PostScript file 233
Viewing and printing a PDF file 234
Using Adobe Acrobat Reader 235

Table of Contents

All That Jazz 235
    The Internet connection 235
    Playing a CD 235
Using Sound Mixer 237
    Selecting a particular track 237
    Changing the time display 238
    Getting the sordid details about your favorite recording artist ...238

Chapter 15: Cruising in Cyberspace 241

Cruising in Cyberspace 242
Up, Up, and Away! Launching Netscape 243
    Going from link to link 245
    Typing an Internet address 245
    Selecting a recently typed address 245
    Going back and forth 246
    Stopping and reloading pages 246
I Know It's out There Somewhere! 246
    Searching the current page 247
    Bookmarking your favorite places 247
    Adding a bookmark 248
Checking Out Corel's Online Services 249
Telling Your Browser Where to Start and How Much to Remember 251
Getting Your Advanced Navigator's License 252
Taking File Manager for a Cyber-Ride 252
Transferring Files from a Remote Site 254

Chapter 16: You've Got Mail! 255

E-Mail Facilities in Corel Linux 256
Putting up Your Mailbox 256
How Your Personal Mail Is Organized 260
Picking up Your E-Mail 260
    Printing and saving messages 261
    Viewing e-mail links and attachments 261
    Picking up new messages 261
Configuring Your Messenger Display 261
Addressing Your Needs 262
Creating and Sending E-Mail 263
    Sending messages later 265
    Drafting a message 265
    Replying to a message 265
    Forwarding a message 266
    Selecting multiple messages 266
    Deleting and organizing messages 266
Participating in Newsgroup Discussions 267
    Subscribing to newsgroups 267
    Putting in your two cents 269
    Starting a new thread 270
    Marking threads as read 271
    Searching for messages on a vital topic 271

Corel Linux For Dummies

Chapter 17: Upgrade Madness 273
Updating (Or Adding) with a Smile 273
Installing Debian Packages from Your Hard Drive 278
Getting Rid of Stuff You Don't Use 279

Part V: The Part of Tens 281

Chapter 18: Ten Cool Desktop Tricks 283
Autohiding Your Panel and Taskbar 283
Moving a Window to the Top of the Pile 284
Using Multiple Desktops 285
Using Sticky Windows 286
Dancing around with the Desktop Manager 286
Iconifying Windows 287
Going for the Max 287
Doing the Incredible Right-Click 287
Changing Your Color Scheme 288
Adopting a New Theme 289

Chapter 19: Ten Things I Circled in the Book 291
Logging In as a Regular User 291
Changing Your Boot Order 292
Creating Program Nicknames 292
Adding Programs to Your Menus 293
Using the Find-the-Window Keyboard Trick 294
Sounding Off 295
Putting on the Pixels 296
Customizing Your File Manager View 297
Moving Files with Drag and Drop 298
Fishing Stuff out of the Trash 298

Chapter 20: Ten Places to Get Free Help 301
Subscribe to Support Newsgroups 302
Start from the Corel Community Web Site 302
Search Corel's Knowledge Base 303
Join Your Local Linux User Group 303
Find KDE Support and Documentation 303
Get Help at Linux Online 303
Look through the Linux Documentation Project 304
Connect with the Debian Support Site 306
Join Other Linux Newsgroups 306
Visit IDG's LinuxWorld 306
Browse Online and Print Magazines 306

Chapter 21: Ten Places to Get Free Stuff ... 309
Getting Free System Updates ... 309
Satisfying Your Theme Hunger ... 309
Getting Free Updates to Corel's Apps ... 310
Setting Up a Hard Drive on the Web ... 310
Subscribing to Free E-Mail ... 312
Getting Fresh Apps at Freshmeat ... 312
Finding Everything Cool at Tucows Linux ... 312
Looking around at Linux Online ... 312
Cruising CNET for Corel Linux and More ... 314
Installing Corel Linux from This Book's CD ... 314

Part VI: Appendixes ... 315

Appendix A: Commands to the Rescue! ... 317
Command Anatomy 101 ... 317
Essential Linux Commands ... 318
Revealing a Command's Secret Powers ... 321
Rescue Missions ... 322
    Where did my letters go? ... 322
    Moving some system files ... 323
Editing Configuration Files ... 324

Appendix B: Glossary ... 329

Appendix C: About the CD ... 339

Index ... 347

IDG Books Worldwide End-User License Agreement ... 372

Installation Instructions ... 379

Book Registration Information ... Back of Book

Foreword

The arrival of *Corel Linux For Dummies* is a harbinger of Linux's spring. The success of Linux is inevitable because of the gigantic, global team effort behind it. We at Corel are especially proud to deliver a desktop version of the Linux OS for the millions of potential users addressed by Steve Harris's book.

Corel Linux received a rave reception, and it's selling like hotcakes in the retail channels. Corel Linux was named CNET's "Editor's Choice" as the best of seven major Linux distributions reviewed. And according to TUCOWS.com Inc., the Internet's leading distributor of digital content, Corel attained the highest percentage of downloads in December, 1999, at 37 percent, almost double the percentage of the nearest contender.

The publication of *Corel Linux For Dummies* can only add to this momentum. Here, you'll find clear, step-by-step instructions for installing, configuring, and updating Corel Linux. Readers of *Corel Linux For Dummies* will find hundreds of tips and tricks on everything from customizing your desktop to managing your files and cruising the Internet.

"The Part of Tens" highlights some great Corel Linux tricks and shows you where to get all kinds of stuff for free. Best of all is the "Ten Places to Get Free Help" chapter, which brings home the point that Corel Linux is not just a bunch of program code but an open community of support as well.

It's amazing when you think of it — you get the Corel Linux OS, Netscape Communicator, Adobe Acrobat Reader, and a collection of themes all for the price of this great *For Dummies* title. Don't you love Linux! Corel is thrilled to be such a major player in Linux, and I'm delighted that Steve and Erwin are part of our team.

Enjoy the freedom!

> Mike Cowpland, president and CEO
> Corel Corporation

Introduction

Welcome to *Corel Linux For Dummies*! I hope it's half as much fun to read as it was to write! It's not every day that a *...For Dummies* book falls into an author's lap, and to do a *...For Dummies* book on Corel Linux, well, that's just the cinnamon and sugar on the donut. Yup, this is history in the making, my friend. Let's have a moment of silence to bear witness to this awesome event.

About This Book

Have no fear, dear reader — this is a Linux book for you and me. *Corel Linux For Dummies* is not a mind-numbing, post-graduate course in disguise, with all those weird hieroglyphics that only a computer geek can love. Corel Linux is easy to use, and this book makes it even easier.

Note to nerds: Don't despair, the command line's still there, and Corel Linux is pure Debian — the most powerful Linux yet!

I figured IDG Books would charge at least 50 bucks for *Corel Linux For Dummies*, but they said, "No, $24.99 is our price point — we make it up on volume." What a steal! Look what you get:

- A special *Corel Linux For Dummies CD* that includes the download edition of Corel Linux, plus the full Netscape Communicator suite, Adobe Acrobat Reader, and a hand-picked selection of spectacular desktop themes.
- Clear, concise descriptions and step-by-step instructions. Lots of helpful pictures too.

Conventions Used in This Book

I follow standard shorthand when asking you to do something. Here's all you need to know:

- Key1+Key2 (such as Ctrl+V) means that you press and hold the first key, press the second key, and then release both keys.
- Command 1➪Command 2 and so on (for example, Tools➪QuickCorrect➪SmartQuotes) means to click the items in succession.

- Text you type is in **bold**.
- New terms appear in *italic*.
- Commands appear like this: `mount -t msdos /dev/fd0 /mnt/floppy`. Luckily, you won't see stuff like this often.

You need a mouse or other pointing device to get around a graphical desktop. The standard mouse actions are

Action	What You Do
Point	Move the mouse to place the pointer on a screen item.
Click	Press and release the left mouse button once.
Double-click	Quickly press and release the left mouse button twice.
Right-click	Press and release the right mouse button. In many cases, a shortcut menu of context-sensitive choices appears.
Drag	Point to what you want to drag, press and hold the left mouse button, move the mouse, and then release the button. You can also drag across text to select it.

A *click* becomes a *tap* if you're using a pen device; *left* becomes *right,* and vice versa, if you're using the left-handed mouse setup.

What You're Not to Read

Because Corel Linux is so easy to set up and use, you don't need a machete to slash through a jungle of instructions on your way to the fun stuff. And after you're set up, this book is strictly nonsequential. Where your busy brain hops, the page can flop.

Foolish Assumptions

Authors have a lot of artistic freedom when writing a ...*For Dummies* book, but this section is mandatory, as in "you must make some foolish assumptions." Makes me think of those tired technical support tall tales that endlessly circulate the Internet, such as

- The woman who thinks the mouse is a foot pedal (gender for illustration purposes only).
- The man who tries to fax a letter by holding it up to the monitor.

          Introduction   3

- The man or woman who calls to say that his or her computer isn't responding, and when asked to read the serial number says, "Wait a minute while I get a flashlight, the power is out."

I will assume that you are none of the above, but that you do have one or both of the following purposes in mind:

- You want a clear, friendly guide to Corel Linux.
- You want to install Corel Linux on your computer, using the CD that's in the back of the book.

In either or both cases, you've come to the right place!

How This Book Is Organized

Half the battle of writing a computer book is getting it organized. The great thing about Corel Linux is that it doesn't take three-quarters of the book to install the darned thing. In this section, you get a bird's-eye view of *Corel Linux For Dummies*.

Part I: Leaping to Linux

After an inspiring sales pitch for Corel Linux, you'll be fired up and raring to go! In Part I, you check out your hardware, back up any existing data, and then break the sacred seal at the back of the book. You stick the CD in your computer, and the rest is easy, thanks to Corel's super-cool Install Express (and this super-cool book). After a quick look around, you can set up the rest of your stuff, such as your printer and your Internet connection or network access. (Even if someone already installed Corel Linux for you, this part is a painless and interesting read.)

Part II: Taking the Grand Tour

Corel Linux is sure to be as exciting as your first kiss, bungee jumping, hang-gliding, or maybe the first rainbow you saw as a child. Even if you're a veteran Linux user, you'll be thrilled by what you see as you start up Corel Linux and explore the desktop. After the grand tour in Part II, you can wow your Windows friends with some tricks they won't believe!

Part III: Linux the Way You Want It

Let's say you just moved into a beautifully furnished house. How can you call it home until you move the furniture around, haul in boxes of books, hang pictures on the wall, put dirty dishes in the sink, throw your clothes on the floor, and install a cat or a dog? Same in Part III with the Corel Linux desktop.

Part IV: Doin' Your Own Thing

Like the automobile, the beer can, and the telephone, computers change the way we live, work, and communicate. In Part IV, you see how the Corel File Manager makes organizing your stuff a breeze. But "Where did I put it?" you ask. Well, tracking stuff down is easy too. Want to get in touch? Here you get to link, browse, e-mail, and discuss. You see how to lay down some words with the text editor and sticky notes. Looking for the latest and greatest? Thanks to Corel Update it couldn't be easier!

Part V: The Part of Tens

In the finest *...For Dummies* tradition, I've put together lists of the handiest information imaginable (with a little help from my friends). You'll find them all here — ten cool desktop tricks, ten neat things to do, ten places to go for help, and ten place to get all kinds of free gifts. Come and get it!

Part VI: Appendixes

I know Corel Linux is a graphical environment, but sometimes Linux commands can come in handy too. They're here in Part VI in an appendix when you want to use them. Computer jargon driving you bonkers? Check out the compact glossary terms, and then drop a couple at the next staff meeting or party. Last, but hardly least, all the software talked about in this book is on your *Corel Linux For Dummies* CD. How's that for an unbeatable bargain! To find out more about the CD, check out Appendix C.

Icons Used in This Book

Here's what to make of the various icons you'll encounter, just in case they aren't obvious.

A shortcut or neat idea I'm especially proud of.

Important information that qualifies this page for a sticky note, to make it easy to find. If you borrowed this book from a friend, you'll have to transfer this information to sticky notes on your desktop (see Chapter 13).

Cool stuff you'll find on the Web.

Mind-numbing stuff to feed the nerds, although some of this is interesting.

Warns you when you can lose data or damage your setup if you aren't careful (heaven forbid!). It might also tell you what to do if things get messed up.

Corel Linux and other valuable stuff on your *Corel Linux For Dummies* CD. Lucky you!

Where to Go from Here

You get the last word! I've never met bug-free software or a bug-free computer book. Any comments, suggestions, criticisms, corrections, or requests will be gratefully received. Please e-mail Steve at `steveh@wkscreen.com` or Erwin at `E.L.M.Zijleman@cpb.nl`.

Part I
Leaping to Linux

The 5th Wave — By Rich Tennant

"It was at this point in time that there appeared to be some sort of mass insanity."

In this part . . .

Some are born great, some achieve greatness, and some show up with the right stuff at the right time.

Install Corel Linux from your *Corel Linux For Dummies* CD, tweak a few settings, and make your own bit of computing history.

Chapter 1
I Can't Believe It's Really Better!

In This Chapter
- Finding out how to pronounce *Linux*
- Discovering why Linux in not just another OS
- Revealing what's special about Corel Linux
- Savoring the four flavors of Corel Linux
- Exposing the power of Corel Linux
- Getting the answer to "Can I still use Windows?"
- Preparing yourself to install Corel Linux

*T*he first thing you'll want to know about Linux is how the heck to pronounce it. Okay, stretch your mouth back and repeat after me, "lee-nucks, lee-nucks, lee-nucks!"

Now that the hard part's over, we can get on with the rest of the book.

All Right, What Is Linux?

Just what is Linux and where does it come from? Linux is the brainchild of Linus Torvalds, who decided to write a compact version of the powerful UNIX operating system while he was a student at the University of Helsinki in Finland.

What's an *operating system* (or OS), you ask? It's a program, such as Linux or Windows, that controls your computer and manages everything from keyboard and mouse input to monitor, disk, and printer output — and everything in-between. It also maintains security and acts as a traffic cop to keep programs from tripping over one another.

Until now, Linux has served as a low-cost computing workhorse, powering many networks and servers behind the scenes. Although it has been around less than a decade, its capabilities have grown at a prodigious rate. For example, the animations for the Oscar-winning movie *Titanic* were produced on Linux systems. And when the U.S. Department of Energy built the world's most powerful supercomputer, guess what operating system they used!

Linux is powerful, but it can be cute and cuddly too, as shown in Figure 1-1.

Figure 1-1:
Linux's cute and cuddly side.

Chapter 1: I Can't Believe It's Really Better!

Born free

Instead of trying to get rich by selling Linux, Torvalds gave it away. He had the foresight to make Linux into a pioneering *open source* operating system that anyone can modify, as long as the enhancements are made available to all. Thousands of programmers from all over the world joined Linus in his crusade to create a sophisticated, complex, and powerful operating system that is forever free.

Yes, Linux is free. The latest Linux *kernel* (core programs), as well as many supporting programs, can always be downloaded free of charge — or $1.95 if you buy a CD with a Linux *distribution* (complete package with installation).

But clever you, you bought this book, so you got the CD with Corel Linux for nothing! (If you're reading this book in the store, you may now proceed to the checkout counter.)

No more software criminals

One great result of free software (along with falling hardware prices) is that you no longer have to belong to the richest one percent of the world's population to have access to a personal computer. A nation such as Korea, South Africa, or Mexico can think about putting computers in all their schools.

This is an important point for the future of cyber-democracy. When you have to pay a $200 software tax to join the ranks of the computing elite, you have a cyber-plutocracy instead. You might argue that folks in the Third World can get by with pirated software, but isn't that a sad commentary on our times? You can't pirate Linux — it's always free!

Sure, but what about the applications? True, commercial programs and games are available for Linux, as they are for any other operating system. But you can legitimately get a surprising number of applications for free, and the list grows longer by the day. You can get a free Star Office for Linux, complete with a word processor, a Web editor, a spreadsheet, a database, and drawing, charting, image editing, and mail applications. You can even get a free version of Corel's venerable WordPerfect 8 for Linux.

Why Should I Use Linux?

Linux is powerful and Linux is free, but what can if offer you? Take a look at these benefits:

- A true, stable, *multitasking* environment that can run several programs at once
- An intuitive, graphical alternative to the Windows and Mac interfaces
- Hundreds of software applications, most of which you can download free of charge
- Built-in support for networking and Internet access
- An operating system that runs like greased lightning — even on an old machine

Linux improvements are being made even as you read this page. If you're having a problem, you can expect to find a fix within hours or days.

What's So Special about Corel Linux?

Why should you use Corel Linux rather than Red Hat, Mandrake, OpenLinux, or SuSE? Glad you asked.

Simple to use

Corel's Install Express is a snap, and the geeks-only Linux interface is gone. You won't have to identify the chip on your graphics card to get Linux to work, and you won't have to type mind-bending commands such as `mount -t msdos /dev/fo0 /mnt/floppy` to do the simplest thing. This frees your brain for important things, like making a peanut-butter-and-jelly sandwich, and means your desk won't collapse under the weight of a stack of manuals.

Smoother than Windows

Corel gives you a Windows-like desktop, but it's faster and smoother than Windows! You can click away on a graphical interface that is a joy to use and includes ingenious file and update managers. Linux veterans will especially appreciate many small details that remove the mind-boggling mystery and aggravation of other distributions. Your floppy and CD-ROM drives are automatically mounted, and you can drag a simple slide bar to adjust your video resolution!

The Debian advantage

What you don't see is as important as what you do see. Corel Linux is powered by Debian GNU/Linux, generally regarded as the purest Linux version available. Debian is maintained by volunteers who are dedicated to the "Free Software" ideal and put together a distribution meeting the strictest Linux file system standards. Debian is rock-solid.

Debian is also technically superior in how its *packages* (components) are stored and organized. They're sorted in standardized directory structure, in which relationships among packages are carefully monitored. This assures trouble-free updates that no other distribution can provide.

Updates don't get easier than this!

When you install a Debian package, other packages upon which it depends are also automatically installed, and so on down the line. You also have the option of updating all your installed packages at once, either from a CD or directly from your favorite Internet location. Should your network connection be cut in the middle of a download, you can seamlessly pick up from where you left off. The knock on Debian was that their package managers were difficult to use, but that obstacle's gone with the graphical Corel Update!

The Four Flavors of Corel Linux

Corel released a free download version of Corel Linux — before the release of the packaged versions. It turned into an instant hit, as thousands of users jammed the Internet sites hosting the 325MB download.

Your *Corel Linux For Dummies CD* includes the Download Edition of Corel Linux plus other goodies described in Table 1-1.

Table 1-1	What's Included in Corel Linux			
Component	**Free Download**	**...For Dummies CD**	**Standard Edition**	**Deluxe Edition**
Corel LINUX OS — based on Debian 2.2 kernel	Yes	Yes	Yes	Yes
Enhanced KDE desktop	Yes	Yes	Yes	Yes
Corel Install Express	Yes	Yes	Yes	Yes

(continued)

Table 1-1 (continued)

Component	Free Download	...For Dummies CD	Standard Edition	Deluxe Edition
Corel File Manager	Yes	Yes	Yes	Yes
Corel Update Package Manager	Yes	Yes	Yes	Yes
Installation technical support (30 days)	No	No	E-mail	E-mail & phone
Netscape Communicator	No	Yes*	Yes	Yes
Adobe Acrobat Reader	No	Yes*	Yes	Yes
Instant Messenger — ICQ compatible client	No	No	Yes	Yes
Bitstream and Type 1 fonts			20	200
WordPerfect 8 for Linux		Light version	Full version	
eFax Plus service — three months free	No	No	No	Yes
OSS enhanced sound drivers	No	No	No	Yes
CIVILIZATION: Call to Power strategy game — Limited Edition	No	No	No	Yes
BRU backup software	No	No	No	Yes
User Guide	No	Yes†	Yes	Yes
WordPerfect 8 for Linux User Manual	No	No	No	Yes
Open circulation source code CD	††	††	Yes	Yes
Bonus desktop themes	No	Yes	No	No
3½-inch Linux penguin mascot	No	No	No	Yes

*See Appendix C for installation instructions.
† Corel Linux For Dummies instead of the Corel User Guide.
†† Source code is not included with the free download or the Corel Linux For Dummies CD-ROM, but it's freely available on the Web.

All versions of the program include a slew of other programs and utilities to let you play games, create graphics, set up a network or Web server, and even create your own Linux programs.

Corel Linux Is Less Powerful, Right?

If Corel Linux is so easy, surely it's less powerful. Right?

Wrong! If anything, Corel Linux is more powerful than other versions, with such tools as the Corel File Manager, a super-clever update facility, and a souped-up Control Center. It might be aimed at the desktop user, but you can still set up a Web server or install a zillion packages, and the command line is there for any geek who needs it.

And don't forget, the Debian engine powers Corel Linux!

Can I Still Use Windows?

Perhaps you're saying, "I have Windows installed, with my favorite word processor, Web browser, and drawing program — and I crash only two or three times a day. Can I use Corel Linux, but keep the (ugh) Windows stuff for now?"

Certainly! Having two operating systems on one machine is not as simple as, say, two word processors, but most Linux vendors provide the tools to do just this. Hey, Linux is the new penguin on the iceberg — it's gotta get along with its neighbors!

Corel Linux offers some nice possibilities:

- You can set up a *dual-boot* machine, where you can choose which operating system — Linux or Windows — you want to run on startup.
- You can take Corel Linux for a test drive, without reformatting your hard drive or creating a Linux partition. This is a relatively safe way to try out Corel Linux on a Windows machine.
- Corel Linux lets you read and write to files in folders set up by Windows programs. (From Windows, you can only read Linux files — and it takes a third-party utility to do so.)
- If your machine is on a Windows network, you can set up Corel Linux to access the network too.

Preparing for Takeoff

You don't have to give up Windows to use Linux. Many folks will have Linux and Windows coexisting for the next couple of years. Linux is coming on fast and has some great advantages, but it's still playing catch-up in some areas. For example, you might be using a speech program or scanning software that, as yet, has no equivalent in Linux.

Or perhaps you've paid for Windows and a bunch of other programs that you have no intention of giving up. Then there's the adage, "If it ain't broke, don't fix it." That's one I've never managed to follow, but boy, does it ever apply to computers!

Enough said. Join in the fun and games! Take a deep breath . . . or run around the block to get rid of your excess energy before turning to Chapter 2. Setting up Corel Linux is a snap, but you should be at your mental and physical best. If Corel Linux is already installed on your machine, take a free pass to Part II or anywhere else you want to go. You can stop by the refrigerator along the way.

Chapter 2

Up, Up, and Away! Installing Corel Linux

● ●

In This Chapter
- ▶ Performing a hardware reality check
- ▶ Taking precautions before you start
- ▶ Deciding what to install
- ▶ Figuring out where to put it
- ▶ Finding out when free space ain't free
- ▶ Starting Install Express
- ▶ Making your install selections
- ▶ You made it!

● ●

I'll bet you can't wait until you get Corel Linux installed! You probably feel like one of those Olympic sprinters, tensed up and ready to spring from the starting block. "On your mark! Get set! . . ." Well, we'll take this one step at a time.

On Your Mark . . . (Considering Your Needs and Options)

Do you get cold and clammy at the thought of installing an operating system? Relax, the Corel Linux Install Express provides a sweat-free install. Just a little planning and a few precautions are all you need.

You can install Corel Linux on any working PC, and you don't need a current operating system to begin. For example, you can install Corel Linux on a brand new machine or on an old machine on which you installed a new hard drive.

The essentials

No sense installing if you ain't got the right hardware. As far as the computer itself goes, the requirements are minimal. You might even want to get in the closet and dig out that old computer that can no longer run Windows (it's under the sneakers and boots) and give it a go. Here are the minimum requirements for Corel Linux:

- A Pentium 90 (or equivalent) processor
- 24MB of RAM (64MB recommended)
- 500MB of unpartitioned hard drive space (or free space to install on a Windows partition) — you can get by with as little as 200MB by using a custom install
- A 2MB VGA PCI graphics card
- A CD-ROM drive
- A 3½-inch floppy disk drive (required if your CD-ROM drive is not bootable)
- A mouse or other pointing device

I suppose a keyboard and a monitor could come in handy, too.

Some things you might want to do with Corel Linux require additional hardware:

- A modem for dial-up Internet access (and an Internet service provider to dial up to)
- A network card for network hookup
- A sound card and speakers and maybe a microphone

Hardware reality check

Although Corel Linux requires fewer resources than Windows, its support for particular disk drives, modems, printers, mice, and other hardware is not yet as broad. Linux does not yet support internal ISDN cards and some DVD drives. This situation is improving rapidly as the Linux kernel evolves and as the mushrooming interest in Linux spurs hardware vendors into action.

Avoid Windows-only hardware such as Winmodems, which employ software to grab your computer's memory for basic operations rather than run them from an on-board chip. Some of these modems will be supported by upcoming versions of Linux, but don't count on it. A similar problem arises with some Windows-only (GDI) printers, but they're much less common than Winmodems.

The video cards that display stuff on your monitor can also be a problem. Some cards don't have Linux versions of *software drivers* (programs to operate computing devices), but this situation is improving quickly. Likewise with sound cards and other multimedia hardware.

When Corel Linux doesn't have a driver for your particular piece of hardware, it substitutes a generic version that lets you utilize most, if not all, of its capabilities.

Many hardware devices come with utilities that run under Windows, but no utilities that run under Linux. Windows-only examples might include a scanner that comes with page managing and copying software and a CD-RW drive that arrives with programs to back up data and burn audio CDs. As with hardware drivers, Corel Linux or third-party equivalents might be available that are just as good, but finding them might take a bit of looking. For example, Corel Linux Deluxe comes with the versatile BRU backup program for performing tape backups.

Getting hardware help

If you experience a Linux hardware predicament, take solace in the fact that thousands of open source programmers are resolving these issues with astonishing speed. Linux is the "Little Kernel That Could"!

Meanwhile, Corel has compiled a huge list of compatible and incompatible hardware. You can find the list at

```
http://linux.corel.com/products./linux_os/hardware.htm
```

If you're having hardware troubles, don't despair. Take a look at all the support options described in Chapter 20, especially the support newsgroups. It's easy to find other users having the same problems, and experts who are more than happy to help!

Don't engage in unprotected installs

If you already have stuff on your computer, when was the last time you backed it up? Well, do it now! When you move a new operating system into your computer, you're doing some heavy-duty lifting and arranging of existing software furniture. Corel's Install Express is well tested and easy to use, but no matter how sure-fire the software and how careful you are, something can always go wrong. Believe me, I've learned the hard way!

Can I remove Corel Linux after it's installed?

Remember, installing an operating system such as Corel Linux is a final act, more so than adding a software application such as WordPerfect. Normally, the only ways to remove an operating system are to reformat your hard drive, or use partitioning software such as Partition Magic to surgically remove the Linux partitions, without affecting others. (If you select the option to install in DOS/Windows Partition, described later in this chapter, you delete the Corel Linux folders instead.)

What's automatic and what ain't?

Until recently, installing Linux was way too complicated for the average user without a degree in computer engineering. Linux books devote literally hundreds of pages to such delightful topics as partitioning drives, checking package dependencies, selecting the right X server for your video card, installing the Linux loader . . . the list goes on and on.

Sure some folks enjoy the sport, just as others love to climb Mount Everest or compete in a triathlon. The rest of us can think of other ways to spend a few months.

Automatic

Corel Linux automatically detects your hard drive, CD-ROM, sound card, video, mouse, and other hardware as it installs and then sets up a Linux driver to operate each component. If a particular component doesn't have a Linux driver, Corel Linux installs the most appropriate generic driver instead.

Corel Linux detects standard, PCI-based cards only.

When you add new hardware, Corel Linux recognizes it the next time you start the computer.

Not automatic

Linux doesn't support every piece of hardware, and some hardware that Linux does support might not be automatically detected by Corel Linux.

During the install, you have a chance to change the default selections, such as what to install, and you are asked to supply a bit of information, such as a user name. After Install Express does its thing, you have to supply a bit more information to do such tasks as connect to a Windows network or dial up to the Internet, as explained in Chapter 4.

What Should I Install?

Before you get started, let's preview the important install selections you'll make as to what to install and where to put it. Table 2-1 summarizes the pros and cons for the "What" selections, which are in the upcoming "Step 4: What do you want to install?" section.

Table 2-1		What to Install
"What" Option	*Pros*	*Cons*
Default desktop	Recommended choice for most users	Won't have all the libraries to perform advanced operations, such as recompiling the kernel
Minimum desktop	Saves disk space	Might miss out on handy tools and features
Desktop Plus	What you need to create your own programs	More stuff than most users need
Server	Stuff to set up server and develop programs	More stuff than most users need
Custom	Lets experts choose exactly what's needed, including stuff not in other options; Handy when space is extremely limited	It's easier to instead customize after the install, by using Corel Update to add and remove packages

Where Should I Put It?

Your "What to install" selections can always be adjusted after the fact, through the Corel Update facility. Your most fateful install decision is where to put Corel Linux, especially if Linux is sharing your machine with another operating system. Table 2-2 summarizes your options for the upcoming "Step 5: Where do you want to put it?" section.

Part I: Leaping to Linux

Table 2-2   **Where to Install**

"Where" Option	Pros	Cons
Take over disk	Simple, clean way to set up a Linux-only machine	Wipes out existing systems and data
	Zero sweat if you're starting from a virgin machine	Leaves no room for another operating system
Use free disk space	Preserves existing systems and data	Must have unpartitioned space not used by another OS; see the "When free space isn't free" section
	Lets Linux coexist with another OS	Existing disk structure may not allow this, even where there is space
Edit partition table	Lets you allocate separate partitions for specific files (user directories, additional programs, temporary files, and so on), especially on a multiuser system or network server	Can destroy existing systems and data with one mouse click
	Lets you escape limitations of your system BIOS, especially when the kernel resides below cylinder 1023	Extra partitions can waste space
	Allows you to reinstall Corel Linux or remove another version of Linux before installing	You can't resize existing partitions to free up space with Install Express
Install in DOS/ Windows partition	Lets you try Corel Linux in Windows 95/98 without reformatting all or part of your disk	Inefficient way to run Corel Linux
		Awkward to reboot between Linux and Windows

TIP: If Corel Linux will share space with an existing Windows system, it helps to defragment your hard drive before you begin. In Windows, choose Start⇨Programs⇨Accessories⇨System Tools⇨Disk Defragmenter.

When free space isn't free

To install Corel Linux, Install Express must find find free space on your hard drive that it can format as a Linux partition, to hold your operating system and Linux files.

Suppose you have a typical Windows PC with, say, a 5GB hard drive fully allocated to your Windows c: drive. If you've installed only 2GB of programs and files, you're left with 3GB of free space as far as Windows programs are concerned.

Unfortunately, this 3GB of space isn't free space to Install Express because it's part of a Windows partition that's off limits to the Linux file system. Corel Linux is really looking for *unpartitioned space* that's not being used by Windows.

You have three ways out of this predicament:

- **Option 1:** Let Corel Linux reformat your hard drive, wiping out Windows and any existing data as it does.
- **Option 2:** Use the Corel Linux trick of installing to that "free space" on your Windows 95/98 partition. Corel Linux will be awkward to launch and you'll take a huge performance hit, but at least you'll get a taste of Corel Linux.
- **Option 3:** If you're a computer guru, you can use a third-party disk partitioning utility, such as PowerQuest's PartitionMagic or the open source FIPS utility, to reduce the size of your Windows partition, thus creating true unpartitioned free space that Corel Linux can use.

Don't use a disk partitioning tool unless you really know what you're doing. With such a tool, you can easily destroy an existing system.

If you want to run both Windows and Linux on one machine but you're not happy with any of these options, Corel Linux is probably not for you at this time.

Waddaya mean I can dual boot?

When you install Corel Linux to share your machine with an existing OS, you get a *dual-boot* machine that let's you choose which OS to use on boot-up. (However, if you go the "Install in DOS/Windows partition" route, you'll have to boot to Windows before you can get to Linux.)

Corel Linux sets up its *LILO* (Linux loader) so you can choose which OS to use on boot-up. The default is Corel Linux, but you can change that (see Chapter 4).

> LILO is installed in your *Master Boot Record* (MBR), generally the preferred location. But there's no option to install in the first sector of the root partition (where the Linux system files and kernel reside). This can knock out another boot manager, such as BootMagic or System Commander.

Peace, brother OS! (Linux and Windows under one roof)

Before you let Install Express blast away at your computer's innards, take a moment to reflect on how Corel Linux is physically installed on your computer — especially if Corel Linux and Windows will be living under one roof.

Linux and Windows will get along well enough, but each has to have its own room, or *partition,* on your hard drive. Linux partitions have a different format (ext2) from Windows partitions.

If you want to have a Linux-only machine, you can simply let Install Express take over your entire hard drive. But if you intend to also install Windows or another operating system, you'll want to choose the "Use free disk space" option, to leave room for the other system. Likewise, if you're installing Corel Linux on a machine that already has Windows 95 or 98, you wouldn't want to choose the "Take over disk" option — unless you intend to wipe out Windows and all your existing data.

> Actually, Install Express normally creates two Linux partitions, one for your programs and data and a swap partition to soup up your Linux engine. You can create additional partitions by selecting the Edit partition table option.

Just to add to the confusion, the unique Corel Linux option to install in a DOS/Windows partition does so without changing the partition to the Linux format. This is a great way to test out Corel Linux on a Windows 95/98 machine, though it's not an efficient way to run Linux. Corel Linux will be awkward to launch, and performance will be much slower than in a native Linux partition.

Get Set . . . (Making Your Selections)

Are you ready? Then it's time to start the install! I assume you've been waiting patiently for this moment, resisting the urge to break the seal at the back of the book — like not opening a present before your birthday.

Corel lays claim to a three- or four-step install, depending on whom you're listening to. Well, Install Express is pretty impressive, but not quite *that* simple — I counted eight steps, plus you might need to do some post-install configuration, which is covered in Chapter 4.

Breaking the sacred seal

Go on, break the sacred seal at the back of this book and extract the CD! If you happen to have more than one Corel Linux CD, you can use the extras as coasters. This idea originated with America Online.

Step 1: Booting the installation CD

The first step in the install is to boot your installation CD. If your CD-ROM is already bootable, this step is automatic. If the automatic way doesn't work, you can either create a boot floppy (Alternative A) or change your machine's boot sequence (Alternative B).

TIP

If you put in the CD while you're running Windows, you'll be told to reboot your system in order to proceed.

Does your CD boot automatically?

Try booting the automatic way first:

   1. **Insert the Corel Linux CD-ROM (the Installation CD from a boxed set).**
   2. **Shut down and restart your computer.**

If your computer restarts without loading Install Express, go to Alternative A or B.

Alternative A: Boot from a floppy

To create an installation floppy and boot from it:

   1. **Write** Corel Linux Boot Install **on a blank, 3½-inch, high-density disk (1.4MB), and insert it in a working computer.**

      Any data on the disk will be erased.

   2. **Insert your installation CD and do *one* of the following:**

      - In Windows, when Corel Linux Autorun appears, follow the instructions to create a boot floppy and then reboot.
      - In a (non-Corel) Linux system, log in as root, open a command shell, and type the following (to mount the CD)

Part I: Leaping to Linux

```
mount -t iso9660 /dev/cdrom /mnt/cdrom
```

and then type

```
dd if=/mnt/cdrom/boot/boot1440.img of=/dev/fd0
```

3. **Put the floppy *and* the Corel Linux CD in your computer.**

4. **Shut down and restart your computer.**

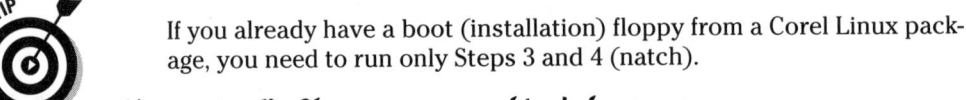

   If you already have a boot (installation) floppy from a Corel Linux package, you need to run only Steps 3 and 4 (natch).

Alternative B: Change your machine's boot sequence

To boot directly from the CD-ROM (without using a floppy), you might have to change the *boot sequence* in your computer's *BIOS* to load from the CD rather than from your hard drive (and then set it back when you're finished.) Refer to your computer's manual and the on-screen messages for how to do this.

Changing the boot sequence is easy if you know how, but remember, I didn't tell you to do this. Don't mess with the factory settings of your computer's BIOS unless you know what you're doing.

You're on your way!

Yeah, you're on your way! You should see the following messages in the mythical penguin world of Figure 2-1:

```
Loading Corel Linux...
Starting Corel Linux...
Detecting hardware...
```

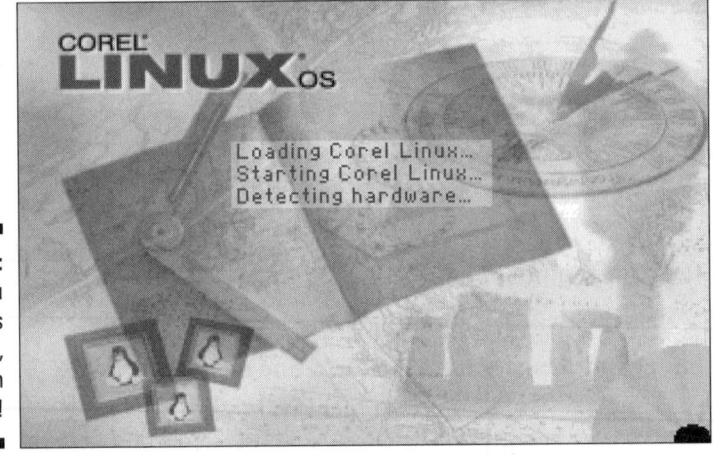

Figure 2-1: When you arrive at this scene, you're on your way!

Chapter 2: Up, Up, and Away! Installing Corel Linux 27

The "detecting hardware" part means that Corel Linux is doing the hard part for you — automatically probing your system to find out what type of video, sound card, tracking device, and other hardware you have. This is where much of the pain of the traditional Linux installs is removed. This step takes a while — please be patient.

Step 2: Agree to the onerous terms

Next you arrive at the inevitable license agreement. Read the agreement and click Accept to become an indentured servant to Corel or click Decline and remain a slave to Microsoft.

Step 3: Who are you?

Think you can fill in the name entry in Figure 2-2? This is the name you want Corel Linux to know you by. It can be up to 16 letters and numbers, but no capital letters please. On a multiuser system, it's common to use your first name plus the first letter of your last name (such as janed for Jane Doe).

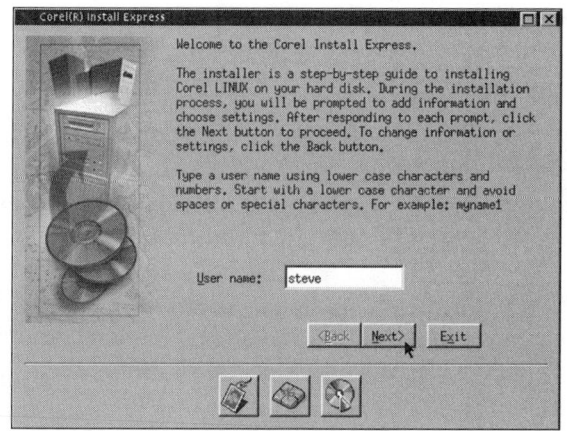

Figure 2-2: What's your name?

This is your working name. Every Linux system also has a *superuser* named root, who can access all the settings and muck about with the system.

Step 4: What do you want to install?

Now that you've figured out your name, click Next to choose what to install, as shown in Figure 2-3.

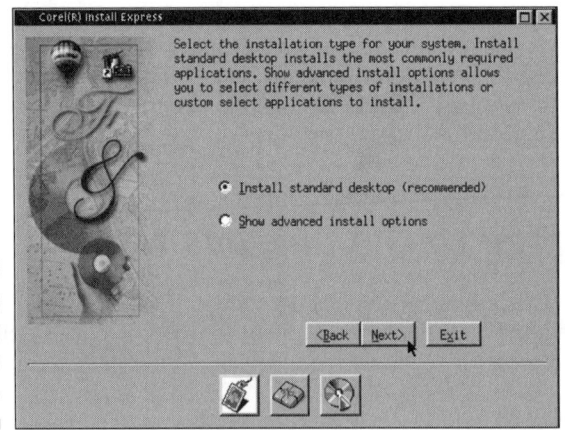

Figure 2-3: Selecting what to install.

In most cases, the recommended setup (Install standard desktop) is fine. You can always add and remove stuff later (see Chapter 17). If you're installing the standard desktop, go to Step 5 now.

If you plan to do such expert tasks as setting up a server or creating Linux programs, do the following:

1. **Click Show advanced install options and then click Next to view the advanced install options shown in Figure 2-4.**

2. **Click one of the following:**

    - **Desktop (minimum installation)** to install only the essential Linux and desktop components.

    - **Desktop Plus (development tools, editors)** to install the default desktop plus the workstation environment for developing or modifying programs.

    - **Server (Web, file, print, Ftp)** to install all Linux server components, including http, ftp, and Samba servers. Includes minimal system components plus the development tools.

    - **Custom (choose one or more applications)** to choose the precise components, known as *packages,* you want to install from various categories.

Step 5: Where do you want to put it?

After you've selected what to install, you're ready for the *big* decision: where to put the stuff. This decision is *irreversible* and, depending on your selection, can wipe out an existing system and its accompanying data. Unless you're using the "Install in DOS/Windows partition" option, Corel Linux grabs all or part of your drive and formats it to suit the Linux file system.

Chapter 2: Up, Up, and Away! Installing Corel Linux 29

Figure 2-4: Advanced selections let you set up everything from a minimal desktop to a server environment.

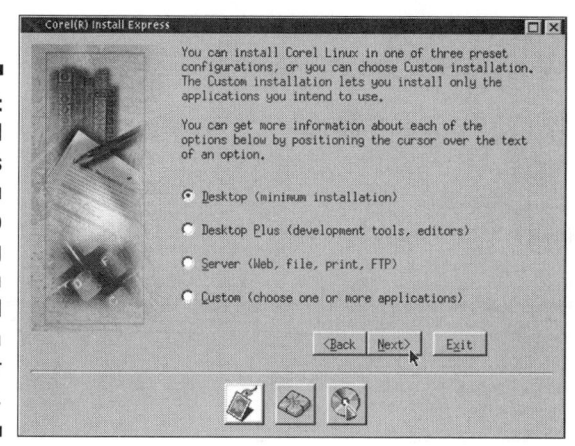

Are you ready? Then click Next to display the "where to" choices in Figure 2-5 and choose from the following:

- **Take over disk (erases all existing information)** to *totally destroy* existing data on your hard drive, creating a clean machine with nothing but Corel Linux. (If you have multiple disks, only one disk is wiped clean — you're asked which disk you want to erase and install Corel Linux on.)

  Does your hard drive contain data that you want to keep? Have you backed it up elsewhere? Click Exit if you have any doubts!

- **Use free disk space (keeps existing information)** preserves existing data, and Corel Linux will not take over your entire hard drive. You must have at least 200MB of free (unpartitioned) space if you choose the default setup.

- **Edit partition table (for advanced Linux users)** lets you delete or create partitions that you specify. As with the "Take over disk" option, be sure that information you don't want to lose is backed up elsewhere.

  Editing partitions is a dangerous procedure that can destroy existing data or make your system unusable. Make sure you know what you're doing before you begin.

  Install Express doesn't let you resize existing partitions. You need a separate utility such as PartitionMagic or FIPS for that.

- **Install in DOS/Windows partition** lets you run Corel Linux from MS-DOS mode under Windows 95/98. As with the "free space" option, existing data is preserved but you must have at least 200MB of free space on your Windows 95/98 partition for the default setup.

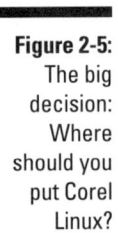

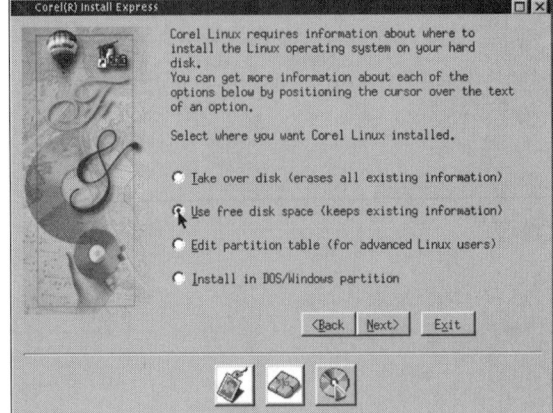

Figure 2-5:
The big decision: Where should you put Corel Linux?

Step 6: Reviewing your selections

Now click Next to review your install selections, as shown in Figure 2-6. Look them over carefully, especially if Corel Linux will be sharing your PC with another system. You may click the Back button to change your selections or click Back and then click Exit to quit.

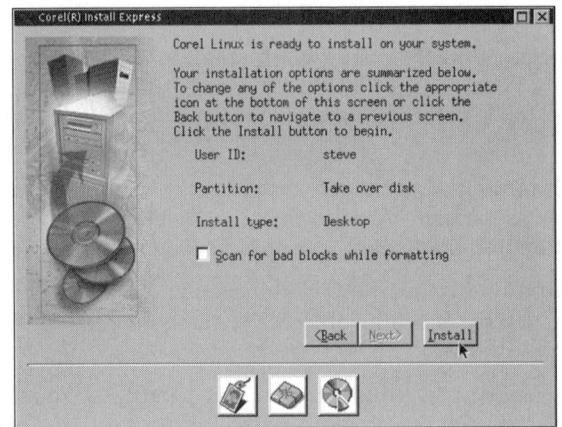

Figure 2-6:
Reviewing your install selections.

Note the check box titled Scan for bad block while formatting. It's best to put a check here, even though doing so makes your install longer, to be sure you're not installing to an unusable portion of your disk.

Go!

The decisive moment has arrived! After you proceed to Step 7, there's no turning back.

Step 7: Off you go!

The decisive moment has arrived! If you are really, really, really, sure, click Install to start the process. The Installing Components screen of Figure 2-7 tells you what's happening as it partitions your hard disk and installs your base system and packages.

Figure 2-7: You're on your way!

Coffee break time! How long does the installation take? That depends on you hardware and your installation selections, but figure between ten minutes and half an hour. Don't be alarmed if the install seems to hang at some place, such as 25% or 98%; the install isn't adept at calculating its progress.

Step 8: Entering the promised land

When the installation is finished, remove the floppy (if you used one). Click OK to reboot Corel Linux. You are presented with the startup selections in Figure 2-8. You made it (enthusiastic applause)!

Figure 2-8: You made it! Choose Corel Linux to enter the sacred realm.

If you changed the boot sequence in your computer's BIOS in Step 1, did you remember to set it back?

Press Enter to activate the Corel Linux selection. (If you don't make a selection within 30 seconds, Corel Linux starts by itself.)

If you have other operation systems on your PC, they should appear in the list of selections. (If you installed in a DOS/Windows partition, you'll have to run Corel Linux from the Windows command mode instead, as explained in Chapter 3.)

The other startup selections — VGA mode, Console, Debug, and Expert — are various safe modes, similar to the Windows safe mode, that you can use when your graphical interface or some critical part of Corel Linux is acting up. Chances are you'll never need them, but Appendix A tells you what to do when you can't get into graphical mode.

The startup screen in Figure 2-9 keeps you informed as Corel Linux loads, starts, initializes, and then mounts and checks the filesystems. The first time around, you have an additional wait as the system goes through a one-time configuration process.

When that's over, the login dialog box appears, as shown in Figure 2-10. Click the drop-down list to select either root or your personal user name and then click Login.

Figure 2-9: Hang around while the system does its initial configuration.

Figure 2-10: Select root or your user name then click Login.

Wow . . . this is exciting! One last thing: You're asked to change your password, even though you were never asked before to enter a password. Type and retype your password in the boxes shown in Figure 2-11 and then click OK.

Passwords can be from five to eight characters, are case sensitive, and may include any combination of letters, numbers, and punctuation marks. Linux has only a few reserved words you can't use.

Welcome to Corel Linux!

Wonder of wonders, here you are in Corel Linux! Sit back, relax, and admire the landscape in Figure 2-12. Let the games (and work) begin!

Figure 2-11: Oops, almost forgot: Type and retype your user password.

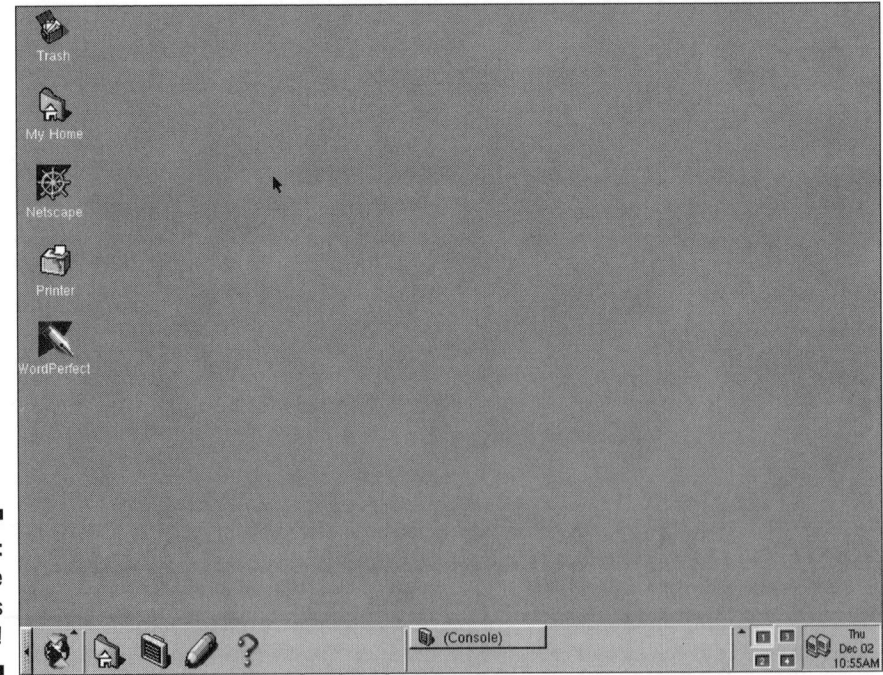

Figure 2-12: Let the games begin!

Chapter 3

Starting Up, Doing Things, and Shutting Down

● ●

In This Chapter

▶ Starting Corel Linux and logging in
▶ Starting Windows or another OS instead
▶ Starting Corel Linux another way
▶ Launching WordPerfect and other applications
▶ Checking your disk space
▶ Issuing commands
▶ Shutting down Corel Linux

● ●

After Corel Linux starts up, it might never go down — at least not on its own, as is the habit with other systems. Still, you'll want to know how to start Corel Linux and log in and then exit the desktop and shut down.

And while you're there, you might want to launch WordPerfect or Netscape or maybe play a little minesweeper or poker.

Starting Up and Logging In

For most Corel Linux installations, getting to the desktop is a breeze:

   1. **Turn on your computer.**

      The splash screen and menu in Figure 3-1 appear.

Part I: Leaping to Linux

Figure 3-1: Press 1 or Enter to start Corel Linux, or come back in 30 seconds.

2. **Press 1 or Enter.**

   If you're too lazy to press a key, Corel Linux launches itself in 30 seconds. The login dialog box shown in Figure 3-2 appears.

Figure 3-2: To log in, select your user name and enter the magic word.

3. **Click the User name list (or press F4) and select your name. Then type the magic password.**

   Only asterisks (*****) appear, to protect you from foreign spies.

4. **If you belong to more than one network domain, select one from the Domain name list.**

5. **Click Login (or press Enter) to go to the Corel Linux desktop.**

> ## Logging in as root
>
> As a rule, avoid logging in as the root superuser because this gives you the power to screw up critical system files. Log on as plain dick or jane when you're not performing system tasks. This type of system security is an unknown concept in the land of Windows 95/98.
>
> I usually let you know whenever root access is required, such as to add a user or change your boot defaults. In some cases, it's not obvious that you have to log in as root. For example, as a longtime Windows user, it took me a while to figure out that I had to log in as root to add fonts to WordPerfect 8.
>
> So when you do need root access, get in the habit of logging out when your root tasks are finished and then logging back in under your regular user name.
>
> Where the program is smart enough, you don't have to log in as root to perform a system task. For example, when using Corel Update as a regular user, you're asked to supply the root password for temporary rights to update the system.

Starting Windows or Another OS

If you have a dual (or multiple) boot machine, simply choose the operating system you want from the list when you boot up.

Starting Corel Linux in a DOS/Windows Partition

If you installed to a DOS/Windows partition, launching Corel Linux is a bit more complicated:

1. **From Windows, choose Start ⇨ Shut Down and then choose Restart in MS-DOS mode.**
2. **If Corel Linux is installed to a different drive than the one you're in, type** d**: and press Enter, where** d **is the name of the drive.**
3. **Type** cd \cdl **and press Enter to go to the Corel Linux folder.**
4. **Type** startcdl **and press Enter.**

   This reboots your computer and starts Corel Linux.

TIP

Type **Exit** in DOS mode to reboot to your normal Windows mode.

Part I: Leaping to Linux

Launching WordPerfect and Other Programs

WordPerfect

After you're in the desktop, launching WordPerfect and other programs is a cinch. If your Corel Linux installation puts a WordPerfect icon on your desktop, as shown in Figure 3-3, just click the icon to launch WordPerfect.

That wasn't hard, was it? If you don't have WordPerfect, click the Help button on the panel to open online help instead.

Now click the Application Starter button on the left of the panel. This pops up a menu of selections, with submenus for online services and many types of applications. Click the program or utility you want, and off you go!

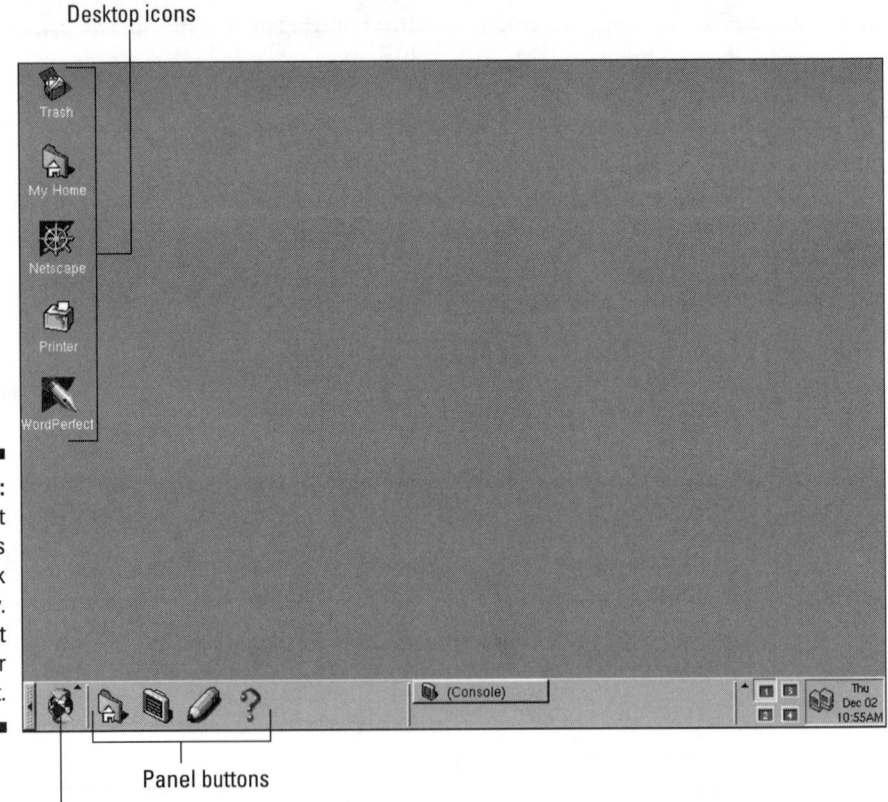

Figure 3-3: WordPerfect or Help is just a click away. Doesn't get any simpler than that.

Desktop icons

Panel buttons

Application Starter

Chapter 3: Starting Up, Doing Things, and Shutting Down 39

Managing System and User Tasks

Okay, your Linux system seems to run fine. But you really want to be in control. You can use the Task Manager to find out about every process and program running on your system and terminate any that are misbehaving. Choose Application Starter⇨Applications⇨System⇨Task Manager, and then do any of the following:

✔ To terminate a particular task, click the task and then click the Kill task button, as seen in Figure 3-4.

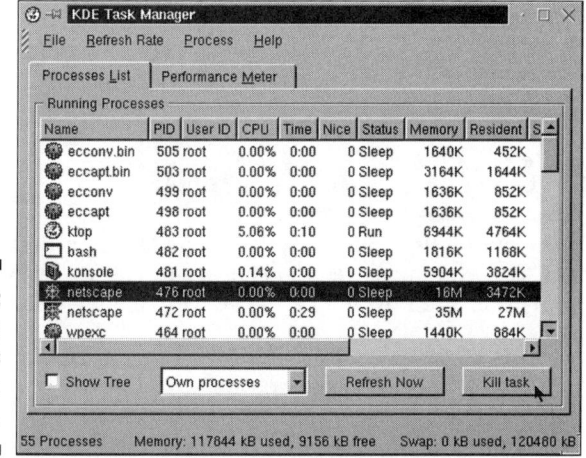

Figure 3-4: Terminating a task that's giving you trouble.

The root user can terminate any user or system process. Other users can terminate only the processes they own.

✔ Click the buttons at the top of the listing to sort tasks by name, user ID, memory, and so on.

✔ Choose the Show Tree option to view groups of dependent processes. Click the nearby drop-down list to show all processes, all user processes, your own processes, or system processes.

✔ Click the Performance Meter tab to view your system's processor (CPU) load and memory usage, as seen in Figure 3-5.

Part I: Leaping to Linux

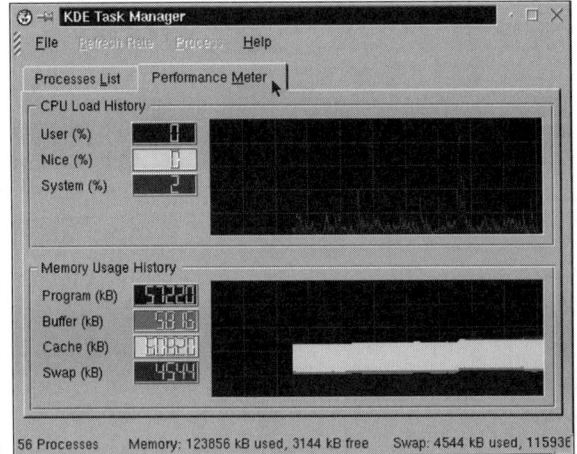

Figure 3-5: Viewing your system's processor load and memory usage.

Am I Running Out of Disk Space?

Afraid you're running out of disk space? Click the File Manager button on the panel and then click The System, as seen in Figure 3-6. This shows you the total size of each partition and how much free space remains in each.

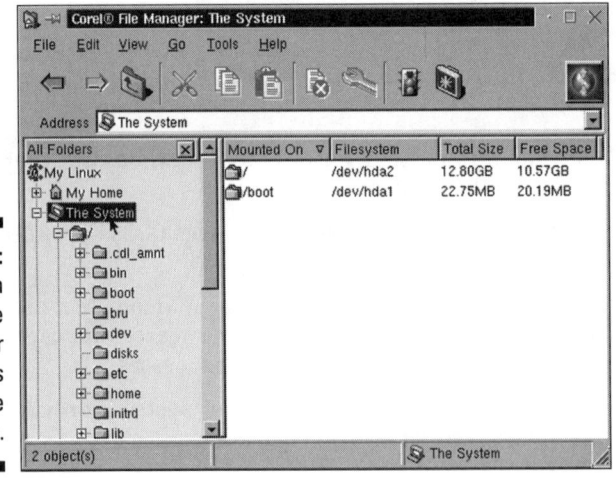

Figure 3-6: The System in File Manager displays your free disk space.

My Kingdom for a Command Prompt!

The graphical interface is a wonderful thing, but experienced Linux users often work from the command line. Why? Because a number of command-line Linux programs don't have a graphical interface. Plus, some utilities offer a lot of command-line options, or parameters, that might not be found in the graphical mode. For example, even though my screen capture utility has a graphical interface, I find it much quicker and easier to perform sophisticated capture operations in command mode.

Sometimes you have no choice but to use commands, such as when something goes haywire with your graphical system. Hey, all Linux once had was the command line, just like DOS in the good old days — it's nothing to be afraid of. Indeed, after you perform some magic from the command prompt, you'll feel a much closer bond with the operating system.

You can enter commands from the Corel Linux desktop in two ways:

- Click the Console button on the panel to enter commands and view their results, as seen in Figure 3-7.

    Press the up arrow to scroll through your previous commands.

Figure 3-7: Entering commands in the Console.

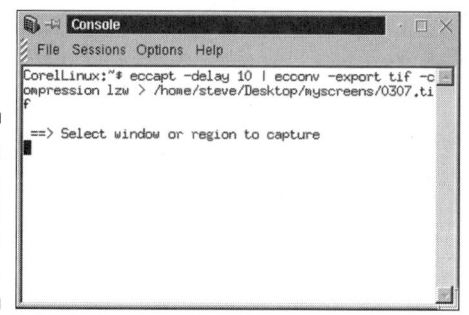

- Press Alt+F2 (or choose Application Starter➪Run) and enter the command you want to run, as seen in Figure 3-8. (Choose the Run in Terminal Window option to view the results in the Console.)

Figure 3-8: Press Alt+F2 to enter the command you want to run.

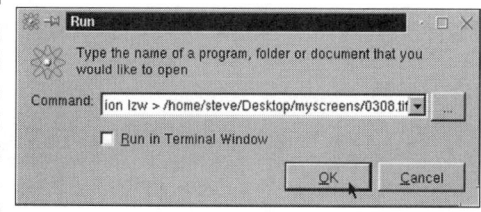

Part I: Leaping to Linux

TECHNICAL STUFF: The Console lets you access the command line in three modes: Linux Console (the default), Shell, and Midnight Commander, the revered DOS-like file manager. See the Console's online help for details.

For details on working with Linux commands, see Appendix A.

Logging Out of the Desktop and Shutting Down

You need to log out of the desktop to switch users, shut down the system, or boot to another OS:

TIP:
1. **Choose Application Starter➪Logout.**

    Or right-click the desktop and then choose Logout.

    If any applications are running, you might see the warning in Figure 3-9 that data might be lost.

Figure 3-9: You are warned if data might be lost when you log out.

2. **If in doubt, click Cancel to go back and exit the programs gracefully.**
3. **Click OK to log out.**

Chapter 3: Starting Up, Doing Things, and Shutting Down

After you log out of the desktop, you can do either of the following:

- Click Login to reenter the desktop as the same or another user.
- Click Shutdown, as shown in Figure 3-10, to either shut down your computer, or shut down your computer and restart to Windows or another OS.

Figure 3-10: Click Shutdown to shut down your computer or restart to another OS.

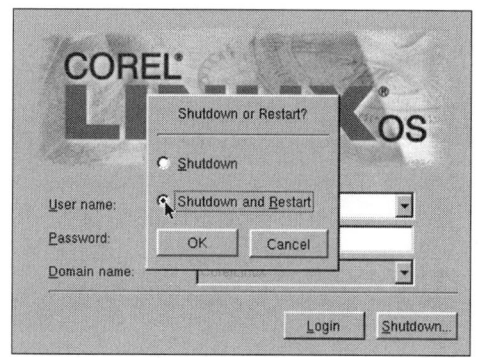

Notice I didn't say to use shutdown and restart to clean up the mess with your current Linux session. That's a Windows trick you can unlearn when using Linux!

In the "never say never" department, it's not unknown to have a software problem in Linux that logging out and back in can correct or a hardware hiccup where it pays to restart your system.

Chapter 4
Post-Install Tweaking

In This Chapter
- Checking out the settings in the Control Center
- Using other languages
- Changing keyboard and mouse configurations
- Changing the date and time
- Setting up printers
- Hooking up to the Internet or a local network
- Adding new users
- Finding out about boot defaults
- Installing Acrobat Reader and Netscape Communicator too

After you've installed Corel Linux and romped around in its dazzling desktop, your next reaction might be "Hey, this is great so far, but how do I hook up my printer and connect to the Internet? The time is wrong, how do I change that? How do I set up accounts for the kids?"

Well, well, well, well, well, you came to the right place. Here, I take care of post-install tweaking and a few questions besides.

Welcome to Mission Control

So where do you go to tweak? Most settings are conveniently gathered under the big tent of the Corel Linux Control Center, similar to the Windows Control Panel. The one exception in this chapter is the dial-up Internet connection, made through the Dial-Up utility on the Network submenu.

Without further ado, click Application Starter (shown in the margin) and then choose Control Center from the main menu. Simply click the plus sign (+) to view the details for the various groups of settings described in Table 4-1. You can also double-click the headings.

Table 4-1	Control Center Settings	
Setting	*Lets You . . .*	*See*
Desktop	Customize desktop aesthetics to your heart's delight, including eye-popping themes that will be the envy of your Windows brethren — plus, choose from 34 interface languages	Chapters 9 and 10
Input Devices	Select international keyboards and set options for your keyboard and mouse	Chapter 4
Keys	Customize your keyboard shortcuts	Chapter 9
Network	Hook up your computer to a network	Chapter 4
Sound	Enable system sounds and assign sounds to particular operations, such as maximizing a window	Chapter 10
Windows	Customize window controls, placement, focus, and other properties	Chapter 9
Password	Change your password	Chapter 4
Date & Time	Set the date, time, and time zone	Chapter 4
Printers	Add, remove, and customize printers	Chapter 4

As you explore the Control Center settings, click OK or Cancel to exit one group before going on to the next. Otherwise, the group will reappear after you close the next group. Very confusing.

Using Other Languages in Corel Linux

Corel Linux lets you change the entire interface to whichever language you like! You can choose anything from Breton to Turkish, with Chinese, Dutch, German, French, Japanese, Korean, Russian, Spanish, and 24 other languages in-between. I'm talking about the menus, dialog boxes, online help — the works.

Hard to believe? Yeah, afraid so. Only a few KDE applications in the initial Corel Linux are in more than one language, and all help leads to the Corel

Chapter 4: Post-Install Tweaking 47

Linux help, initially only in English. (And to think that KDE started in Germany.) But, as with everything else in the Linux world, this too is changing quickly, and you can expect the language support to proliferate as Linux spreads throughout the world. So try the settings now, if only to see what you have to look forward to.

Changing your preferred language

To change the preferred language for your menus, dialog boxes, and online help:

1. **Choose Application Starter ⇨ Control Center (KDE Kontrollzentrum), double-click Desktop, and then choose Language (Sprache).**
2. **Select your first language and then select your second and third backup languages in order of preference, as shown in Figure 4-1.**
3. **Click OK to change the language for any applications you now open.**

If the first language is not available, Corel Linux tries your second and third choices. If none of your preferred languages is available, Corel Linux uses the default, which is Esperanto. Just kidding, the default language is English.

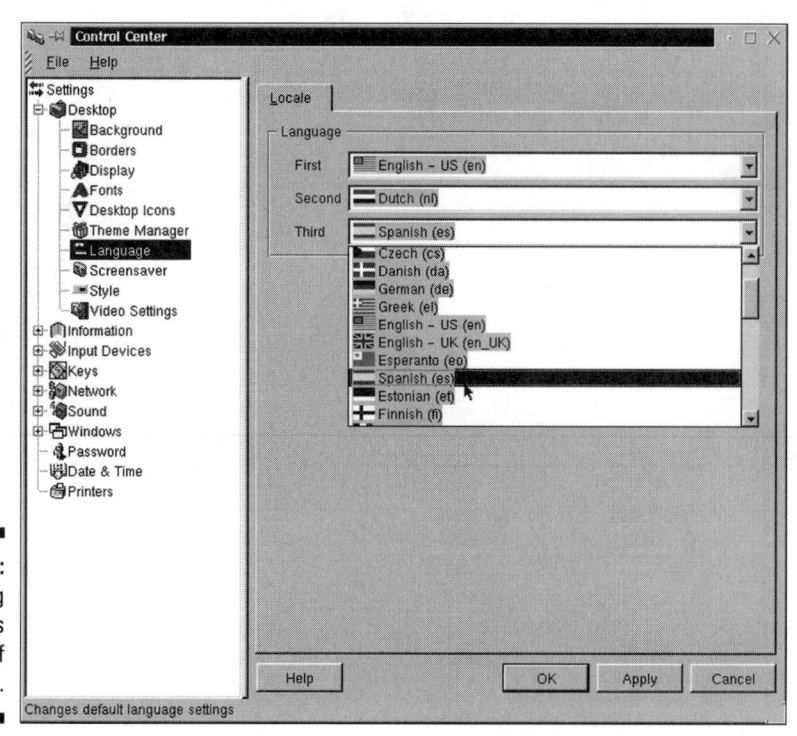

Figure 4-1: Selecting languages in order of preference.

Using international keyboards

To go along with your multilingual menus and dialogs, you can use international keyboard maps to type in languages with non-English characters:

1. **Choose Application Starter ⇨ Control Center, double-click Input Devices, and then choose International Keyboard, as shown in Figure 4-2.**

2. **For each keyboard you want, click Add and select the keyboard from the drop-down list.**

3. **You can select a keyboard in the listing and then click the Up or Down button to change its position in the keyboard pecking order.**

4. **Click the StartUp tab and then choose**
   - **Autostart** to have your first international keyboard load when you log into the desktop
   - **Docked** to place the keyboard selection button in the docking station (see Chapter 5) to the right of the panel instead of in one of the desktop corners

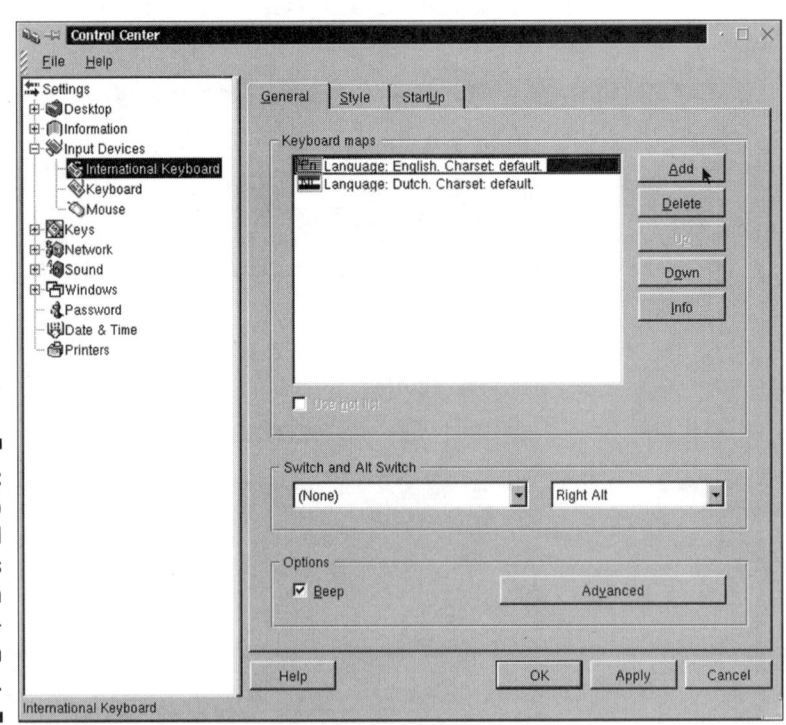

Figure 4-2: Setting up international keyboards so you can type non-English characters.

Chapter 4: Post-Install Tweaking

5. **If you want to change the colors or font for the keyboard selection button, click the Style tab.**
6. **Click OK to use the new list of keyboards.**

The next time you log in (if you selected Autostart and Docked), you can click the keyboard selection button on the desktop or panel to switch keyboard language maps.

Configuring Your Keyboard and Mouse

In addition to your international keyboards, Input Device settings give you a few keyboard and mouse options:

1. **Choose Application Starter ⇨ Control Center and then double-click Input Devices.**
2. **Choose Keyboard to turn keyboard repeat onnnnnnnnn or off, as shown in Figure 4-3. Slide the volume up if you want to hear annoying clicks as you type. Click OK.**

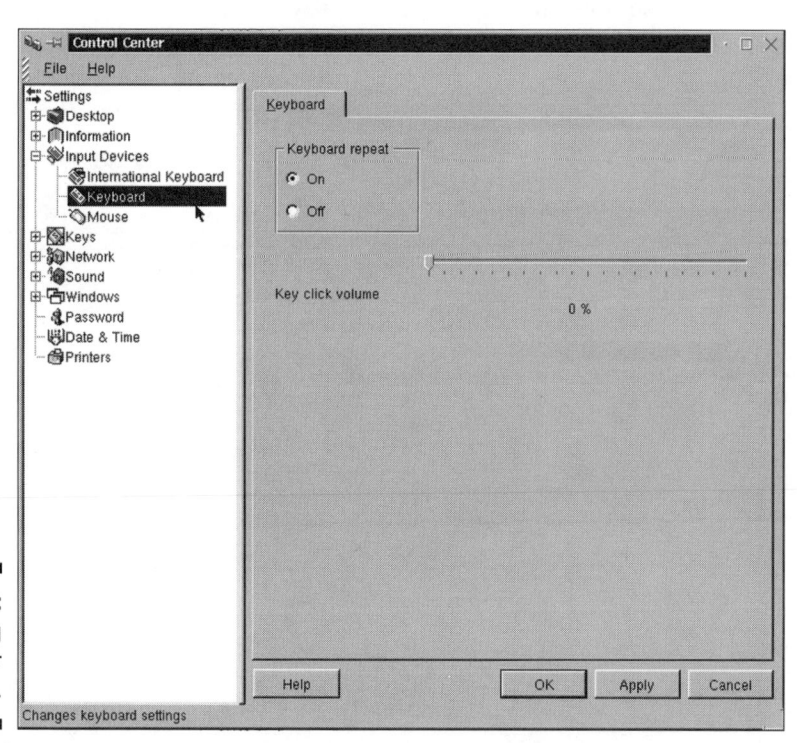

Figure 4-3: Configuring your keyboard.

Part I: Leaping to Linux

3. **Choose Mouse to adjust the following:**
   - **Acceleration,** how fast the mouse goes
   - **Threshold,** how quickly the mouse responds when you move it
   - **Button mapping** for right-handed or left-handed (left and right button actions reversed)

4. **Click OK to use the new mouse settings.**

In Chapter 9, you can find a bunch of mouse settings related to window activities.

Setting the Date and Time

Isn't it great to be on vacation and not even worry about the date and time? Wake up, you're at your computer, and it's time to synchronize! You wouldn't want to stamp the wrong date on your files or the wrong time on your e-mail messages, would you?

To prevent such temporal discord:

1. **Choose Application Starter ⇨ Control Center ⇨ Date & Time, as shown in Figure 4-4.**

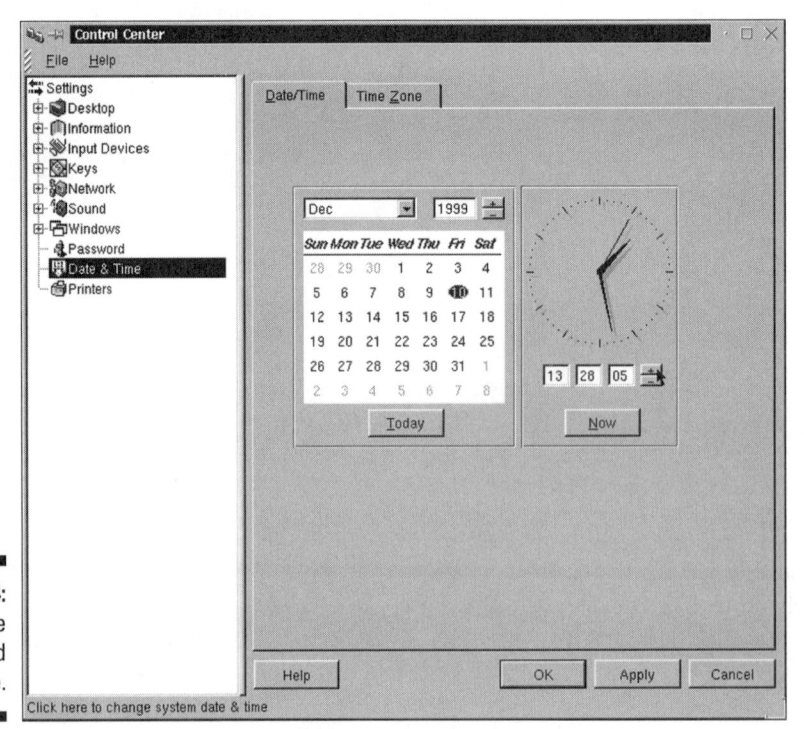

Figure 4-4: Setting the date and time.

2. **Select the month from the list, click the day, and then type the year. Or click the +/- buttons to adjust it.**

   Click Today to restore the current settings.

3. **Click the hour, minute, and second boxes and type the correct time. Or click the +/- buttons to adjust it.**

   It's a 24-hour clock, so 10 P.M. is 22 hours. Click Now to restore the current time.

4. **To keep in sync with the rest of the world, click the Time Zone tab and select your time zone from the list.**

5. **Click OK to make your changes.**

Setting Up Printers

So, you wanna print stuff, too? You have to set up your printer first. Not to worry, getting your printer to work in Corel Linux is easy. *How* your printer works, however, is not always so easy because not every printer has a custom-tailored driver for Linux; you might have to use a close substitute instead.

To set up one or more printers:

1. **Choose Application Starter ⇨ Control Center ⇨ Printers, as shown in Figure 4-5. If you're not logged in as root, supply the root password when asked.**

2. **Click Add and choose either**

   - **Locally on my Computer** for a printer hooked up to your machine. You are asked to give the printer a nickname and choose the port it uses (if in doubt, use lp0), as shown in Figure 4-6.

   - **Remotely on the Network** to access a printer connected to the network. You are asked to give the printer a nickname, specify the hostname of the server that controls the printer, and choose whether it's a Windows or UNIX/Linux network. (For a Windows network printer, you are asked to supply your network name and password.)

   > **TIP:** To install a network printer, you must to set up your network first.

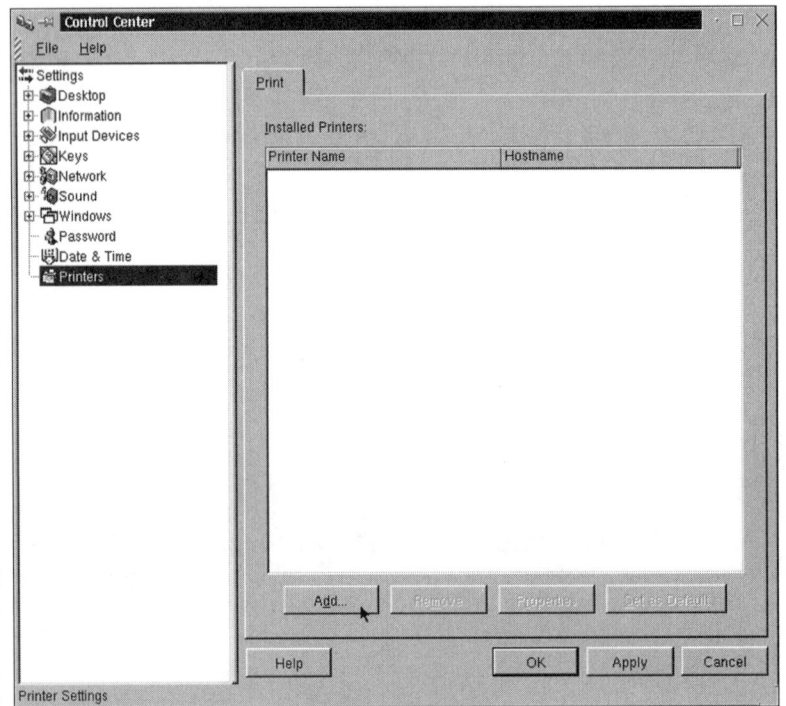

Figure 4-5: Setting up a printer.

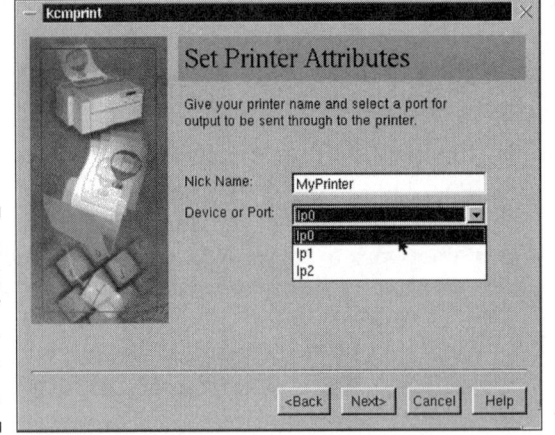

Figure 4-6: Naming your printer and assigning the correct port.

 3. **Click Next and then select the manufacturer and printer model from the drop-down lists, as shown in Figure 4-7.**

Chapter 4: Post-Install Tweaking   53

> **TIP:** If your printer's not listed, check your printer's documentation for other compatible printers you can select. You can also check with the manufacturer for the latest Linux drivers.

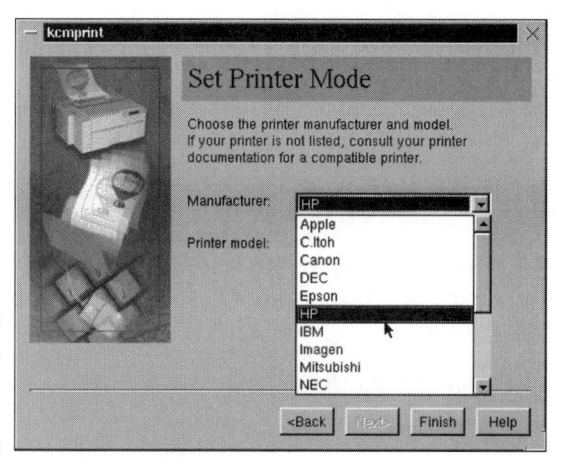

Figure 4-7: Choosing your printer.

4. Click Finish.

5. Select the printer from the list and then click Properties to change any default advanced or output settings, as shown in Figure 4-8.

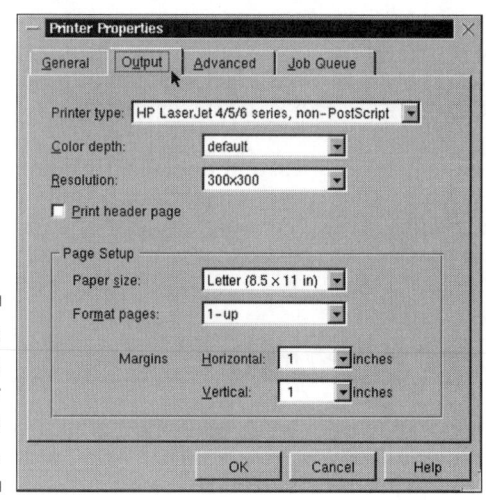

Figure 4-8: Tweaking your printer's settings.

6. **If you have more than one printer and want to change the default printer used by your Linux applications, select the printer and click Set as Default.**

7. **Click OK to keep your new printer setup.**

You should now be able to use your printer from most Linux applications. Test it out by using the Text Editor in the panel.

Connecting to the Internet

You *do* want to connect to the Internet, right? And you do have an idea of what it is, like some super-stupendous network that in some mysterious way lets millions of folks all over the world

- E-mail letters with attached photos
- Chat (not on camera, please!)
- Discuss
- Conspire
- Research
- Shop
- Form beautiful (and sometimes cantankerous) relationships

In one way or another, we're all getting connected, either through an Internet dial-up connection, a network, or (if you're so lucky) some other high-speed connection, such as ISDN, cable, ASDL, fiber optics, or satellite.

I can't cover all the high-speed possibilities, and they mostly come with some high-powered setup help anyway, such as your next-door neighbor's high-school kid. I stick to the dial-up (modem) access that most of us have (sigh), and see how to hook into a network further on.

Essential dial-up hardware

Stripped down to the bare essentials, a dial-up connection requires

- A Linux-compatible modem to transmit and receive data
- A telephone line

I know, I know, a telephone line's pretty obvious. (Please, no dumb technical-support-call jokes about the woman — never a man! — who uses the mouse as a foot pedal.) What's not so obvious is that you might want to spring for a separate line if you plan to use the Internet a lot. And who doesn't? The nice thing about a lot of high-speed options is that they combine phone (voice) and data in one.

As for the modem, most computers come with them nowadays, so you're likely to have an *internal* one, buried somewhere in your computer's innards. You'll also see *external* modems that plug into one of your machine's outlets, like a serial port or a USB connection. Then there's the PCMCIA modem on a little PC card, used mainly with portable PCs.

External modems are a bit more expensive, and I find their external wires to be a pain. Looks like a snake pit behind my computer as it is! That said, you'll rarely have a problem configuring Corel Linux to use an external modem.

If you have an ISDN modem, you have to recompile the kernel to enable support for ISDN (and your specific hardware). After that, you can use Corel Update to download and install the ISDN utility package.

Another essential: Your ISP

If you're dialing into the Internet, who're you gonna call? That'll be your friendly *Internet Service Provider* (ISP) who hooks you up to e-mail, browsing, and other Web services. If you don't have an ISP, you might check with your friends and neighbors for the best bets in your area.

Dialing into a local network, say from your home to the office, is much like dialing an ISP, so the same principles apply.

Your ISP will supply you with the essential setup information. Normally this entails

- A phone number to dial for access.
- The alphabetic domain name of your ISP.
- Primary and secondary Domain Name Server (DNS) numbers, in the 123.456.789.0 format.
- Your login ID and password.
- Your e-mail address, usually in the form *username@domain name*. The username is often the same as the login ID.

Part I: Leaping to Linux

> **TIP:** See whether your ISP can provide multiple e-mail addresses, for your spouse, 2.3 kids, dog, and cat.

- A POP3 server name, for receiving messages on your machine.
- An SMTP server name, for sending messages out.
- A newsgroup server name, to participate in Internet discussions covering every conceivable topic.

The first four items are required to connect to your ISP and browse the Web (though you don't always need the domain name.) The last four are needed to set up your e-mail application and newsreader, such as Netscape.

Sorry if it sounds complicated. You need the same information when dialing from Windows, if that's any comfort.

Configuring your dial-up connection

Got all the stuff: modem, phone line, Internet Service Provider, and essential hookup info? Okay, you can now proceed with your modem hookup:

1. **Log in with your normal user ID.**

   Each user has a separate dial-up configuration.

2. **Choose Application Starter ⇨ Applications ⇨ Network ⇨ Dial-Up.**

   The Dial-Up dialog box appears, as shown in Figure 4-9.

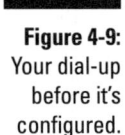

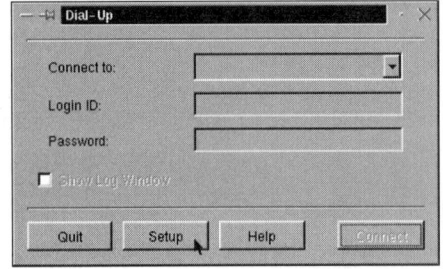

Figure 4-9: Your dial-up before it's configured.

3. **Click the Setup button.**

   The Dial-Up Configuration dialog box appears, as shown in Figure 4-10.

4. **Click New and make up a connection name for your ISP. Then enter the phone number your ISP gave you, as shown in Figure 4-11.**

Chapter 4: Post-Install Tweaking *57*

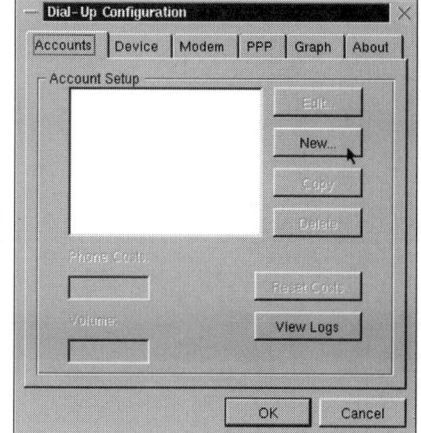

Figure 4-10: You configure your dial-up from here.

> You'll find tons of weird entries under various tabs when you're configuring your dial-up, but chances are the ones I'm describing are all you need. Need more info on a particular entry? Right-click the item and click Quickhelp.

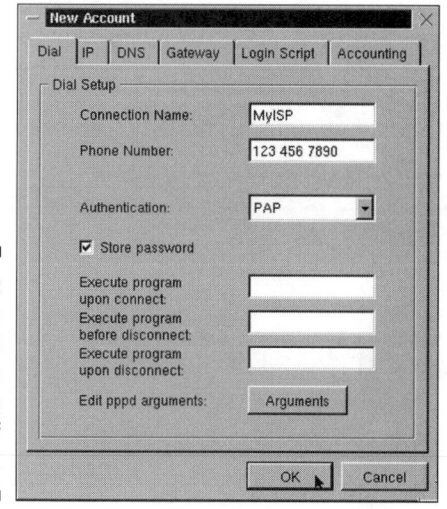

Figure 4-11: Make up a name and enter the phone number of your ISP.

5. **Click the DNS tab. In the DNS IP Address box, enter the primary and secondary numbers you got from your ISP. Click Add (or press Enter) to place each number in the list, as shown in Figure 4-12.**

   Normally, leave the Domain Name entry blank and leave the Disable existing DNS Servers during Connection option unchecked.

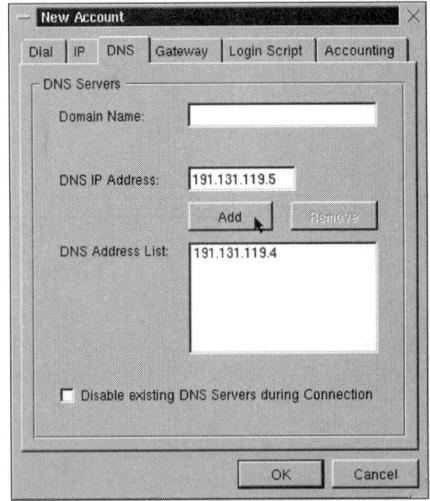

Figure 4-12: Entering the DNS numbers you got from your ISP.

6. **Click OK to return to the Dial-Up Configuration dialog box.**

7. **Click the Device tab and then select your modem device from the drop-down list, as shown in Figure 4-13. Start with /dev/ttyS0.**

    This takes a bit of explaining because usually the "modem" device at the top of the list doesn't work. Instead, select the specific communications port (COM) your modem is using. Just for laughs, these go by the names ttyS0, ttyS1, ttyS2, and ttyS3 for COM1, COM2, COM3, and COM4, respectively. Not to worry, that's just four choices, and you can use good old trial and error.

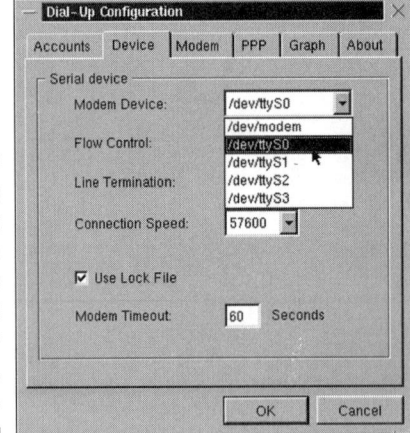

Figure 4-13: If the first modem device doesn't work, try the next, and so on.

8. **Click the Modem tab and then click the Query Modem button, as shown in Figure 4-14.**

Chapter 4: Post-Install Tweaking 59

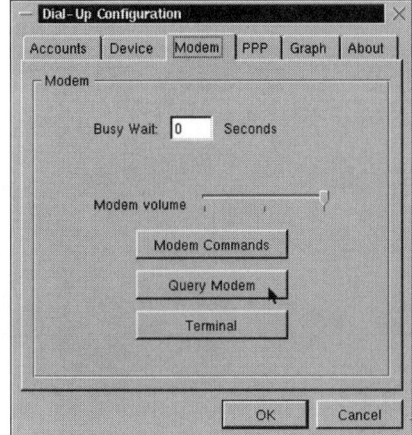

Figure 4-14: Querying your modem to see whether it works.

9. **If you get an apologetic "Sorry, can't open modem" or "Sorry, the modem doesn't respond," click the Device tab, select another device, and try again.**

10. **When you get "Modem Ready," followed by a mysterious probing, followed by a Modem Query Results display as shown in Figure 4-15 — bingo! — chances are you're ready to go. Click Close.**

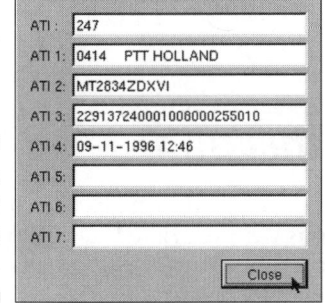

Figure 4-15: Bingo! Your modem is talking back.

TIP

Didn't make it this far? Don't give up, unless you have one of those horrible Winmodems described in Chapter 1. (Although I expect these too will be supported by Linux soon.) Check your modem's documentation or contact technical support at the modem maker or at the place you bought your computer. There may be a way out, such as by changing jumper settings or using a different port in the event of a hardware conflict.

11. **Ready to see whether it works? (Uh, you did hook up the phone wire to the modem, didn't you?) Enter your login ID name and password, as shown in Figure 4-16, and then click Connect!**

60 Part I: Leaping to Linux

> ### Trashing your dial-up options
>
> When you tried to connect, did you get an error that pppd died unexpectedly (what a phrase!) or timed out? If so, contact your ISP to ask what options need to be set in the /etc/ppp/options file.
>
> In many cases, an empty options file — or no file at all — does the trick. As root, rename the /etc/ppp/options file to options.old in case you need to return to the original. Then create a new /etc/ppp/options and leave it empty or don't create a file at all!

Figure 4-16: Okay, let's connect!

Please, tell me you made it! If so, you're ready for a cyberspace cruise in Chapter 15.

Connecting and disconnecting

After you have the dial-up working, connecting to your ISP is a no-brainer. Choose Application Starter ➪ Applications ➪ Network ➪ Dial-Up and then click Connect. Unless you changed the default setting, Dial-Up remembers your login ID and password from the previous session.

The Connect button becomes Disconnect after you're in. Simply click Disconnect when you want to end the session. The session also terminates if you log out of the desktop.

Hooking into a Local Network

Dialing up from home to your ISP is one form of networking. Usually when we speak of a *network* though, we're talking about a *local area network (LAN),* found in corporate skyscrapers, your local health clinic, or even in a home office. A local network consists of

- A *server* computer that runs the show
- Terminals, computers, printers, and other devices

All the devices (nodes) on a local network are physically linked together through *Ethernet* (network) cards and cables, so that they can communicate with one another and share files, programs, and other resources.

Some LANs don't even have a server. Smaller networks often use a peer-to-peer architecture of computing equals, rather than the client/server architecture of larger networks. This is your typical home network if, say, you network a Linux PC and a Windows PC.

Two types of local network hookups

The Corel Linux Control Center has two types of local network hookups:

- **TCP/IP,** which uses industry-standard means of transmitting local network and Internet data. UNIX/Linux machines usually run this type of network.
- **Windows Workgroups,** which can share resources on a Windows-based network.

Corel Linux works perfectly with either or both!

Getting hooked up

"Whoa," you say, "stop right here! I'm over something-teen years old. I can't do this!" Wrong! As long as you have a supported network card, Corel Linux automatically detects it during installation and sets things up so it will work. All that's left for you to do is hook up the cable and fill in a few blanks with identifying details.

Take a clean notepad over to your network administrator (the drudge who keeps the data flowing), and have the administrator write down the information you need. Promise pizza, bonbons . . . whatever's his or her weakness. If you're the one who set up the network, you still deserve a reward!

Hooking up to a TCP/IP network

To hook up to a TCP/IP network, here's what you do:

Part I: Leaping to Linux

1. **Wedge the notepad with the administrator's weird scribbles between your keyboard and the right side of your monitor.**

2. **Log out, if necessary, and log in as root.**

3. **Choose Application Starter ➪ Control Center and then double-click Network.**

4. **Choose TCP/IP and then enter the hostname (the name of your computer) and the domain name (the name of the local network), as shown in Figure 4-17.**

   This tells your computer who to connect to, and tells the network who you are, so you can get on the office joke list.

5. **Click the IP Address tab and then click to select the Enable ethernet option, as shown in Figure 4-18.**

   The Ethernet interface selection is in case you have two cards. If so, select the card your cable is hooked up to.

   You can uncheck (disable) Ethernet to save on resources if you don't plan on running on a network. You might also want to disable Ethernet to secure a machine, such as a point-of-sale terminal, so that information doesn't get out to the network.

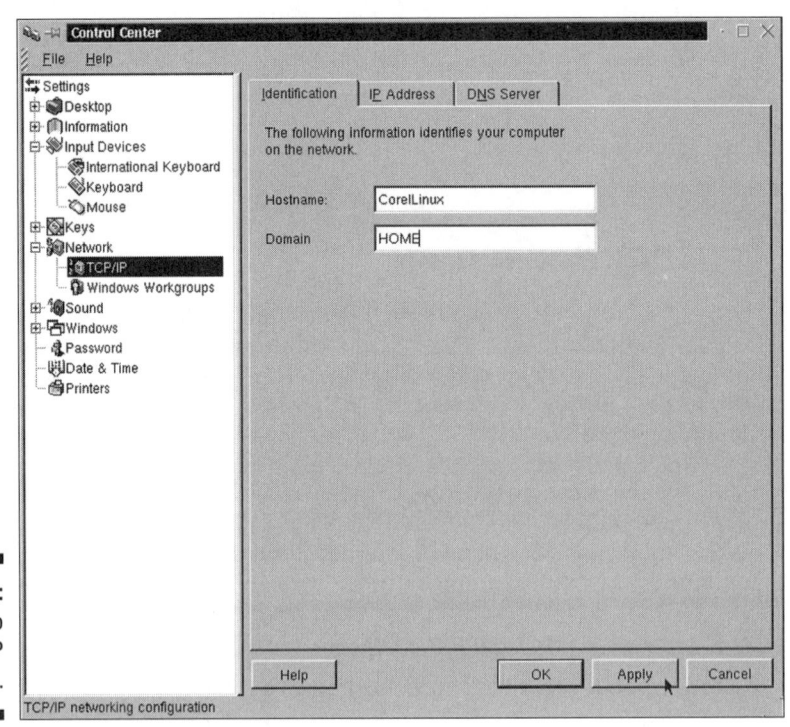

Figure 4-17: Hooking up to a TCP/IP network.

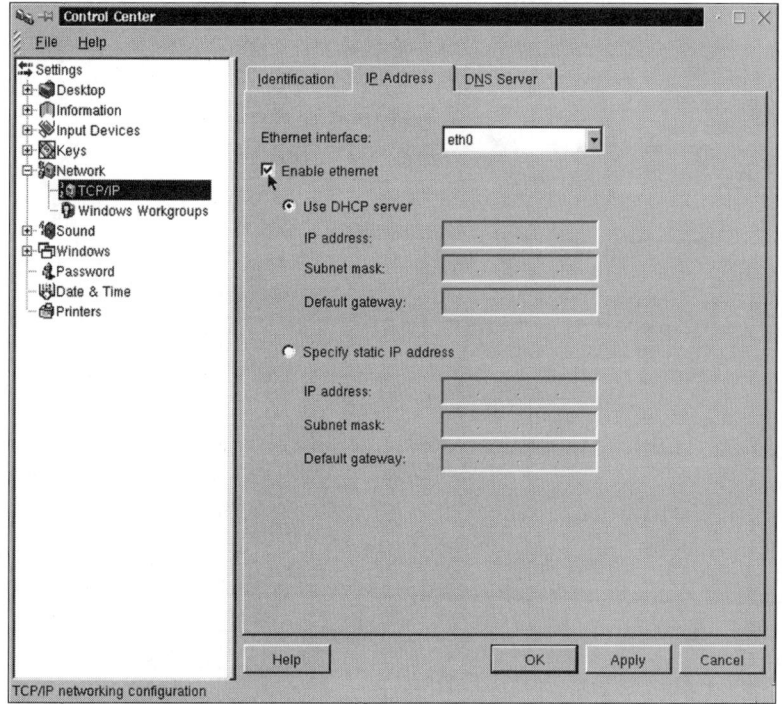

Figure 4-18: Enabling your Ethernet connection.

6. Next, do *one* of the following to provide your computer's network address:

    - Choose **Use DCHP server** if the network server assigns a different IP address to your computer each time you connect. (You won't need to enter the IP address, subnet mask, and default gateway.)

    - Choose **Specify static IP address** and enter the address if an IP address is permanently assigned to your computer. (Check with your system administrator for the information required here.) If your network contains subnetworks, fill in the IP address of the subnet mask and default gateway so your computer can access the entire network.

7. Click the DNS Server tab. Then click Add to enter the IP address for each Domain Name Service (DNS) server your local network uses, as shown in Figure 4-19. Click OK.

    The DNS server resolves host and domain names into IP addresses.

8. Click OK to save your TCP/IP network setup.

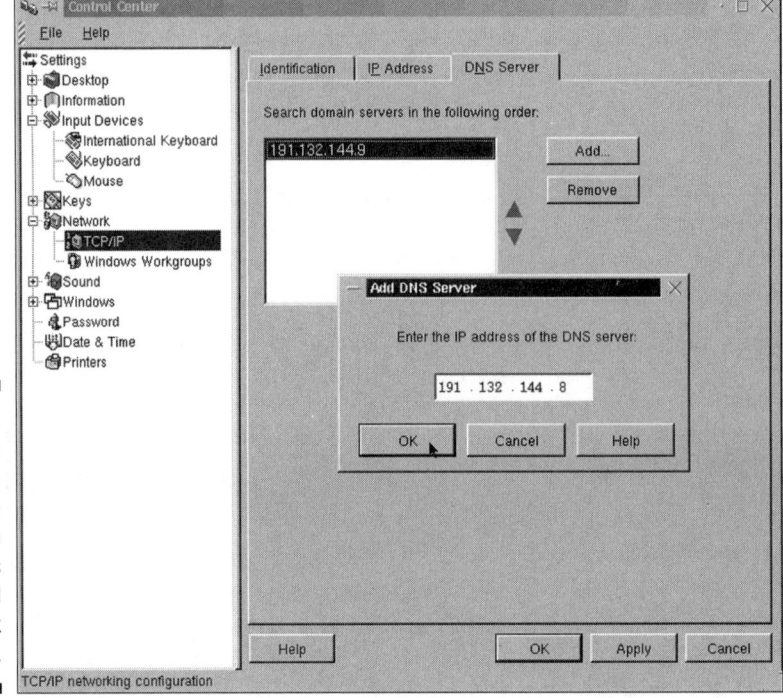

Figure 4-19: Adding the Domain Name Service addresses your local network uses.

Hooking up to a Windows Workgroup

After you've pried a little information out of your network administrator, hooking up to a Windows Workgroup is a slice of pie:

1. **Log out, if necessary, and log in as root.**

2. **Choose Application Starter ⇨ Control Center and then double-click Network.**

3. **Choose Windows Workgroups.**

4. **Click to check Enable Samba, as shown in Figure 4-20, and then enter the following identifying information:**

    - **Description** of your computer
    - **Workgroup** to which your computer belongs
    - **WINS server** (if your network has one) to quickly locate another computer on the network through its current network address

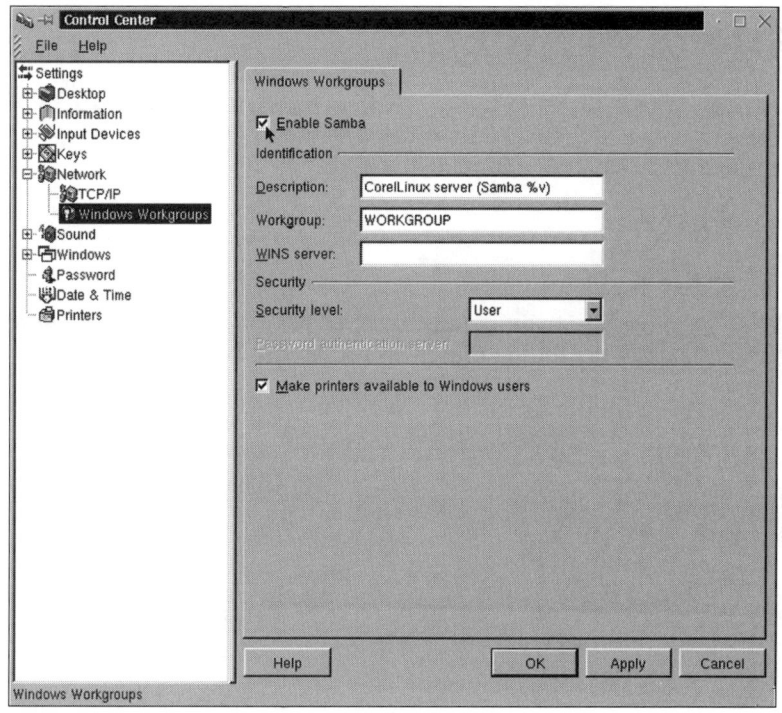

Figure 4-20:
Hooking up to a Windows workgroup.

5. **Choose the security level.**

   This is normally User unless your administrator says otherwise.

6. **Choose whether or not you want to make printers attached to your machine available to other users on the network.**

7. **Click OK to save your Windows Workgroup setup.**

Samba rocks on a Windows network

Samba client software is installed automatically with Corel Linux. What is Samba? It's your secret weapon for invading a Windows network.

Samba lets your Corel Linux system share files and printer services on a network with other UNIX/Linux computers and with computers on a Microsoft Windows network.

After you physically plug your machine into the Windows network and identify it to the network through the Windows Workgroup setup, your Linux machine becomes part of the Windows network. Remote drives and folders to which you have access magically appear in the Corel File Manager. You can immediately print stuff on a network printer. Samba rocks!

Part I: Leaping to Linux

Is Anyone Missing?

Your kids are tired of playing Windows games? Set them up with their own user IDs (so they can't do any harm to your personal or system files) and let them romp around in Corel Linux!

To add a user:

1. **Log in as root.**
2. **Choose Application Starter ➪ Applications➪System➪User Manager to display the dialog box shown in Figure 4-21.**

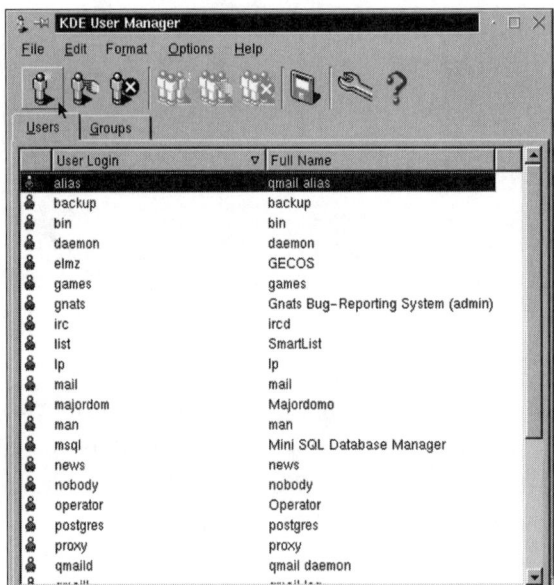

Figure 4-21: Go to the User Manager to add a new user.

3. **Click the Add User button and assign a name for the user in the User login box, as shown in Figure 4-22.**

   The login shell and home directory are filled in automatically. The personal user information is not required.

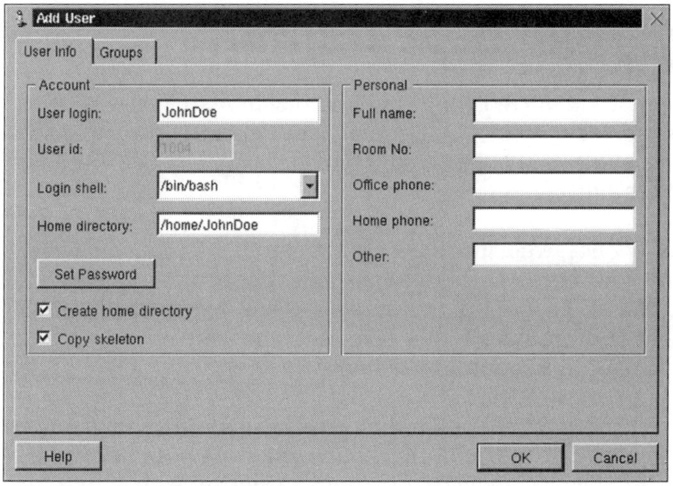

Figure 4-22: Adding a user.

4. **Click the Set Password button to assign a user password, as shown in Figure 4-23. Type and retype the password and then click OK.**

5. **Click OK to add the user.**

Users you add are assigned to a primary group set up by the system.

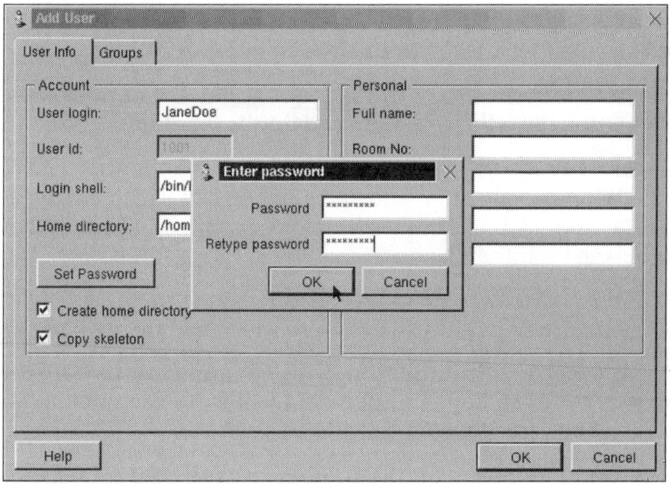

Figure 4-23: Setting the user password.

Changing Your Boot Defaults

Let's say you converted your Windows machine to a dual-boot Linux/Windows system. You normally boot up and do all your work, Web browsing, and e-mail in Linux, and only occasionally use Windows programs when there's no close substitute.

But your spouse, well, just hasn't gotten around to changing from the old ways and goes berserk when the machine boots up to Linux. "I don't want this . . . how do I get out of this screen!" (How come kids never say that?) The best way out of trouble, in this case, is to change your Corel *Linux Loader (LILO)* to boot to Windows by default.

This is an advanced operation that involves messing with your *master boot record*. If you screw up, your machine might not boot until you restore the boot record. I'm assuming that you're a responsible child or maybe an adult. Otherwise, how did you get root access?

If you have an inkling of what you're doing, here's the trick:

1. **Log in as root, click the Text Editor button on the panel, and open the /etc/lilo.conf file.**

2. **Among the list of boot selections, find the label for the multiline section describing your Windows boot partition, as shown in Figure 4-24.**

    The label is probably near the bottom of the OS pecking order. You'll see the likes of label=dos or, in this example, label=MS_Windows.

3. **On a line near the top of the file, above the list of boot selections, add** default=dos **(or whatever the selection is labeled).**

    In Figure 4-25, I added the line Default = MS_Windows, to match the label of the Windows partition shown in Figure 4-24. I also changed the boot-up delay from 300 to 100 (10 seconds). For more on using the Text Editor, see Chapter 13.

    A trickier way to make Windows the default is to move the section describing the Windows selection to the top of the pecking order.

4. **Do you want to adjust the time your computer waits before going on if you don't press a key? Change delay=300 (30 seconds) to another value, as I did in Figure 4-25.**

5. **Click the Save button on the toolbar to save your changes.**

Chapter 4: Post-Install Tweaking 69

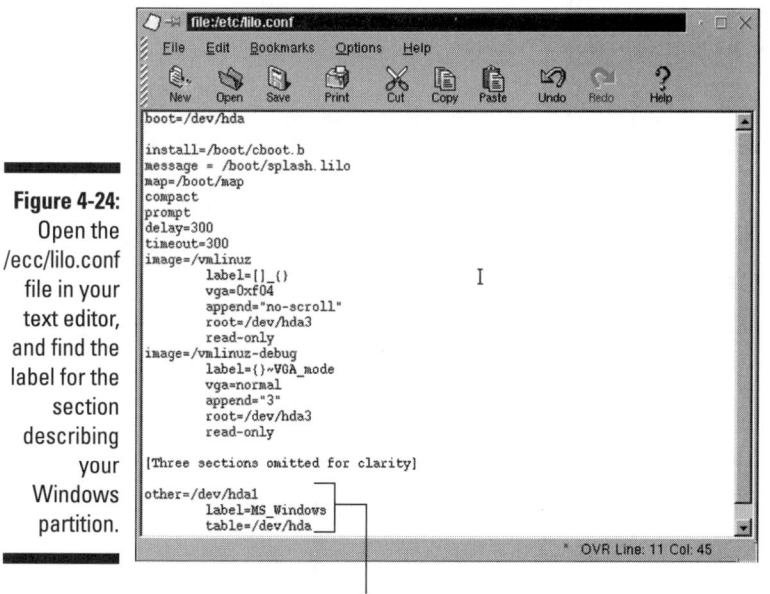

Figure 4-24: Open the /ecc/lilo.conf file in your text editor, and find the label for the section describing your Windows partition.

```
boot=/dev/hda

install=/boot/cboot.b
message = /boot/splash.lilo
map=/boot/map
compact
prompt
delay=300
timeout=300
image=/vmlinuz
        label=[]_()
        vga=0xf04
        append="no-scroll"
        root=/dev/hda3
        read-only
image=/vmlinuz-debug
        label=()~VGA_mode
        vga=normal
        append="3"
        root=/dev/hda3
        read-only

[Three sections omitted for clarity]

other=/dev/hda1
        label=MS_Windows
        table=/dev/hda
```

Section describing Windows boot partition

Entry to change the default boot selection

Change in the boot-up delay

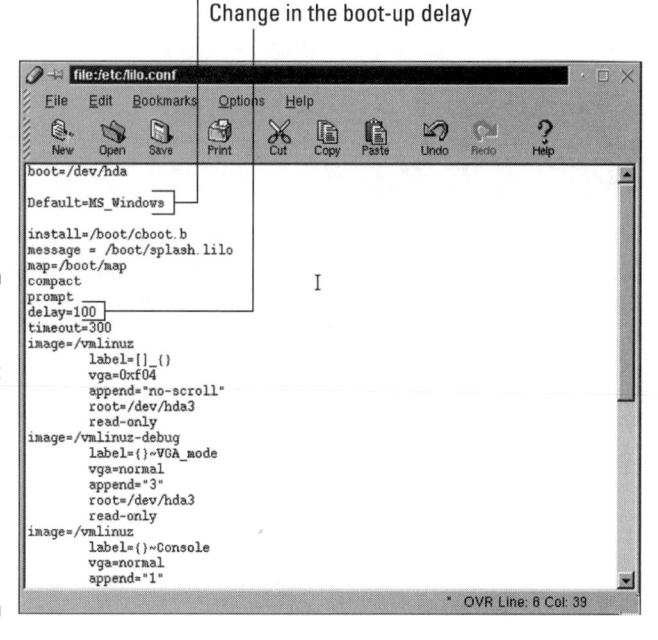

Figure 4-25: Changing the default boot selection as well as the time the system waits before choosing the default.

```
boot=/dev/hda

Default=MS_Windows

install=/boot/cboot.b
message = /boot/splash.lilo
map=/boot/map
compact
prompt
delay=100
timeout=300
image=/vmlinuz
        label=[]_()
        vga=0xf04
        append="no-scroll"
        root=/dev/hda3
        read-only
image=/vmlinuz-debug
        label=()~VGA_mode
        vga=normal
        append="3"
        root=/dev/hda3
        read-only
image=/vmlinuz
        label=()~Console
        vga=normal
        append="1"
```

Part I: Leaping to Linux

6. **Click the Console button on the panel. Then type** lilo **as shown in Figure 4-26, and press Enter.**

   This writes your changes to the master boot record. The Console displays a list of your boot choices, with an asterisk next to your default Windows selection.

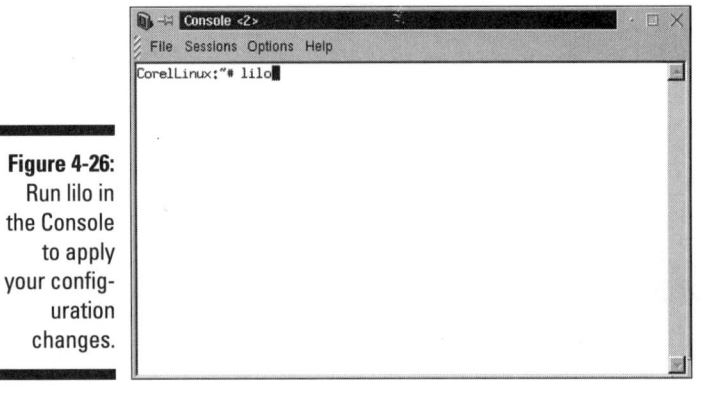

Figure 4-26:
Run lilo in the Console to apply your configuration changes.

The next time you boot up, your Windows selection should appear at the top of the list and automatically load after the specified delay if you don't touch a key.

Installing Acrobat Reader and Netscape Communicator

If you installed the Download Edition of Corel Linux from your *Corel Linux For Dummies* CD, you can also install Adobe Acrobat Reader and the full Netscape Communicator Suite. See Appendix C for details.

Part II
Taking the Grand Tour

The 5th Wave — **By Rich Tennant**

MODERN MARRIAGE
©RICHTENNANT

"WE'RE AGREED ON THE SILVER PATTERN, WALLPAPER AND CARPET SCHEME, BUT WE'RE STILL HASHING OUT THE OPERATING SYSTEM."

In this part . . .

Somehow, the words *grand tour* recall a visit to the magnificent Chateau de Versailles outside Paris. Corel Linux is a bit more utilitarian than those palatial ballrooms and salons, one hundred sixty-eight dish banquets, and folks loaded down with about three kilos of lace.

Wonder what Louis XIV would make of the desktop?

Chapter 5

Dancin' on the Desktop

In This Chapter
▶ Meeting a lovely (inter)face
▶ Controlling operations from the panel
▶ Launching anything and everything from the program menu
▶ Switching programs with a single click
▶ Juggling multiple desktops
▶ Discovering the keys to success
▶ Finding help

*W*arning to old-time Linux or UNIX users: The Corel Linux desktop may short a few circuits in your brain! Aw, you won't need them anyway. If you're new to Linux, just saunter onto the desktop and survey the beautiful scene. A few rungs from perfection perhaps, but state-of-the-art cool and easy to use.

There's stuff here that Windows users can only dream about, such as multiple desktops and zany themes. What is this, a desktop or a playground? The latter perhaps, when you find out about all its graphical tricks (in Chapters 7 and 8) and how you can customize the desktop to your exquisite tastes (in Chapters 9 and 10).

Tell your friends that Corel Linux has a great GUI (graphical user interface). Be sure to pronounce it "gooey" when you do. (It got that name from those annoying types who eat jelly doughnuts while leaning over your shoulder to touch the screen and say, "you have a spelling mistake there!")

Wow! This Is Linux?

Are you on the lovely graphical desktop in Figure 5-1? If not, log in now so we can admire it together.

Figure 5-1:
Wow, wow, wow!

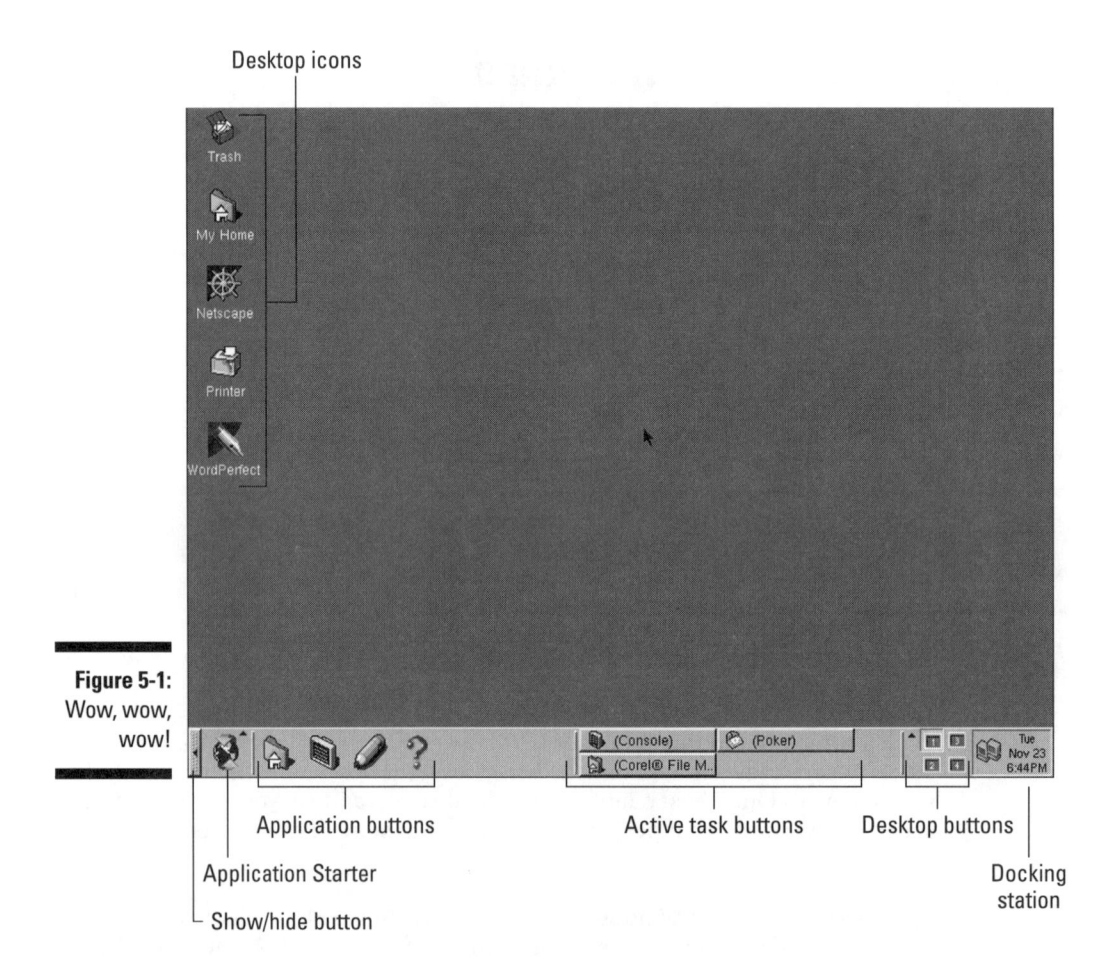

Desktop icons — Trash, My Home, Netscape, Printer, WordPerfect

Show/hide button
Application Starter
Application buttons
Active task buttons
Desktop buttons
Docking station

Wow, this is Linux? Corel Linux is cooler than a Mac or a Windows machine!

Panel Discussion

Pretty clean screen, no? First, you have a few "nickname" shortcut icons for quick access to your favorite tools and applications, such as the trash can for discarded files. North American users generate tons of waste, so they get a dumpster instead.

Chapter 5: Dancin' on the Desktop

Second, you get an all-purpose panel is at the bottom of the screen. The panel is your desktop center of operations, so let's give it a little test run:

- ✓ Click the little *show/hide button* on the left to scoot the panel out of the way. Click the button again to bring it back.

  When you slide the panel off the screen, a miniature Application Starter and window list appear in the upper-left corner of the screen.

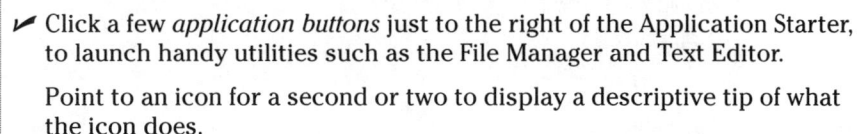

- ✓ Click *Application Starter* to locate and run various programs.

- ✓ Click a few *application buttons* just to right of the Application Starter, to launch handy utilities such as the File Manager and Text Editor.

  Point to an icon for a second or two to display a descriptive tip of what the icon does.

- ✓ Note how for each program you launch, a *task button* appears in the middle of the panel. Click the task buttons to switch between applications.

- ✓ Move further to the right and click a *desktop button*. Behold, you can switch entire virtual desktops, each with its own applications, just as easily as you switch applications on a single desktop! (We'll get to virtual desktops in a few minutes.)

- ✓ Finally, you see the good ol' date and time in the *docking station* on the right, plus a handy icon to click when you're in the mood to twiddle your display settings. You'll notice that other programs you run, such as notes and international keyboards, place icons here for easy access.

There you have the panel essentials. Oh, try this: Click a blank spot in the panel and then hold the mouse button as you drag the panel to the top or side of the screen. For a bunch of other panel tricks, check out Chapter 9. You tell me this isn't fun!

Launching Programs

Icons on the desktop and panel are great for launching your favorite programs and utilities. If you're looking for everything but the kitchen sink, however, go to the program menu instead:

1. **Click the Application Starter.**
2. **Click your way through the menus and then click the program you want to launch, as shown in Figure 5-2.**

Part II: Taking the Grand Tour

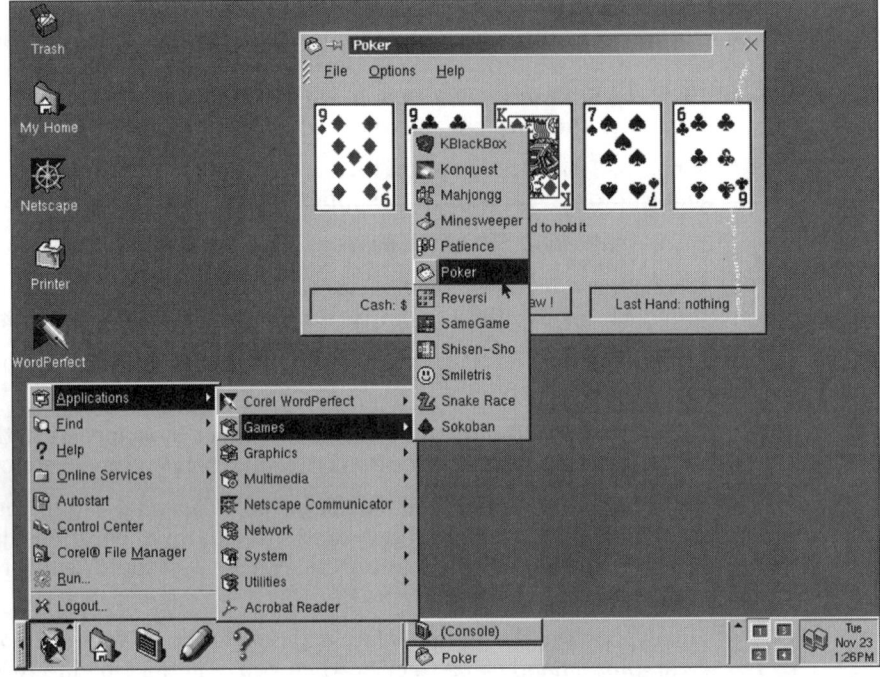

Figure 5-2:
Click the Application Starter, browse the menus, and then click a program to launch it.

Notice how the top selections on the main Application Starter menu have little triangles on the right that branch out to *submenus* of additional selections. The Applications selection, in turn, branches out into more categories, for Games, Graphics, Multimedia, and so on.

Take a minute to explore the menus to see all the stuff on your system. Jump to Chapter 6 if you care to hang out there for a while. Okay, you can play Snake Race, but come back soon — there's more stuff to see in the rest of this chapter!

Switching between Programs

Back so soon? Want to find out about more tricks?

Because Linux is a true multitasking environment, you can run a bunch of programs at one time without fear that they'll trip over one another or crash the system. But how do you switch from one active program to another, such as from your word processor to your Internet browser?

Couldn't be easier. Just click the program window you want to use, as shown in Figure 5-3.

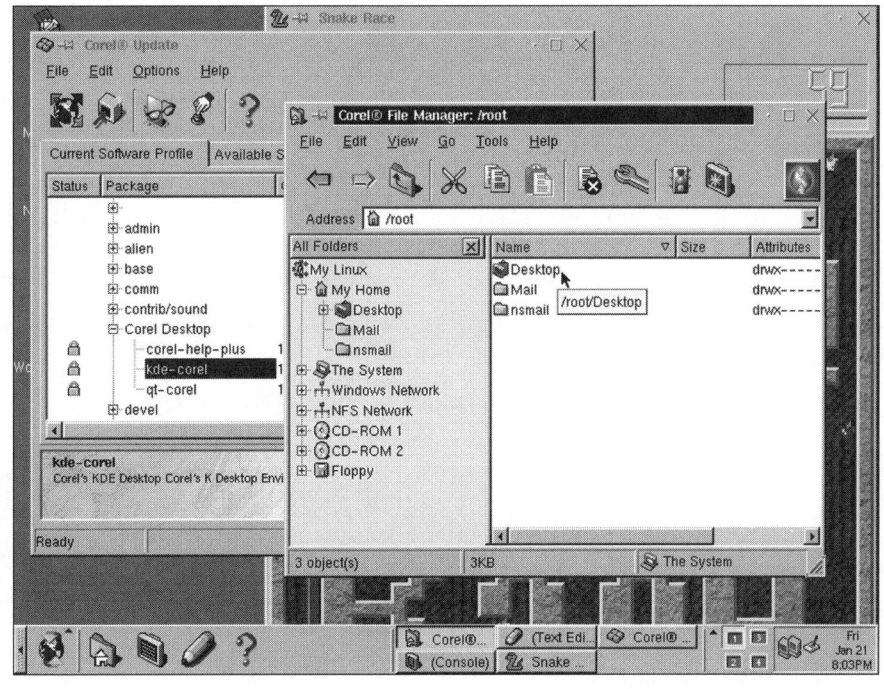

Figure 5-3: To use a program, just click its window.

If the program you want isn't visible, you can always click its task button on the panel. Note how the task button for the active program appears pushed in.

TIP

Drag a program window by its title bar (the top part with the name) to position it on the screen.

Tired of using the mouse? Press Alt+Tab to switch between the active programs on your desktop. (Press Alt+Shift+Tab to switch in reverse.)

Did Someone Say "Multiple Desktops"?

So, you think running multiple programs is handy? Try running multiple desktops! Corel Linux lets you run as many as eight desktops at once, and each desktop can have its own program windows.

Want to play Asteroids at work when your boss isn't looking? Click the 2 button on the panel and play Asteroids in Desktop 2. Then click the 1 button when you hear footsteps, to jump back to your regular work. It's that simple!

Even when you're not playing games, multiple desktops are a handy way to reduce clutter and arrange what you're doing. You might use Desktop 1 for a full-screen display of the report you're writing, Desktop 2 for your graphics programs, Desktop 3 for browsing the Internet, and Desktop 4 to run a Web server. The possibilities are endless and entirely up to you.

I know, you can't keep a single Windows desktop from crashing, so it's hard to believe that Linux can handle multiple desktops with aplomb. You'll just have to get used to it! Desktops come in twos, so you can have either two, four, six, or eight. Chapter 9 shows how to change this and other desktop settings.

Sticky windows

Now here's a cute trick:

1. **On Desktop 1, open the poker game and play with it a bit.**
2. **Click the pushpin at the upper left to "stick" the poker game on all your desktops.**
3. **Click the 4 button on the panel to switch to Desktop 4 and then play a few more hands.**
4. **Go to Desktop 3 and click the pushpin again. This "unsticks" the poker game, so it appears only in Desktop 3.**
5. **Try this on a Windows machine (just kiddin').**

Note that the result (aside from losing $50) was that you moved the poker game from Desktop 1 to Desktop 3. Another way to move a window is to right-click its title bar, click the To Desktop option, and then choose another desktop, as shown in Figure 5-4.

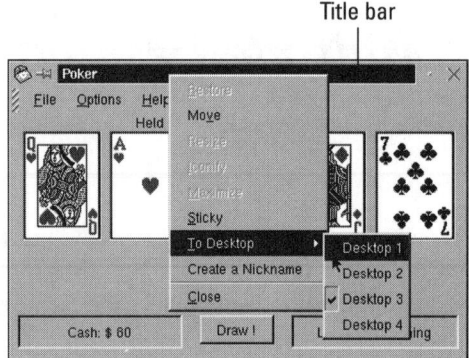

Figure 5-4: Right-click the title bar to move an application to another desktop.

Desktop Manager tricks

I saved the best desktop tricks for last. Still playing poker on Desktop 3? Well, just to the left of the desktop buttons on the panel, find the little button with an arrow. Click the button to pop up the graphical Desktop Manager. Then drag the miniature display of the poker game from Desktop 3 in the upper right to Desktop 2 in the lower left, as shown in Figure 5-5. Way cool, or whatever superlative you care to use!

Figure 5-5: The pop-up Desktop Manager lets you drag your poker game to another desktop!

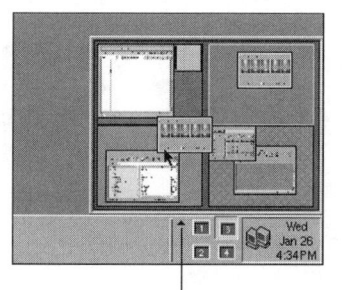

Click here to display Desktop Manager

The Desktop Manager gives you a nice visual display of what's on all your desktops. You can switch desktops from there with a click of the mouse. Again, folks, don't try this on Windows.

Your Keys to Success

For those of us who hate to memorize keystrokes and birthdays, the graphical interface is a godsend. Like a kid in the candy store or a tourist in a foreign land, we just point (and click) to get what we need.

Nonetheless, most graphical operations have keystroke equivalents that you might want to use for any of these reasons:

- You hate using a mouse or other pointing device.
- Your speed demon hands can't stand the constant interruptions of mousing around.
- You have a physical limitation that makes pointing and clicking a difficult or impossible task.
- You want to show your friends how good you are at memorizing stuff.

Part II: Taking the Grand Tour

If you're old enough to have used a typewriter, you know it's an excellent device for entering text. But the computer keyboard, shown in Figure 5-6, has it all over the typewriter. It has the features described in Table 5-1 that make it a powerful, versatile tool.

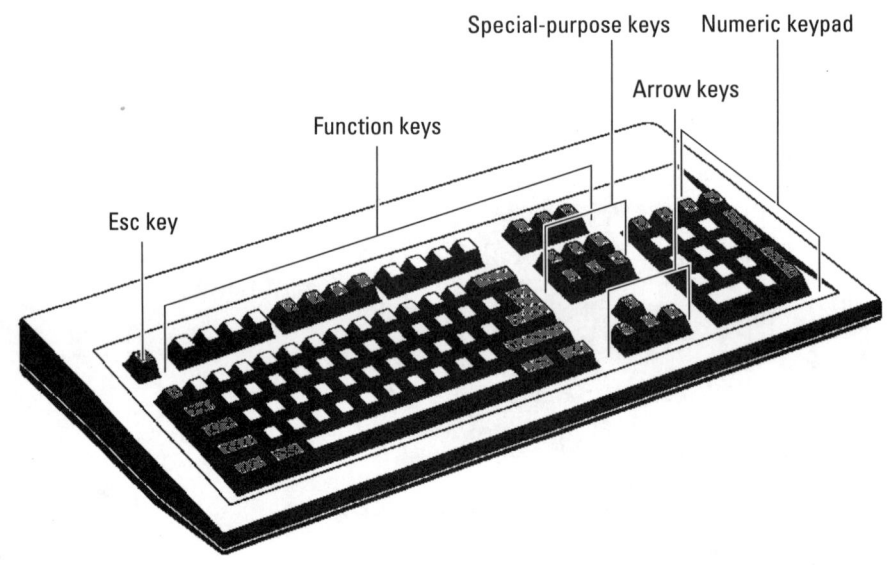

Figure 5-6: Your computer keyboard is a powerful, versatile tool.

Table 5-1	Keyboard Features
Type of Key	*Operation*
Numeric (keypad)	Found on most full-sized keyboards, lets you perform calculations and enter numbers (make sure Num Lock is on).
Function	The pre-mouse standard for performing specific program operations. The most notorious function key is F1, for Help.
Shift	Enables all keys, including the function keys, to perform two operations.
Ctrl and Alt	Enables the other keys to do multiple functions, just as the Shift key does. When used in combination with Shift, they provide more possibilities than you'd care to remember.
Arrow	Gets you anywhere on the screen in two seconds flat. Like most other keys, the arrow keys repeat when you hold them down.

Type of Key	Operation
Special-purpose	Insert, Delete, Home, End, Page Up, and Page Down are special-purpose keys. They can be especially handy when used with other keys (such as Ctrl, Alt, and the arrow keys).
Esc	A quick way out of dialog boxes, menus, and other tight places.

Corel Linux has two types of keyboard shortcuts:

- Global keys for chugging around the desktop and managing windows
- Standard keys for when you're working in many programs

Here are the cheat sheets to the global (desktop) and standard (program) keystrokes. You can customize these to your liking, as described in Chapter 9. Some programs, such as WordPerfect, have separate settings for their keyboard shortcuts.

Global (desktop) keyboard shortcuts

Table 5-2 provides a handy cheat sheet to the global (desktop) shortcut keys.

Table 5-2	Handy-Dandy Global (Desktop) Keystrokes
Keystroke	Does This Desktop Trick
Ctrl+Tab	Switches desktops; hold the Ctrl key and keep pressing Tab till you arrive at the desktop you want
Ctrl+F1 through Ctrl+F8	Switches to desktop 1 through 8
Alt+Tab	Switches between active applications; hold Alt and press Tab till you arrive at the one you want
Alt+F1	Pops up the program menu; you can then search the menus by using the arrow keys and press Enter to run the highlighted program
Alt+F2	Enables you to type a Linux command, as described in Chapter 3
Alt+F3	Displays a menu of window operations, such as maximizing the window to fill the entire desktop, resizing it with the arrow keys, or moving it to another desktop

(continued)

Table 5-2 (continued)

Keystroke	Does This Desktop Trick
Alt+F4	Closes the current window
Alt+F7	Moves the window by using the arrow keys
Alt+F8	Resizes the window by using the arrow keys
Alt+F9	Makes the current window an icon
Alt+F10	Maximizes or restores the current window
Ctrl+Esc	Displays the list of tasks you can switch to
Ctrl+Alt+Esc	Kills the next window you click without saving any work

Alt+Ctrl+Fx and Alt+Ctrl+Shift+Fx (where Fx is any function key) result in a new Linux login, like using another machine, and you might not be able to find your way out. Stay away from these keystrokes!

What, you didn't listen? Okay then, press Alt+Ctrl+F7 to return to your cozy Corel Linux desktop.

Standard (program) keyboard shortcuts

Table 5-3 provides a handy cheat sheet to the standard (program) shortcut keys.

Table 5-3   Handy-Dandy Standard (Program) Keystrokes

Operation	Keystroke
Close	Ctrl+W
Cut	Ctrl+C
Copy	Ctrl+X
End	Ctrl+End
Find	Ctrl+F
Help	F1
Home	Ctrl+Home
Insert	Ctrl+Insert
New	Ctrl+N

Chapter 5: Dancin' on the Desktop

Operation	Keystroke
Next	Page Down
Open	Ctrl+O
Paste	Ctrl+V
Print	Ctrl+P
Prior	Page Up
Quit	Ctrl+Q
Replace	Ctrl+R
Save	Ctrl+S
Undo	Ctrl+Z

Getting Help

In case your *Corel Linux For Dummies* book ever walks away, just click the Help button on the panel to pop up a Navigator window with the Corel Linux *User Manual* displayed, as shown in Figure 5-7.

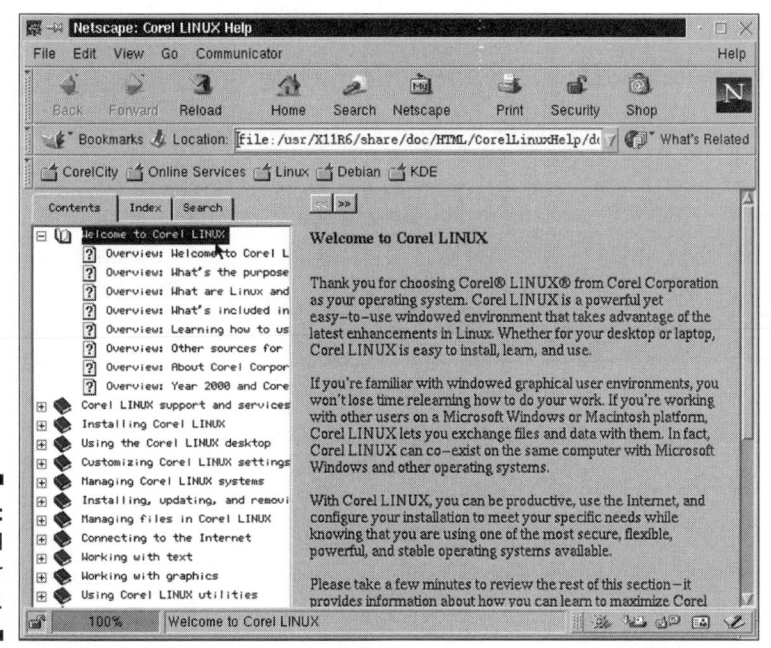

Figure 5-7: The Corel Linux *User Manual.*

You can browse the contents, look up a topic in the index, or do a keyword search.

Need more help? Check out the fabulous lineup of free help resources in Chapter 20 — from support newsgroups to online documentation, and more.

Chapter 6

Meet the Stars!

In This Chapter
- Checking out the program stars on your desktop
- Finding out who's costarring on the main menu
- Meeting the supporting cast of submenu selections
- Discovering the installed extras not on the menus
- Giving the command line its due
- That's just the tip of the iceberg of program talent

Although Corel Linux is a wonderful operating system, it's still only a means to an end. I'm sure you came here with a purpose — maybe to write a letter, play Smiletris, draw a picture, or browse the Web.

Thousands of Linux programs are out there, with more arriving every day. Choosing the ones to put on your system is sort of like wandering the supermarket aisles with a shopping cart: text editors on your left in aisle 2; games in aisle 4; spreadsheets in aisle 7. Most of the goods in this supermarket are free, so if you're like me, you're tempted to drive home with a truckload of stuff.

How do you choose which programs to use? Rather than overwhelming you with every text editor or game out there, Install Express does your shopping for you and then serves up a carefully prepared feast of applications.

Of course, none of these programs will do you much good if you don't know where they are or how to run them. That's where the graphical interface comes in. If you'll allow me to switch metaphors, we can think of the available programs as a hierarchy of film or stage actors:

- The stars, with desktop icons or panel buttons
- The costars on the main menu
- The supporting cast, on the submenus
- The installed extras, not on the menus
- The waiting-on-tables-and-driving-cabs crowd of uninstalled programs

Part II: Taking the Grand Tour

This chapter shows you what programs you have, with handy cross-references to the chapters that show how to use them.

Stars on Stage

Your star programs are always on stage as the desktop icons and panel buttons shown in Figure 6-1.

Desktop icons

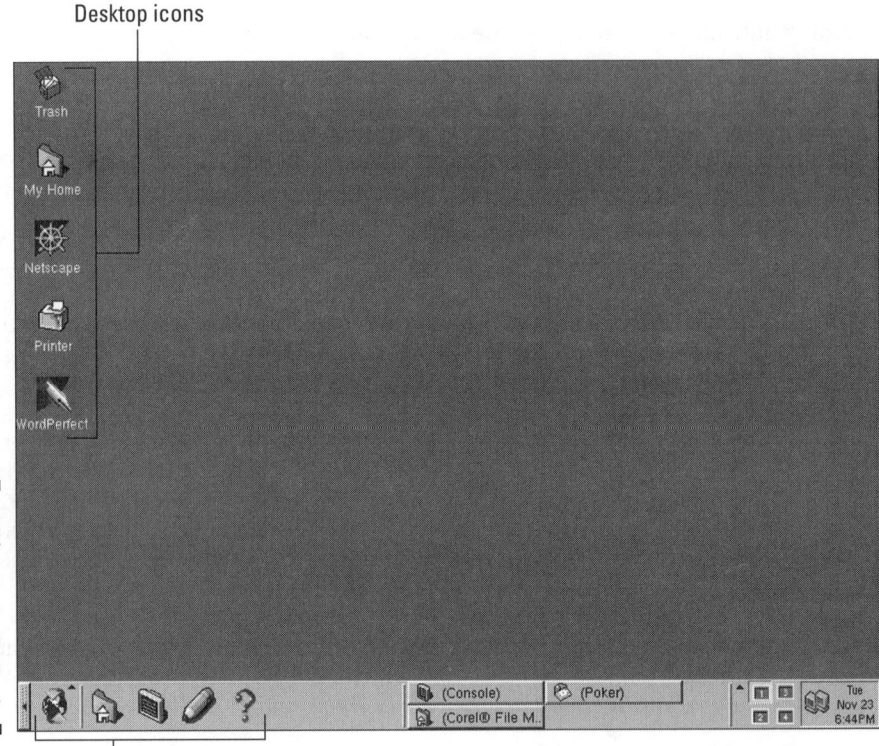

Figure 6-1: Your program stars on stage are just one click away.

Panel buttons

You can figure that if the Corel folks saw fit to put them front and center, they're pretty essential for most users. If you're not one of the "most users," you can add, remove, and rearrange the cast as you see fit. But that's a subject for Chapter 9. For now, let's look at these star programs as described in Table 6-1.

Chapter 6: Meet the Stars!

Table 6-1   Star Programs with Desktop Icons or Panel Buttons

Icon or Button	Its Name	Lets You...	See
Trash	Trash	Dig discarded files out of the trash	Chapter 11
My Home	My Home	Open the File Manager at your home folder	Chapter 11
Netscape	Netscape	Browse the Web, go shopping, and so on	Chapter 15
Printer	Printer	Install and configure your printer	Chapter 4
WordPerfect	WordPerfect	Write books or anything else	WordPerfect's online help
	Application Starter	Access everything on your menus	This chapter
	Corel File Manager	Open the File Manager at your home folder	Chapter 11
	Console	Go nongraphical by typing your Linux commands in the Console window	Chapter 3
	Text Editor	Use kwrite to create and edit basic text files	Chapter 13
	Help	Get help	Chapter 5

The WordPerfect icon appears only if you installed the Standard or Deluxe boxed editions of Corel Linux.

Part II: Taking the Grand Tour

Costars on the Main Menu

Your costar programs are one click behind the stars. Click the Application Starter to display these selections on the main menu, as shown in Figure 6-2 and described in Table 6-2.

Figure 6-2: Your main menu costars — one click behind the stars.

Table 6-2	Costars on the Main Menu	
Selection	*Lets You . . .*	*See*
Applications	Select from the supporting cast of applications on the submenus	The next section
Find	Find files on your computer or locate a computer on your network so you can access its files	Chapter 12
Help	Get user or administrator help	Chapter 5
Online Services	Connect to a growing network Connect to a growing network of services, freebies, and help for Corel Linux, including the office and drawing apps	Chapter 21
Autostart	Automatically launch programs when you enter the desktop	
Control Center	Adjust all your desktop and system settings from one convenient location	Chapters 4, 9, and 10
Corel File Manager	Open File Manager at your home folder	Chapter 11
Run	Enter one-line Linux commands, such as to launch a program not on the menus	Chapter 3
Logout	Exit the Corel Linux session	Chapter 3

Supporting Cast on the Submenus

Choose Application Starter ⇨ Applications, as shown in Figure 6-3, to hobnob with the supporting cast of programs on the submenus, which are described in Table 6-3.

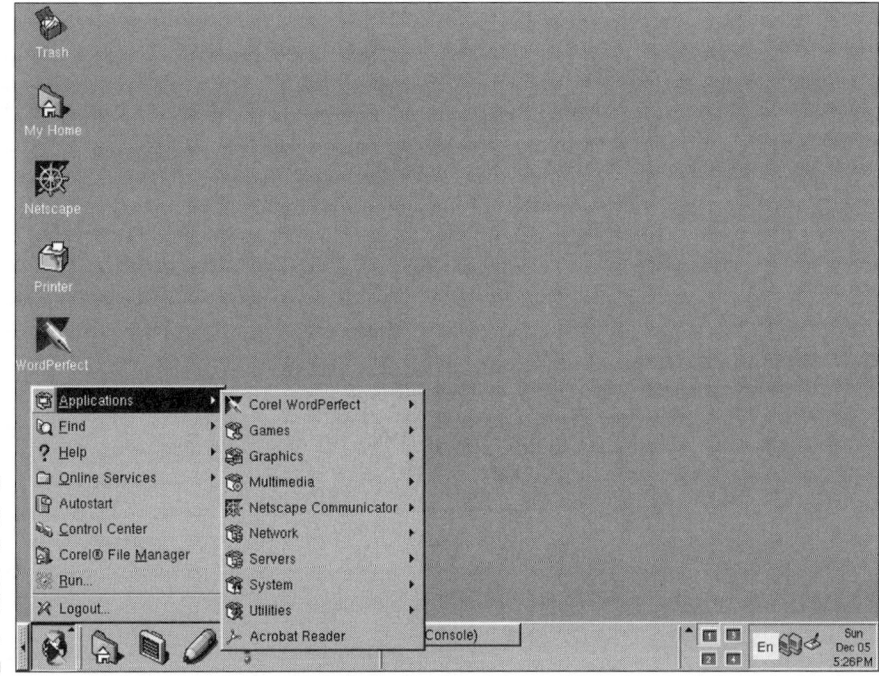

Figure 6-3: Here's the supporting cast of programs.

Table 6-3	Supporting Cast of Programs on the Applications Submenus	
Submenu of Applications	*Lets You . . .*	*See*
Corel WordPerfect*	Use WordPerfect and associated utilities	WordPerfect's online help
Games	Engage in addictive amusements	Each game's online help

(continued)

Table 6-3 *(continued)*

Submenu of Applications	Lets You . . .	See
Graphics	Use tools such as The Gimp (for graphics creation and editing), screen grab, and image viewers	Chapter 14 and online help
Multimedia	Play CDs and multimedia files, sing along with the Karaoke Player, and use the sound mixer	Chapter 14 and online help
Netscape Communicator	Browse the Web, send and receive e-mail, join discussions and chats	Chapters 15 and 16
Network	Dial up your Internet service provider and use the KDE chat and newsgroup facilities	Chapter 4 and online help
Server (root user on server installation)	Set up a Samba server to hook into a Microsoft Windows network; set up a network mail server	Online help
System	Manage fonts, processes, and tasks; edit mime types	Chapter 5 and online help
System (root user only)	Use additional utilities to update, add, and remove programs, view system events, and manage user accounts	Chapter 17 and online help
Utilities	Use miscellaneous utilities to create archives of compressed (zip) files, do mathematical calculations, format floppies, edit text and hexadecimal files, and create sticky notes	Chapters 12, 13, and online help
Acrobat Reader	Read documents in the popular Adobe PDF format	Chapter 14

* Standard and Deluxe boxed editions of Corel Linux only

Chapter 6: Meet the Stars! 91

Installed Extras Not on Your Menus

When the Install Express sets up your system, it doesn't put everything on your menus. The omissions on my system included the menu editor of all things! Kind of amusing — or frustrating — depending on your mental state. A classic Catch-22 that's solved in Chapter 9.

Of course, if everything were on the menus, we'd be overwhelmed by choices when we start using Corel Linux. For example, why put five or six command-line text editors on the menus when we already have the fabulous, graphical, kwrite editor on the panel? Still, some biggies didn't make it on my install, including korganizer, the KDE calendar and appointment utility, and, the e-mail client.

Although you wouldn't want everything on your menus, it's hard to discover the things that aren't. That's why I give you Table 6-4, showing some of the end-user extras that aren't on your menus after a default install. (It doesn't include system and programming tools.) Your results may vary depending on your edition, install choices, and perhaps the date of your Corel Linux release.

Most of these programs can be found in either the /usr/bin or /usr/X11R6/bin folders.

Table 6-4 Some Installed End-User Extras Not on Your Menus

Installed Extra	Lets You . . .
Fun stuff	
fortune-mod	Serve fortune cookies on demand
oneko	Have a cat chase your cursor
xfishtank	Turn your screen into an aquarium
xmountains	Generate random fractal (mathematical) mountains
Games	
3dchess	Play 3-D chess on three boards with 96 pieces
blast	Blow holes in programs to vent your frustrations
cgoban	Play computerized Go with others
lincity	Build and maintain a city or a country
netris	Play a version of Tetris over a network

(continued)

Table 6-4 (continued)

Installed Extra	Lets You . . .
Games (continued)	
pacman	Gobble up dots in a labyrinth
xasteroids	Change big rocks into little ones
xblast	Blast away at your opponents
xgalaga	Play a space-invader-like game
xgammon	Play backgammon
xjig	Create and put together jigsaw puzzles
xpat2	Play patience with different rule sets
xpilot	Join in a multiplayer shoot-em-up
Graphics	
gnuplot	Create plots
kfract	Generate fractals
libtiff-tools	Convert and manipulate TIFF graphic images
netpbm	Convert images between a variety of formats
xli and xloadimage	Graphics viewer
Multimedia	
cdrecord and cdwrite	Write CDs
freeamp	Listen to MPEG audio
Kmedia	Play digital audio (WAV) files
splay	Play MPEG audio files
wav2cdr	Convert WAV sound files to audio CD format
wavtools	Record, play and compress WAV sound files
Network	
efax and Hylafax	Send and receive faxes
KArchie	Search and access files stored in anonymous ftp Web directories
KBiff	Be notified when mail arrives
Kmail	Send and receive mail

Chapter 6: Meet the Stars! 93

Installed Extra	Lets You . . .
krn	Participate in newsgroups
lynx	Browse the Web in text mode
ncftp and Wxftp	Transfer files to and from a remote site
Xbiff	Put a cute mailbox on your screen
Server	
apache	Run the world's most popular server
fetchmail	Gather and forward mail
System	
fileutils	Manage files using various utilities
gawk	Scan and process using language patterns
ktop	Monitor your system
klpq	Manage your print queue
m4	Automate with macros
mc	Use the DOS-like Midnight Commander file manager
Utilities	
ae (Anthony's Editor)	Use a tiny, full-screen editor
alien	Convert Red Hat, Stampede, and Slackware packages to Debian for installation
dosemu	Run DOS programs under Linux
ed, nvi, and vim	Use three old-style (nongraphical) UNIX text editors
gv	View PostScript and PDF files
gzip	Manage compressed files
Karm	Keep track of the time you spend on various tasks
Kclock	Float a wall clock on your desktop
Kddat	Create tape backup archives
Kfax	View and print fax files
Kmenuedit	Edit your program menus
Korganizer	Keep your calendar, with appointments, events, and to-dos

(continued)

Table 6-4 *(continued)*

Installed Extra	Lets You . . .
Utilities (continued)	
	Convert Microsoft Word docs to HTML
tar	Create archive files in the tar format
xdaliclock	Tell time in melting digits
xeyes	Have eyes follow your mouse pointer
Xf86config	Manually configure your system's graphics
XF86setup	Configure your system's mouse, keyboard, graphics card, monitor, and graphics mode
xlock	Lock your screen and display wild graphics instead
xmag	Magnify a selected portion of your screen
xscreensaver	Keep your screen busy while you're away
xphoon	Display the current phase of the moon on the root desktop
xscreensaver	Configure and run screensavers
Find	
findutils	Find files using various utilities
Help	
doc-debian	Read Debian manual, FAQs, and other documents
doc-linux	Read Linux HOWTOs, mini-HOWTOs, and FAQs
Kdehelp	Get help on the K desktop environment
xman	Browse X Windows system manual

Good Old Command-Line Extras

Once upon a time, most Linux programs were run from the command line, without the nice, intuitive, graphical interfaces that we've come to expect today. Perfectly good, even powerful programs, mind you, but many as easy to use as their graphitized brethren. For example, who would want to use a command-line text editor, such as vi, when you have the graphical kwrite instead. Command-line stalwarts say vi is faster after you master its tricks, but I have enough to do figuring out my VCR remote.

Chapter 6: Meet the Stars! **95**

That said, some Linux pros resort to command line utilities for some of the powerful options they provide. They're also great to have in emergencies, as described in Appendix A. For example, suppose your system's graphics go wacky and you (or some computer guru) must drop into Linux repair mode to fix your settings with that little editor we just scorned. Aha!

Program Wannabes

ON THE CD

Install Express puts a choice selection of applications on your system, but it's the tip of the iceberg of the thousands and thousands of talented programs floating around. You can find a huge waiting-on-tables-or-driving-cabs crowd of uninstalled programs on your *Corel Linux For Dummies* CD, at the Corel Linux distribution site, or at another distribution site. Chapter 17 shows you how to discover what's out there and how to add, remove, and update programs with Corel Update.

Chapter 7
Graphical Gizmos

In This Chapter
- Going bar hopping
- Freeing up brain cells with the incredible right-click
- Holding a dialog
- Selecting stuff
- Deleting stuff — and getting it back

A dog does tricks to please its master. A cat does tricks to please itself. You do tricks to have fun. There's no getting around it. I could say that the techniques in this chapter will make you 37 percent more productive, but the real reason I present them is because it's out-and-out fun to teach your mouse new tricks.

But more productive you will be! Computing curmudgeons can spout off about how efficient they were at pre-Windows computing. They neglect to tell you that it took seven years to learn the commands, when they could have been going to movies or walking their mouse.

One favor I ask is that you please try out these tricks as you go along. This is a practical guide, not a theoretical treatise. That said, grab your mouse and hang on!

Jumping into Windows

Most business in a graphical environment is conducted in windows, custom decorated by each program for the tasks at hand. While doing a research report on potato chips, for example, you might have WordPerfect and calculator windows open in Desktop 1, while using Dial-Up and Navigator on Desktop 2 to get the latest news from chip central. Figure 7-1 gives you the anatomy of the sophisticated window you see when you open a document in WordPerfect 8.

Part II: Taking the Grand Tour

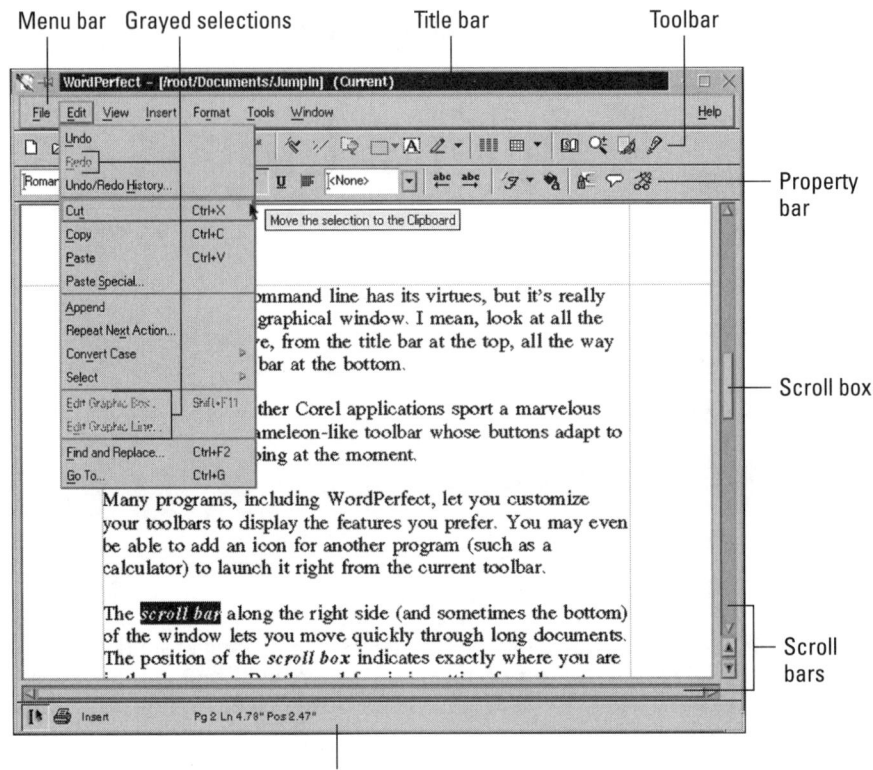

Figure 7-1: Anatomy of a window.

Labels on figure: Menu bar, Grayed selections, Title bar, Toolbar, Property bar, Scroll box, Scroll bars, Status bar

A lot of window business is transacted at bars, so I expect you'll be right at home. Click the stubby pencil on the panel at the bottom-left to open the Text Editor, so you can go on a stroll and check out the saloons.

Opening and closing times

Did you notice those little doodads with diagonal lines to the left of the menu bar and toolbar in the Text Editor? A lot of Linux programs have these. Click the doodad to alternately open and close your bars, as shown in Figure 7-2. Clever!

> **TIP:** For bars without doodads, such as those in WordPerfect, look for selections on the View or Options menu to alternately view or hide your bars.

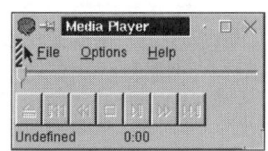

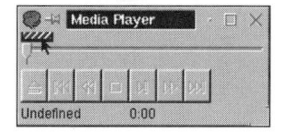

Figure 7-2:
Click those little doodads to open and close your bars.

A quick look in the title bar

The *title bar*, as its name implies, provides descriptive information, such as the name of the program or the file you're working on. It blew me away to see that when the title can't fit in the bar, its text slides back and forth so you can view the complete title! Corel Linux is full of these pleasant little surprises.

Now try these title bar tricks:

- Click and hold the title bar and then drag the window around your desktop.
- Double-click the title bar to alternately *shade* (roll up) and *unshade* the window. Too much!

    The window shade sounds are a hoot! To activate sounds, see Chapter 10.
- Right-click the title bar to select from a list of everything you can do with the window.

Big things from little buttons

Mustn't overlook those little buttons to the left and right of the title bar. Table 7-1 shows you the big things that those little buttons can do. Give them a try!

Table 7-1	Big Things from Little Buttons	
Click This Button		To . . .
	Upper-Left Buttons	
	Window menu button (miniature program icon)	Get an all-purpose list of everything you can do with the window, such as iconify, maximize, close, or move.

(continued)

Table 7-1 *(continued)*

Click This Button		To . . .
Upper-Left Buttons		
	Sticky button	Stick the window to make it appear in all your desktops. Click again to unstick the window and make it appear in only the current desktop.
Upper-Right Buttons		
	Iconify button	Make the window get out of the way. Click its button on the panel to get it back.
	Maximize button	Enlarge (maximize) the window to fill the entire screen, minus the panel.*
	Restore button	Return a maximized window to its previous size.*
	Close button	Close the window.

*Maximize and restore are alternating states of the same button.

> **TIP:** If you're using a different desktop theme (see Chapter 10), your buttons might take on a wacky appearance, but they'll do the same things.

Dropping in at the menu bar

If you're really hungry, especially if you're looking for an oddball delicacy such as chocolate ants, drop in at the *menu bar*. There you'll find nearly every program offering, logically arranged under the menu categories of File, Edit, and so on. Many menu selections lead to submenus (File ⇨ Open Recent) or dialog boxes (Options ⇨ Default Style). These selections are indicated by right-pointing triangles for submenus or ellipses (...) for dialog boxes.

To mouse around the menu bar:

1. **Click a menu bar selection, such as File or Edit.**

2. **Move the mouse to browse through the menu and submenu selections.**

   Point to the menu bar selections to move from menu to menu.

3. **Click to select the delicacy of your choice.**

> **TIP:** If a menu selection appears *grayed out*, you can't use it at the moment. In WordPerfect, for example, the Cut selection on the Edit menu appears grayed out if you haven't selected any text. The little KDE text editor hasn't learned this yet.

If you're not into mousing, peruse menus with the keyboard:

1. **Choose a menu by pressing the Alt key plus the underlined letter.**

    Press the Alt key alone to go to the top of the leftmost menu, which is usually File.

2. **Scroll the menus by using the arrow keys.**

3. **Press Enter to select the highlighted item.**

To exit a menu without making a selection, click outside the menus or press Esc.

Getting fast food from the toolbar

Toolbars are sort of a fast food drive-through, with one-click access to frequently used features. Instead of the vast buffet of the menus, toolbars have an eye-catching selection to satisfy ravenous appetites.

> **TIP:** Corel programs for Linux sport a *property bar* beneath the toolbar. This chameleon-like toolbar presents a set of features pertaining to the current task (such as drawing, tables, or outlining). If you're in WordPerfect, select some text or create a table and note how the property bar selections change, while the standard toolbar items remain the same.

Going for a scroll (bar)

The *scroll bar* along the right side (and sometimes the bottom) of the window lets you move quickly through long documents. The position of the *scroll box* indicates exactly where you are in the document.

The real fun is in getting from here to there:

- Click the **scroll arrows** at either end of the bar to move line by line or row by row. Hold an arrow down to scroll continuously.
- Drag the **scroll box** to quickly move to another location.
- Click a **blank spot** above or below the scroll box to scroll a screenful of information at a time.

Grabbing the latest gossip at the status bar

Drop in at the *status bar*, at the bottom of the window, to hear the latest on what's happening in your program. For example, when you click a folder in the File Manager, the status bar shows you the number of files in the folder and their total size, as shown in Figure 7-3.

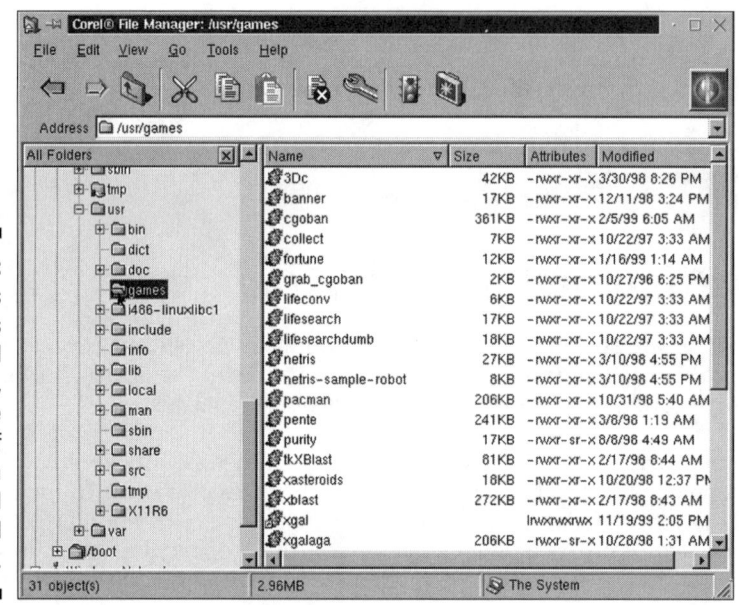

Figure 7-3: The status bar displays useful information, such as the number of files in a folder and their total size.

Various programs display different things on the status bar. The WordPerfect status bar (which it calls the application bar) shows what documents you have opened, your location in the current document, and whether your shadow cursor is on. When you're working on a table, it tells you which table and cell you're in.

The Incredible Right-Click

One amazing thing about a graphical interface is that programs seem to know where you are and what you're doing and can guess what you want to do next. The buzzword for this omniscient clairvoyance is *context sensitive*.

Chapter 7: Graphical Gizmos   *103*

This context-sensitiveness can make your life a lot easier. Plus, it gives your right mouse button something to do. Try this: Right-click the desktop, as in Figure 7-4. Now, you wouldn't do this to add a new user. Instead, the program figures that you might want to arrange your icons, create a nickname or folder, or log out of the system because dinner is getting cold.

Figure 7-4: When you right-click the desktop, the program figures out what you want to do.

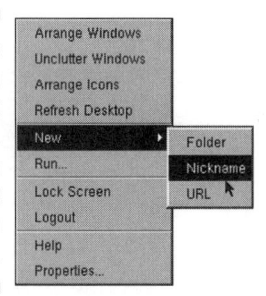

When you right-click in WordPerfect, you get such likelies as center your text, run a spell check, or change the font. Pop quiz: Where are you going to right-click to customize your panel? That's the beauty of right-click — it usually pops up what you're looking for, thus saving tons of memorizing and hunting around. Enjoy your dinner.

Conducting a Dialog

When you do something in Corel Linux, such as change the font or search for a file, your choices are often presented in the form of a dialog box, or *dialog* for short, as in Figure 7-5. The dialog allows for back-and-forth between you and the program. The program says "here are the things from which to choose," and you say "thanks, these are the things I'm choosing and here are their names."

Consulting a wizard

A sophisticated cousin to the dialog box is the *wizard*, which offers a relatively foolproof method to accomplish a complex task. A good example is the Installation Wizard of Chapter 2, which lets you install an entire operating system in a few easy steps. The selections you make in Step 2 of a wizard may affect your choices in Step 3, and so on till you complete the task.

Another example of a wizard is the one used to add a printer, described in Chapter 4.

Part II: Taking the Grand Tour

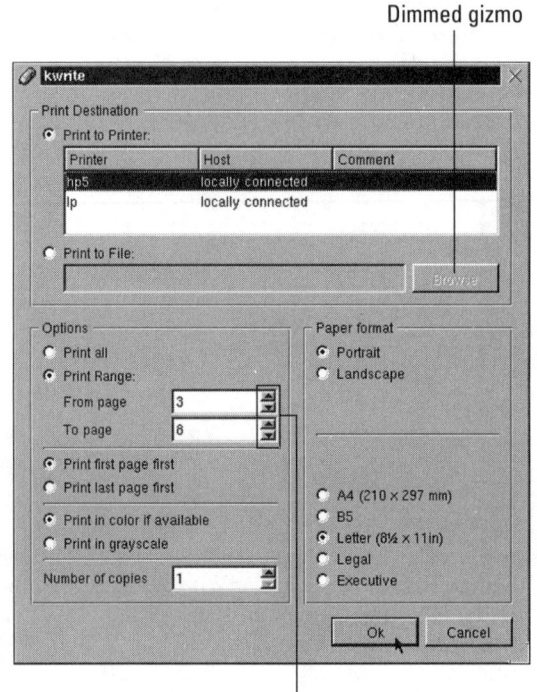

Figure 7-5: Letting your wishes be known through a dialog box.

(Callouts: Dimmed gizmo; Spin boxes)

You'll get the idea quickly enough, so no need to attend night classes at dialog school. Table 7-2 summarizes the gizmos you can find in a dialog and how they're used. To see more examples of these gizmos, check out Figures 7-6, 7-7, and 7-8.

Table 7-2	Gizmos for Conducting a Dialog
Dialog Gizmo	**How to Use It**
Check box	Click to check the options you want. You can select more than one.
Radio button	Click the option you want. You can select only one.
Text box	Type your entry or selection.
Selection list	Scroll the list, if necessary, and then click your selection (hold Ctrl to select more than one).
Drop-down list, opened	Scroll the list, if necessary, and then click your selection.
Spin box	Type a number or click the tiny arrows to change the value.

Chapter 7: Graphical Gizmos 105

Dialog Gizmo	How to Use It
Slider	Drag the little lever to adjust a value, such as the audio volume or the screen resolution.
Tab	Click the tab for the set of selections you want.
Palette	Click to trigger a visual display of colors or tools from which to choose.
Preview area	View the effect of your selections before they're applied.
Command button	Click to perform an immediate action. Some buttons take you to lower-level dialog boxes.
Dimmed gizmo	Not available for the current situation, such as the Browse button for Print to File if you're printing to paper instead.

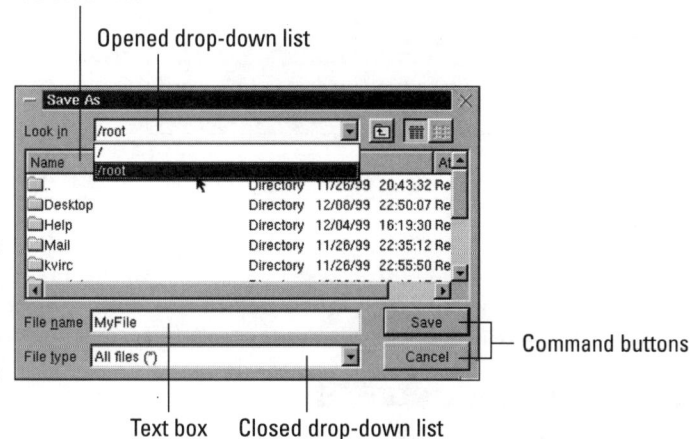

Figure 7-6: More dialog gizmos.

More tricks? Where?

The Corel Linux environment can be an intuitive and fun place. In this chapter, you just scratch the surface of the graphical tricks you can perform, both on the desktop and in particular applications. Here are some more tricks and where they're described:

- Using multiple desktops (Chapter 5)
- Your keys to success (Chapter 5)
- Juggling windows (Chapter 8)
- Creating an efficient workplace (Chapter 9)
- Customizing windows (Chapter 10)

Part II: Taking the Grand Tour

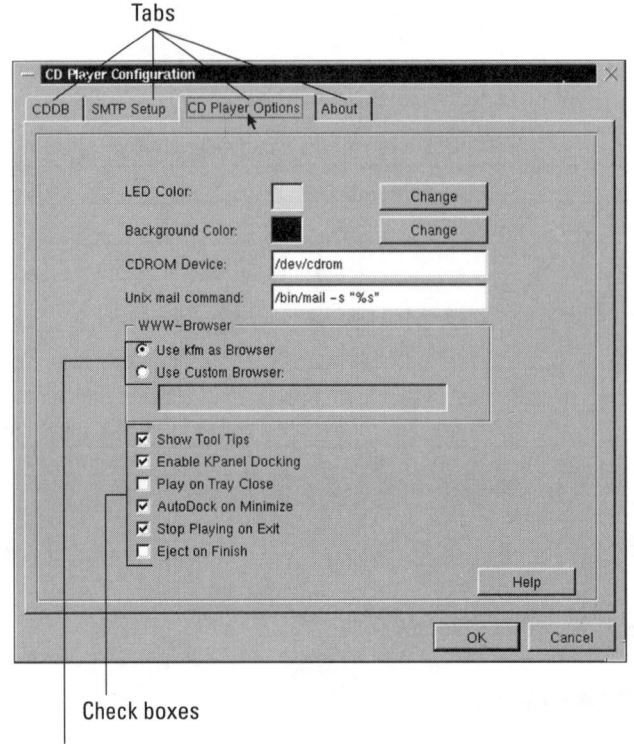

Figure 7-7: And more.

Tabs · Check boxes · Radio buttons

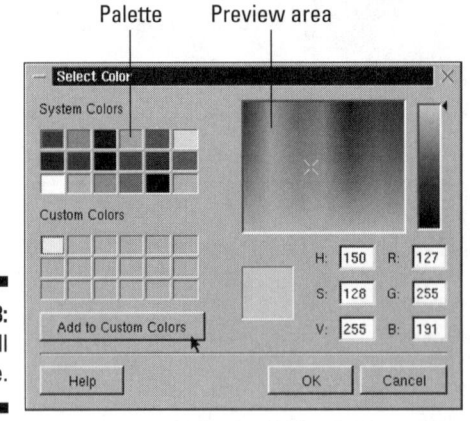

Figure 7-8: And still more.

Palette · Preview area

Working with Selected Stuff

The remainder of this chapter deals with some basic tricks of the trade in a graphical environment such as Corel Linux or Windows. You take a look at how you can select text and graphics and then cut, copy, and paste stuff all over the place. I use WordPerfect 8 for illustration, but the same principals apply in other applications.

Selecting text and graphics

One of the most powerful and flexible features of a program such as WordPerfect is its capability to perform operations on selected (blocked) text and graphics. You can move, copy, or delete highlighted information or change the format of your text. You can even save your block as a file.

You may use many selection tricks, but here are two basic techniques:

- **Using the mouse,** simply drag across the text and graphics you want to select, as shown in Figure 7-9, and then release the mouse button.

- **Using the keyboard,** place the insertion point where you want to start selecting and then press F8 or hold the Shift key (in WordPerfect) and use the arrow keys to extend your selection.

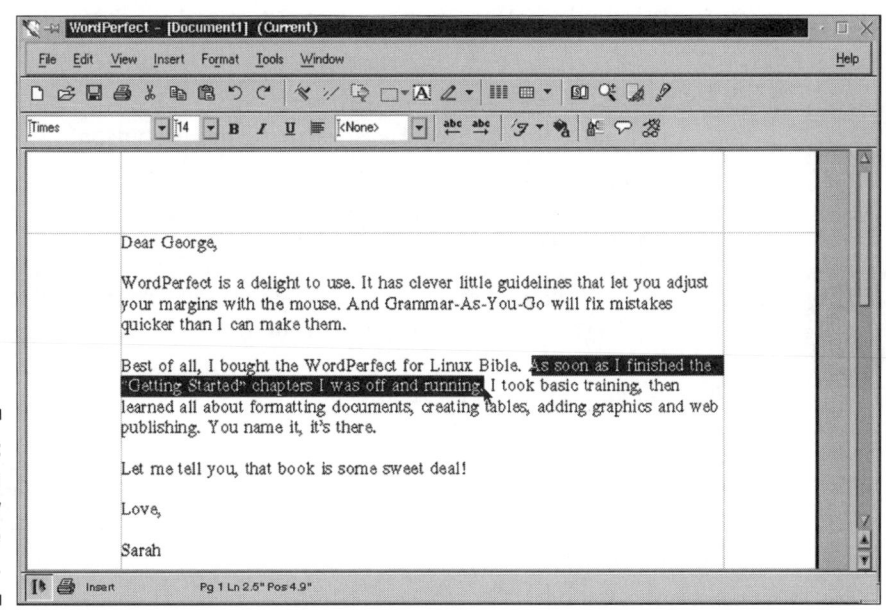

Figure 7-9: Selecting text by dragging the mouse.

Again, you may select things in many ways, depending on the program you're using, but mouse dragging is almost universal.

Try Edit ⇨ Select All to select everything in the window.

Moving and copying selections

After you select stuff, you can do many things with it. After you select text in WordPerfect, for example, you can change its format, font, and other properties.

Best of all, you can move your selected text around to rearrange your ideas or copy it to avoid retyping it. Essentially, you have two ways to move and copy:

- **By cutting or copying** the selected information (text or graphics) to the clipboard and then **pasting** it to the new location
- **By dragging the information** with the mouse and dropping it into place

Drag and drop with the mouse

For nearby moving or copying of text, try using the mouse to drag and drop:

1. **Drag to make your selection and then release the left mouse button.**
2. **Put the mouse pointer on the selected text and then drag it to the new location.**
3. **Do one of the following:**
    - To move the information, release the mouse button.
    - To copy the information while leaving the original intact, hold down the Ctrl key while you release the mouse button. (The mouse pointer usually looks different when you press Ctrl.)

Drag and drop is okay for short-haul moving of small selections. For long-distance moving and copying, use cut, copy, and paste.

Move and copy with the clipboard

Although you can't drag and drop in every program, you can nearly always move and copy your selections with a clipboard. A *clipboard* is a holding area (or buffer) to which you can cut and copy information and then paste it to another location in the current file, in another file, or even in another file in another application.

To move or copy using the clipboard:

1. **Select the information.**
2. **Place the selection on the clipboard in either of two ways:**
    - To move the information, click the Cut (scissors) button on the toolbar. (You can also press Ctrl+X or click Edit ➪ Cut.) The selection disappears from the document and is transferred to the clipboard.
    - To copy the information, click the Copy button on the toolbar. (You can also press Ctrl+C or click Edit ➪ Copy.) The selection remains in its place in the document, and a copy of the selection is placed on the clipboard.
3. **Move the insertion point to where you want to put the information.**
4. **Click the Paste button on the toolbar.**

    You can also press Ctrl+V or click Edit ➪ Paste.

You can paste the clipboard multiple times.

Deleting Information and Getting It Back

Deleting zaps your stuff for good, *without* placing it on the clipboard. Use the Delete or Backspace key to delete one character at a time. The same Delete and Backspace keys can also delete a whole selection.

"Egad, I didn't mean to delete (move, copy) that! How do I put my stuff back the way it was?" If you just performed the regretted action, you're in luck (in most text editors or drawing programs):

1. **Click the Undo button to reverse your last editing action.**

    You can also click Edit ➪ Undo or press Ctrl+Z.

2. **Repeat Undo to backtrack your editing session, one action at a time, for as many Undos as your program permits.**

To undo the Undos, click the Redo button on the toolbar. (You can also click Edit ➪ Redo.) When there are no more Redos, the Redo arrow on the toolbar appears dim.

Undo and Redo work with any editing change. For example, if you just changed your font or margins, Undo can put them back to the way they were.

Chapter 8
Window Wonders

In This Chapter
▶ Diving for windows
▶ Cleaning up your desktop

The great thing about the Corel Linux desktop is that you can do dozens of tasks at the same time — word processing here, a Reversi game there, with maybe a little dial-up, Netscape, file find, help, Control Center, and Corel Update thrown in. Before you know it, you have windows all over the place, and the one you really want — Reversi — has disappeared from view.

Window Washers to the rescue! This chapter lets you in on tricks for taking control of this visual clutter of buttons, bars, and other graphical gimcracks. You have two categories of solutions:

- Go diving for the window you want
- Clean up the place a bit

Before you try out the tricks in this chapter, go about your normal business to make an unsightly mess of your desktop. That's not a hard assignment, is it?

Now that you've made a mess, you can try the various window diving and cleanup techniques.

Window Diving

If you're like me, you usually open applications all over the place, without any thought as to their sensible arrangement. This isn't really as bad as it sounds because you can perform several diving tricks to come up with the window you want.

Part II: Taking the Grand Tour

Moving a window to the top of the pile

Sometimes all you see on your desktop is a collage of overlapping windows. Your active window is in full view, but the poker game you want is at the bottom of the pile, with a bit of its title bar protruding, as shown in Figure 8-1. That little bit is yelling "I'm here, click me!" Click the title bar. Whoosh! The poker game flies into view, ready for action.

TIP

You can have your mouse automatically bring a window to the fore and make it active, just by pointing. To change this and other window settings, see Chapter 9.

Pushing the panel button

Is the little window you want completely obscured by other window-hogging apps? No need to push the panic button. Push the *panel button* instead, as shown in Figure 8-1. I can't believe they pay me to write jokes like this.

I'm here. Click me!

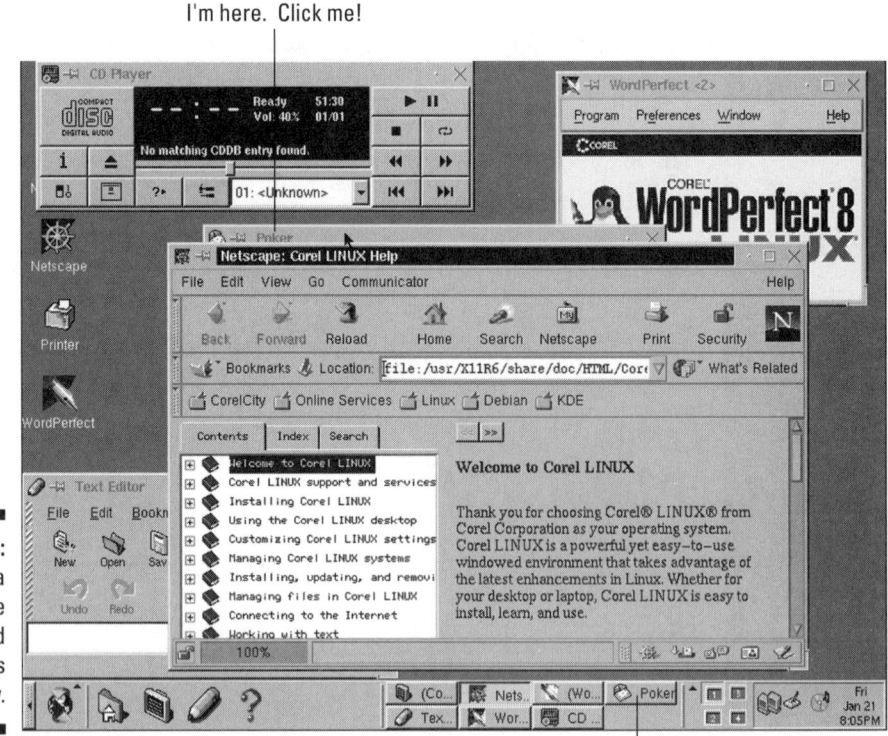

Figure 8-1:
Click a piece of the window and it whooshes into view.

Or click the panel button.

Keyboard to the rescue

Did you forget that you can do more than type with your keyboard? Well, let's put that neglected utensil back into action. When you lose sight of the window you need, try this keyboard-to-the-rescue trick:

1. **Hold down the Alt key and press Tab till you find the window you want, as shown in Figure 8-2.**
2. **Let go and up pops your window!**

Figure 8-2: Hold down Alt and press Tab till you come to the window you want.

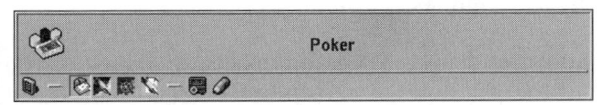

Wait, here's another:

1. **Press Ctrl+Esc to display a list of all the windows on all your desktops.**
2. **Scroll the list with the arrow keys. When you come to the window you want, press Enter to switch desktops and pop up the window.**

   Or, if you must use your mouse, double-click a window in the list.

Cleaning Up the Place

Cleaning your desktop is about as exciting as cleaning your abode, but it does make it easier to work. So grab your virtual broom and dustpan and follow me as we toss windows out, move them around, whisk them under the rug, or sweep them into neat piles. We can shrink and enlarge them too, but not to fit in the metaphor.

Close the window!

Close that window! (Only don't do it now.) When I'm finished with an application, I try to remember to get rid of it, so that it doesn't get in the way of what I want to do next. As with junk mail, don't let it hang around to distract you.

Okay, closing a window to clean up is pretty obvious — but sometimes the obvious is easy to forget.

Moving windows around

Another way to arrange your desktop is to grab your windows by their title bars and move them around, as shown in Figure 8-3.

Notice how a window snaps to the desktop border, though you can move it beyond the border too. Windows also snap to the edges of other windows.

To move the current window using the keyboard, press A+F7, position the window by using the arrow keys, and then press Enter.

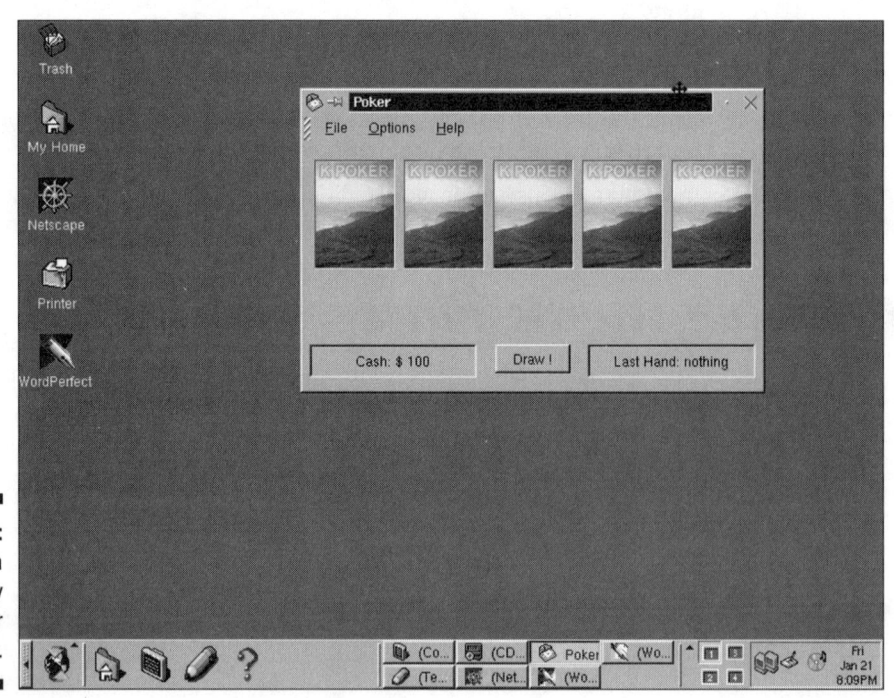

Figure 8-3: Grab a window by its title bar to move it.

Roll up the window

Think, for a moment, of an app window not as a window but as a windowshade. Want to roll up the window? Double-click its bar, as shown in Figure 8-4. This keeps your window where it is, but gets it out of the way of other windows. Double-click the title bar again to unroll the window.

Iconify, iconify!

Iconify, iconify! I like that word, so I wrote it twice. Shading is fun, but the best way to make a window disappear is to click its iconify button, as shown in Figure 8-5. This removes the window from view, but leaves its task button behind on the panel. When you click the task button on the panel, the window pops right back to its previous location, ready for action.

TIP

To iconify the current window, you can also click its task button on the panel or press Alt+F9.

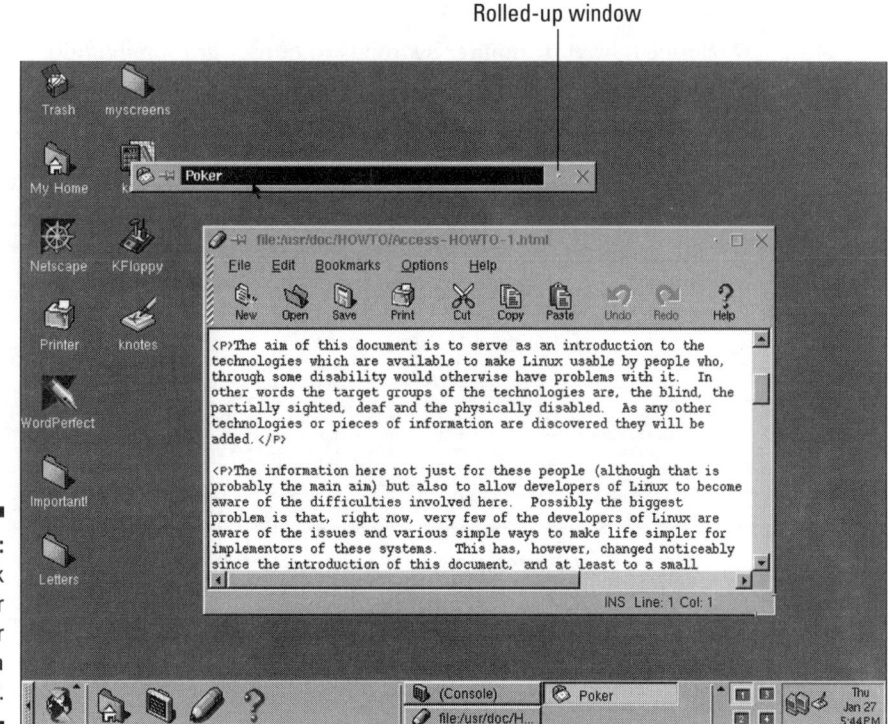

Figure 8-4: Double-click the title bar to roll (or unroll) a window.

Part II: Taking the Grand Tour

Figure 8-5: Click the Iconify button to get a window out of the way.

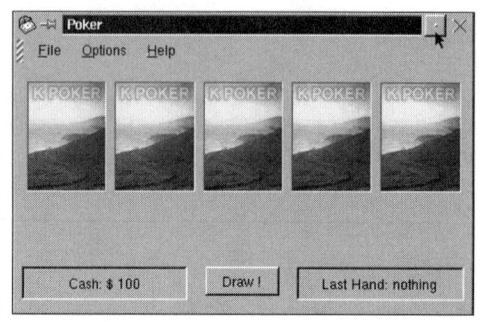

Making the window BIGGER (Or smaller)

Is the size of your current window cramping your style? Then make it bigger. Or if the current window is in the way of other windows, make it smaller. Doing either is really simple:

1. **Position the mouse pointer over the window border you want to move. Or for two-dimensional enlarging or shrinking, point to a corner, as shown in Figure 8-6.**

   Notice how your pointer switches to border-grabbing mode.

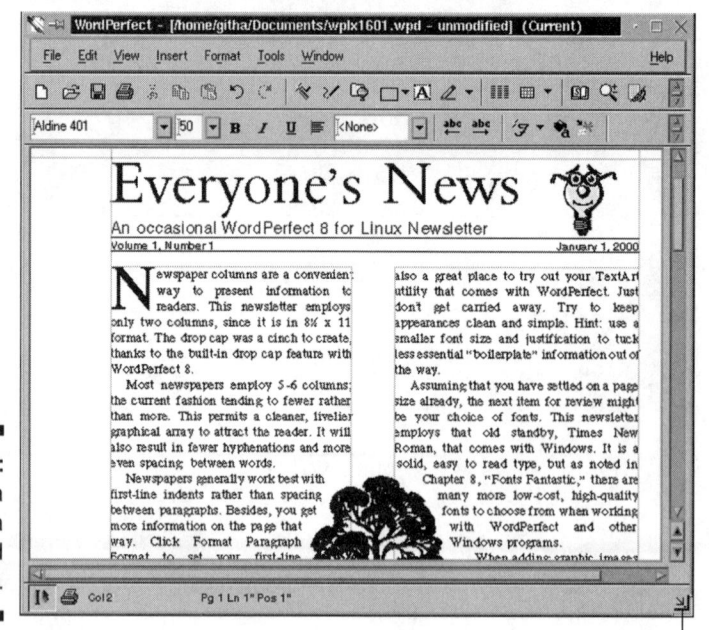

Figure 8-6: Point to a side or a corner and then drag.

Pointer in border-grabbing mode

2. **Click and drag to enlarge or shrink the window and then let go.**

   Keyboard alternative: Press A+F8, enlarge or shrink the window by using the arrow keys, and then press Enter.

TIP

The current size and shape of each application's window is remembered from session to session.

Going for the max

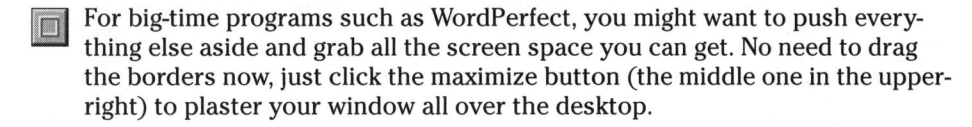

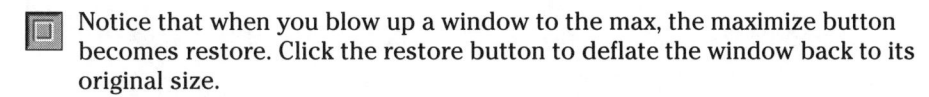

For big-time programs such as WordPerfect, you might want to push everything else aside and grab all the screen space you can get. No need to drag the borders now, just click the maximize button (the middle one in the upper-right) to plaster your window all over the desktop.

Notice that when you blow up a window to the max, the maximize button becomes restore. Click the restore button to deflate the window back to its original size.

Keyboard alternative: Press Alt+F10 to alternately maximize and restore the current window.

Arranging and uncluttering windows

As you open windows, notice how your desktop normally follows a "smart placement" policy of putting the window in the largest vacant desktop space. Try this: Close all your open windows and then open the Text Editor. Notice how it's placed in the upper-left of your screen. Now close the Text Editor and then open the Console and Help. Open the Text Editor again, and you see how it does the best it can to find a new location, away from the other windows.

Smart placement is a big help. But when things get really messy, you can try the arrange and unclutter options:

1. **Go to a blank spot on your desktop (if you can find one!) and right-click.**
2. **Choose either of the following:**
   - **Arrange Windows,** to place your windows in a (relatively) neat pile, as shown in Figure 8-7, where you can click the one you want.
   - **Unclutter Windows,** to restore a semblance of smart placement after you've moved windows around, as shown in Figure 8-8.

Part II: Taking the Grand Tour

Figure 8-7: Right-click a blank spot and choose Arrange to make a neat(er) pile of your windows.

Figure 8-8: Right-click a blank spot and choose Unclutter to restore a semblance of smart placement.

Organizing the mess into multiple desktops

The best clutter-control trick is to organize the mess into multiple desktops. That way, you can do word processing in one desktop, Web browsing in another, graphics in a third, and so on, and they'll never bump into each other. See Chapter 5 for various multiple desktop tricks.

Part III
Linux the Way You Want It

The 5th Wave — By Rich Tennant

"I think the cursor's not moving, Mr. Dunt, because you've got your hand on the chalk board eraser and not the mouse."

In this part . . .

Decisions, decisions:

- Paper or plastic bags at the supermarket checkout?
- Should we finally put studded tires on the car this winter?
- What shall we have for dinner?

I suppose the decisions in this part aren't quite as momentous as the above, but sometimes it's fun to deviate from the Corel Linux desktop defaults. You also might find some useful tricks here.

Chapter 9
Desktop Dynamics

In This Chapter

▶ Tailoring your desktop
▶ Customizing the keyboard
▶ Moving the panel and taskbar
▶ Improving your desktop operations
▶ Customizing your window operations

The Corel Linux desktop is a great place for most people to work and play. You're not "most people"? No problem. This chapter shows you how to arrange the furniture in your desktop environment in a way that's most efficient — and fun — for you.

The idea here is to experiment — try stuff out and choose the settings you like best. Remember, though, that lots of work went into designing the Corel Linux environment, so in most cases you should be quite happy with the program's defaults.

Still, desktop settings aren't the meat-and-potato critical settings of Chapter 4, where you connect to the Internet or hook into a local network. Think of them as delectable graphical desserts to fine-tune desktop operations and make programs easier to launch.

It's Your Desktop!

Think of your desktop as *valuable real estate*. Just as a prime time television commercial gets quick access to millions of susceptible brains, vendors of potato chips and SUVs would love to grab a place on your upwardly mobile monitor.

But guess what? You're tuned into Linux, so your channels are off-limits to Crispy Foods and Mogul Motors. The closest you come to commercialism in Corel Linux is the trail of cookie crumbs scattered on the Online Services menu, leading to various Corel Web pages.

Yup, the desktop is yours and yours alone, both as a work-and-play place and as a launching pad for whatever you want to do. If you use, say, the Gimp graphics program a lot, give it a prominent place. That's your choice, not the dictates of Cyclops Software.

Keeping your desktop from session to session

One aspect of your desktop settings that is totally automatic is called *session management*. You should still be aware of how session management works, however, to make the most of it.

Suppose you want to log out of the system, but you're in the middle of running some screen captures from the command line in the Console and copying files from one folder to another in File Manager. Rather than close everything down, just leave your desktop as-is when you exit. The next time you log in, the File Manager automatically opens to the same folder and the Console is there, ready to continue where you left off.

Be aware, however, that you can lose your work in certain applications if you don't save it before you exit. You get a warning that shows the open applications when you exit the desktop.

You can even single out groups of windows to exclude from automatic session management. See "Filtering windows for special treatment," later in this chapter.

Putting nicknames on your desktop

Nicknames, as their name implies, are the quickest way to get from here to there. Desktop nicknames come in three flavors, as shown in Figure 9-1:

- **Folders**, which place a file folder right on your desktop
- **Program nicknames**, which execute programs
- **URL nicknames**, which take you straight to Internet locations

Chapter 9: Desktop Dynamics *125*

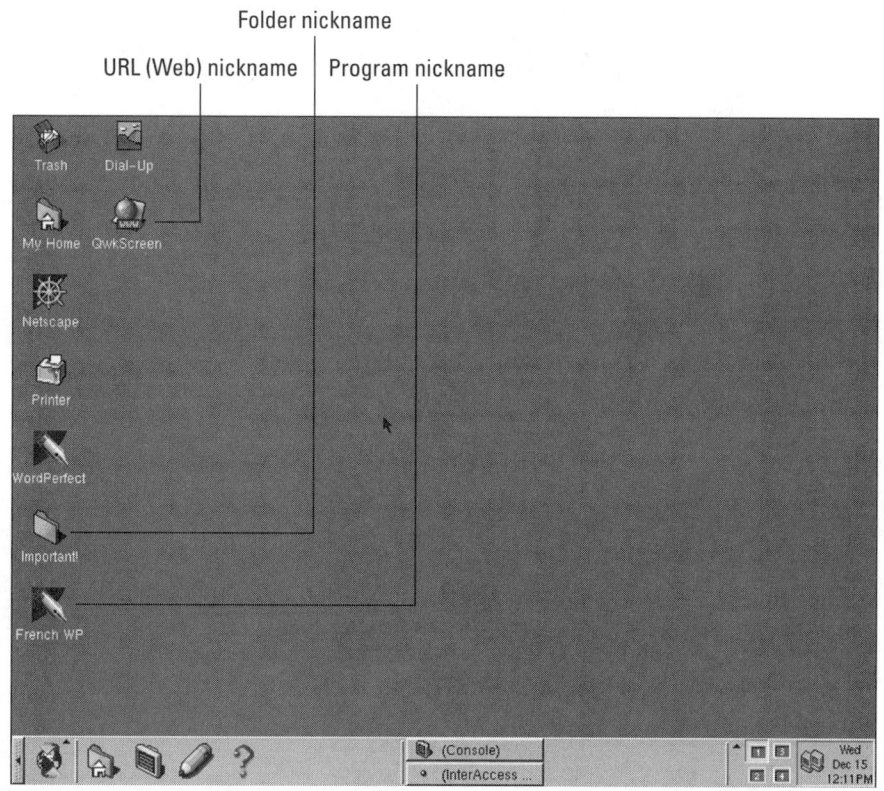

Figure 9-1: Desktop nicknames to folders, programs, and Web locations.

Creating folder nicknames

You can place folders right on your desktop, for direct access to important files:

1. **Right-click on your desktop and choose New ➪ Folder.**
2. **Give the folder a name and then click OK, as shown in Figure 9-2.**

Figure 9-2: Creating a desktop folder for direct access to a bunch of files.

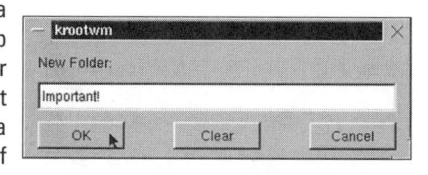

Nicknames or shortcuts?

Linux *nicknames* are similar to *shortcuts* under Windows. I prefer the more user-oriented Windows term, but nobody asked me!

You can save files to a desktop folder just like any other folder. You can also drag and drop existing files to the folder, to move, copy, or link the files.

To go straight to your files, simply click the folder, as shown in Figure 9-3.

Creating program nicknames

Putting program nicknames on your desktop is a great way to launch your favorite applications. For example, if you use Dial-Up a lot, you can put its nickname right on your desktop, so you don't have to hunt in your menus.

What's especially handy is that you can configure your program nicknames to launch with specific parameters. For example, you can have one WordPerfect icon for the English interface and another for the French one.

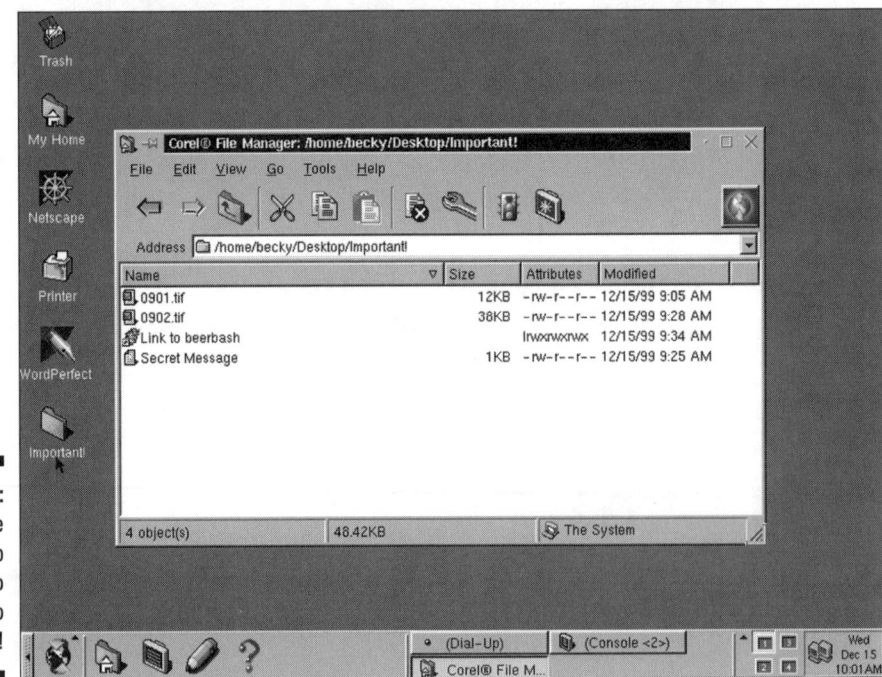

Figure 9-3: Click the desktop folder to go straight to your files!

Chapter 9: Desktop Dynamics

To put a program nickname on your desktop:

1. **Log in as the user for whom you're creating the nickname.**
2. **Do either of the following:**
    - Open the program for which you're creating the nickname.
    - Open File Manager and locate the program.

    Nicknames created by root appear only on root's desktop.
3. **Right-click the title bar of the program's window or the program in File Manager and then choose Create Nickname, as shown in Figure 9-4.**

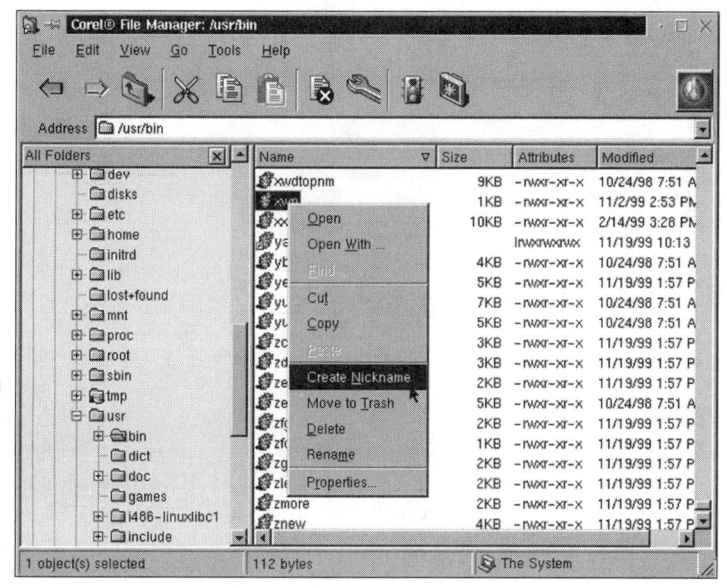

Figure 9-4: I'm creating a nickname to a program.

4. **Type the nickname as you want it to appear on the desktop.**
5. **Specify any command-line options, as shown in Figure 9-5.**

    When in doubt, leave the Command-line options text box blank.

6. **If you want to customize the desktop icon, click Change icon. Select an icon from one of the lists, as shown in Figure 9-6.**
7. **Click OK.**

Figure 9-5: Enter the nickname and any command-line options.

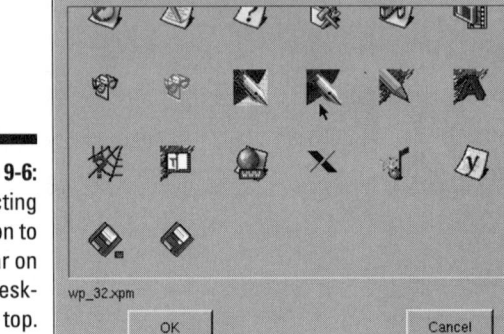

Figure 9-6: Selecting the icon to appear on your desktop.

> The xpm icons you select can be found in /usr/X11R6/share/icons and the subfolders of /usr/X11R6/share/apps. You can also create your own by using a bitmap editor, such as Gimp. Icons you create or find on the Web can then be put in the /usr/X11R6/share/icons folder, so they'll appear among your icon selections.

> You can also right-click on your desktop to create a program nickname and then browse to select the program.

Creating URL nicknames

If you put URL nicknames on your desktop, you can go directly to your favorite Web pages and FTP (file transfer protocol) sites. Just follow these steps:

1. **Open the location in the File Manager.**

   See Chapter 15 for details.

2. **Right-click in the window and then choose Create Nickname, as shown in Figure 9-7.**

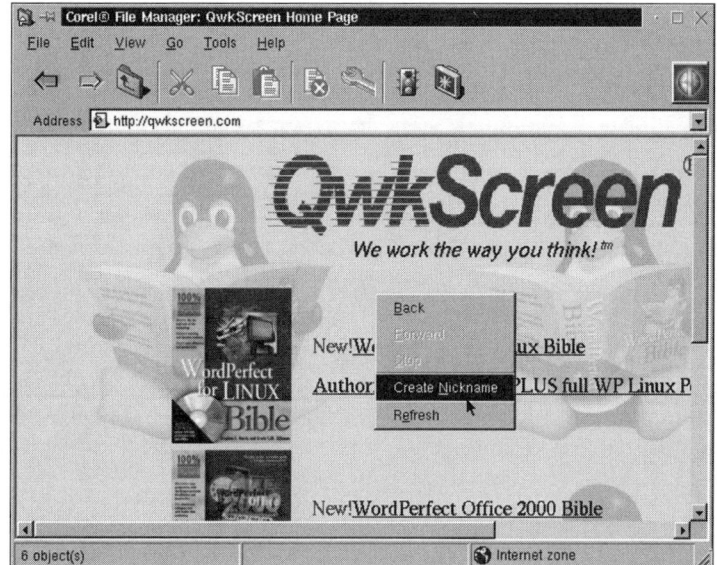

Figure 9-7: Right-click in the window to create your URL nickname.

3. **Type the nickname as you want it to appear on the desktop and specify the target location, as shown in Figure 9-8.**

4. **Click OK.**

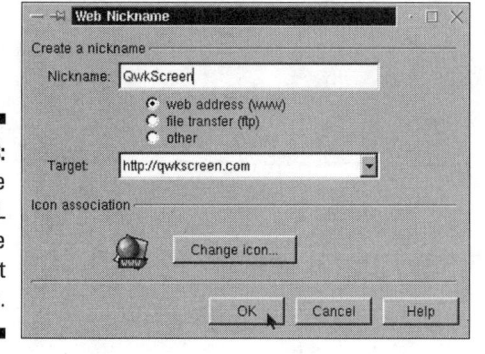

Figure 9-8: Enter the URL nickname and target location.

130 Part III: Linux the Way You Want It

> **TIP:** You can also right-click your desktop to create a URL nickname. If you have the location in Netscape at the time, you can cut and paste the URL location from there.

Removing and editing nicknames

To remove a nickname from your desktop, simply drag it over to the Trash icon. You can also right-click the icon and choose Move to Trash.

To edit a desktop nickname, right-click its icon and choose Properties.

> **TECHNICAL STUFF:** Each program and URL nickname has an associated kdelnk file in the user's Desktop folder. The root user can, for example, copy kdelnk files to the Desktop folders belonging to various users, to give them the same nicknames.

Putting links on your desktop

Desktop links are similar to nicknames, as you can see in Figure 9-9. Links are straight from-here-to-there deals, without the nicknames' configuration options.

Figure 9-9: Desktop with links to folders, files, programs, and Web sites.

The basic varieties of desktop links are easy to create:

- **Folder links** open folders in File Manager. The folder you link to can be anywhere, unlike a nickname folder, which always resides on your desktop.
- **File links** open files. For a known file type, the file opens in its associated program, such as WordPerfect for a WP doc or the Text Editor for a text file.
- **Program** links launch the application you're linked to.

Notice how the link icons include little link arrows in the lower-left, to distinguish them from the originals from whence they came. If you move the original program, folder, or file, the link no longer works.

To create a desktop link:

1. **Open File Manager and locate the folder, file, or program.**
2. **Drag and drop the item on your desktop.**
3. **Choose Link from the menu that appears, as shown in Figure 9-10.**

Figure 9-10: Drag and drop and then choose Link.

Pretty simple. Now just click the link whenever you want to go to the folder or file or launch the program.

You can drag the nicknames and links around your desktop to rearrange them. Then right-click on your desktop and choose Arrange Icons to line them up straight.

Customizing your menus

Let's face it, you can have only so many nickname icons on your desktop. After a point, sparks start bouncing around your eye sockets, making things harder to find, not easier. The best way to dig a program out of the haystack is to cruise through a nice set of menus, clearly arranged by topic.

Part III: Linux the Way You Want It

> **Linking to links**
>
> One cute trick I discovered is that you can link to the KDE link files, created for menu selections and other items. For example, I created the links for Web sites in Figure 9-9 by doing a file find on *.kdelnk to locate the entries for the Online Services menu and then right-clicking those. Clicking the resulting link opens Netscape and takes me straight to the site, just as if I had made the menu selection.

Why isn't a program you use on the menus? Either because it wasn't put there in the first place (see Chapter 6) or because you've since added the program to your repertoire, through Corel Update (see Chapter 17).

The basic operations of adding or removing folders and applications are simple ... once you know how. It's also simple to move applications from one submenu folder to another. More sophisticated menu editing tasks require the KDE menu editor.

Adding submenu folders and applications to your menus

As I said, it's simple to add submenu folders and applications (nicknames) to your menus. Unfortunately, the easy way works only for the root user in the initial release of Corel Linux. The KDE menu editor doesn't have this restriction, so the first thing you'd do is add the KDE menu editor to your Utilities submenu:

1. **Log in under root, assuming you're allowed to do so.**

    Remember, root access gives you power to mess up system files, so log out and then log back in under your normal user ID as soon as possible.

2. **Choose Application Starter ⇨ Applications ⇨ Utilities.**

3. **Right-click Utilities, and choose New ⇨ Nickname, as shown in Figure 9-11.**

    To add a subfolder instead of an application nickname, choose Folder when you right-click and give the subfolder a name.

4. **In the Nickname box, type** Menu Editor, **as shown in Figure 9-12.**

Chapter 9: Desktop Dynamics *133*

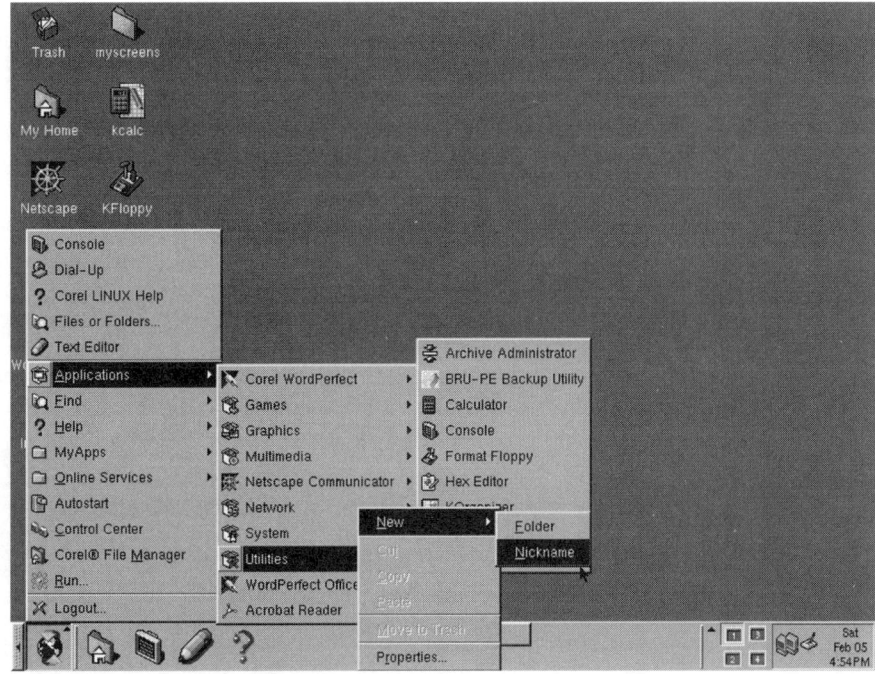

Figure 9-11: Adding a nickname to the Utilities submenu.

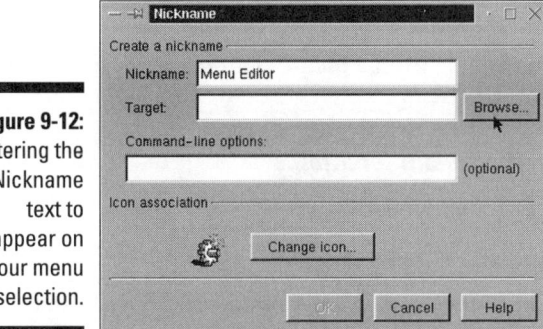

Figure 9-12: Entering the Nickname text to appear on your menu selection.

5. Click the Browse button and go to the /usr/X11R6/bin folder. Then select kmenuedit and click OK, as shown in Figure 9-13.

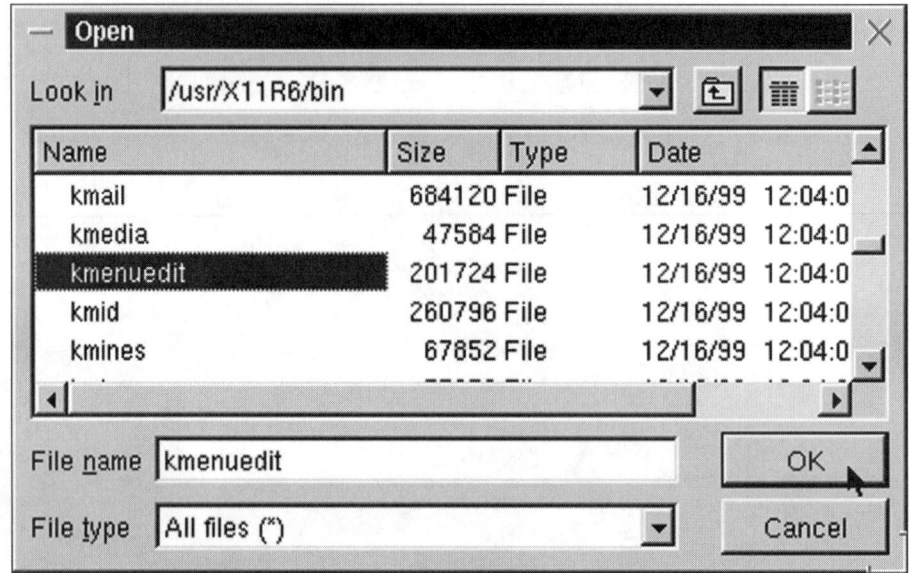

Figure 9-13: Selecting the menu editor application.

6. If you want to browse and select another icon, click Change icon.
7. Click OK to add the menu editor to your Utility submenu selections.

Removing a subfolder or a nickname from your menus

To remove a subfolder or a nickname from a menu, right-click the subfolder or nickname and choose Move to Trash.

Moving a nickname to another menu location

To move a nickname to another menu location, do the following:

1. Right-click the nickname and choose Cut.
2. Right-click the subfolder you're moving the nickname to and then choose Paste.

Use copy and paste to copy a nickname.

Unfortunately, you can't move submenu folders in the initial release of Corel Linux, even if you're logged in as root. Another task for the KDE menu editor.

Using the KDE menu editor

Now that you've added the menu editor to your Utilities submenu, let's give it a go:

Chapter 9: Desktop Dynamics   *135*

1. **If you're adding items to everyone's menus, log in under root. If you're changing only your personal menus, log in under your regular user ID.**

2. **Choose Application Starter ➪ Applications ➪ Utilities ➪ Menu Editor.**

3. **When you start the KDE menu editor for the first time, it asks you to identify the base directories for your menus. The default should be fine, so click OK.**

   The menu editor in Figure 9-14 appears, with an empty personal menu on the left and the system default menu on the right. Note that if you don't have root privileges, the default entries appear grayed. You'll be able to view or copy entries, but not add or edit them.

4. **To add an item to your menus, right-click EMPTY or another location and choose Change.**

5. **In the Type drop-down list, as shown in Figure 9-15, select the type of item (other than Swallow) you want to add:**

   - **Separator** delineates a group of menu selections.
   - **Submenu** adds a folder to the selected menu.
   - **Application** adds a program nickname.
   - **Link** specifies a Web address.
   - **Device** adds a disk drive or other device.

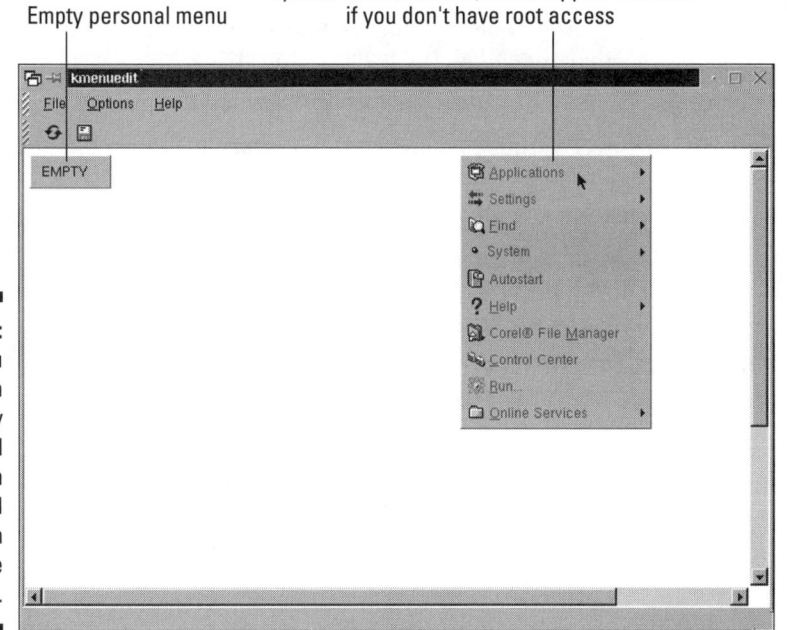

Figure 9-14: The menu editor with an empty personal menu is on the left and system defaults are on the right.

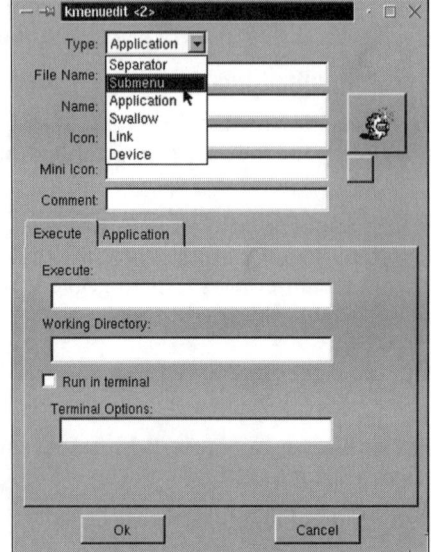

Figure 9-15: Selecting the type of item to add to your menus.

6. Follow the dialog boxes and online help for the item you selected, and then click the Save button on the menu editor toolbar to add the item.

Rearranging menus and other menu editor tricks

When you're in the KDE menu editor, here are some tricks you can employ:

- ✔ Click submenus to display succeeding levels of entries. Click again to close a submenu and all the levels below it.
- ✔ Drag a menu item to another location to copy it.
- ✔ To start over without saving your changes, click the Reload button on the menu editor toolbar.
- ✔ Right-click entries; then move them by cutting and pasting or copy them by copying and pasting.
- ✔ Drag, cut, copy, and paste submenus just like you do individual entries. This lets you rearrange submenus to suit your preferences.
- ✔ Drag an item to another location by holding the middle mouse button (or both the left and right buttons).

The menu editor takes some getting used to, so play around with it to get the feel of how it works. One trick you might try is to copy an entry similar to the one you want to add and then right-click and choose Change to customize it. You can always click the Reload button to start over or simply discard your changes.

Adding buttons to the panel (not)

In a normal KDE environment, you can add buttons to the panel similar to the way you add desktop icons, such as by dragging a program from File Manager to the panel. Unfortunately, this feature isn't present in the initial release of Corel Linux.

The closest you can come to adding a button to the panel is to create a desktop nickname (not a link) and then drag the nickname to the panel to create a button. However, you can't then remove the desktop icon, leaving just the panel button, because deleting the icon deletes also the kdelnk file used by the panel button.

You can rearrange your panel buttons, if you're so inclined. Right-click a button, choose Move, and then drag the button to another location in the row.

It's Your Keyboard, Too!

Keyboard shortcuts often get short shrift in a graphical environment. They take a bit of memorization, whereas the graphical ways are usually staring you in the face. That said, if you look over the keystroke tables in Chapter 5, you'll find a lot of handy tricks that can speed up your work, such as

- Global desktop keys such as Ctrl+Tab to switch desktops and Ctrl+Esc to display and switch tasks
- Standard program keys such as Ctrl+C for copy, Ctrl+V for paste, Ctrl+S for save, and Ctrl+P for print. I almost forgot: Ctrl+Z (Undo) comes in handy a lot!

You can modify your global and standard shortcut keys. The best way to do this is by setting up custom keyboard schemes. Before you go and do that, keep in mind a few points:

- Keyboard changes and custom keyboard schemes apply to each particular user but are not desktop-specific.
- You can't change your function keys (F2, F3, and so on).
- You can assign actions to any Shift, Ctrl, or Alt key combinations with another key. If a combination is already taken, the editor lets you know.
- Standard keyboard changes do not apply to all programs. For example, if you change save to Ctrl+A, you might still find that certain programs still insist on using Ctrl+S to save.

Creating a custom keyboard scheme

The method for creating custom keyboard schemes is the same for both global and standard keys:

1. **Choose Application Starter ⇨ Control Center.**
2. **Double-click Keys and choose either the Global Keys or Standard Keys, as shown in Figure 9-16.**

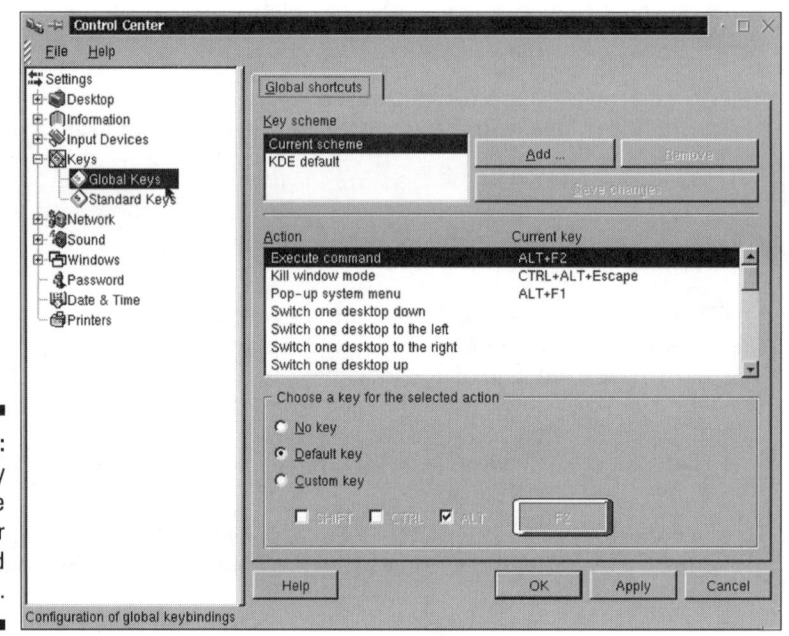

Figure 9-16: You may customize the global or standard keys.

The Current scheme is the same as the KDE default at this stage because there is no other keyboard and no changes have been made.

3. **Click the Add button, give your custom keyboard a name, and then click OK, as shown in Figure 9-17.**

Figure 9-17: Naming a custom keyboard.

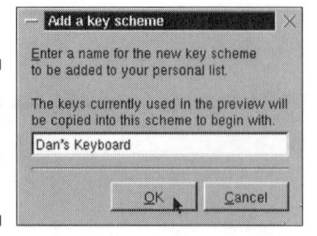

4. **Choose the action you want to customize, as shown in Figure 9-18, and then do one of the following:**

    - Choose the **No key** option to remove the keystroke assignments.

    - Choose the **Default key option** to restore the KDE default to a key you've changed. (This option appears dimmed for actions not assigned to the default KDE keyboard.)

    - Choose the **Custom key** option, choose the SHIFT, CTRL, and ALT options you want, and then click the button to the right and press the key to use in combination with the keys you checked. As you can see in the figure, I chose Ctrl+Down.

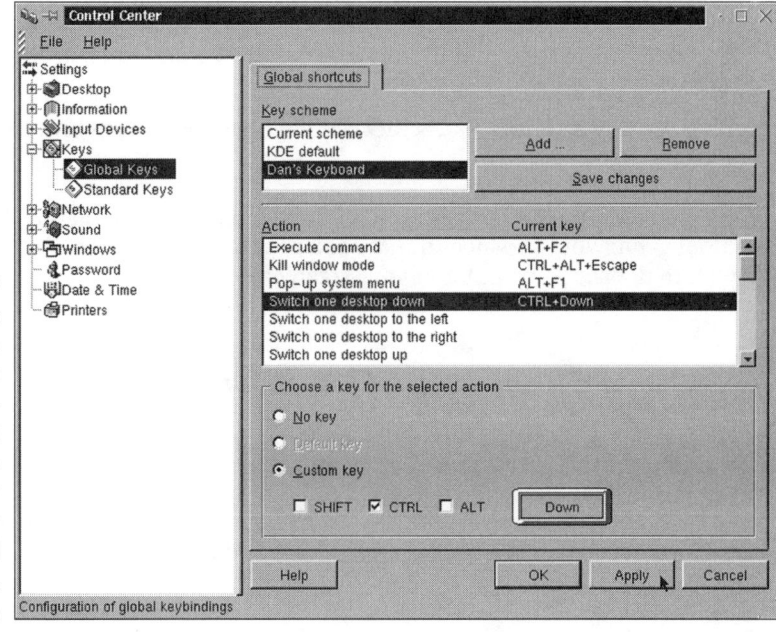

Figure 9-18: Choose the action you want to customize and then choose the keys for your selected action.

5. **Repeat Step 4 for any other action keys you want to add or change.**
6. **To save your custom assignments, click the Save changes button.**
7. **To use your new scheme now, click Apply.**

Switching keyboard schemes

When you have multiple keyboard schemes, either for the global or standard keys, you may switch among them:

1. Choose Application Starter ⇨ Control Center.
2. Double-click Keys and then choose either Global Keys or Standard Keys.
3. In the Key schemes list, select the keyboard you want and then click Apply.

Deleting a custom keyboard scheme

To delete a custom keyboard scheme:

1. Choose Application Starter ⇨ Control Center.
2. Double-click Keys and then choose either Global Keys or Standard Keys.
3. In the Key schemes list, select the keyboard you want and then click Remove.

When you click the Remove button, your keyboard is immediately deleted, without giving you a chance to reconsider the fateful decision. Removing the keyboard doesn't even put it in your trash can.

Fine-Tuning Desktop Operations

The desktop works just fine out of the box or off the CD in the back of this book. If you want, however, you can customize desktop operations to suit your tastes in a lot of little ways. It's fun to experiment with the settings described here. Who knows? You might just latch onto something that improves the quality of your computing life.

For me, the biggest bonus of the bunch is to autohide the panel. Please, don't get me wrong; the panel is lovely — I just don't want to stare at it all day.

Changing the location and size of the panel and taskbar

Before we get to autohiding the panel, did you know that you can move it around and change its size?

You can also separate the taskbar from the panel and let the panel go its merry way, as shown in Figure 9-19. This can be disorienting, to say the least, but some folks can get used to anything.

Chapter 9: Desktop Dynamics *141*

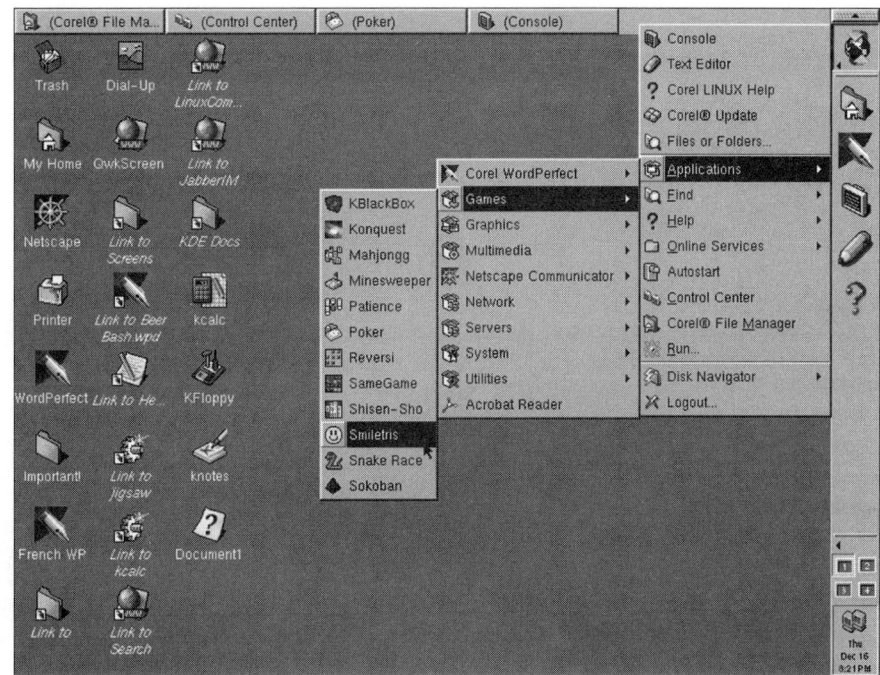

Figure 9-19: Wild stuff you can do with your panel and taskbar.

Just for fun, try fooling with the locations and size of your panel and taskbar:

1. **Right-click a blank spot in the panel or taskbar and choose Configure.**

   The dialog box shown in Figure 9-20 appears.

2. **In the Location area, select a panel location at the top, left, bottom, or right of your screen.**

3. **In the Style area, choose a panel style (size).**

   Large doesn't buy you anything, but tiny is sleek and discreet, as shown in Figure 9-21.

4. **In the Taskbar area, click a location for the taskbar, either docked in the panel or on its own.**

   The Hidden selection zaps the taskbar — not to be confused with auto-hide.

5. **Click Apply to keep testing different options.**

6. **When you're finished, click OK.**

You can also move the panel with your mighty mouse. Just grab an empty spot in the panel and drag it to the top, bottom, or either side of the screen.

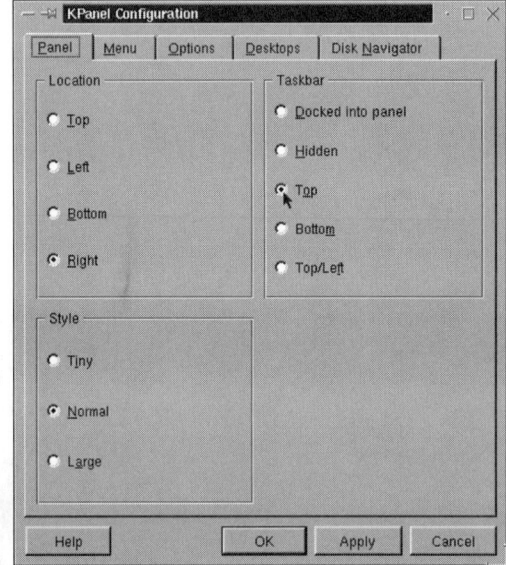

Figure 9-20: Go ahead, play with your panel and taskbar.

Figure 9-21: A sleek, discreet, tiny panel.

Autohiding the panel

When you autohide the panel it stays discreetly out of view, like a faithful attendant, ready to pop into view whenever you point:

1. **Right-click a blank spot in the panel and choose Configure.**
2. **Click the Options tab.**
3. **Choose the Auto hide panel option to do just that, as shown in Figure 9-22.**

   You can then drag the sliders to adjust the autohide delay and speed. If the taskbar is separate from the panel, you can also autohide that and adjust its delay.

   I like a very small autohide delay. That gets it quickly off the screen when it's not needed, especially when I accidentally pop it up.

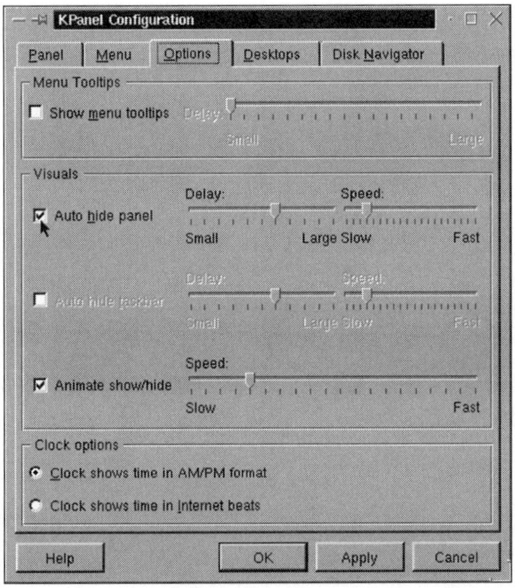

Figure 9-22:
My favorite desktop trick: Autohiding the panel.

4. **Choose the Animate show/hide option and adjust its speed.**

   This setting animates the panel's disappearance and reappearance when you click the flyout tab at the end.

5. **To keep testing different options, click Apply.**

6. **When you're finished, click OK.**

If your taskbar is separated from the panel, you can autohide that as well.

Fine-tuning your menu display

Corel Linux keeps track of the programs you run and turns the ones you use most (or used most recently) into *Quick Start* entries at the top of your main menu. You can change the number of Quick Start entries and other menu configuration options, although you might never know it because the settings are accessed through the panel configuration:

1. **Right-click a blank spot in the panel and then choose Configure.**
2. **Click the Menu tab to display the settings in Figure 9-23.**

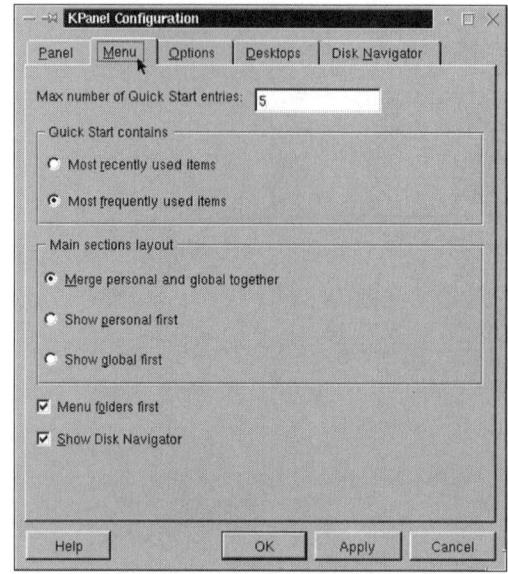

Figure 9-23: Your menu settings, accessed by right-clicking on the panel.

3. **Specify the number of handy Quick Start entries you want to display at the top of the main menu.**

   You may display anywhere from 0 to 20 Quick Start entries, but 8 to 10 is a reasonable limit.

4. **In the Quick Start contains area, make a selection.**

   You may choose to display the programs you either used most recently or use most often.

5. **In the Main sections layout area, make a selection.**

   You may keep together or separate your personal and main selections. If you want to separate them, choose whether to put your personal or global selections first.

6. **If you want to display your menu folders (submenus) first, click to add a check mark to the Menu folders first option.**

   Otherwise, folders and individual selections are merged into one alphabetical list.

7. **If you want Disk Navigator on your menu, click to add a check mark to Show Disk Navigator.**

   Doing so results in a hierarchical display of your system, including recently used files and folders.

8. **When you've finished making your selections, click OK.**

How many desktops did you say?

Having multiple desktops is a fabulous feature that alone would be worth the price of Linux, if it weren't free. The default four is a reasonable number of desktops, but you can have anywhere from two to eight:

1. **Right-click a blank spot in the panel and then choose Configure.**
2. **Click the Desktops tab.**
3. **In the Visible list, choose the number of desktops you want, as shown in Figure 9-24, and then click OK.**

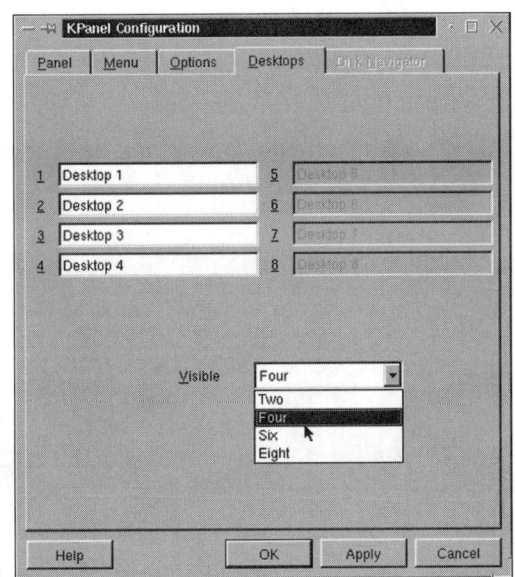

Figure 9-24:
How many desktops did you say?

Renaming your desktops

You may rename your desktops (Desktop 1, Desktop 2, and so on) to anything you choose — although I'm not sure how doing so would affect the quality of your computing life. Right-click a blank spot in the panel and choose Configure. Then click the Desktops tab, type the new names, and then click OK.

Customizing Window Operations

Holy smokes! You can customize window operations too. I'm not talking about appearances here — beautification is covered in Chapter 10. I'm talking about things that affect everyday window operations. These options are all found in the Control Center, though their arrangement is somewhat bewildering.

Setting keyboard window controls

You can customize the Ctrl+Tab and Alt+Tab keystrokes for walking thorough windows:

1. **Choose Application Starter ⇨ Control Center.**
2. **Double-click Windows and then choose Advanced.**
3. **If you want Ctrl+Tab to walk you through desktops, click to select the first option on the Advanced tab, as shown in Figure 9-25.**

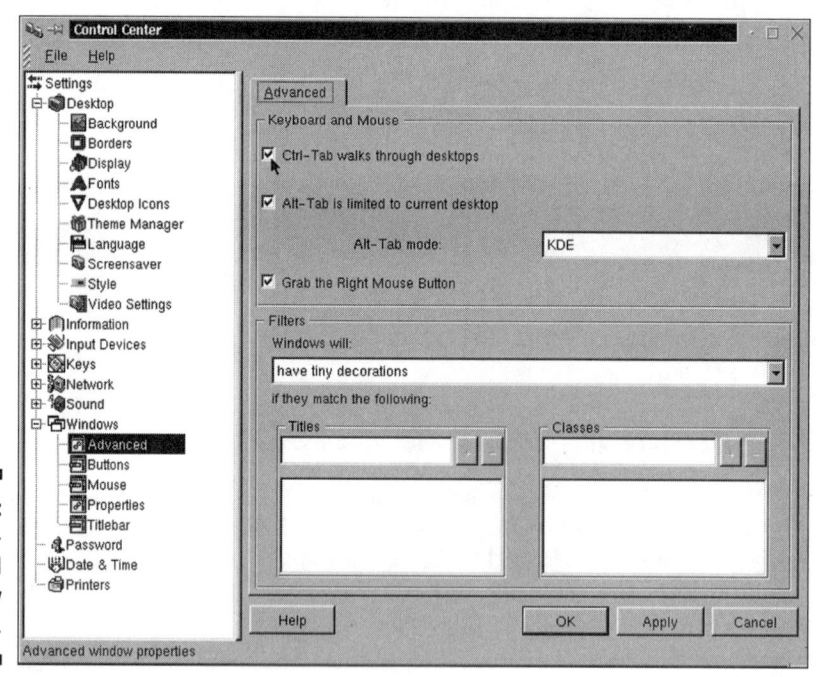

Figure 9-25: Setting keyboard window controls.

4. **If you want Alt+Tab to walk you through just the windows in the current desktop, click to select the second option.**

   Otherwise, Alt+Tab walks you through all the windows in all the desktops.

   TIP: The option to use the CDE mode for your Alt+Tab walkthroughs doesn't work in the initial release of Corel Linux. Also, leave the Grab the Right Mouse Button option checked to allow certain programs to use their own right mouse button settings when necessary.

5. **When you've finished making your selections, click OK.**

Changing how your mouse behaves around windows

You can change two types of mouse behavior around windows:

- What happens when you click various buttons on various window spots
- The way windows come into focus as you point to them

Retraining your mouse buttons

You can specify what each mouse button does when you click various places on active and inactive windows. Before you start, here are the operational terms:

- **Raise** brings the window to the top of the pile.
- **Lower** pushes the window down to the bottom.
- **Activate** switches the focus from the active window to the one you click.
- **Pass click** both activates the window and does the operation on the active window with one click.
- **Operations menu** gives you a list of all the window tricks you can perform, including move, iconify, and sticky.

To retrain your mouse buttons:

1. **Choose Application Starter ⇨ Control Center.**
2. **Double-click Windows and then choose Mouse.**

   The various click operations are displayed, as shown in Figure 9-26.

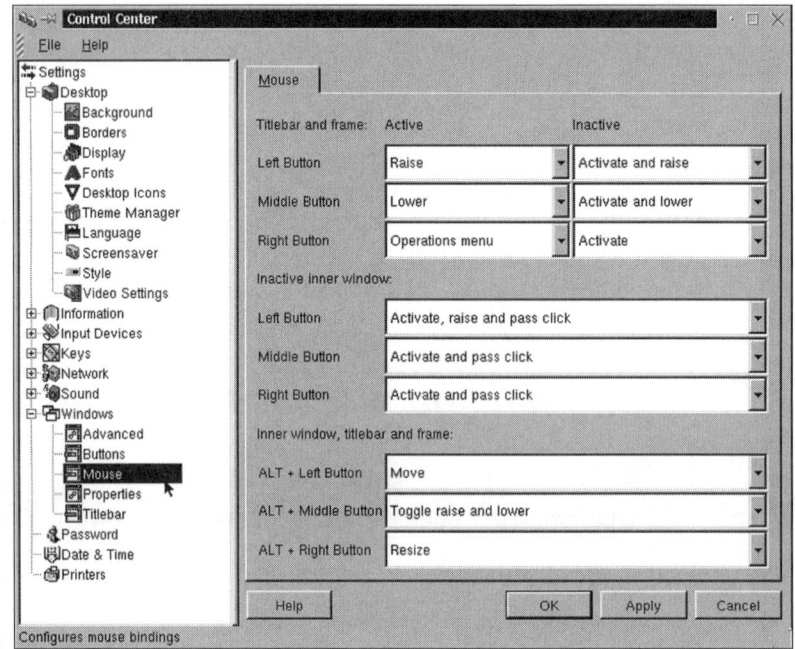

Figure 9-26: Retraining your mouse buttons.

3. **Make your selections in the three areas of the dialog box:**

    • In the top area, choose what the various buttons do when you click the title bar or frame of active and inactive windows.

    • In the middle area, choose what the various buttons do when you click an inactive inner window.

    • In the bottom area, choose what the various buttons do when you hold the Alt key and click a window.

    If you have a two-button mouse, try simultaneous clicks of the left and right buttons to perform the middle button operations.

4. **Click Apply to test various settings.**

5. **Click OK when you're finished.**

Changing what happens as you move the mouse

To change what happens as your mouse moves around a bunch of windows, do the following:

1. **Choose Application Starter ⇨ Control Center.**

2. **Double-click Windows and then choose Properties.**

    The screen shown in Figure 9-27 appears.

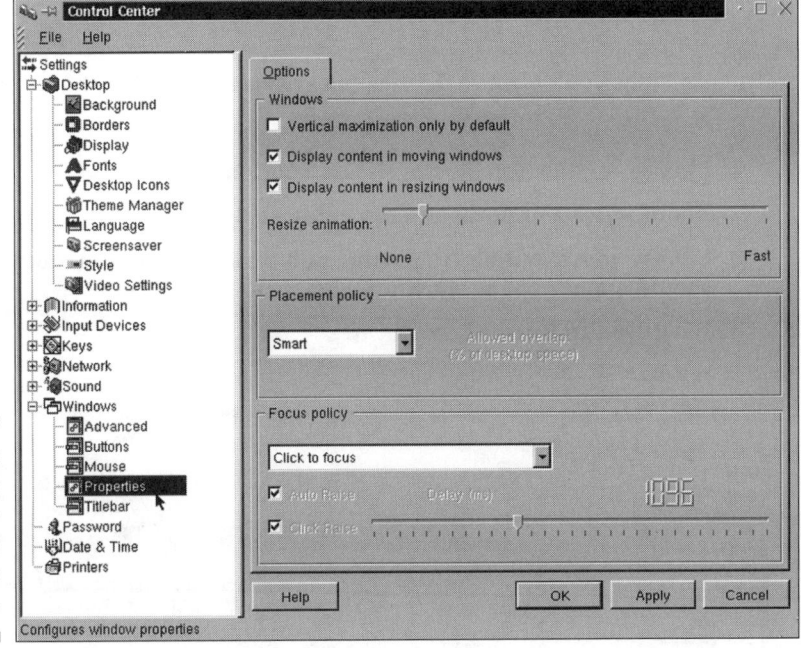

Figure 9-27: Changing what happens as you move the mouse.

3. In the Focus policy area at the bottom of the screen, click in the list and choose from the following:

    - **Click to focus** lets you click a window to make it active.
    - **Focus follows mouse** lets you point to a window, without clicking, to make it active.
    - **Classic focus follows mouse** lets you point to a window to make it active and then point to the desktop and deactivate the window.
    - **Classic sloppy focus** lets you do the same as Focus follows mouse, that is, point to a window to make it active and keep it active until you point to another window.

4. For all but the Click to focus policy, you can choose Auto Raise to automatically bring the active window to the fore. You can then drag the Delay slider to adjust (in thousandths of a second) how long you must point before the window pops up.

5. If you're not using Auto Raise, you can choose the Click Raise option to pull up the window, as you do with the Click to focus policy.

6. Click OK when you're finished.

Setting your window button display

You probably won't want to do this, but you can configure what window buttons you display and where:

1. **Choose Application Starter ➪ Control Center.**
2. **Double-click Windows and then choose Buttons.**
3. **Choose which buttons to display and which side of the toolbar they should appear on, as shown in Figure 9-28.**
4. **When you're finished, click OK.**

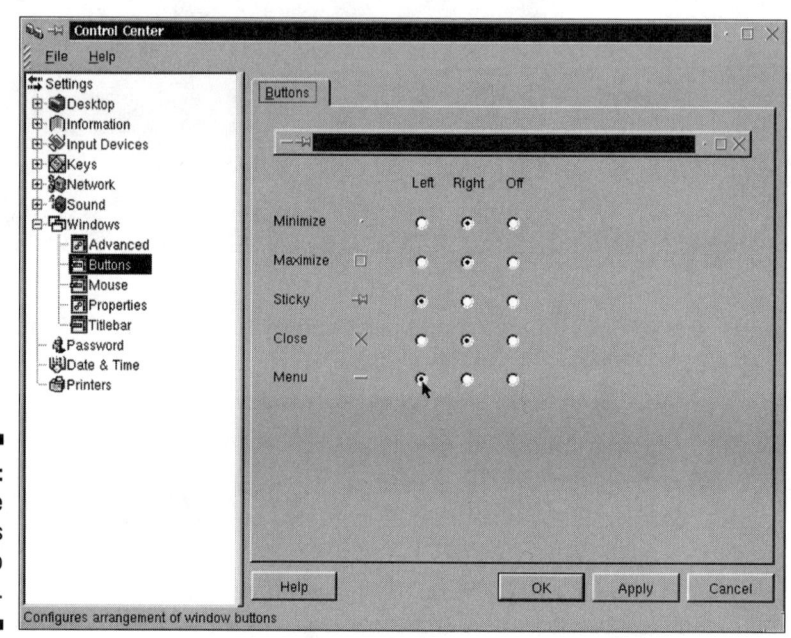

Figure 9-28: Choose the buttons you want to display.

Making order out of window chaos

You can even choose the policy by which you attempt to maintain a semblance of order amidst the window chaos:

1. **Choose Application Starter ➪ Control Center.**
2. **Double-click Windows and then choose Properties.**

Chapter 9: Desktop Dynamics   151

3. **In the Placement policy area of the screen, click in the list, as shown in Figure 9-29, and select from the following policies:**

   - **Smart** puts windows in the largest vacant desktop spaces.
   - **Cascade** places windows on top of one another so that their title bars are visible.
   - **Interactive** uses smart placement unless there's too much window overlap, in which case you place them manually.
   - **Random** opens windows in random locations.
   - **Manual** has you drag windows when you open them and then click to place them.

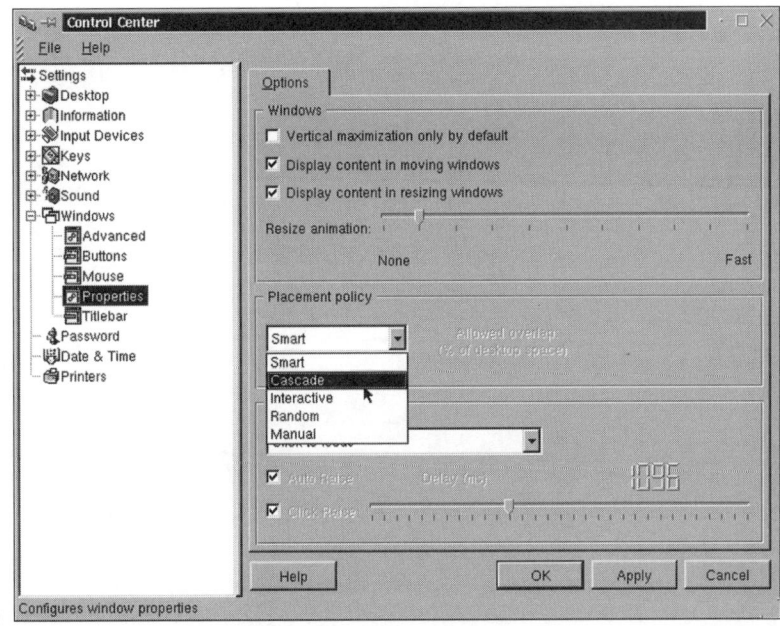

Figure 9-29: Choosing how to maintain order amidst window chaos.

4. **If you choose the Interactive mode, you can then set the percentage of desktop space the windows can overlap, before you set them manually.**
5. **When you're finished, click OK.**

As you can see, you can do a lot with your desktop! No need to be in a hurry to change things, though, because the default settings are aimed at what most folks like.

Chapter 10
Decorating Your Desktop

In This Chapter
▶ Wallpapering or painting your backgrounds
▶ Coloring your window
▶ Fooling around with screen fonts
▶ Rearranging your desktop icons
▶ Styling yourself after other operating systems
▶ Adopting a whole new theme
▶ Sounding off
▶ Resolving your resolution

Do you suffer from the Desktop Doldrums? Tired of looking at the same old interface? Then it's time to add a little color to your computing life — and a little sound, a little style. Maybe a lot of color, a lot of sound, and a lot of style. In fact, why not go totally crazed with some Fantasy, SciFi, or Nature theme, as shown in Figure 10-1!

Can't promise the stuff in this chapter will make you 23 percent more productive or even 3 percent more productive, but you will have a good time.

Okay, I'm going to risk sounding like a spoilsport or, yuck, a prude. A lot of careful design and testing went into the default desktop to create a pleasant and productive environment. A completely wacko desktop makeover can make you decidedly less productive. Still, you gotta try out the themes!

Figure 10-1: Pasteurized pixels.

Customizing Your Desktop Backgrounds

Tired of staring at the same old wall? Then customize your desktop backgrounds to use one color, two colors, or maybe a zany wallpaper. Each desktop can provide a characteristic backdrop, such as a single color for Desktop 1, two colors for Desktop 2, and different wallpapers for Desktops 3 and 4. Not a bad idea, really, because the background will immediately alert you to which desktop you're in.

Painting your backgrounds

To use color backgrounds for your desktops:

1. **Choose Application Starter ⇨ Control Center.**

   You can also click the display icon on the right of your panel for most desktop appearance settings.

2. **Double-click Desktop and then choose Background.**

   The settings shown in Figure 10-2 appear.

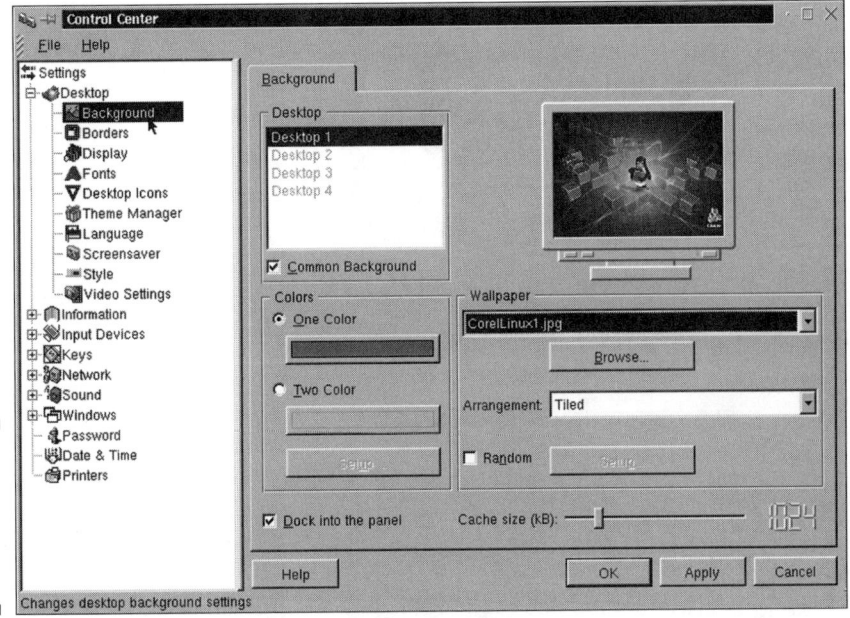

Figure 10-2: Customizing your desktop backgrounds.

3. **Do one of the following:**

    - To apply your settings to all backgrounds, click to add a check mark to the Common Background option.

    - To change a particular desktop, leave the Common Background option unchecked and click the desktop in the list.

4. **To use a color background, do one of the following:**

    - Choose One Color and then select a color from System Colors or Custom Colors.

        To create a custom color, click the large window to choose a color, click the narrow window to fine-tune its shade, click a blank spot in the Custom Colors palette, and then click the Add to Custom Colors button, as shown in Figure 10-3.

    - Choose Two Color, select both colors, and then click the Setup button to blend the colors or create a pattern, as shown in Figure 10-4.

5. **Click OK to apply your changes.**

Figure 10-3: The artist within creates a custom color.

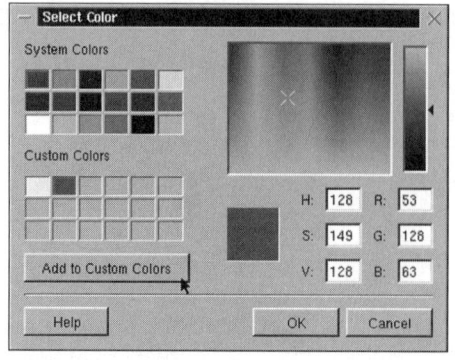

Figure 10-4: Applying a blend or pattern to your two-color background.

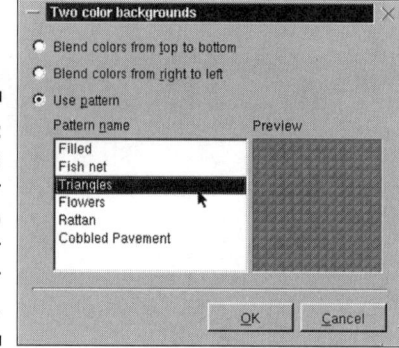

> **TIP:** When you choose a light color for your desktop background, change your icon text to a darker, contrasting color. See "Customizing Your Desktop Icon Display," later in this chapter.

Wallpapering your backgrounds

To wallpaper your desktop backgrounds, follow these simple steps:

1. **Choose Application Starter ⇨ Control Center.**
2. **Double-click Desktop and then choose Background.**
3. **Do one of the following:**
    - To apply your settings to all backgrounds, click to add a check mark to the Common Background option.
    - To change a particular desktop, leave the Common Background option unchecked and click the desktop in the list.
4. **In the Arrangement list, select the wallpaper arrangement you want to use, such as tiled, centered, or mirrored.**

Chapter 10: Decorating Your Desktop *157*

TECHNICAL STUFF: Many wallpapers are no more than little bitmaps, designed to repeat to fill the whole screen. Select the nonrepeating Scale option instead to see what I mean.

5. **Do one of the following:**

    - In the Wallpaper list, select a wallpaper from the wallpaper folder. Or click the Browse button to select a bitmap from elsewhere.

    - To arrange a rotating background show, choose the Random option and then click the Setup button. You have several options, as shown in Figure 10-5. To rotate the files in a wallpaper folder, choose the Pick files from directory option. To rotate wallpapers in a custom list, to which you can add and delete entries, make sure that the Pick files from directory option is not selected. You can also set the time between switches and whether the selection should be in order or random.

6. **Click OK to apply your selections.**

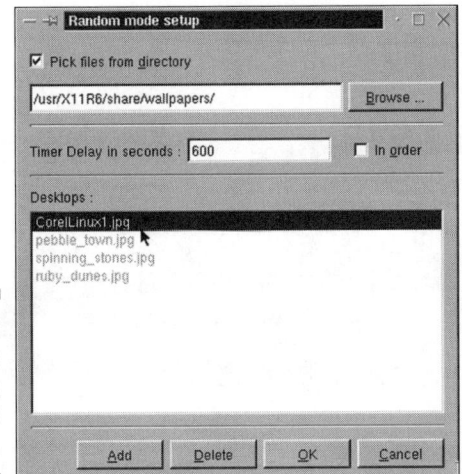

Figure 10-5: Setting up a rotating background show.

A Few More Background Options

You have a few other background options, not specific to a particular display:

1. **Choose Application Starter ⇨ Control Center.**
2. **Double-click Desktop and then choose Background.**
3. **Click to add a check mark to the Dock into the panel option.**

    The Display Settings icon is added to the right of your panel.

Part III: Linux the Way You Want It

4. **Drag the slider to adjust the size of your background cache.**

   A larger cache can speed up display if you're using large wallpaper bitmaps, but it also takes system resources away from other tasks.

5. **Click OK to apply your changes.**

Changing Your Window Colors

You can change the colors of all your window widgets, such as title bars, title text, general background, and window background and text. You can also select color schemes of coordinated widget colors and create custom schemes of your own.

To change your window colors:

1. **Choose Application Starter ➪ Control Center.**
2. **Double-click Desktop and then choose Display.**

   The color settings in Figure 10-6 appear.

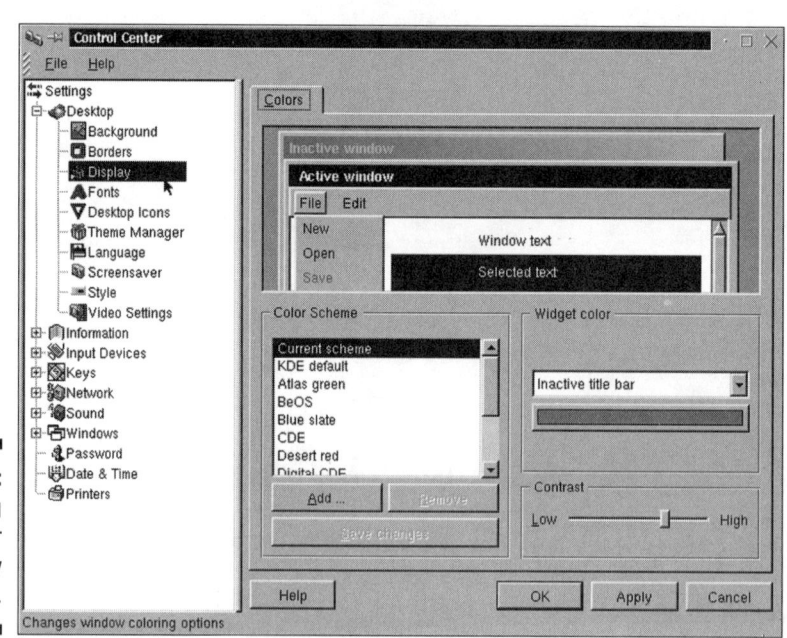

Figure 10-6: Changing your window colors.

3. **In the Color Scheme list, select a coordinated color scheme that most nearly suits your tastes, as shown in Figure 10-7.**

    The preview window shows what the scheme looks like.

 4. **In the widget color list, select various widgets to refine their colors.**

    Your selections appear in the preview window.

 5. **If you want to make your color contrasts higher or lower, move the Contrast slider.**

 6. **If you want to save your custom colors to a new scheme, click the Add button to give your scheme a name, as shown in Figure 10-8.**

    You can't change or remove the system color schemes, but you can save them as custom schemes that you can then edit or remove.

 7. **Click OK to apply your changes.**

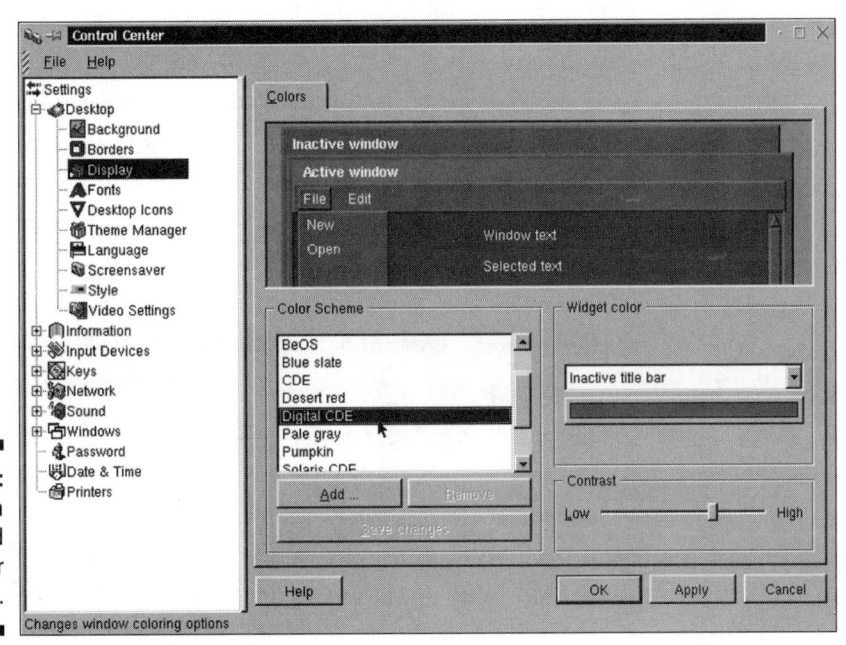

Figure 10-7: Selecting a coordinated color scheme.

Part III: Linux the Way You Want It

Figure 10-8: Saving your custom colors to a new scheme.

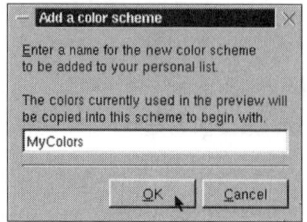

Changing Your Screen Fonts

You can change various fonts used in your desktop display, such as the font that appears in your window title bars. Here's how:

1. **Choose Application Starter ⇨ Control Center.**
2. **Double-click Desktop and then choose Fonts.**

   The settings in Figure 10-9 appear.

3. **Select the type of font you want to change.**
4. **Select the typeface, size, and other characteristics.**
5. **Repeat Steps 3 and 4 for other fonts you want to change.**
6. **Click OK when you're finished.**

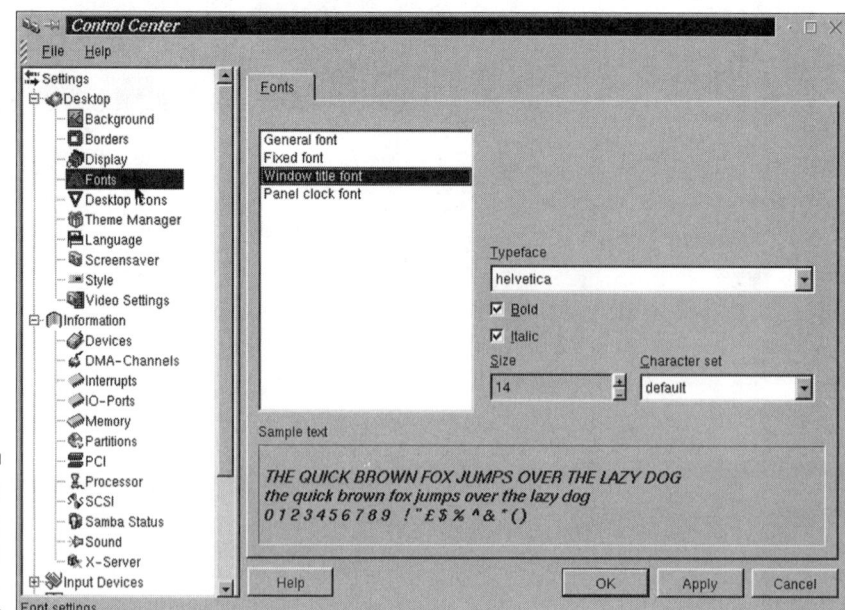

Figure 10-9: Changing your screen fonts.

Customizing Your Desktop Icon Display

Try dragging a few desktop icons around. Then right-click on your desktop and click Arrange Icons. Notice how your icons snap to attention in neat columns and rows. You can also change the spacing between your rows and enhance visibility of their text:

1. **Choose Application Starter ➪ Control Center.**
2. **Double-click Desktop and then choose Desktop Icons.**

   The settings in Figure 10-10 appear.

3. **Set the horizontal and vertical spacing, in pixels, to either scrunch your icons together or spread them apart.**
4. **If you want your icons to have transparent text, choose the Transparent Text for Desktop Icons option.**

   Transparent text actually refers to a transparent text *background* that lets your desktop color or wallpaper show through. If you remove this check mark, you can then select the Icon background color option, which is background for just the text, not the entire icon. Confused? It's easier to just do it than to explain it.

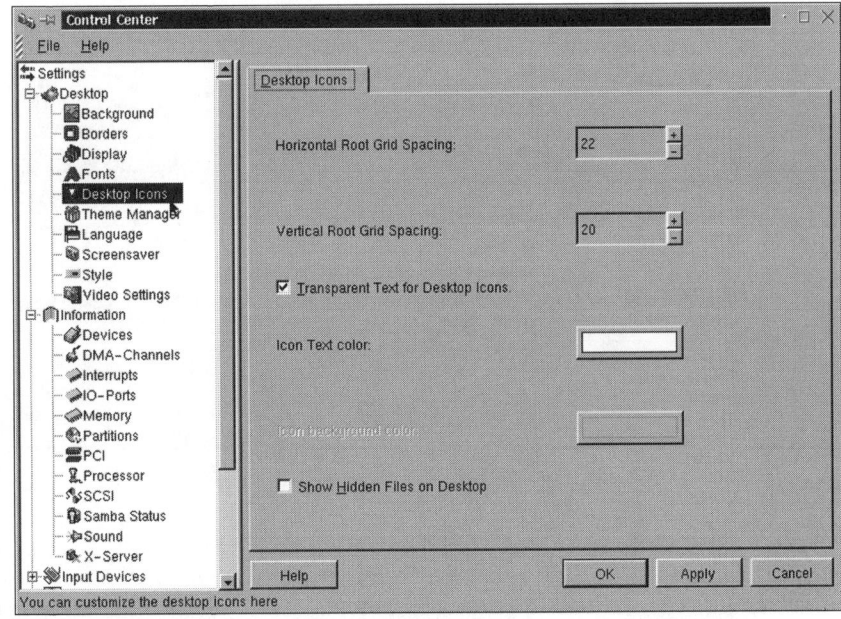

Figure 10-10: Customizing your desktop icon display.

Part III: Linux the Way You Want It

5. **Select an icon text color — preferably one that contrasts with the background.**

6. **If you want to show hidden files on your desktop, choose the Show Hidden Files on Desktop option.**

   Hidden files are files and folders with names beginning with a period (.). These aren't likely to be on your desktop anyway.

7. **Click OK to apply your changes.**

   You see the results the next time you log in. To apply a new spacing, you'll have to right-click on the background to arrange your icons.

Putting on the Style

The Corel Linux desktop has a chameleon-like nature that lets it take on characteristics of other operating systems:

1. **Choose Application Starter ⇨ Control Center.**
2. **Double-click Desktop and then choose Style.**

   The settings in Figure 10-11 appear.

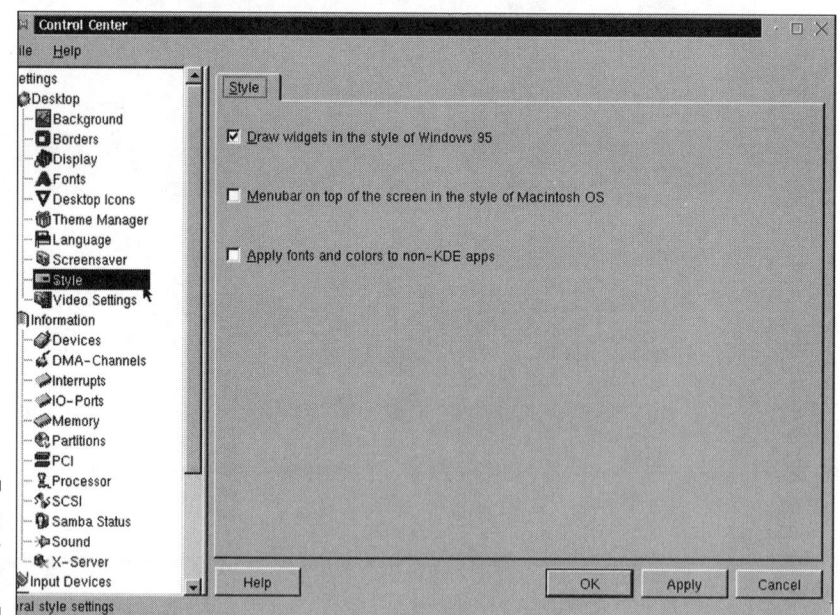

Figure 10-11: What's your style?

3. **Choose any of the following:**
   - **Draw widgets in the style of Windows 95** uses Windows-like check boxes, drop-down lists, and the like.

     Hey, I like to kid about Windows, but this setting is a must! Remove the check mark and click Apply if you don't believe me.

   - **Menubar on top** is for folks who think the Macintosh interface is divine.

   - **Apply fonts and colors to non-KED apps** brings within the fold programs that are not part of Corel Linux.

4. **Click OK to apply your changes.**

Throwing a Theme Party

You're invited to a theme party! To attend, you have to dress up your desktops in all kinds of crazy outfits. *Themes* are all-in-one packages with everything from custom colors and wallpapers to borders, icons, sounds, and more. Some theme party outfits are sedate and formal; others are totally wacky and wild!

Your theme outfits come wrapped in packages — compressed archives containing all the elements for that theme. The archive names are in the form of *Themename*.tgz or *Themename*.tar.gz.

Let's go party!

1. **Choose Application Starter ➪ Control Center.**
2. **Double-click Desktop and then choose Theme Manager.**
3. **Select various themes in the list to preview them, as shown in Figure 10-12. Then select the one you want to apply.**
4. **Click the Contents tab and choose the various theme parts you want to apply, as shown in Figure 10-13.**

   Click to remove or add a check mark.

5. **Click Apply to wear your new desktop outfit.**

164 Part III: Linux the Way You Want It

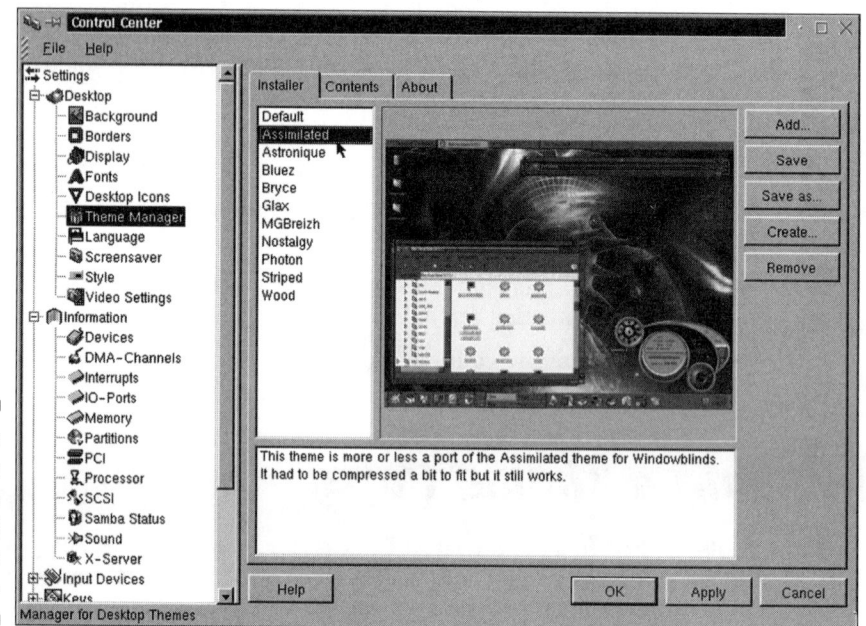

Figure 10-12: Click the themes to see the wild effects you can apply.

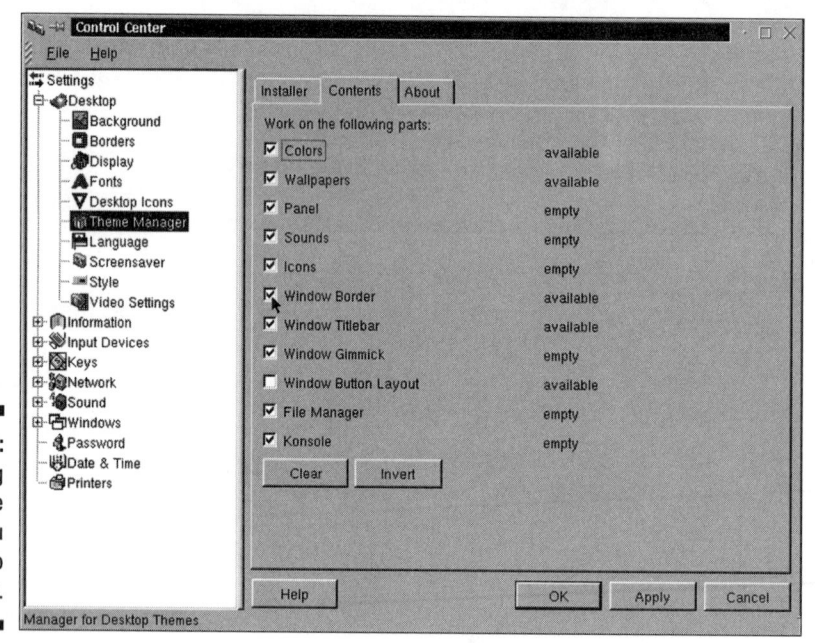

Figure 10-13: Selecting the theme parts you want to apply.

Chapter 10: Decorating Your Desktop *165*

TIP

You can mix parts from various themes. Suppose you want the Wood theme (which doesn't have sounds) and you want the sounds from the MGBreizh theme. Apply the Wood theme, choose the MGBreizh theme, click the Contents tab, choose the Sounds option, and then click the Apply button. Voila!

TECHNICAL STUFF

The Default theme selection consists of the KDE default settings with no special theme elements. This selection is the easiest on system resources.

Satisfying your theme hunger

ON THE WEB

After seeing some of the stupendous effects of some themes, you're bound to be hungry for more. To satisfy your visual appetites, head over to the `kde.themes.org` Web site, as shown in Figure 10-14. You can download themes to your heart's content and then add them to your list.

TIP

You might be tempted to go after wild, dark, and mysterious themes. If you're still using your computer for work and not just play, look for the small, simple, elegant makeovers. They won't leave you buried in foliage or squinting at the screen to make out the text.

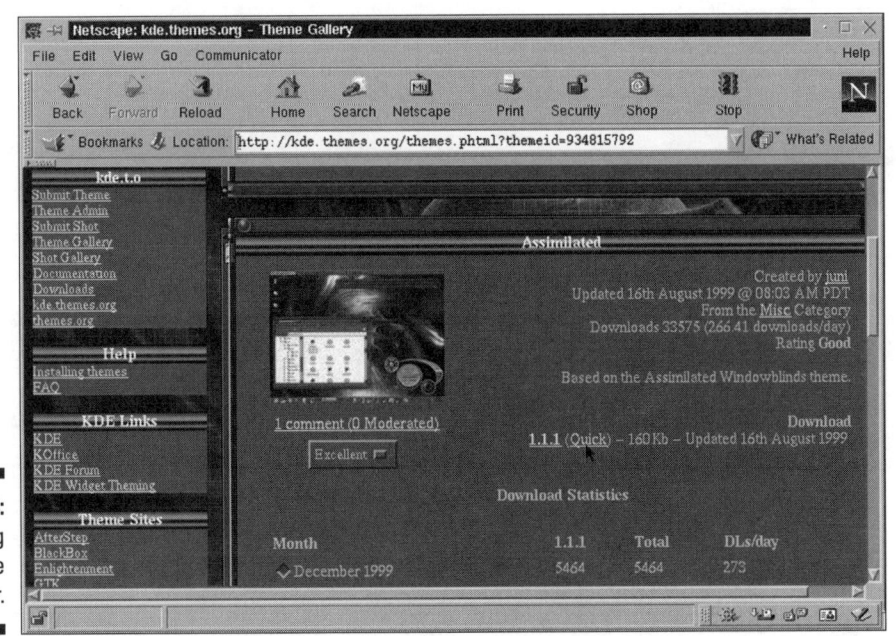

Figure 10-14: Satisfying your theme hunger.

Adding and removing themes

Suppose you just downloaded a bunch of jazzy new themes. To use them, you must add them to your list:

1. **Choose Application Starter ➪ Control Center.**
2. **Double-click Desktop and then click Theme Manager.**
3. **Click the Add button.**
4. **Select the theme package and then click OK to add it to the list, as shown in Figure 10-15.**

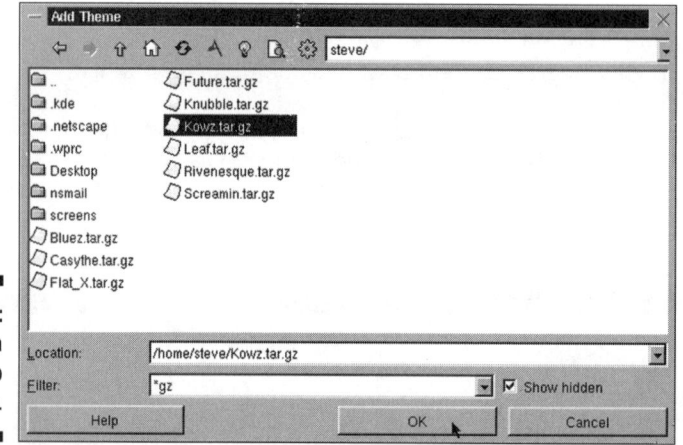

Figure 10-15: Adding a theme to your list.

To remove a theme, select the theme in the Theme Manager and then click the Remove button. Removing the theme from the list does not delete the theme package file.

Themes are usually saved in each user's home folder. The themes in the global folder at /usr/X11R6/share/apps/kthememgr/Themes automatically appear in everyone's list and can't be removed by anyone except the root user.

Creating your own themes

The Theme Manager has a tempting Create button, but it doesn't get you too far. However, creating your own themes is not so difficult, assuming you're among the artistically gifted. Go to the kde.themes.org Web site for complete instructions with examples.

Chapter 10: Decorating Your Desktop   *167*

Making a Joyful Noise

If you don't want the pizzazz you can still have the jazz. Here's how to add a little noise to your computing life:

1. **Choose Application Starter ➪ Control Center.**
2. **Double-click Sound and then choose System Sounds.**
3. **Click to add a check mark to the enable system sounds option.**

   The events and sounds shown in Figure 10-16 appear.

4. **In the Events list, select an event to which you want to apply a sound.**
5. **In the Sounds list, select an associated sound.**

   To turn off sound for a particular event, select the (none) option.

6. **Click Apply.**
7. **For additional event and sound associations, repeat Steps 4 through 6.**
8. **When you're finished, click OK.**

System sounds are in the /usr/X11R6/share/sounds folder. The files you add to the folder, as root, appear in the list of selections.

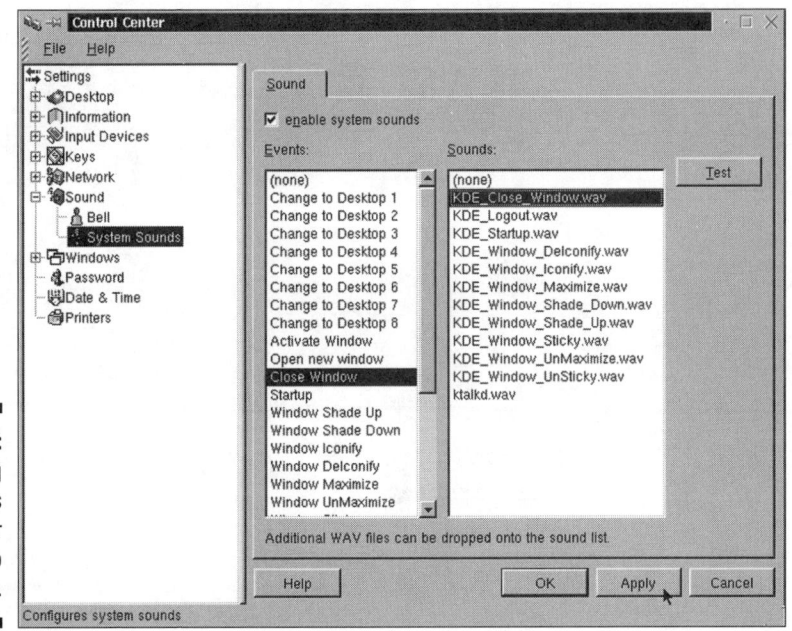

Figure 10-16: Associating sounds with your desktop happenings.

Putting on the Pixels

Most of the old, low-resolution, 14-inch monitors are long gone — and not missed. In the bad old days, you had to press your nose to the screen to see what was there, meanwhile getting zapped with a dose of radiation.

If you're using a desktop computer, chances are that the mysterious measurement of your monitor is 15 inches, 17 inches, or even 19 inches or larger. If so, the amount of information you display on your screen is a matter of personal preference. Depending on your graphics card, you can go from the minimal 640 x 480 screen pixels (recommended only for crash recovery) to the 1280 x 1024 pixels in Figure 10-17 or higher.

The greater the number of pixels on your screen, the sharper the images appear. On the other hand, you might end up squinting at dialog boxes, toolbars, and other screen objects because their fixed number of pixels will take up less screen space on a particular monitor. Corel Linux seems to be most comfortable at 800 x 600 pixels, the resolution used for the figures in this book, or at 1024 x 768.

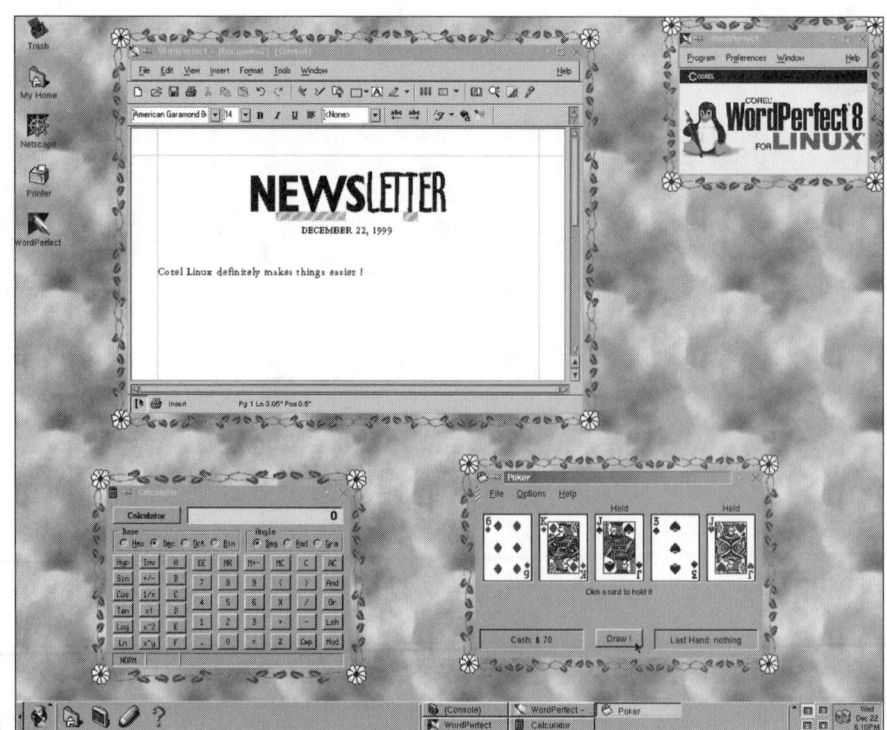

Figure 10-17: Putting on the pixels — a screen resolution of 1280 x 1024.

To change your resolution and other video settings:

1. **Choose Application Starter ⇨ Control Center.**
2. **Double-click Desktop and then choose Video Settings.**
3. **Click the Screen Resolution slider to move it to a lower or higher resolution, as shown in Figure 10-18.**
4. **In the Colour Depth list, select something that your graphics card and monitor can support.**

   The greater the depth, the richer the colors but the more memory your video card will need. If in doubt, don't increase the color depth.

5. **In the Frequency list, select the refresh frequency your monitor supports at the resolution you selected.**

   Higher frequencies eliminate visible screen flicker.

6. **In the Available Monitor Types list, select your monitor. Or, if you don't see your monitor, select the default option.**

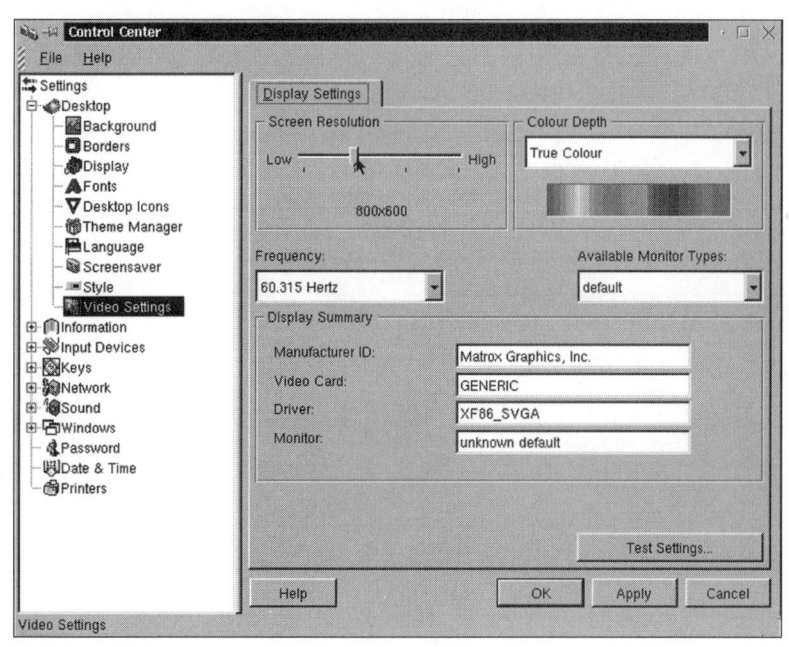

Figure 10-18: Sliding over to another resolution.

7. **Click the Test Settings button to see whether the settings you chose are supported by your hardware.**

   The test may adjust one or more selections, based on your hardware's capabilities.

   Be sure to click Test Settings *before* you click Apply! Otherwise, you might end up with settings not supported by your video adapter. When that happens, you might be forced to start Corel Linux in low-resolution VGA mode. Or worse yet, you could end up in command-line mode with no graphics at all!

8. **Click Apply to use your new settings.**

9. **If you get a message to do so, save your work and exit your applications, and then press Ctrl+Alt+Backspace to exit the desktop and restart your X graphics server.**

Part IV
Doin' Your Own Thing

The 5th Wave — By Rich Tennant

"I failed her in Algebra, but was impressed with the way she animated her equations to dance across the screen, scream like hyenas and then dissolve into a clip art image of the La Brea Tar Pits."

In this part . . .

A couple of years ago, I wouldn't have dreamed of doing the stuff here using Linux, rather than Windows or a Mac. Time to hop onboard the Linux Express!

Chapter 11

Managing Your Files

In This Chapter
- Seeing out what types of files you have
- Finding out where everything is kept
- Going to your home folder
- Uncovering more than files in File Manager
- Swinging through the folder tree
- Granting file permissions, sorting the folder view, and more
- Renaming, copying, moving, and deleting files and folders — and still more

A nice thing about computers is that all your documents and files are always within easy reach . . . if you can find them. With Corel Linux, you're in luck because it comes with the best file manager in the business. Before you know it, you'll be swinging from branch to branch on your folder tree like a pro!

The focus of this chapter is the Corel File Manager, but keep in mind that you'll be managing files in plenty of other places as well, such as WordPerfect, the Text Editor, and graphics programs.

What Kinds of Files Are We Talking About?

Now, what kinds of files are we talking about? Your system is full of different types of files, but some of the more important ones are

- **System files** make everything tick in Corel Linux; they include a number of text configuration files.
- **Programs** are the files you use to do stuff.
- Personal **user files** are letters, reports, photographs, and so on.

Part IV: Doin' Your Own Thing

System files are generally off-limits to all but the root user. No need to mess with them unless you're fixing a problem, updating your system, or performing some other administrative task, such as managing user accounts.

WARNING! I've said this before, but I'll say it again. Do not log in as root unless you absolutely have too. Access to system files gives you the power to screw things up.

Like system files, programs are generally installed and left alone. Although this chapter explains where you can find system files and programs, the user files are the focus of your day-to-day file management activities.

Going Home

Before you get started with managing files, you should check out how they're organized. Log in as a regular user and then click the My Home shortcut on your desktop to open File Manager at your home base, as shown in Figure 11-1. (If File Manager is already open, click My Home in the left pane.)

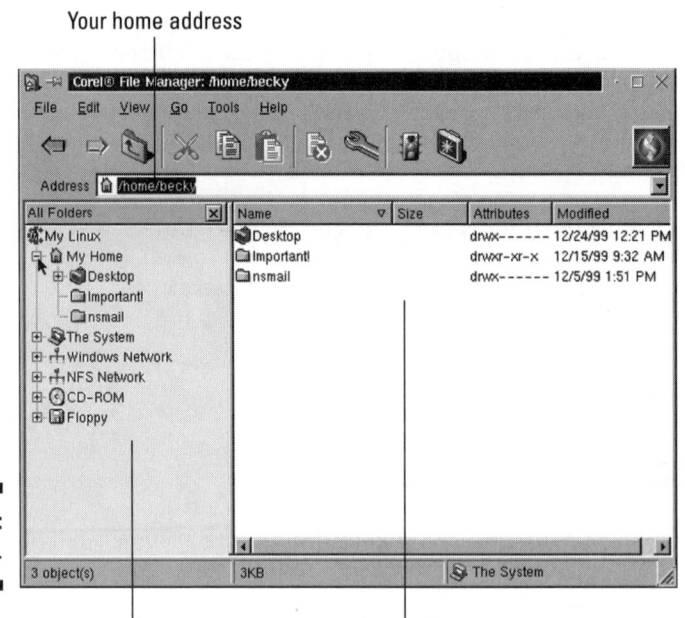

Figure 11-1: Going home.

You'll notice a little house in the Address list just below the toolbar, followed by /home/*username*, with your ID as the username.

Also note how File Manager has two panes: on the left is a *tree view* of all the folders on your system, and on the right is a detailed view of the contents of the selected folder. Click Desktop in the tree view to display the contents of your Desktop folder.

> If you don't see the tree, choose View ⇨ Tree. Make sure Show the System selection on the View menu also has a check mark because we'll be looking at the system files in a moment.

What's All This Other Stuff in the File Manager?

When you look at the tree view in the File Manager, you see not only My Home and The System but also a bunch of other stuff, including removable media such as floppies and CD-ROMs, and possible network connections. This is an indication that your file system is popping out of your computer's case and hauling in stuff from outside. In our increasingly networked and Web-enabled world, you can access outside information as if it were right there on your hard drive!

Look for the following virtual folders in the tree view:

- **Windows Network,** to access files and folders on a Windows network, if your machine is connected to one. See Chapter 4 for hook-up details.
- **NFS Network,** to access outside files and folders if you're hooked into a standard UNIX or Linux local network. See Chapter 4 for more information.
- **CD-ROM** and **Floppy** (and other removable media). Before Corel Linux, it was a real pain to access removable media in Linux. Now they appear automatically in File Manager.
- **Web Browser**, to access recently visited Web locations. Yup, File Manager can be used as a Web browser too!
- **V-Drive**, soon to make an appearance in File Manager. Choose Application Starter ⇨ Online Services ⇨ Corel vDrive to sign up for free virtual hard drive space that you can access from anywhere.

Poking around Your Folders

The programs, documents, graphics, and other files on your system are stored in folders. Folders can also contain subfolders, so that files can be organized in a logical hierarchy, or *tree*, much as you organize the drawers, sections, and folders of a filing cabinet. Note how your home folder in Figure 11-1 has separate Desktop, Important!, and nsmail subfolders. (I added the Important! one.) The Important! and nsmail subfolders can, in turn, have subfolders of their own, and so on.

Your desktop isn't pictured as a folder in the tree, but it's still a folder.

The virtue of virtual neatness

Folders are very useful. I tend to throw all the papers on my desk into one big vertical pile. When I need something, I *hope* to find it near the top of the pile. I usually don't, though, and end up shuffling through everything in a fruitless search.

Same goes for letters, reports, graphics, e-mail, and other stuff you store in your machine. If you threw everything into one big folder, you'd be searching for the needle in the haystack all the time. A virtual mess in your machine is the same as the real one on the top of your desk.

Field guide to folder trees

Let's take a closer look at your folder tree:

- Unlike its arboreal counterpart, your Linux file tree starts with a single root folder, denoted by a single slash (/).
- The tree itself is a logical, rather than a physical, structure. For example, your floppy drive, CD-ROM, and hard drive partitions are all *mounted* on your tree as so many branches. Even Windows and network drives can appear on your Linux file tree.

Revealing the tree

When you go to your home folder, what you see in the tree view isn't the tree at all but visual shortcuts to various branches. To see what I mean, double-click The System in the tree view and then double-click the root folder (/), as shown in Figure 11-2. Ah-ha, there it is!

Chapter 11: Managing Your Files *177*

Are they folders or directories?

When the Windows interface was plastered over DOS, *directories* were renamed *folders* and given cute little folder icons that you could click open with your mouse. Although traditionalists objected, *folder* is a much more useful concept, especially in a graphical environment. Think about it: A real-life directory, such as a phone directory, is just a book. In a file cabinet, you often put folders inside of folders, and you certainly don't put a book inside a book! Anything's possible, I suppose.

So I'm glad to see that the Corel File Manager uses the folder terminology to go along with the visuals. For now, you'll see many more Linux references to *directories* instead of *folders*. The terms are interchangeable.

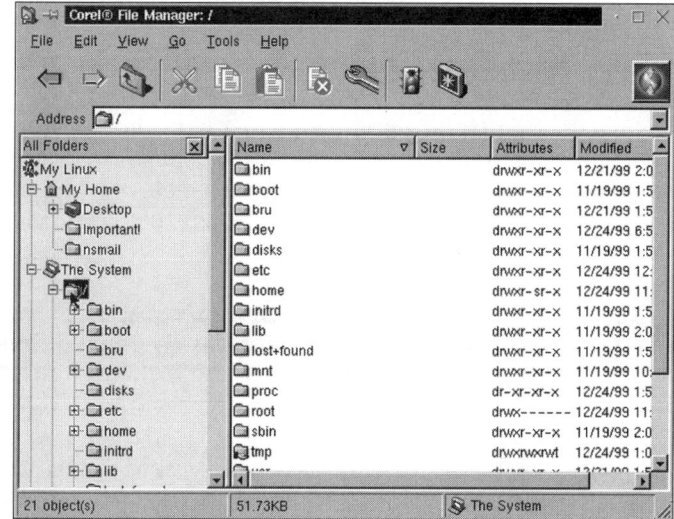

Figure 11-2: Going to the root of the file system tree.

Note how the Address line in File Manager now shows only /, to indicate that you're in the root folder.

You can also click the little plus and minus signs to the left of the folders to expand or collapse tree branches and then click to select the folder you want.

Beating a path to your files

Now that Linux has gone graphical, you can see everything in front of you as you thread your way among the folders. As you go deeper and deeper into the woods, you'll notice that a lengthening *path* appears in the Address line in File Manager. For example, if you organize your letters into various folders, you might see the following path emerge for your personal essay:

/home/becky/letters/school/
PersonalEssay.wpd

Thus, the address of your personal essay is nothing more than a string of folders, separated by slashes (/). Same thing goes when you're browsing Web addresses. (Just to confuse you, MS-DOS and Windows slashes go the other way, \.)

Simple, right? Handy too. Suppose you want to search for a particular letter. Rather than look all over the system, you can confine your hunt to the subfolders in the /home/becky/letters path.

Climbing the branches

When you open the root folder, you see an intimidating list of subfolders with technical sounding names of bin, boot, dev, disks, and so on. Don't worry, you're not going to be quizzed on the periodic elements of your Linux file system. But take a look at Table 11-1, which explains the type of stuff that goes in the various system folders.

Table 11-1	What Stuff Goes into Various System Folders
Folder	What You'll Find There
/	The logical home of all files and folders, regardless of their physical location. The system root folder is where it all begins. Do not confuse your system root folder with the /root folder further down in this list.
/bin	Linux system programs, including various command-line utilities such as cp, dir, ls, mkdir, mount, and mv.
/boot	The Linux kernel and other essential system files to get you up and running.
/dev	All device files used to represent various system devices, such as disk drives, CD-ROMs, printers, sound cards, and serial ports.
/etc	System configuration files and initialization scripts.
/home	The home folders for all users other than root. For example, the home folder for monica is /home/monica.
/lib	Library files for C and other programming languages.

Will the real root folder please stand up?

Linux is afflicted by the naming calamity, whereby everyone refers to the primeval / folder as the root directory, upon which there hangs another folder named root, for the root user's files. It takes a while to realize that we're talking about two entirely different entities!

It would be less confusing if whoever did this had hung the root user's folder from the /home folder, along with everyone else's, but that's not the way it is.

Folder	What You'll Find There
/lost+found	Folder for lost files.
/mnt	Various mounted file systems, including your automounted floppy disk or CD-ROM.
/proc	Files your system uses to keep track of itself.
/root	The home folder for the root user's files.
/sbin	Various programs to maintain and configure your system.
/tmp	Files that are needed temporarily but are normally deleted each time you boot the system.
/usr	Lots and lots of subfolders for user programs, including games, documentation, and icons. The X11R6 subfolder has many programs from Corel, KDE, and more.
/var	System definition files and status information.

Checking Out Your Folders and Files

The best way to get the hang of using File Manager is to start checking out your folders and files:

1. **Click the File Manager button on the panel.**
2. **Choose View ⇨ Tree, if necessary, to display the tree view.**

Part IV: Doin' Your Own Thing

> **TIP:** Drag the border between the two panes to adjust the width of the tree view.

3. **To expand the system tree, double-click The System, if necessary, or click the plus (+) sign to its right.**

4. **Go along the tree and click to open the usr folder, then click the X11R6 folder within that, and finally click the bin subfolder.**

   The contents of /usr/X11R6/bin are listed in the right panel, as shown in Figure 11-3.

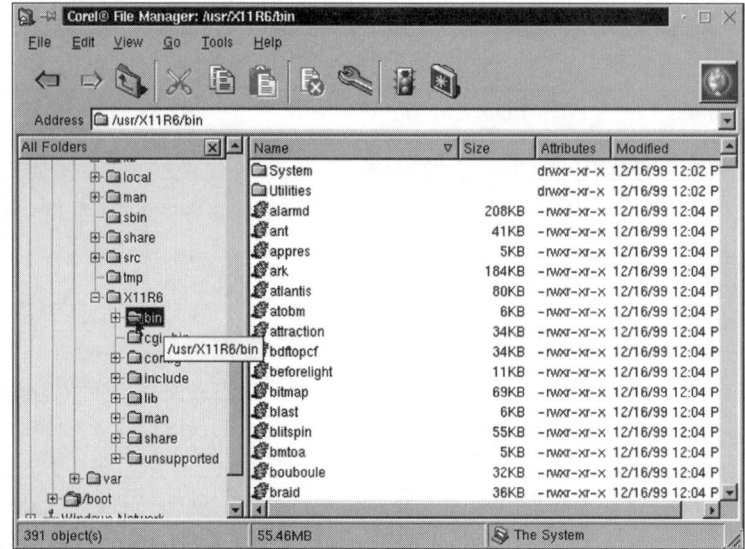

Figure 11-3: Poking around your folders.

File Manager clicking school

You have several click choices while browsing folders in File Manager. They're all pretty intuitive, but you might want to practice them a bit:

- Click the + and − buttons in the tree view to alternately expand and collapse the tree branches.

- Click a folder in the tree view to display its contents in the right pane of File Manager.

- Double-click a folder to both alternately expand or collapse its branch *and* display its contents in the right pane.

- Double-click a folder in the contents display to view that folder's contents *and* expand its branch in the tree view.

Try all these tricks and observe what happens and then send away for your Clicking School diploma.

I didn't want to see them anyway! (Granting permissions)

As you swing from branch to branch on the system tree as a regular user, you'll land on folders where File Manager shows you nothing but a blank gray panel with an Access denied message, as shown in Figure 11-4. Geez, at least it could say I'm sorry and display a smiley face or a pastoral scene.

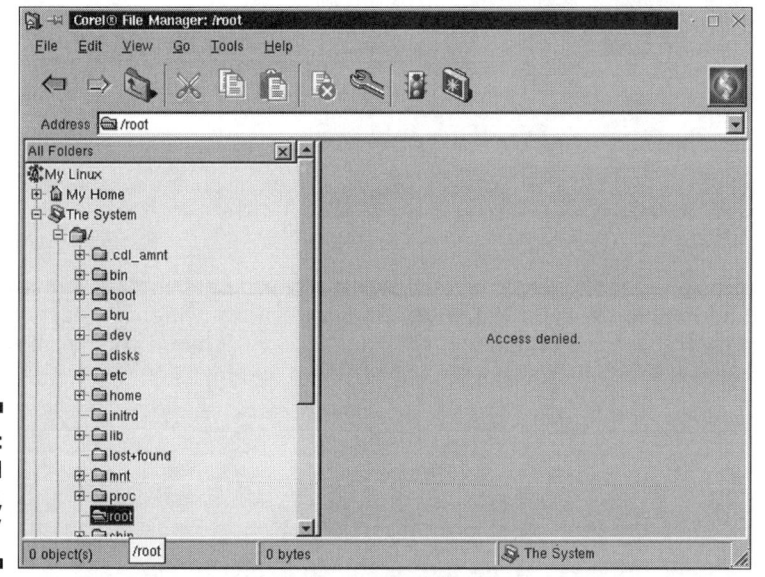

Figure 11-4: Linux could at least say, "I'm sorry."

To put it bluntly, this message means that the contents of this folder don't belong to you. It means also that the owner hasn't granted you permission to read, write, or execute any of its files.

When you land on a gray wasteland, click the Properties button on the toolbar to reveal the permissions for that folder or file, as shown in Figure 11-5. Notice the Permissions:

```
drwx------
```

The *d* just means it's a directory, but the six hyphens (-) at the end mean that nobody but the owner has permission to view, write to, or search the folder.

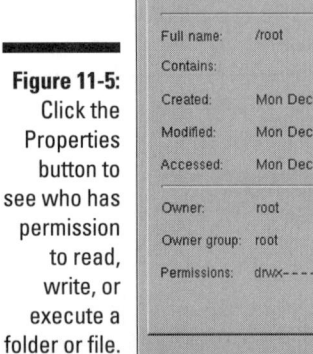

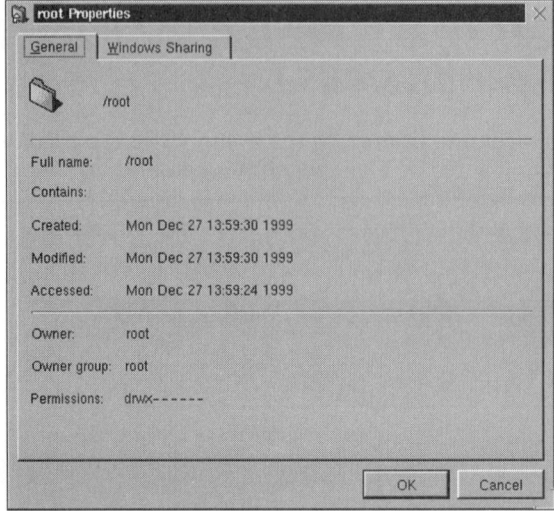

Part IV: Doin' Your Own Thing

Figure 11-5: Click the Properties button to see who has permission to read, write, or execute a folder or file.

This is all as it should be in a multiuser environment such as Linux. Normally, you don't have to worry about these permissions, which are part of the properties of every folder and file. You can, however, change the permissions as to who gets to muck about with the folders and files you own.

To set permissions on a file that *you* created:

1. **Select the file.** 
2. **Click the Properties button.**
3. **Click the Permissions tab, as shown in Figure 11-6.**

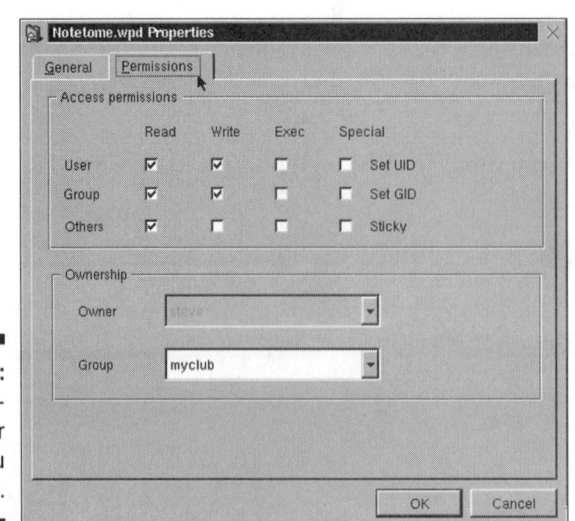

Figure 11-6: Setting permissions for a file you created.

4. **Click to add or remove a check mark from the options to grant or deny the following permissions to you (because you're the user), group, or others:**

    - **Read** (view the file)
    - **Write** (modify the file)
    - **Execute the file** (if it's a program)

5. **When you're finished setting permissions, click OK.**

> **TIP:** Removing read access provides the highest level of security and lets you hide from others information such as your financial records or the invitation to your spouse's surprise birthday party. Write protection keeps folks from changing the file, but they can read or copy it to another name or place. Note that you can prevent yourself from modifying your own file! This lets you preserve for your records the original form of a report you wrote or a letter you sent.

Now select one of your folders just as you did the file. Click the Properties button and then click the Permissions tab, as shown in Figure 11-7. Here, you set the following permissions for the user, group, and others:

- ✔ **Show entries,** to view the folder's contents
- ✔ **Write entries,** to add files to the folder
- ✔ **Search,** to allow the folder's contents to appear in search results

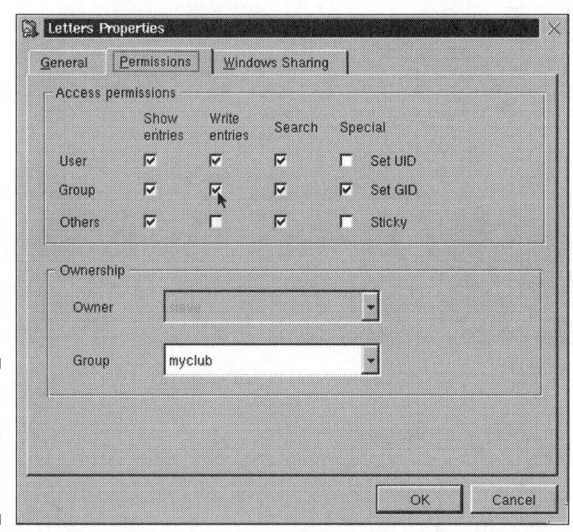

Figure 11-7: Setting folder permissions.

Part IV: Doin' Your Own Thing

> ### Root doesn't ask anyone!
>
> The root user doesn't need anyone's permission to view any folder or file on the system. They don't call root *superuser* for nothing! In fact, root has the power to lock you out of your own folders and files and even to change their ownership!

Sorting your folder listing

Click the buttons above the listing on the right side of File Manager to sort the folder's contents by Name, Size, Attributes, and Modified date. Click the same button twice to sort the listing in reverse order. Figure 11-8 shows the list sorted in reverse order by size. Note how the little sort triangle moved over to the Size button and now points upward.

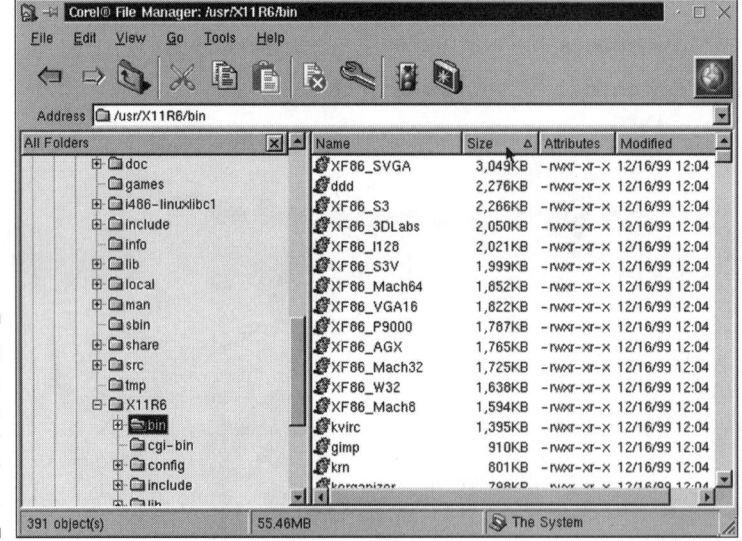

Figure 11-8: Click a button to sort your folder listing.

Retracing your steps

You can use the handy navigation arrows on the File Manager toolbar to go back and forth between folders you've visited. Click the Back arrow on the left to retrace your steps.

Chapter 11: Managing Your Files   *185*

Click the Forward arrow to come back again. Try both, they're great!!!

To go back up the folder tree toward the root folder, click the Up button on the toolbar successive times.

In case you haven't noticed, your File Manager is a lot like a Web browser. In fact, it *is* a Web browser. When you're online, you can browse through Web pages just as you browse the files on your system.

Here's a great file and Web browsing trick: Click the Address listing, as shown in Figure 11-9, to return to a recently visited folder or Web location. Note how the Web Browser locations also appear in the tree view.

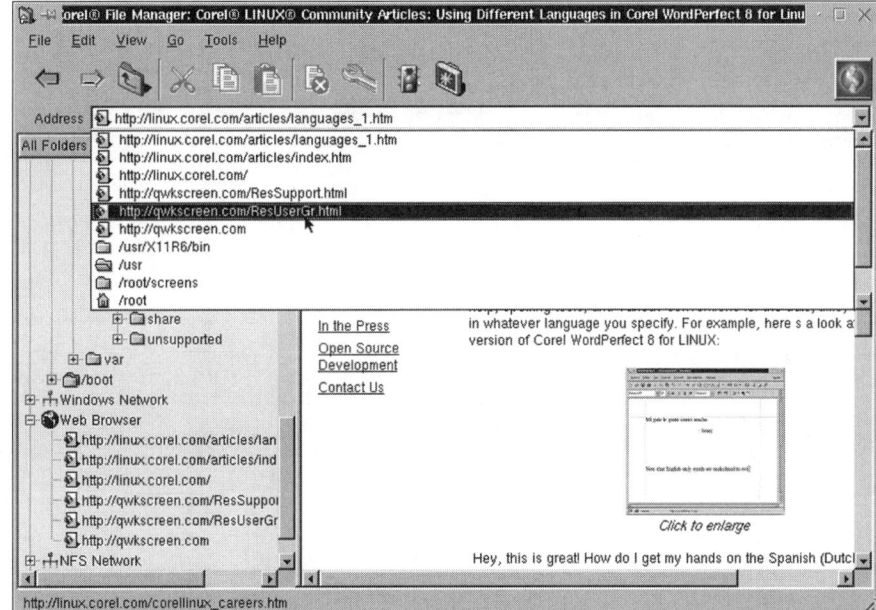

Figure 11-9: Returning to a recently visited folder or Web location.

Customizing your File Manager view

Choose the View menu to alternately display or hide various File Manager elements and types of files, as shown in Figure 11-10. Click an item to add a check mark and display the item; click again to remove the check mark and hide the item. You can also display large icons in place of the file listing, if that suits your tastes.

Part IV: Doin' Your Own Thing

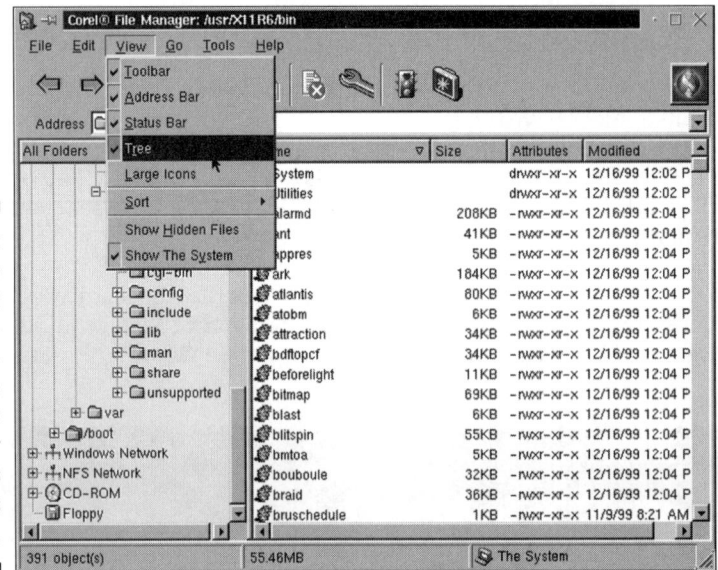

Figure 11-10: Choose the View menu to alternately display or hide various File Manager elements and types of files.

Figure 11-11 shows a bare-bones File Manager shorn of all its optional paraphernalia and without the tree view.

Figure 11-11: A bare-bones File Manager after removing everything from view.

> **TIP**
> You can still navigate in the bare-bones view by double-clicking folders and using the Go menu.

The two file viewing options on the View menu are worth considering:

✔ **Show Hidden Files** refers to files that begin with a period (.), which normally aren't displayed. The idea is if you don't see it, you won't mess with it.

✔ **Show The System** gives you the option to view the entire system, not just your personal folders and files.

Figure 11-12 shows what File Manager looks like when you remove the system from view but reveal the hidden files. Normally, there's no need to mess with hidden files, so you might as well keep them from cluttering up your view. But remember that they're there because sometimes you might need to access a hidden file to, say, change a user setting.

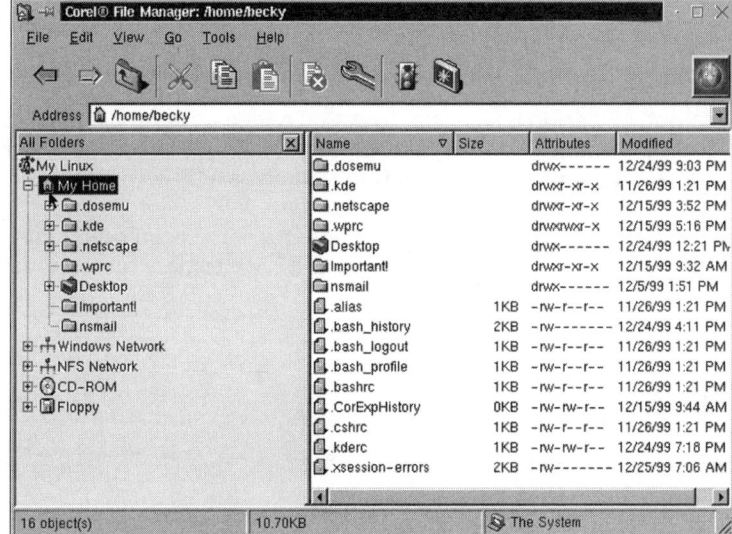

Figure 11-12: File Manager with the system hidden but the hidden files revealed.

Working with Files and Folders

Now that you know your way around the File Manager, it's time see what you can do with folders and files. Note that all the operations in this section assume that you've already opened File Manager and gone to the files and folders you want to work with.

Naming files and folders

Naming files and folders is sort of like naming children, except there are lots more of them so you'd better make them easy to remember and organize. For example, you might create a Schoolwork folder, with subfolders for History, Music, Literature, Physics, Basketweaving, and so on.

Here are the naming rules:

- Names can be longer than you'll ever want (256 characters)
- You can mix uppercase and lowercase letters, numbers, and special characters, such as the underscore (_) and hyphen (-).
- Names are case-sensitive, meaning that your Letters folder could have three subfolders named *Seth*, *seth*, and *seTh*. (Windows, wisely, won't let you do this.)
- A dot, or period (.), is used to set off a filename extension from the rest of the filename. For example, LettertoDan.wpd denotes a WordPerfect document; MyDrawing.xbm is identified as a bitmap graphic.

The full path is used to determine whether a name is unique. Thus, you can copy a file from one folder to another, and have folders for . . . /business/letters and . . . /personal/letters.

Creating folders

To create a new folder within the current one:

1. **Right-click in the folder and then choose New Folder.**

   You can also choose File ⇨ New Folder.

2. **Type a name for your folder and press Enter.**

You can also right-click the desktop and choose New ⇨ Folder to create a desktop folder as described in Chapter 9.

Renaming a folder or a file

To rename a folder or file:

1. **Click the name of the folder or file and then pause a second and click it again.**

Chapter 11: Managing Your Files   189

> **TIP**
>
> You can also click File Rename, or right-click the file and choose Rename.

   2. **Do either of the following:**

      • Start typing to replace the entire name.

      • Click again or press the arrow keys to edit the name.

   3. **Press Enter or click elsewhere in File Manager.**

Launching an application or viewing a file

Try this trick to launch an application straight from File Manager:

   1. **Make your way to the /usr/X11R6/bin folder.**

   2. **Scroll the listing and then double-click the kcalc program, as shown in Figure 11-13.**

      Up pops the calculator, ready to use!

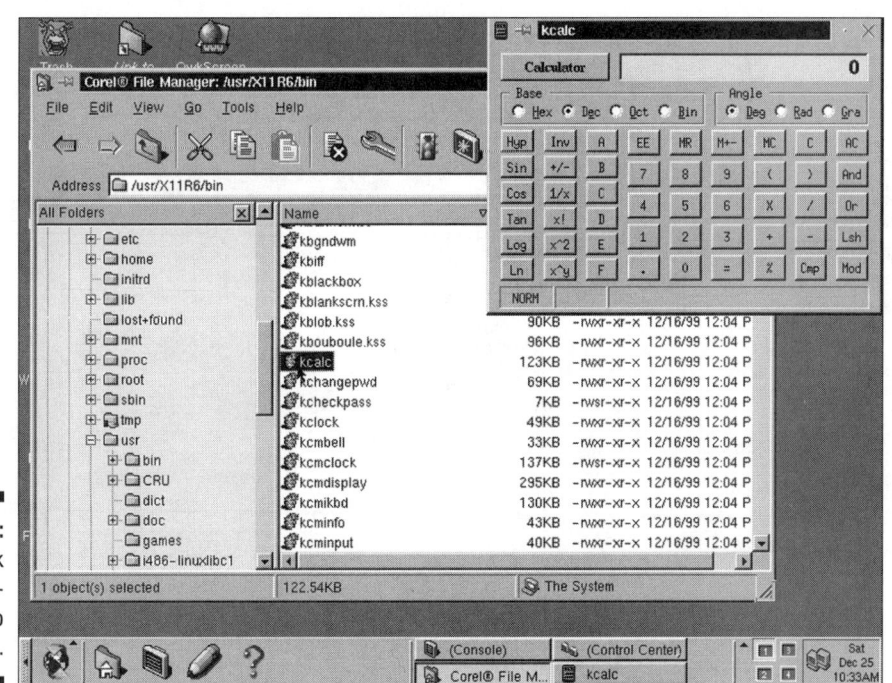

Figure 11-13: Double-click an application to launch it.

190   Part IV: Doin' Your Own Thing

> **TIP**
>
> Double-click the icon, not the name, to avoid accidentally renaming your file.
>
> Likewise, double-click a plain text file, and the file immediately opens in the Text Editor. Double-click a WordPerfect document to open the document in WordPerfect. Double-click a .tar.gz compressed archive to open it in Archive Administrator. Couldn't be easier!

Selecting files and folders

File management operations, such as move, copy, and delete, are performed on selected files and folders. You can select a single file or a whole slew of files and folders at once. Selecting a folder also selects any subfolders within it.

Click individual files (or folders) in File Manager to select them. (An individual folder can be selected in either tree view or the contents listing.)

To select a consecutive group of files, click the first file, hold the Shift key, and then click the last file, as shown in Figure 11-14.

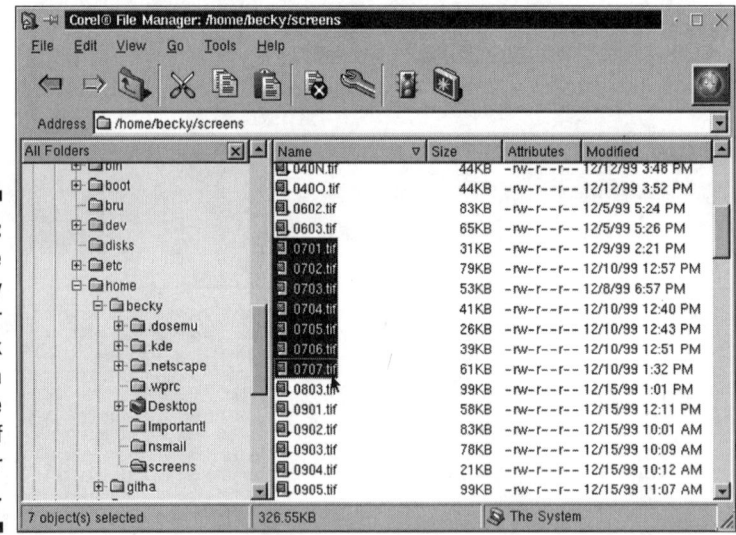

Figure 11-14: Hold the Shift key on your second click to select a consecutive group of files or folders.

To select two or more nonconsecutive files in the File Manager, hold the Ctrl key as you click each file.

Click a blank spot in the listing to deselect all the files or hold the Ctrl key and click files to deselect them one at a time.

Here are a few more tricks:

- Press Ctrl+A or choose Edit ⇨ Select All to select the entire contents of a folder.
- Choose Edit ⇨ Invert Selection to reverse the select state of all the folder's items. For example, if you select one file and then invert the selection, everything but that file will be selected.

Moving files and folders to another folder

To move files or folders to another folder:

1. **Select the files or folders to be moved.**
2. **Click the Cut button on the toolbar (or choose Edit ⇨ Cut).**
3. **Open the target folder.**
4. **Click the Paste button on the toolbar (or choose Edit ⇨ Paste).**

Copying files and folders to another folder

To copy files or folders to another folder:

1. **Select the files or folders to be copied.**
2. **Click the Copy button on the toolbar (or choose Edit ⇨ Copy).**
3. **Open the target folder.**
4. **Click the Paste button on the toolbar (or choose Edit ⇨ Paste).**

How do I cut, copy, and paste thee? Let me count the ways!

Cut, copy, and paste are such ubiquitous file management operations that a whole slew of shortcuts have been invented to carry them out. For example, to copy selected files you can

- Click the Copy button on the toolbar
- Choose Edit ⇨ Copy
- Right-click your selection and choose Copy
- Press Ctrl+C

Same goes for Cut and Paste. Their respective keystrokes are Ctrl+X for cut and Ctrl+V for paste.

This doesn't count the drag-and-drop method, which you get to later in the chapter!

Moving and copying with drag and drop

To move selected files and folders with your mouse, drag them to the new location and drop them into place, as shown in Figure 11-15.

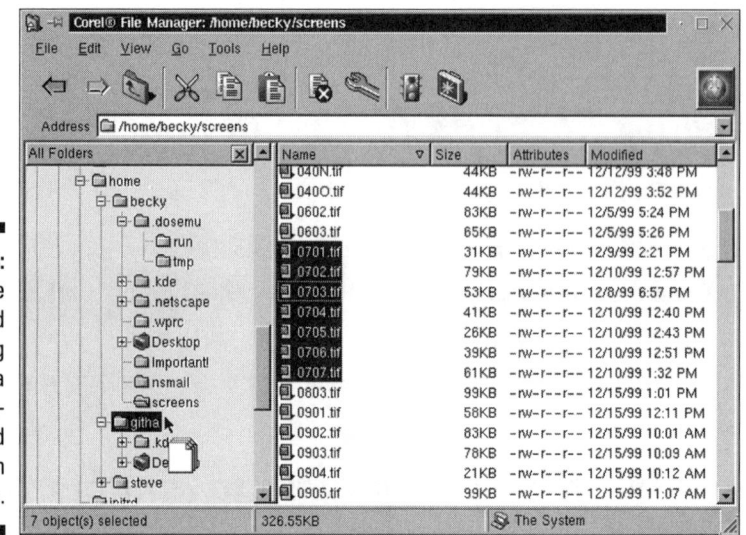

Figure 11-15: To move selected files, drag them to a new location and drop them into place.

To copy the selected items rather than move them, hold the Ctrl key as you drop them into place.

> **TIP:** In the first release of File Manager, the move operation just described copies the files, rather than moves them. No real danger in that, but just be aware that you'll have to go back to the original location and delete the files if you don't want to keep duplicates.

> **TIP:** You can also drag files and folders to the desktop to move, copy, or link to them, as described in Chapter 9.

Dumping stuff in the trash

To dump selected files and folders in the trash:

1. **Click the Move to Trash button on the toolbar (or choose File ➪ Move to Trash).**
2. **When asked to confirm your decision, click Yes.**

Chapter 11: Managing Your Files

You can also drag your selection over to the Trash icon on your desktop or right-click your selection and click Move to Trash.

Fishing stuff out of the trash

Sometimes you dump a file or a whole folder in the trash, and a few minutes later, it dawns on you, "Uh, oh (or some more forceful expression), I didn't mean to do that!" Not to worry:

1. **Click the Trash icon on your desktop.**
2. **Select the files or folders you want to retrieve.**
3. **Right-click and choose Restore, as shown in Figure 11-16, or choose File ➪ Restore.**

   This sends them back from whence they came.

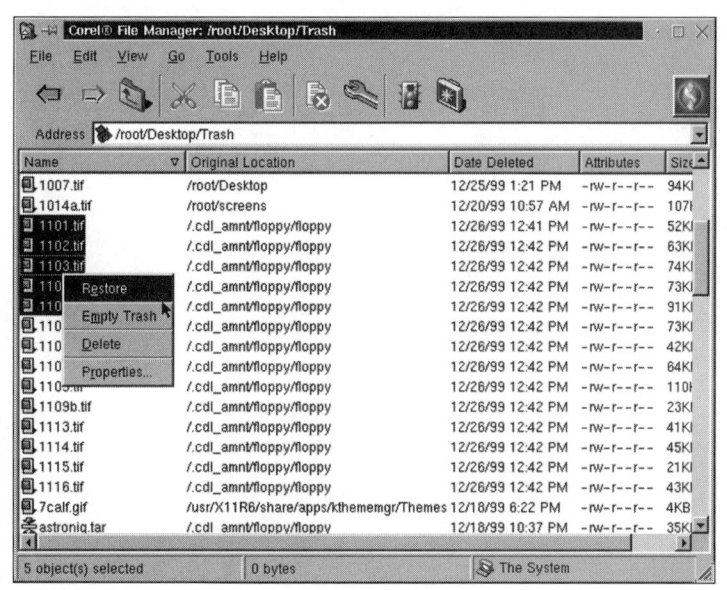

Figure 11-16: Getting your stuff out of the trash.

Emptying the trash can

As I'm sure you noticed, when you trash your folders or files, you're simply moving them to another place — your personal trash folder, to be precise. The files are still there, taking up space on your hard drive. Plus your trash listing gets so long that it's a bit overwhelming. Well, if you're really, really sure you won't be needing something again, you can empty it from your trash:

1. **Click the Trash icon on your desktop.**
2. **Do either of the following:**
    - Choose File ⇨ Empty Trash to toss everything overboard into your hard drive's Bermuda Triangle.
    - Select only the files and folders you're sure you'll never need and then choose File ⇨ Delete to deep-six that part of your cargo.

Unlike the bottles, cans, fliers, and bubble wrap we throw away, dumping virtual trash leads to a cleaner computing environment!

Deleting files and folders

To delete selected files and folders:

1. **Right-click your selection and then click Delete (or choose File ⇨ Delete).**
2. **When asked to confirm your decision, click Yes.**

Deleting stuff removes it immediately and for good. You can't go back and fish it out of the trash can.

Chapter 12
Finding Stuff and Opening Archives

In This Chapter
- Searching for files and folders
- Looking for a computer on your network
- Accessing files on a network
- Unhooking from a network share
- Creating and managing compressed file archives

Life is an eternal quest — no more so than on your computer or network. Well, at least Corel Linux comes with the tools to help you quickly locate stuff on your machine or elsewhere on a network.

Very often, what you find is a collection of related files, such as 96 cauliflower recipes, packaged into one neat, compressed archive. You'll see how to open the archive and cook the cauliflower and then create your own archive of 127 ways to make peanut butter and cauliflower sandwiches, the healthy alternative to peanut butter and jelly sandwiches.

Finding Files and Folders

It's nice to have all your files perfectly classified and organized so that you can always figure out exactly where something should be, but real life isn't so logical and tidy. Besides, you might be searching someone else's files. Perhaps you're looking for a utility on your system or a folder on koalas somewhere on a network drive.

No matter what you're looking for, the Find Files utility is the place to go. You can search for files and folders based on any or all of the following:

- Name
- Location
- Date modified
- File type
- File size
- Text found in the file

Text names are case sensitive (for example, *Cat* and *cat* are not the same). If you're not sure of the exact name or contents, you can use the following wildcard substitutes for particular characters:

- * substitutes for zero or more characters
- ? substitutes for a single character
- [A-Z] or [a-z] substitutes a range of uppercase or lowercase characters for a single character
- [0-9] substitutes a range of numbers for a single character

For example:

```
Te*.wpd
```

matches all WordPerfect documents starting with *Te*. A search on

```
wild*d
```

might find files containing *wildcard* or *wildcatted*. A search on

```
[1-2][0-4]*.tif
```

matches *1417.tif* and *2009.tif* but not *0114.tif* or *2501.tif*, for example.

Doing a basic search

To search for files or folders:

1. **Choose Application Starter ⇨ Find ⇨ Files or Folders.**

    Or in the File Manager, choose Tools ⇨ Find Files or Folders.

2. **In the Named box, type the name of the folder or file you're searching for, as shown in Figure 12-1.**

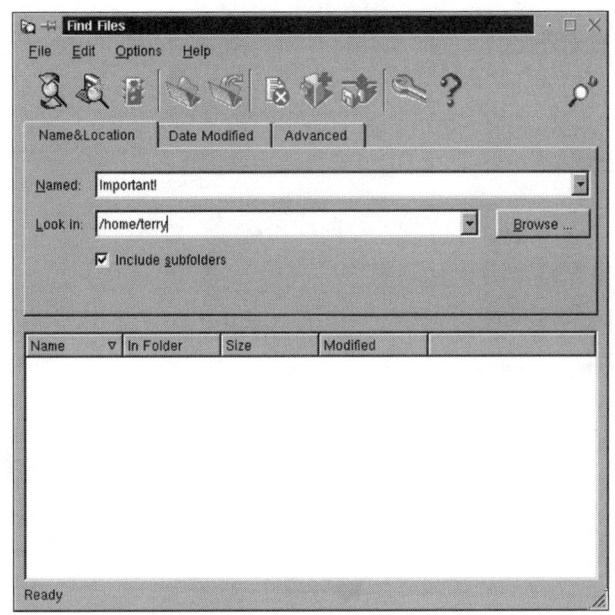

Figure 12-1: Doing a basic search.

You can click the Named drop-down list to select from your previous searches.

 3. Under Look in, specify where you want to start searching from.

Your home folder is filled in by default. You can click the list to select from previous search locations or click the Browse button to locate a folder.

Type / to search your entire system. Leave the Look in box blank to start searching from the /root folder.

 4. To search the entire branch of your file system, starting at the folder you specified, choose the Include subfolders option.

 5. Click the Start Search button. (You can also press Enter or choose File ➪ Start Search.)

You should hear a whirring and clicking as little elves run around to fulfill your search and then deliver the results, as shown in Figure 12-2.

Stopping a search in its tracks

Sometimes you want to stop a search before it's finished. Perhaps what you're looking for has already shown up in the list, or the search is going on forever, or you're searching for the wrong thing. Simply click the Stop Search button to end it now (or choose File ➪ Stop Search).

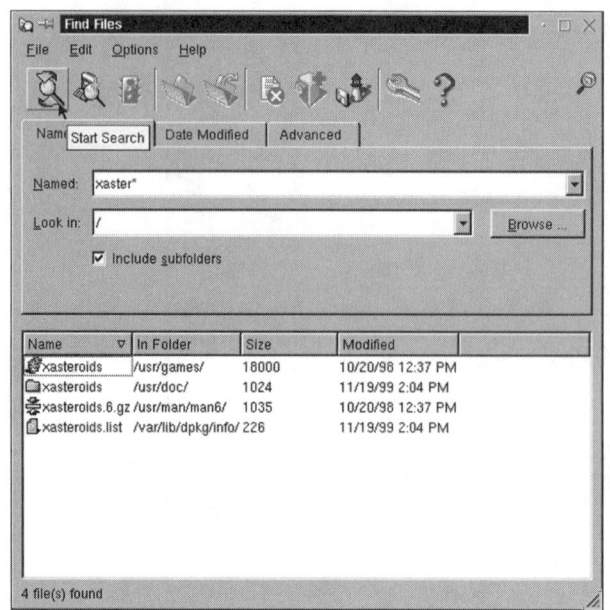

Figure 12-2: Hey, the elves found something!

Clearing your search results

Click the New Search button if you want to clear your search results before starting a new search.

What do I do with the stuff I found?

Okay, you've found what you're looking for. Now what? You can do pretty much do everything you can do in File Manager:

1. **Click an item in the search results listing.**
2. **Click the following buttons to perform various tricks:**

   - **Open** performs the operation associated with the item, such as launch an application, open a folder in File Manager, or open a document in the text editor. You can also double-click an item to perform its open operation.

   - **Open Containing Folder** opens the folder where the item is stored (the parent folder for a folder).

   - **Delete** gets rid of the item for good.

Chapter 12: Finding Stuff and Opening Archives **199**

When you delete an item, it's gone and you can't get it back. For a more cautious approach, drag the item in the listing over to the trash can on your desktop.

- **Add to Archive** adds the item to an existing file archive. (You can't create a new one.)
- **Save Search Results** creates a file of clickable links from your listing.

Sophisticated searching

In most cases, a basic search is all you need to quickly locate something. If you're having trouble, though, try a sophisticated search:

1. **Choose Application Starter ⇨ Find ⇨ Files or Folders.**
2. **Type the name of the folder or file you're searching for, where you want to search from, and whether to include subfolders in your search.**
3. **Choose the Date Modified tab and make your selections.**

   You can specify dates to search between, as shown in Figure 12-3, or you can search during a previous number of months or days.

   Enter "between" dates in the dd/mm/yyyy format.

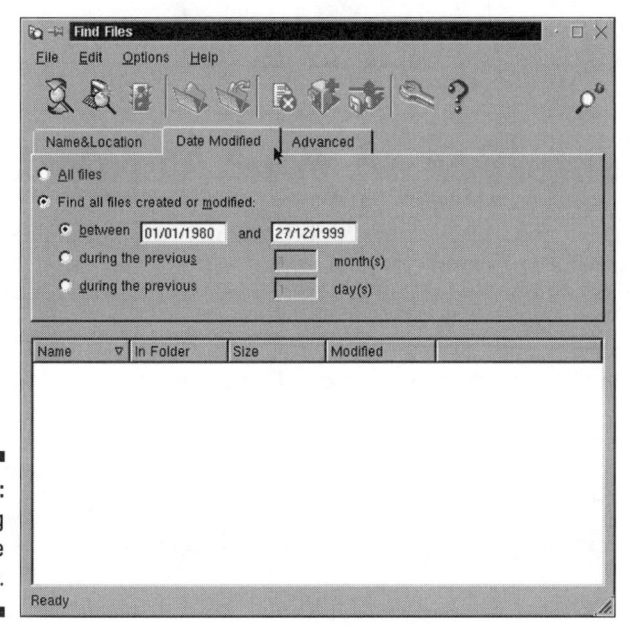

Figure 12-3: Searching on a range of dates.

Part IV: Doin' Your Own Thing

4. **Click the Advanced tab and make your selections.**

   You may select a particular type of file to search for, text to look for if you're searching a document, or a file size no bigger (At Most) or smaller (At Least) than the number of kilobytes you specify, as shown in Figure 12-4.

5. **Press Enter or click the Start Search button.**

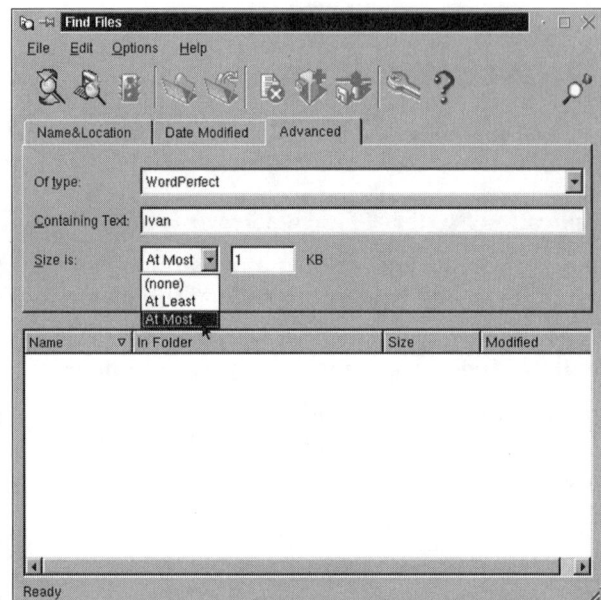

Figure 12-4:
Specifying advanced search options.

Finding a Computer on Your Network

If you need stuff from another computer on your network but you don't know where the computer is located, you can search to find its location. You'll then be able to access its files and create a desktop link so you won't have to search again:

1. **Choose Application Starter ⇨ Find ⇨ Computer.**

   Or in the File Manager, choose Tools ⇨ Find Computer.

2. **Type the name of the computer you're searching for and then click the Start Search button.**

   All computers found are listed, as shown in Figure 12-5.

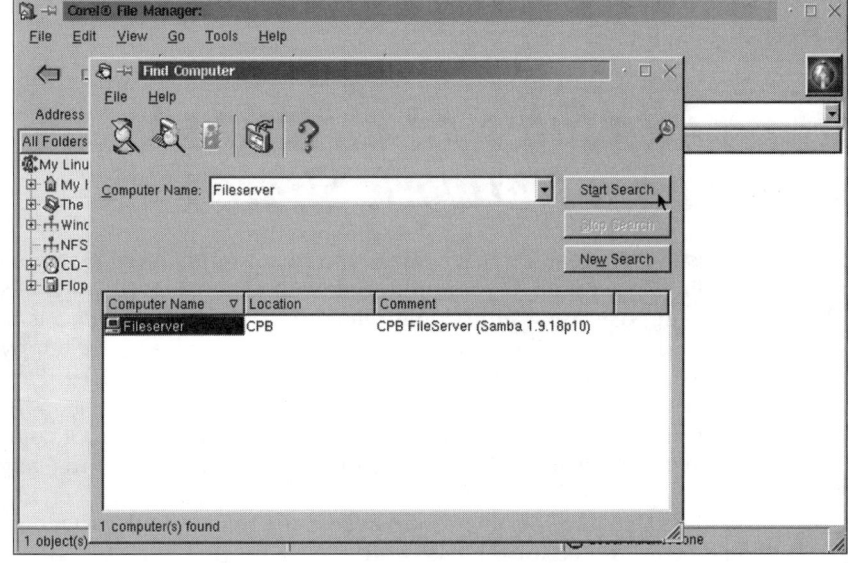

Chapter 12: Finding Stuff and Opening Archives 201

Figure 12-5: Searching for a computer on your network.

3. **Select a computer in the listing and then do any of the following:**

    - Click the Open Computer button to view the computer's files.
    - Choose File ➪ Explore to show the computer's files in File Manager, as shown in Figure 12-6.
    - Choose File ➪ Create Desktop Link to put a link on your desktop so that you won't have to search again.

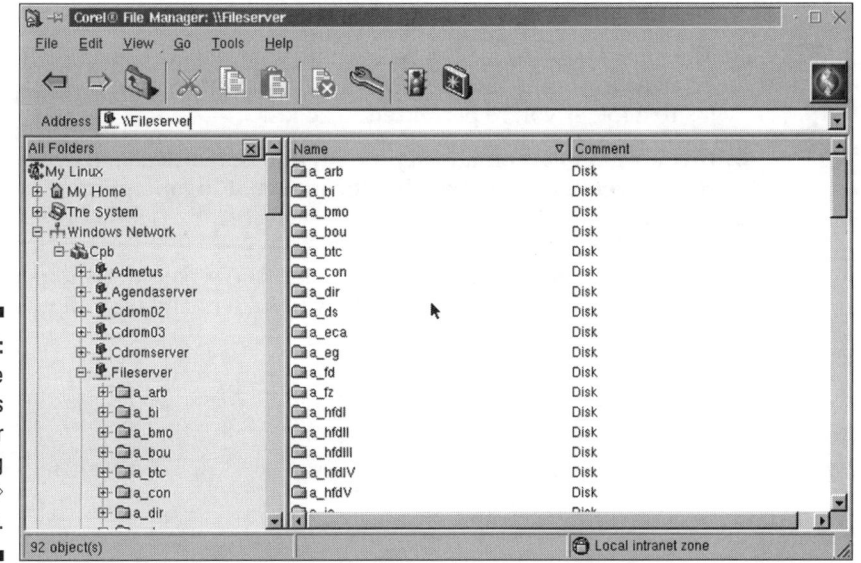

Figure 12-6: Viewing the computer's files after choosing File ➪ Explore.

4. Click the Close button to exit Find Computer.

Getting into Files on a Network (Mounting a Network Share)

Because you're reading this, I guess you're not intimidated by technical sounding terms such as "mounting a network share." And now that you're here, I suppose you want to know what it means. Well, *mounting* is the process of taking a file system from somewhere, such as your floppy or CD-ROM, and plugging it in as a branch of your file system tree. The *network share* part is nothing more than a folder on another computer, so here we're talking about making a remote folder part of your local tree. Of course, this section is useless if you have a machine that's not hooked into a network.

You must also have permission to access the remote folder to mount it. If not, you'll be prompted for the password.

Still sounds complicated? Well, it isn't hard to do:

1. **Click the File Manager button on the panel.**
2. **In the tree listing (on the left), choose either a Windows network or an NFS network, as shown in Figure 12-7.**
3. **Choose the server, as shown in Figure 12-8, and then locate and double-click the share you want to mount.**
4. **Choose Tools ⇨ Mount Network Share to display your mounting information, as shown in Figure 12-9.**

   The *mount point* in the figure is where your network share will be inserted in your local tree. You can change this mount point, as long as it's to a folder you're permitted to access.

5. **If you want to automatically mount this network share every time you start Corel Linux, choose the Reconnect at logon option.**
6. **Click OK.**

   You can now access the contents of the network folder and perform various file operations, just as you do with folders and files on your local drive.

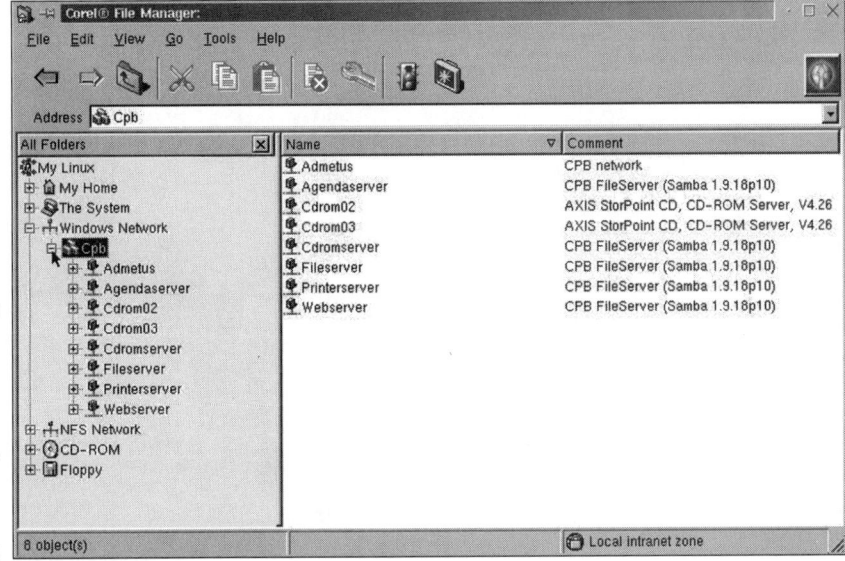

Chapter 12: Finding Stuff and Opening Archives 203

Figure 12-7: Selecting either a Windows network or an NFS network.

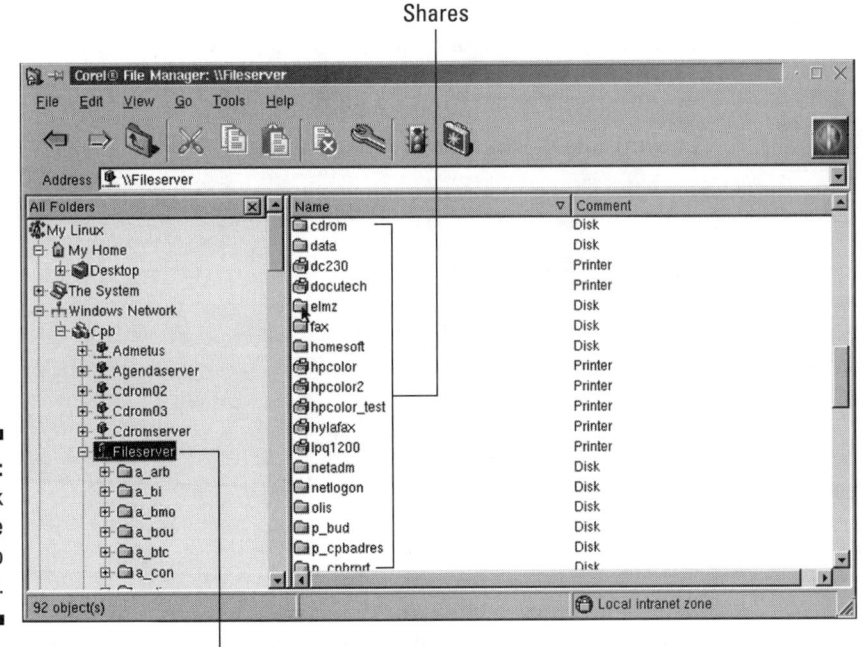

Figure 12-8: Double-click the share you want to mount.

Shares

Server

Figure 12-9: Mounting information for the network share.

Disconnecting a Network Share

You can disconnect a network share if it's no longer needed:

1. **Click the File Manager button on the panel.**
2. **Choose Tools ⇨ Disconnect Network Share.**
3. **Select the share to disconnect, as shown in Figure 12-10.**

Figure 12-10: Select the share you want to disconnect.

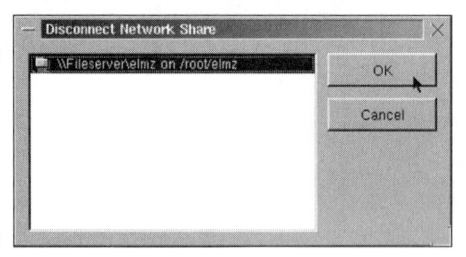

4. **Click OK.**
5. **If you're prompted, click Yes if you want to automatically remount the network share the next time you log in or click No if you don't.**

Chapter 12: Finding Stuff and Opening Archives **205**

Creating and Managing File Archives

Oh, no, another one of those scary headings! No sweat, as soon as you try your hand at creating an archive, you'll see that it's no big deal.

"But, wait, what's a file archive?" Thanks for asking. I like readers like you. An *archive* is a collection of related files, stored as one file, normally in a compressed format. "Why do that?" you ask. Because a single archive is neat, compact, and easy to handle, especially if you're sending it to someone else. For example, when I sent this chapter and all its figures to my editor, I packed them into a single archive and then attached the archive to an e-mail saying "Sorry this chapter's late; the readers asked a lot of questions!"

Another archive example is the desktop themes covered in Chapter 10. Each theme is a single archive containing wallpapers, buttons, sounds, and all kinds of other stuff. Look at the archive for the MGBreizh theme in Figure 12-11 to see what I mean.

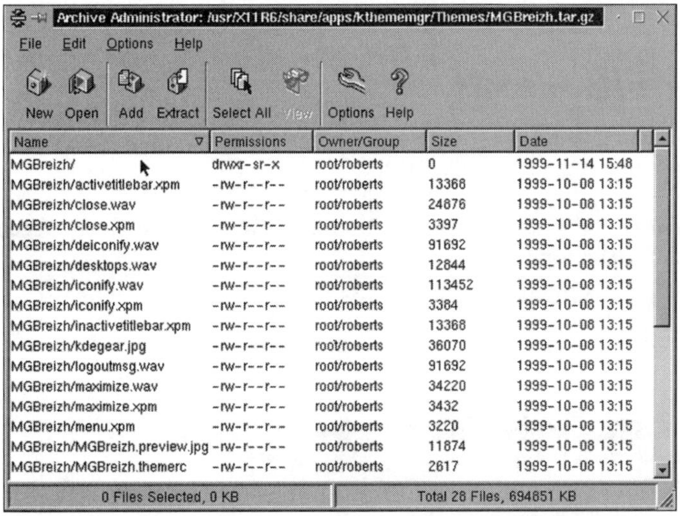

Figure 12-11: The archive of the MCBreizh theme contains all sorts of stuff.

The MCBreizh archive has 28 files totaling 694K. When you look in File Manager, you see that the MCBreizh archive file is only 459K, however, because the files in the archive are compressed. When you select MCBreizh in Theme Manager, the archive is uncompressed for use.

Help! What are all these archive types?

Oops, more technical stuff. Several archive file types are available. Each employs a different technique to squish down a file (or collection of files) for efficient transport and then uncompress it for use after its arrival at the new location.

ZIP is the most popular compressed format in Windowland, Many utility programs, such as WinZip, simplify the task of managing zip archives.

The Corel Linux Archive Administrator employs the *tar* utility, which, in turn, can employ *gzip* and *gunzip* to compress and uncompress archives, respectively.

Compressed files are identified by their respective filename extensions. (An uncompressed tar archive is simply .tar.)

The Archive Administrator can recognize a number of compressed file types, including .gz, .tgz, .tar.Z, tar.lzo, .lzh, .rar, .zoo, and .zip.

Please note that .tgz is short for, and equivalent to, tar.gz. This combined use of tar and gzip is often used under Linux.

Creating an archive

So when you assemble a theme, a chapter with figures, a bunch of photos, or whatever, put them in an archive:

1. **Choose Application Starter ⇨ Applications ⇨ Utilities ⇨ Archive Administrator.**
2. **Click the New button, as shown in Figure 12-12.**
3. **Go to the folder where you want to place your archive.**

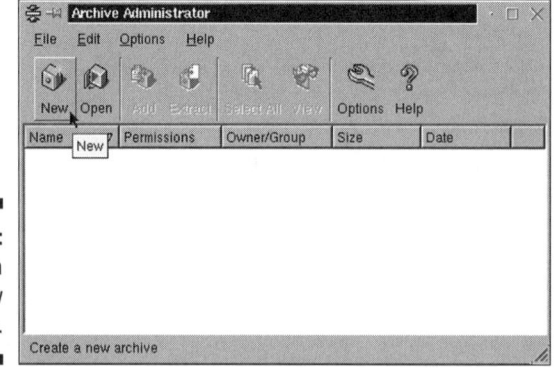

Figure 12-12: Creating a new archive.

Chapter 12: Finding Stuff and Opening Archives   *207*

4. **Type a name for the archive, as shown in Figure 12-13.**

   Typing an extension is optional. If you don't type an extension, .tgz is used, creating an archive compressed with gzip. Specify .tar to create an uncompressed archive.

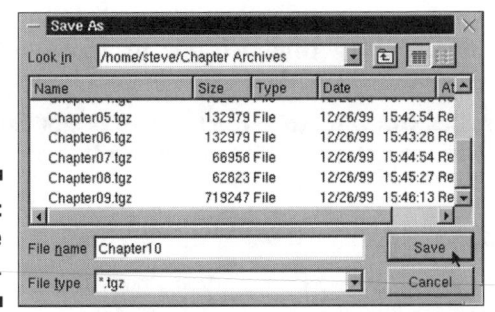

Figure 12-13: Naming the archive.

5. **Click Save.**

6. **Click the Add button. Select the files to add to your archive, as shown in Figure 12-14. Click OK to add the files.**

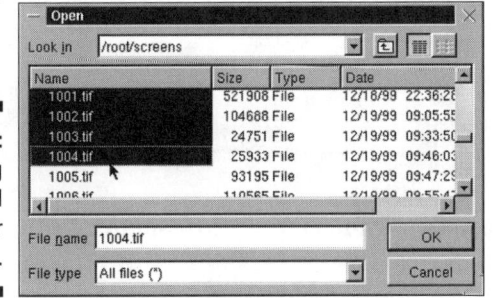

Figure 12-14: Selecting files to add to your archive.

7. **Repeat Step 6 to add files from other folders.**

   The files you add are copied, not moved — the original files remain intact.

8. **Click the Close button to exit the Archive Administrator.**

Extracting an archive

You can extract all or part of an archive to the location you specify:

1. Choose Application Starter ➪ Applications ➪ Utilities ➪ Archive Administrator.

2. Click the Open button in Archive Administrator, browse to select the archive, and then click OK.

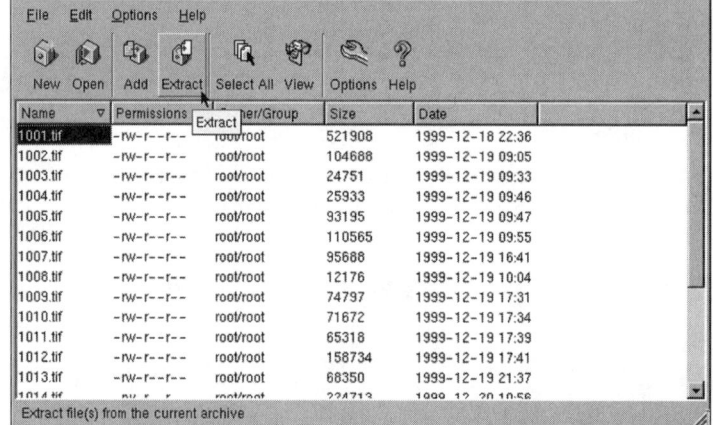

3. Select the particular files you want to extract, if you're not extracting them all, and then click the Extract button, as shown it Figure 12-15.

Figure 12-15: Select the files you want to extract, if necessary, and then click Extract.

4. Type the destination, as shown in Figure 12-16 or click Browse and select it.

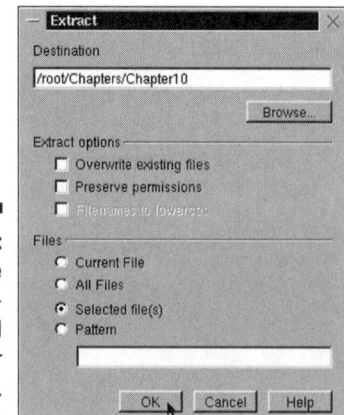

Figure 12-16: Specify the extract destination and other options.

Chapter 12: Finding Stuff and Opening Archives — 209

5. **Click to choose any extract options you want.**
6. **Specify which files you want to extract from the archive, if necessary.**

    You can even enter a pattern, such as *.tif to extract all TIFF files.

7. **Click OK to extract the files to the specified destination, waiting for your perusal.**

Editing and viewing an archive

You can open an archive to add to, remove, or view the files within it:

1. **Choose Application Starter ➪ Applications ➪ Utilities ➪ Archive Administrator.**
2. **Click the Open button in the Archive Administrator, browse to select the archive, and then click OK.** 
3. **Do any of the following:**

    - Click the buttons at the top of the list to sort by name, permissions, owner, and so on. Click a button twice to reverse sort. 
    - Click the View button to perform the operation associated with the item, such as launch an application, open a folder in File Manager, or open a document in the text editor. 
    - Click the Add button to place more files in the archive.
    - Right-click selected files and then choose Delete, as shown in Figure 12-17, to remove the files from the archive.

4. **Click the Close button to exit the Archive Administrator.**

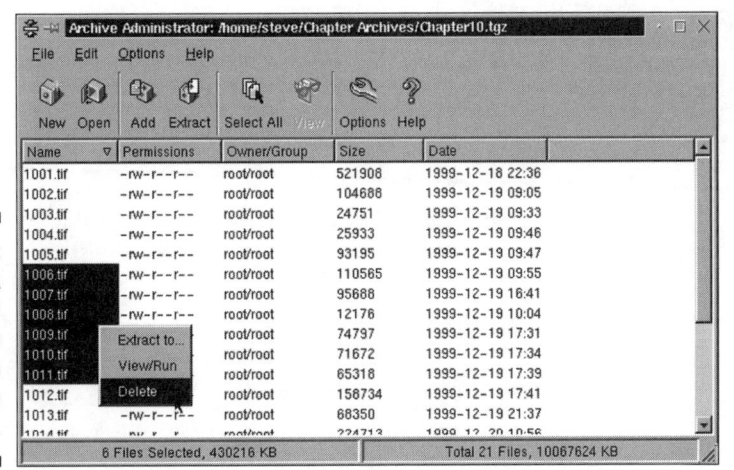

Figure 12-17: Right-click selected files to delete them from the archive.

Setting Archive Administrator options

You can fine-tune various file archiving options for just the current session or permanently:

1. **Choose Application Starter ⇨ Applications ⇨ Utilities ⇨ Archive Administrator.**
2. **Click the Options button.**
3. **Select or modify any of the following options, as shown in Figure 12-18:**
   - **Store full path** recreates the original file paths as you extract the files.
   - **Only add newer files** ensures that when you update an archive, all its files are the latest version.
   - **Location** changes the default location for your archives.
   - **Application name** changes the utility that Archive Manager uses to create and extract archives.
   - **Save settings on exit** uses your new settings in future sessions.
4. **Click OK.**

Figure 12-18: Setting Archive Administrator options.

Now that you see how easy it is to handle archives, you'll probably find lots of uses for them. I couldn't imagine writing this book without them!

Chapter 13
Putting In a Good Word

In This Chapter
- A few words about WordPerfect
- Introducing the Text Editor
- Fine-tuning Text Editor options
- Customizing text selections
- Turning your ideas into sticky notes

A picture might be worth a thousand words, but can you imagine if we communicated only with pictures? I know about the prehistoric drawings on the walls of caves, but even cave folks spoke, didn't they? It's speech that makes us human, and writing is just scribble to represent the noises we make. If cave folks had writing, I'm sure we'd see "I love you, Muttonbrain" scrawled on the walls or maybe "Meet me at the roasting pit when the moon is in the walnut tree."

Yes, there's no substitute for writing, so I expect you'll be doing some in Corel Linux.

The Premier Word Processor

If you bought Corel Linux in a box, you'll have either the Standard Edition's light version of WordPerfect 8 or the Deluxe Edition's full version. If you have WordPerfect, click the WordPerfect icon on the desktop to pop up the most powerful Linux word processor around, as shown it Figure 13-1.

A free, downloadable version of WordPerfect 8 for Linux is available via Corel's Linux Web site at `linux.corel.com`.

I'd like to tell you all about the wonders of WordPerfect 8 for Linux, but that would take a book in itself — such as my *WordPerfect for Linux Bible* (published by IDG Books Worldwide, Inc.). There's also the help menu and the printed *User Manual* that comes with the Deluxe Edition.

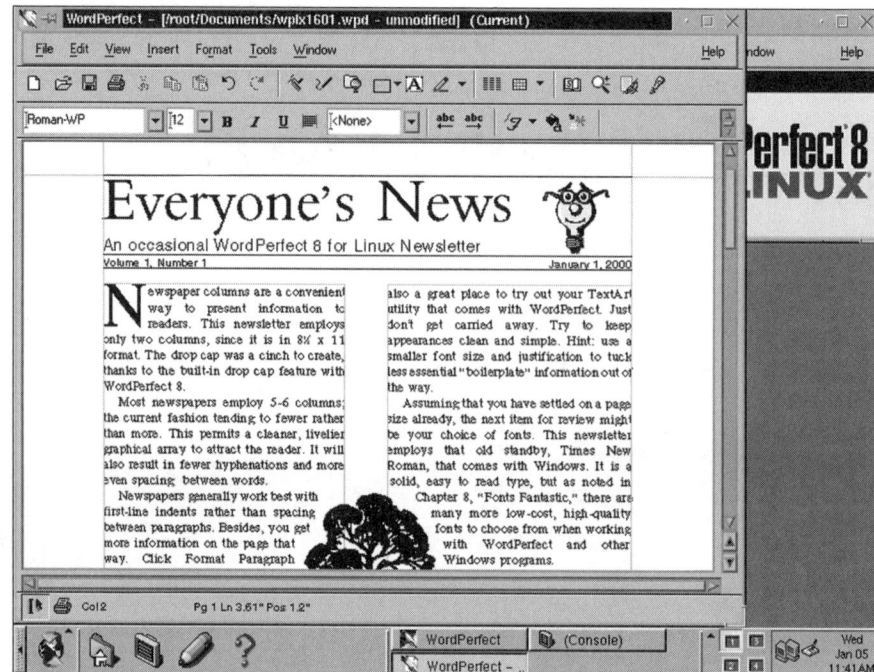

Figure 13-1: The most powerful Linux word processor around.

Your Handy Little Text Editor

Many types of text files don't require all the fancy formatting of your word-processed letters and reports. For these, click the pencil on the panel to pop up the handy-dandy little Text Editor, which is shown in Figure 13-2.

If for some reason your panel isn't around, choose Application Starter ➪ Applications ➪ Utilities ➪ Text Editor.

You can turn off the Text Editor's toolbar or status bar from the Options menu, though there's really no need to. The status bar shows useful information, such as the cursor position, insert or overwrite mode, and whether something such as vertical selection is active.

Is this a word processor we see? No, don't look for a spell checker, graphics, or fancy formatting here. This gizmo is for creating and editing ASCII text files. (ASCII is the standard set of characters used in many text files, including Linux configuration files.) Ah, ha! The Text Editor is also great for jotting down shopping lists, drafting e-mail messages, or anything else where the word is the thing. Think of the Text Editor as a plain pizza, not a gourmet meal.

Chapter 13: Putting In a Good Word *213*

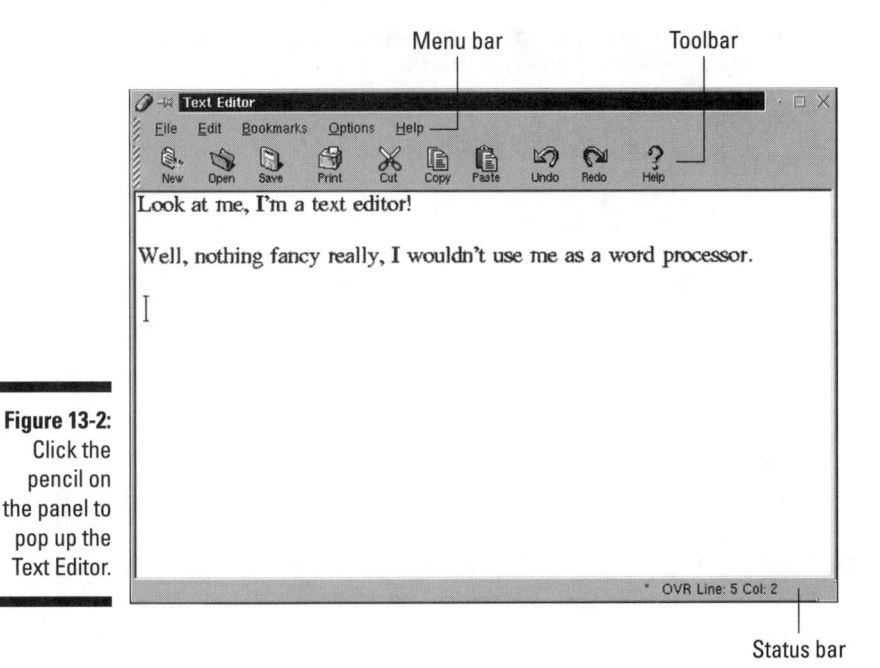

Figure 13-2: Click the pencil on the panel to pop up the Text Editor.

(Figure shows Text Editor window with callouts: Menu bar, Toolbar, Status bar)

Although ASCII characters remain the same, text file formats can vary from platform to platform. For example, the carriage returns in a Linux text file don't appear in the Windows Notepad, so you'll have to add them back if you copy the file to Windows.

The programmer's delight

Hark programmers: This text editor speaks your language! You can choose Options ⇨ Highlight Type to select various language types, including C++, Java, Perl, and HTML, as shown in Figure 13-3. The editor then makes your life easier by automatically applying various highlight styles to keywords, data types, comments, and so on. Very clever!

Creating a text file

To create a text file from scratch, simply click the pencil and start typing. Notice how the *insertion point* (the blinking vertical bar) moves along as you type. As soon as you fill up more than the width or height of the window, scroll bars appear. You can drag these or use the arrow keys to navigate the window.

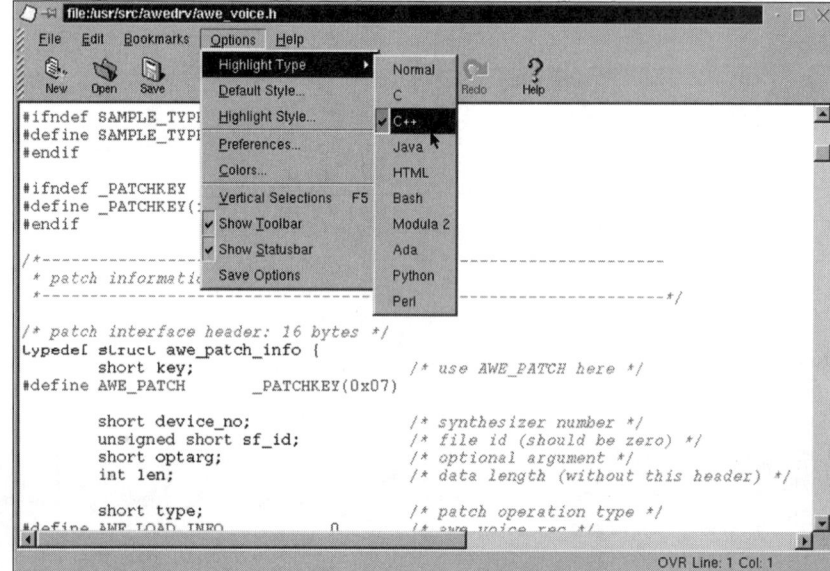

Figure 13-3: The editor highlights program keywords, data types, and other elements.

Setting Word Wrap and Editing Options

If you've ever used a word processor such as WordPerfect, you'll know that if you don't first end a line by pressing Enter, your line of text automatically *wraps* to the next line when it bumps against the right margin. Well, a line in the Text Editor goes on and on and on and on unless you tell it not to. It doesn't have fixed margins of a certain width, but you can tell it to automatically wrap your text when you reach a certain number of characters.

To set word wrap and other editing options, choose Options ➪ Preferences. Then click to choose any of the following options, which also appear in Figure 13-4:

- **Auto Indent** aligns subsequent lines of text to where you tabbed the current line.
- **Backspace Indent** goes back to previous indents when you press Enter followed by Backspace.
- **Word Wrap** wraps lines of text at the number of spaces you specify in the Wrap Words At box.
- **Replace Tabs** resets existing tabs when you change the tab width.
- **Remove Trailing Spaces** removes any spaces at the ends of your lines.

- **Wrap Cursor** makes the cursor go to the end of the next line when you press the down arrow.
- **Auto Brackets** creates sets of brackets when you type [,{, or (.
- **Tab Width** sets the number of spaces between tabs.
- **Undo Steps** sets how many editing changes you can back out of.

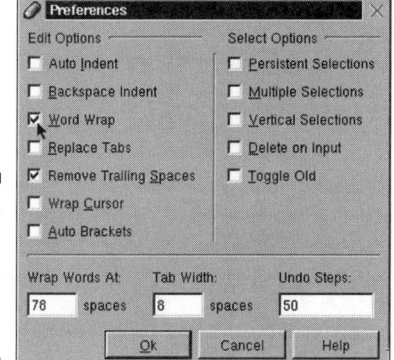

Figure 13-4: Using word wrap and other editing tricks.

Setting Text Selection Options

In the same dialog box that contains the edit options, you'll find several selection options that can come in handy, especially when you're working on program files. Choose Options ➪ Preferences and then choose the options you want:

- **Persistent Selections** keeps selections on screen as you type.
- **Multiple Selections** (with Persistent) lets you make more than one selection at a time.
- **Vertical Selections** selects text in columns rather than line by line.

    Choose Options ➪ Vertical Selections (or press F5) to toggle vertical selections on and off.

- **Delete on Input** deletes selected text upon pressing Enter.
- **Toggle Old** (with Persistent and Multiple) inverts the select state by selecting text again.

Some options, such as Toggle Old, work only in combination with others, so play around with them to see how they work.

Jotting Down Notable Ideas

Word processors are for big ideas, such as an article on "Unidentified Flying Penguins." That's why you go through all the fuss and bother of creating, formatting, spell checking, saving, and naming your documents. "But," you ask, "what do I do when I have a little idea, the size of a sticky note?"

Did I hear *sticky note*? Well guess what? You can now have the virtual sticky notes shown in Figure 13-5. Moreover, they come in whatever size or color you want!

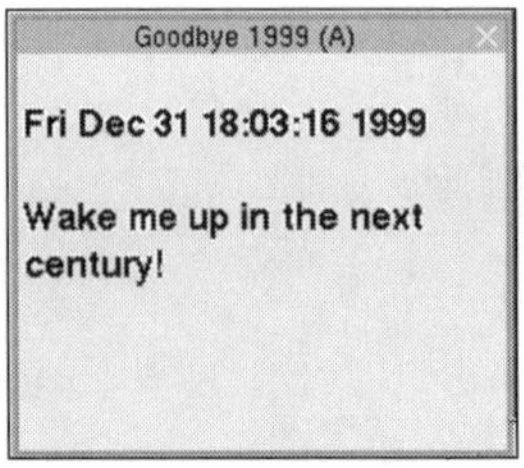

Figure 13-5:
Virtual sticky note.

> Goodbye 1999 (A)
>
> Fri Dec 31 18:03:16 1999
>
> Wake me up in the next century!

These virtual notes also offer distinct advantages over the paper kind:

- You don't need to scatter a bunch of little notepads all over the place, just so you can locate one before your idea fades from view.
- They don't stick where they don't belong.
- They don't cling to the insides of your wastebasket.
- You can attach an alarm to a note so that it will pop up at the appointed time, beep three times, and tell you to walk the dog.
- You can e-mail them to your friends and enemies.

Once it starts, it never stops

One nice thing about the Note utility is that after you start it, it keeps running from session to session, without getting in the way. I don't mean that you can't turn it off. It's just that when the Note utility is running, all you see is a cute little Note icon in the docking station.

To write a note for the first time:

1. **Choose Application Starter ➪ Applications ➪ Utilities ➪ Note.**

   This puts a blank note on the screen and the cute little Note icon in the docking station, as shown in Figure 13-6.

Figure 13-6: Your docking station now has a cute little Note icon.

2. **Type your note: "Wash the dishes before Githa gets home" or whatever.**

3. **Click the Close button in the upper right to save the note.**

Creating a note

To create a note, click the Note icon in the docking station and then click New Knote, as shown in Figure 13-7.

Figure 13-7: Creating a note.

Deleting a note

To delete a note, right-click the note and then choose Operations ⇨ Delete Note, as shown in Figure 13-8.

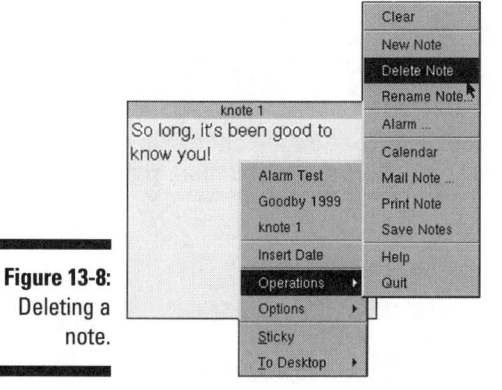

Figure 13-8: Deleting a note.

Renaming a note

As your create notes, they're given the default names of knote 1, knote 2, and so on. To give them meaningful names such as *Shopping List* or *Things to Do*, right-click your notes and choose Operations ⇨ Rename Note.

Mouse dragging operations

Try these dragging operations with your notes:

- Drag a note by its title to move it around the screen.
- Overfill a note with text and then drag a scroll bar to navigate the note.
- For a note with borders, drag a side or a corner to enlarge or shrink the note.

    Right-click a note and choose Options ⇨ 3D Frame to give it a border.

- Drag text to select it.

Cutting, copying, and pasting text

After you select text, you can cut, copy, and paste it in the same note, between two notes, or between your notes and another application, such as the Text Editor.

Cut, copy, and paste are a keystroke-only affairs when you're editing a note:

- Ctrl+X for cut
- Ctrl+C for copy
- Ctrl+V for paste

Inserting the date or a calendar

If you're so inclined, you can right-click a note and then choose Insert Date to insert the current day, date, and time. To insert a minicalendar, right-click and choose Operations ⇨ Calendar.

Alarming notes!

You can use notes as virtual alarm clocks to remind you to walk the dog or watch *The Simpsons*:

Chapter 13: Putting In a Good Word **219**

1. **Right-click the note and choose Operations ➪ Alarm.**
2. **Set the date and time, as shown in Figure 13-9, and then click OK.**

Figure 13-9:
Turning a note into a virtual alarm clock.

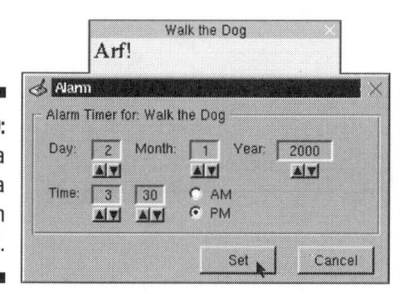

When the alarm sounds, Corel Linux switches desktops, if necessary, and pops the note into view.

Changing the appearance of notes

You can right-click a note and then choose Options to add a 3D frame or change the note's colors and font, as shown in Figure 13-10.

Figure 13-10:
Right-click your note to select options.

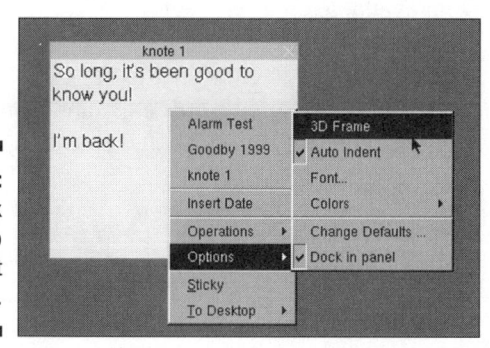

You can also change the default appearances for future notes:

1. **Right-click a note and choose Options ➪ Change Defaults.**
2. **Change any of the options shown in Figure 13-11:**
    - Click the Change buttons to change the color of the text and the note background.
    - Specify the initial width and height, in pixels.

Part IV: Doin' Your Own Thing

- Choose 3d Frame to put a border around your notes.
- Choose Auto Indent and, when you press Enter, your text is neatly lined up with the first non-blank space in the line above.
- Change the mail and print commands, if necessary.

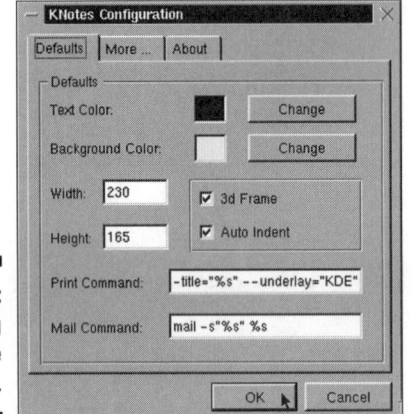

Figure 13-11: Changing default note appearances.

3. **Click the More tab and then choose Change to select the font face (family), size, and other attributes, as shown in Figure 13-12.**

   You can also choose from available character sets.

4. **Click OK to save your changes.**

TIP

Appearance changes do not affect the way your notes copy and print.

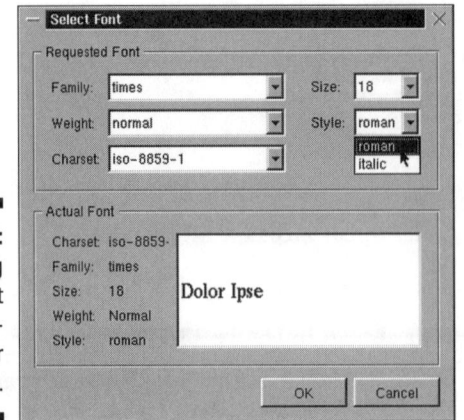

Figure 13-12: Changing default font appearances for your notes.

Printing a note

When subliminal messages like "Buy Crispy Crunches" pop into your brain, you can add the items to your shopping note. Then, when it's time to shop, right-click the note and click Operations ➪ Print Note, so you can take it with you.

Your printer has to be set up to print, as explained in Chapter 4.

E-mailing a note

You can write a shopping list note and then e-mail it to your spouse at another location. Right-click the note, choose Operations ➪ Mail Note, and then specify the receiver's e-mail address.

Exiting the Note utility

Like I said, the Note utility keeps going and going from session to session, until you tell it to stop. If you want to turn it off for some reason, right-click the Note icon in the docking station and choose Exit knotes.

Alarms won't sound when the program is closed.

Chapter 14
Playing with Pictures and Sounds

In This Chapter
- Creating original art masterpieces
- Opening, viewing, and printing PostScript and PDF files
- Playing around with CDs

Although words are a necessity, sometimes, pleasurable pictures, accompanied by a little music, of course, can really liven up that old newsletter or report. In this chapter, you look at some of the things that Corel Linux lets you do in the graphics and sound departments:

- Create graphics with GIMP (fun)
- View and print PostScript and PDF files (serious business)
- Play CDs (a blast!)

GIMPing with Graphics

Digital graphics are all over the place these days, especially with the explosion of Web graphics and digital photography. Corel Linux comes with a powerful image manipulation program known as the *GIMP* that's designed for professionals and amateurs alike, as shown in Figure 14-1.

The GIMP is short for the GNU Image Manipulation Program. It's a freely distributed piece of software that lets you create original images and edit others, such as with photo retouching.

Corel will be porting its signature CorelDRAW powerhouse to Linux in the near future. Now that's something to look forward to!

Figure 14-1: Example of a professional artist GIMPing along.

What GIMP can do

Now just because GIMP is free, don't get the idea that it's not powerful. When I right-click on my original masterpiece, as shown in Figure 14-2, I see enough tools, filters, dialog boxes, and options to make my head spin. This one powerful bitmap, baby!

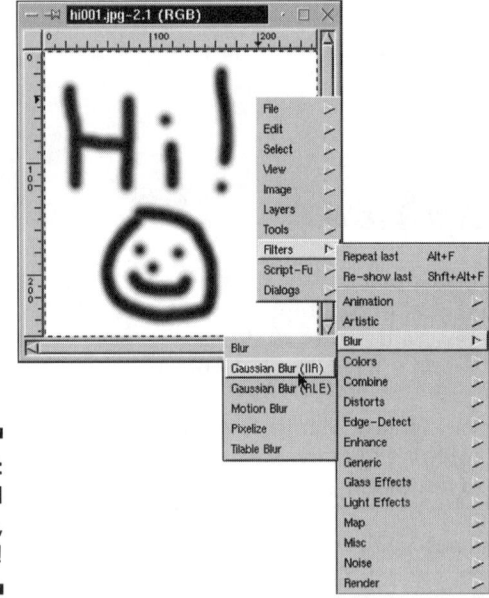

Figure 14-2: A powerful bitmap, baby!

> ## What's GNU?
>
> So what's GNU? Not the animal, but the Free Software Foundation's name for its "not UNIX" UNIX-compatible nonproprietary software. GIMP is a prime example of this software, which anyone can download, modify, and redistribute, as long as they agree not to limit further redistribution.

Just to give you an idea of GIMP's power, I compiled a tip-of-the-iceberg list of features taken from the `GIMP.org` Web site. GIMP features

- A brush, pencil, airbrush, clone, and more
- Tile-based memory management so that image size is limited only by available disk space
- Sub-pixel sampling for all paint tools for high quality anti-aliasing
- Full alpha-channel support
- Layers and channels
- A procedural database for calling internal GIMP functions from external programs, as in Script-fu
- Advanced scripting capabilities
- Multiple undo/redo (limited only by disk space)
- A virtually unlimited number of images may be open at one time
- A powerful gradient editor and blend tool
- The capability to load and save animations in a convenient frame-as-layer format
- Transformation tools such as rotate, scale, shear and flip
- Support for file formats such as gif, jpg, png, xpm, tiff, tga, mpeg, ps, pdf, pcx, and bmp
- The capability to load, display, convert, and save to many file formats
- Selection tools such as rectangle, ellipse, free, fuzzy, bezier, and intelligent
- Plug-ins for the easy addition of new file formats and new effect filters
- More than 100 plug-ins
- Support for custom brushes and patterns
- Much, much more!

Much, much, more for sure, and more features and enhancements with each release. GIMP does screen captures too.

> ### Bitmap and vector images
>
> GIMP handles many kinds of bitmap images. *Bitmaps* are digital images made up of thousands of tiny squares of different-colored picture elements, known as *pixels*. Bitmaps are good for photographs and fine art, with subtle shadings and vivid detail.
>
> Another class of images, *vector* graphics, is used for drawing, charting, and computer aided design (CAD) programs.

Launching GIMP

To start GIMP, choose Application Starter ➪ Applications ➪ Graphics ➪ GIMP. The program sets itself up the first time around, and then loads itself and numerous plug-in extensions, as shown in Figure 14-3.

Figure 14-3: Loading GIMP.

Creating an image

After loading and displaying your GIMP tip of the day, the little GIMP toolbox, shown in Figure 14-4, appears on your screen.

"What," you exclaim, "this is all I get? Oh well, waddya expect for free!" Be patient, from a little acorn a mighty oak can grow. For starters, choose the File menu at the top of the toolbox and then choose New to open an image window. Grab a pencil or brush or some other tool described in Table 14-1, and start creating your bitmapped masterpiece.

When you right-click in the image window, you get the File menu selections plus all the tools, filters, selections, and so on.

Chapter 14: Playing with Pictures and Sounds 227

Figure 14-4: The little GIMP toolbox that appears on your screen.

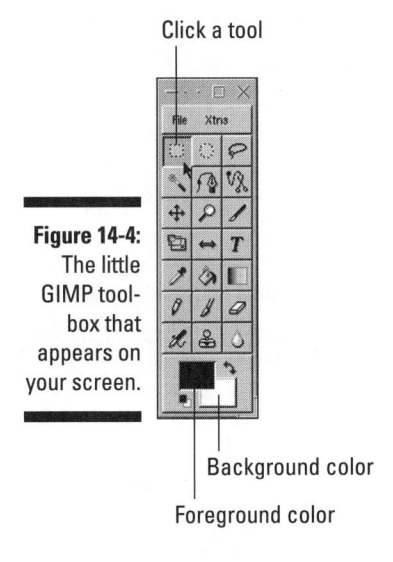

Click a tool
Background color
Foreground color

Table 14-1   Tools for Creating Your Masterpiece

Tool Button	Lets You
	Select rectangular regions
	Select elliptical regions
	Select freehand regions
	Fuzzy select like-colored pixels of contiguous regions
	Select regions using Bezier curves
	Select shapes from an image using intelligent scissors that guess the edges of an object
	Move an image, a layer, or a selection
	Zoom in and on the location you click (hold Shift to zoom out)
	Crop the image to the rectangular area you select
	Transform (rotate, scale, shear, or distort) a selection
	Flip (mirror) the image horizontally or vertically

Table 14-1 *(continued)*

Tool Button	Lets You
T	Add text where you click the image
(eyedropper)	Choose the foreground and background colors from any image you have displayed
(paint bucket)	Fill a selection with the foreground or background (with Shift) color
(gradient)	Fill with a color gradient blend of the foreground and background colors in the direction you drag
(pencil)	Draw sharp pencil strokes
(brush)	Paint fuzzy brush strokes
(eraser)	Erase to background or transparency
(airbrush)	Airbrush with soft, semitransparent spray strokes
(stamp)	Paint with a selected (cloned) image pattern or region
(drop)	Convolve (blur or sharpen) areas of your image
(color selector)	Select foreground color you paint with and the background color when you erase or cut

Toolbox tricks

Try these tricks with various tools:

- Hold the Ctrl key, or the Shift key, or both while using a tool.
- Double-click a tool to choose various options, such as the Transform tool's rotate, scale, shear, or distort option.

- Hold Shift and click when using the pencil to draw straight lines. This technique also works with the paintbrush, eraser, airbrush, clone tool, and convolver.

- Choose File ⇨ Dialogs ⇨ Brushes to choose tips for your pencil, paintbrush, or eraser, as shown in Figure 14-5.

Figure 14-5: Selecting a tip for your pencil, paintbrush, or eraser.

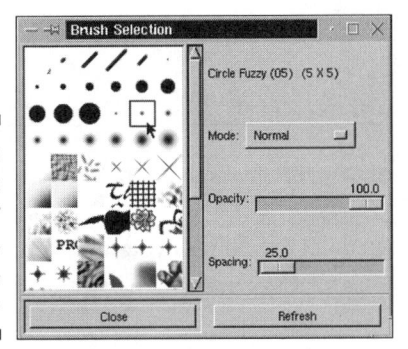

Using the selection tools

The first six tools in the toolbox let you select and manipulate a specific part of your image. The boundary of your selection becomes a blinking dotted line, affectionately known as *marching ants*. Anything you do to the selected part of your image doesn't affect the rest of the image. Click anywhere in the image to turn off the selection.

Selecting foreground and background colors

You can change the foreground color you paint with and the background color that's left when you erase or cut. Do any of the following in the Color Selector at the bottom of the toolbox:

- Double-click the foreground or the background to display the Color Selection dialog box shown in Figure 14-6 and then choose the color you want.

Figure 14-6:
Selecting a foreground or background color.

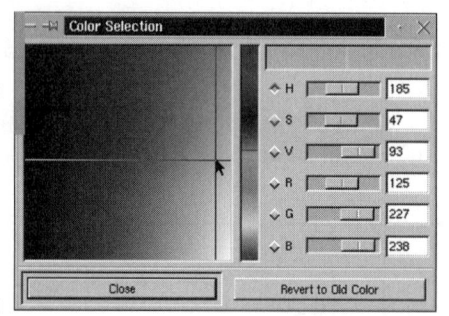

- Click the double arrow to swap the foreground and background colors.
- Click the foreground or background, and then click the Color Picker button to choose a color from any of the images you have on display.
- Click the little black-and-white icon in the lower-left to restore the black-and-white defaults.

Taking an art course

Now choose the Xtns menu in the toolbox (look back at Figure 14-4) to view a huge array of tools and options. Included on the Web Browser submenu are selections to hook you up with the GIMP community, such as updates, plug-ins, and tutorials, as shown in Figure 14-7. Be sure to check out the FAQs (Frequently Asked Questions).

Figure 14-7:
Selecting Web browser hooks to the GIMP community.

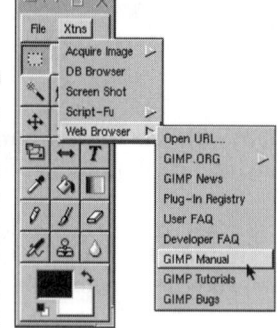

If you go to the GIMP *User's Manual,* shown in Figure 14-8, you'll find detailed instructions, with examples, of many of GIMP features.

Figure 14-8:
Web-based instructions and examples.

Working with PostScript and PDF Files

As you go about your appointed tasks in Corel Linux and on the Web, you'll often encounter the following two common Adobe Systems file types:

- **PostScript** documents display images and fonts as precise scalable graphics that can be sent to high-resolution printers and other output devices.

  Although you need a PostScript printer to take advantage of this graphical precision, PS Viewer (described in the next section) can send output to a standard laser or inkjet printer.

- **Portable Document Format** (PDF) files, produced from a growing number of desktop publishing applications, can be viewed by the recipient in their original format.

Opening and viewing a PostScript file

Corel Linux comes with PS Viewer, which can open and view PostScript files:

1. **Choose Application Starter ⇨ Applications ⇨ Graphics ⇨ PS Viewer.**

   You can also double-click a PostScript file in File Manager to open it in PS Viewer.

2. **Click the Open button, and then locate the folder with your files.**

3. **If you're looking for *.eps files instead of *.ps files (the default), type *.eps in the Filter box and press Enter.**

4. **Select the file, as shown in Figure 14-9, and then click OK.**

Figure 14-9: Selecting a PostScript file to view and print.

5. **Click pages in the listing or use the various navigation buttons to view the file.**

   The Read Down button is especially handy for reading one screen of information at a time.

6. **Click the Zoom buttons to zoom in or out of your document display.**

7. **Click the Flag button to mark the current page as one you want to come back to or print, as shown in Figure 14-10.**

8. **Click the Close button if you want to exit the viewer without printing your file.**

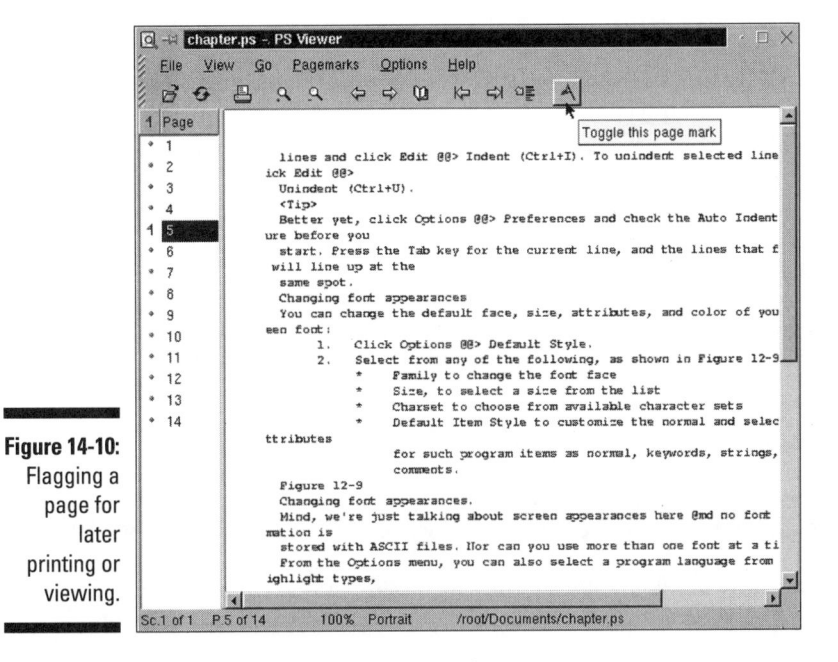

Figure 14-10: Flagging a page for later printing or viewing.

Printing a PostScript file

To print the current file:

1. Click the Print button.

The options shown in Figure 14-11 appear.

Figure 14-11: Selecting your print options.

234   Part IV: Doin' Your Own Thing

2. **Specify any of the following options:**

- **Print to file** to send your print selection to another PostScript file for printing later.

- Print **All** the pages, the **Current** page, only **Marked** pages, or the **Range** of pages you specify.

- **Print the document in reverse order.**

3. **Click OK to print your file or selection.**

Your printer has to be set up to print, as explained in Chapter 4.

Viewing and printing a PDF file

PS Viewer can view and print some Adobe PDF files, but the best tool for the job is, naturally enough, the free Adobe Acrobat Reader shown in Figure 14-12.

Adobe Acrobat Reader is not on the download version of Corel Linux, but it is on your *Corel Linux For Dummies* CD. See Appendix C for installation instructions.

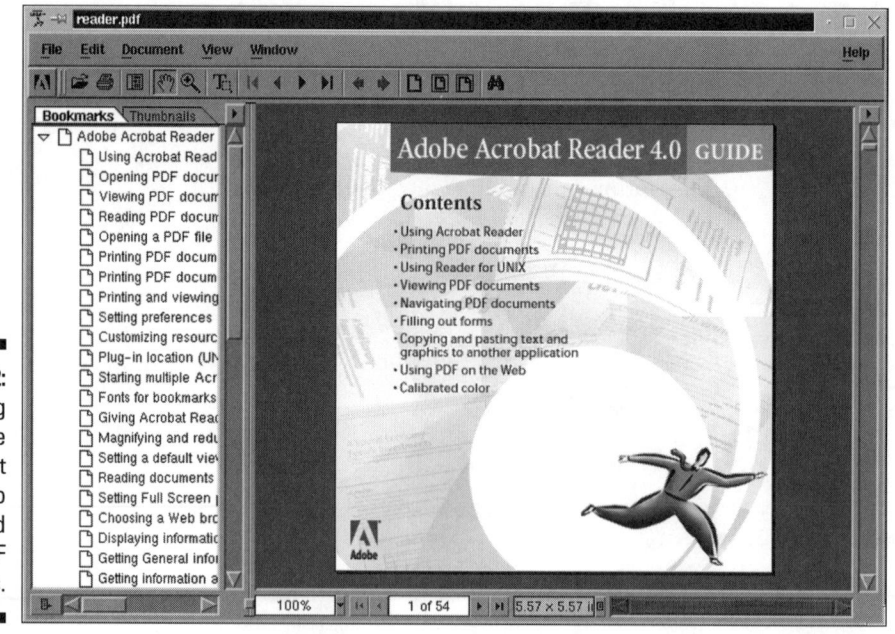

Figure 14-12: Using Adobe Acrobat Reader to view and print PDF files.

Using Adobe Acrobat Reader

You can launch Adobe Acrobat in either of these ways:

- Click Application Starter ➪ Applications ➪ Acrobat Reader
- Double-click a PDF file in File Manager

Any special PDF formatting appears in the reader. If you choose Help ➪ Reader Guide, you'll find a handy guide to all Acrobat features, including the capability to cut and paste selections to other applications.

All That Jazz

After all this graphical intensity, I think it's time for a little music — assuming, of course, that your sound system is up and running, as described in Chapter 4.

The Internet connection

Wouldn't it be great to know what you're listening to? Well, just log onto the Internet and the CD Player automatically gets the information for you! It uses your CD's identification code to access the gigantic CD database (CDDB) of hundreds of thousands of album titles and several million tracks. The player then automatically displays the album, artist, and track names as your CD plays.

After you have the artist's name, you can then get tour and background information from various sources.

What if your CD isn't in the database? You can write up the information yourself and add it to your local collection. If you're in a generous spirit, upload your information to the Internet CDDB for others to share!

Playing a CD

So why not grab a CD and give it a whirl:

1. **Log onto the Internet, if you want to grab information as you play the CD.**
2. **Slide the digital donut into your CD drive.**

3. **Choose Application Starter ⇨ Applications ⇨ Multimedia ⇨ CD Player.**
4. **If you're prompted to enter your local CDDB base folder, click OK.**

   Normally, this should default to /usr/X11R6/apps/kscd/cddb/.

   If your folder exists, you shouldn't be prompted. If necessary, create the folder yourself, as root, in File Manager, and add any of the following subfolders: rock, classical, jazz, soundtrack, newage, blues, folk, country, reggae, misc, and data.

5. **If no exact match is found in the online database, select from a list of one or more entries, as shown in Figure 14-13.**

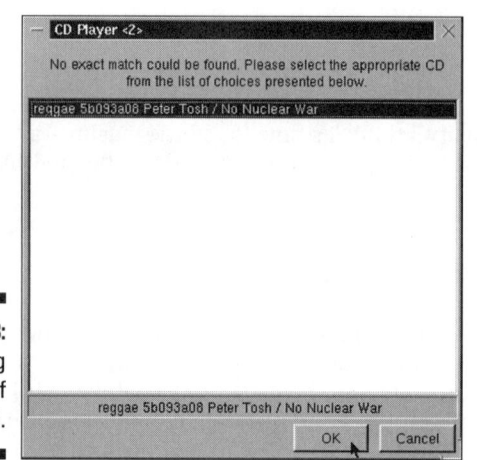

Figure 14-13: Selecting the title of your CD.

If the play list doesn't appear, click the Configure button and make sure Enable Remote CDDB has a check mark.

6. **Click any of the following controls to control the CD play:**

   - **Play/Pause** alternately plays and pauses the CD.

   - **Stop** stops play.

   - **Eject** ejects the CD (not supported on some older CD drives).

   - **Backwards** moves 30 seconds back in the current track.

   - **Forward** moves 30 seconds forward in the current track.

   - **Previous** goes back to the previous track.

   - **Next** advances to the next track.

Chapter 14: Playing with Pictures and Sounds

- **Shuffle** plays the tracks in random order.
- **Loop** plays the CD from beginning to end continuously.

7. **Drag the slider to adjust the volume of play, as shown in Figure 14-14.**
8. **Click the Quit button to exit the CD player.**

Figure 14-14: Drag the slider to adjust the volume of play.

Using Sound Mixer

The volume and balance of your CD Player is also affected by the Sound Mixer's settings. Choose Application Starter ⇨ Applications ⇨ Multimedia ⇨ Sound Mixer Panel to adjust these settings, as shown in Figure 14-15.

Figure 14-15: Adjusting the CD volume and balance in Sound Mixer.

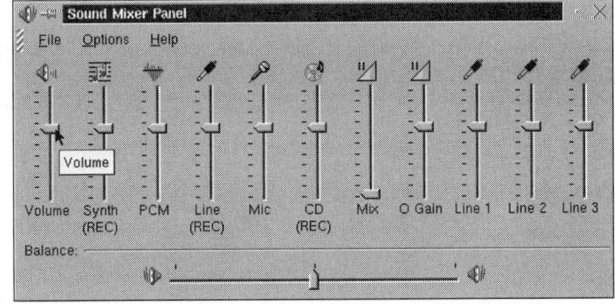

Selecting a particular track

To choose a particular track, click the listing and then select the track, as shown in Figure 14-16.

Figure 14-16: Selecting a particular track.

Changing the time display

Click the Time Display button to toggle the time display between the elapsed time on the current track (the default), the track time remaining, the total elapsed time, and the total remaining time.

Getting the sordid details about your favorite recording artist

After you're connected to the Internet and the artist's name appears in CD Player, click the Information button. Choose from the following, which are shown also in Figure 14-17:

- ✓ **Performances,** to find out about tour dates.
- ✓ **Purchases,** to buy CDs by the artist, though you have only two sites to choose from.
- ✓ **Information,** to tell various search engines to get the biography, photos, and other information on the artist, as shown in Figure 14-18.

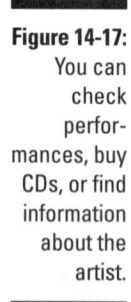

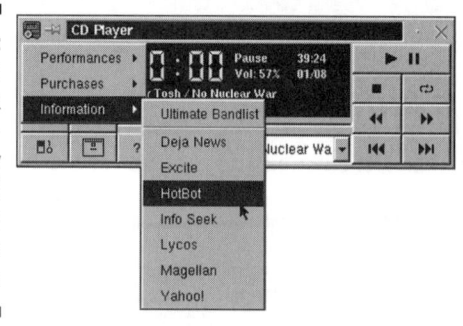

Figure 14-17: You can check performances, buy CDs, or find information about the artist.

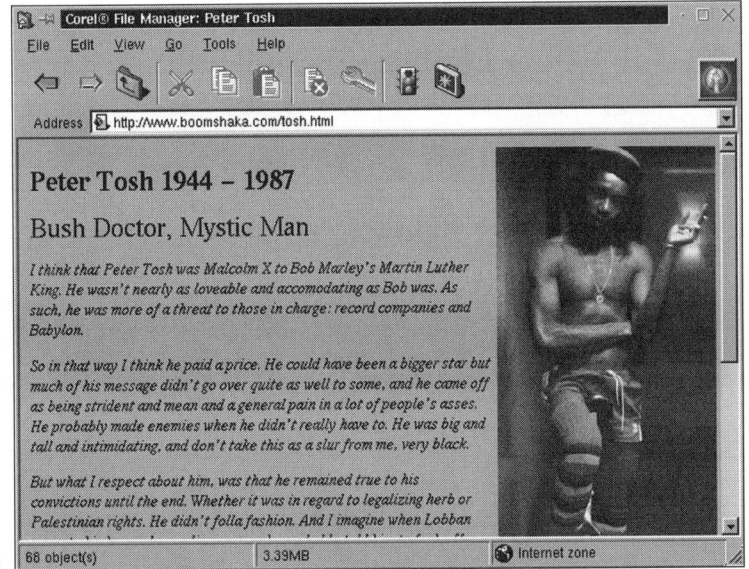

Figure 14-18: Retrieving background information on the artist.

Chapter 15
Cruising in Cyberspace

In This Chapter
▶ Launching into cyberspace
▶ Launching Netscape
▶ Finding a contact lens on the beach
▶ Using Corel's online services to set up a virtual office
▶ Setting your browser preferences
▶ Bookmarking your favorite places
▶ Browsing cyberspace with your File Manager
▶ Transferring files between your place and theirs

*T*he Web is a fabulous way to connect with others around the world and get instant information on *anything*. This chapter has you hopping from Web page to Web page all over cyberspace. And in Chapter 16, you send messages across continents in less time than it takes to print snail mail and stuff it in an envelope.

Cruising in Cyberspace

Netscape Navigator, shown in Figure 15-1, is your ticket to cruising the virtual universe. It comes bundled with all versions of Corel Linux.

And look at Figure 15-2 — you can access Web sites through File Manager as well! A file on your computer, a folder out on the network, or a Web page in Timbuktu — they're all the same to File Manager!

The great thing about the Web isn't the software or the commercial sites — it's the people. Instead of being a couch potato watching television, you can be couch potato communicating with others on the Internet.

Interested in Cajun cooking, raising goats, ridding the Earth of land mines, or tricks on using Corel Linux? You'll find many others on the Web who share your interests and concerns.

What's the Web?

If you're new to the Web, some explanation might be in order. The Web, also known as the World Wide Web, WWW, and W3, has taken the computer industry by storm. Politicians try to censor it and giant corporations vie to control it, but the infant Web (for now) is toddling off in its own direction and growing at its own pace — which happens to be a breakneck speed.

To the user, the great thing about the Web is its simplicity. It appears on the screen one richly formatted hypertext page at a time. The next page you click to can be in the same folder as the current one or on another site a continent away.

A spider's web is an apt metaphor — the Web is the gigantic creation of millions of individuals, universities, companies, and government agencies, and lets you hop from page to page around the globe.

The Web supports

- Information, such as reports, files, and bulletins
- Communication, including e-mail, forums, and conferences
- Services, such as banking, airline reservations, and catalog shopping

Another great thing about the Web is that it's platform independent. It's the only place where all the operating systems meet!

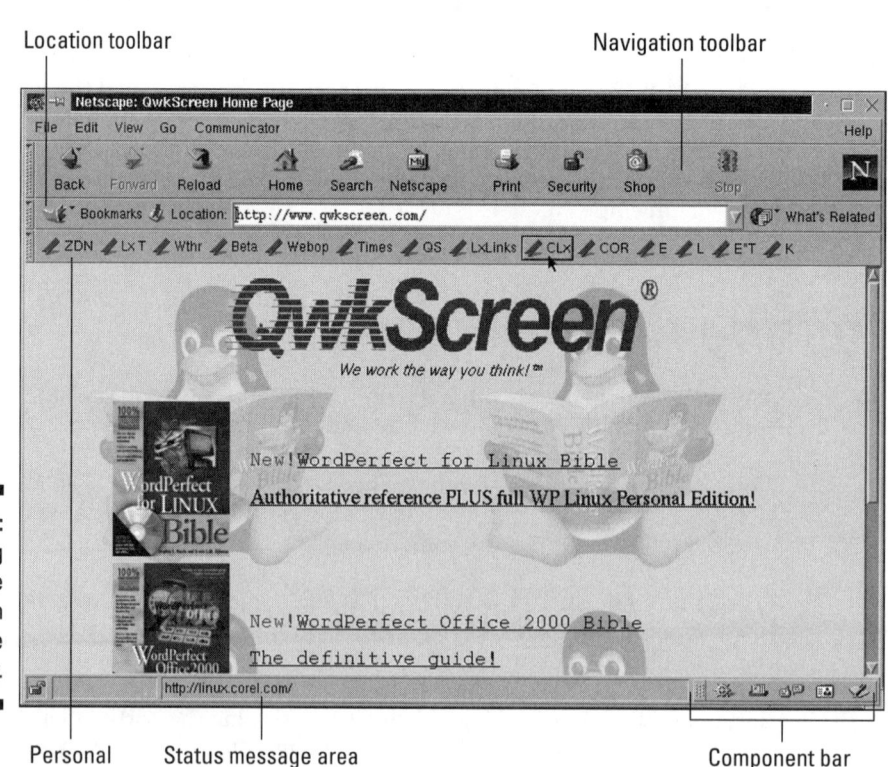

Figure 15-1: Cruising cyberspace with Netscape Navigator.

Chapter 15: Cruising in Cyberspace *243*

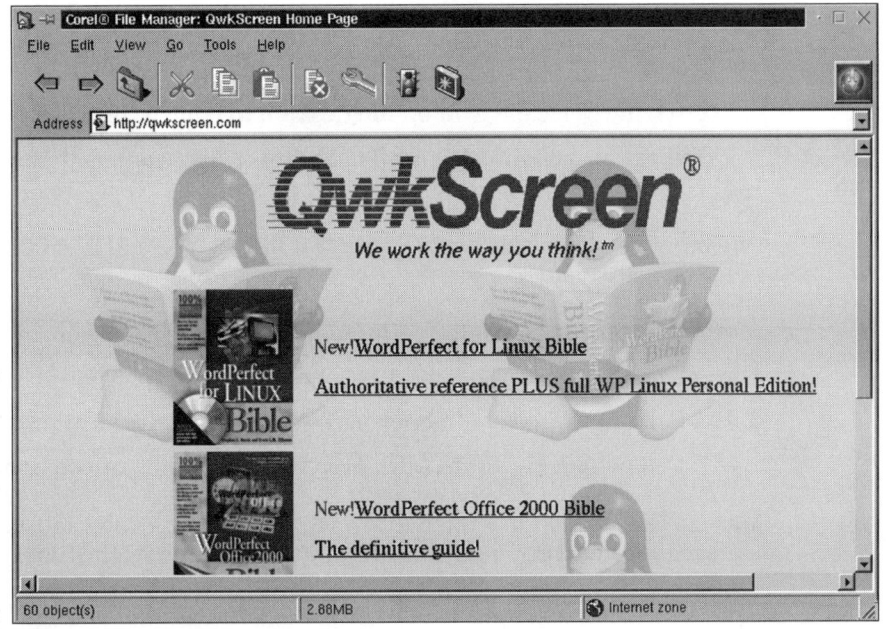

Figure 15-2:
The same Web site viewed in the Corel File Manager.

Of course, the Web has lots and lots of information. You can print a map of Oshkosh, Wisconsin, check train and airline schedules, and research any topic imaginable. Whatever you're looking for, it's there!

Your Web browser can take you to different types of places depending on your *protocol* (means of communication). The predominant places are

- **HTTP sites** to view Web pages
- **FTP sites** for transferring files from a remote location

Up, Up, and Away! Launching Netscape

Strap on your seat belt, if your chair has one, and blast off into cyberspace:

1. **Activate your network or dial-up access, if necessary.**

   For a dial-up, choose Application Starter ➪ Applications ➪ Network ➪ Dial-Up and then choose Connect to ignite your engines.

Part IV: Doin' Your Own Thing

REMEMBER

Of course, your browser won't get too far if you're not wired to the Web. See Chapter 4 for details.

2. **Click the Netscape icon on the desktop to launch Netscape Navigator.**

   You can also choose Application Starter ➪ Applications ➪ Netscape Communicator ➪ Netscape Navigator.

The browser window shown in Figure 15-1 has a menu and four other bars to help you get around:

- A **Navigation** toolbar for performing common browsing operations
- A **Location** toolbar for selecting a bookmark or typing a Web location
- A **Personal** toolbar with bookmarks to your favorite locations
- A **Component** bar to the open primary Communicator components

You can click the left of a toolbar to fold it up into a clickable tab and increase your viewing area. Another way to hide or show the toolbars is from the View menu.

Click the left of the component bar to display it as a floating palette, as shown in Figure 15-3. Click the Close button (the x in the upper right) to dock the component bar again.

Figure 15-3: Look, Ma, the component bar floats!

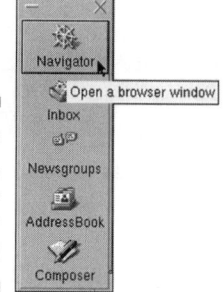

TIP

Click the Navigator button on the component bar to open multiple browser windows.

At the bottom of the browser window, you'll also notice a *status message area*, displaying the progress of your current connection or the address of the current page. You can point to a link to display its address on the status bar.

Going from link to link

Most Web pages contain clickable *links* to other pages or locations. A link might appear as a highlighted word, an image, a bar containing several selections, and other ways. When your mouse pointer is over a link, the pointer changes to a hand with a pointing finger.

Typing an Internet address

You can type an Internet address, such as http://www.corel.com, directly in the Location toolbar and then press Enter to go to that location.

You can omit parts of a standard Internet address. Navigator automatically assumes http:// for the prefix, http://www. for the pathname, and .com for the suffix. Thus, you could simply type **Corel** to go to Corel's Web site.

Selecting a recently typed address

Click the address listing to select from the last ten addresses you typed, as shown in Figure 15-4.

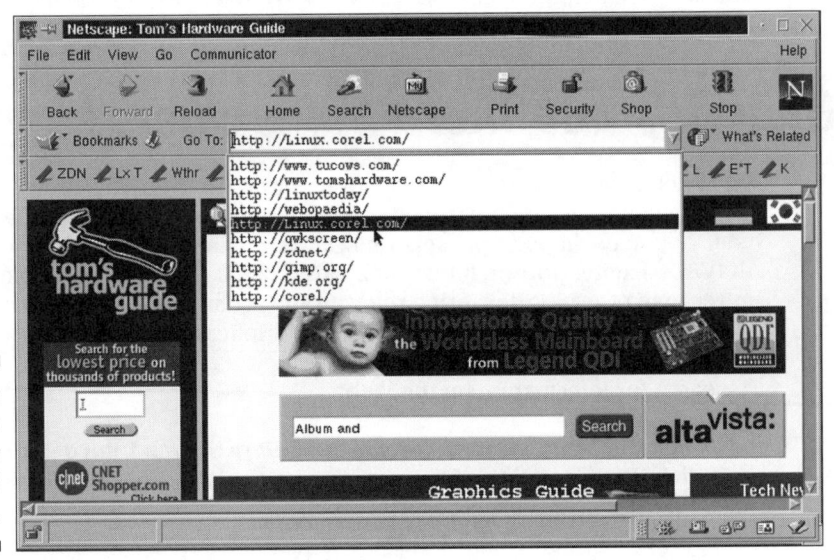

Figure 15-4: Selecting a recently typed address.

Going back and forth

Click the Back button to retrace your steps during a browsing session. Click the Forward button to come back. Click and hold either the Back or Forward button to select from a menu of previous pages.

TIP: You can also right-click in the Web page and then choose Forward or Back from the menu that appears.

Click the Home button to return to the home page at the start of your session. The home page is initially set to `Corelcity.com`, but you can change it to whatever you like. See "Configuring Navigator," later in this chapter.

Click the Netscape button to go to the Netscape home page.

Stopping and reloading pages

Sometimes when you're loading a Web page, things don't seem to connect. When this happens, you can click the Stop button and then try again or go to a more promising site.

Many Web pages are constantly updated, especially news and financial ones. You can click Reload to ensure that you have the latest information.

I Know It's out There Somewhere!

With such a vast amount of information out on the Web, the construction of search engines and their associated databases has become an industry in itself. You may choose from several brands, including (in alphabetical order) AltaVista, Excite, HotBot, Infoseek, Lycos, Magellan, and Yahoo! Some are better than others at delivering relevant hits from your query, allowing custom queries, and eliminating dead and duplicate links.

To search for information on the Web:

1. **Click the Search button (or choose Edit ⇨ Search Internet) and then click the tab or link of the search engine you want.**
2. **Follow the search engine's instructions.**

    Normally, you type a query and click a search button (see Figure 15-5).

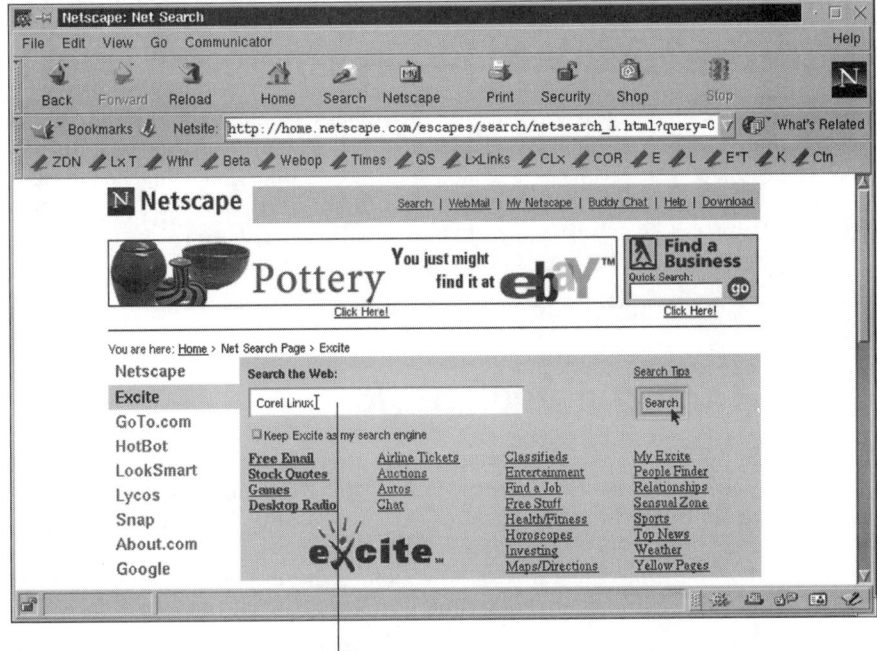

Figure 15-5:
Enter your query to search the Internet.

Type here

3. **Browse the search result listing and click any link that looks promising.**

   If the link isn't what you're looking for, click the Back button to return to the search result listing and try another link.

Searching the current page

To locate text in the current page, choose Edit ➪ Find in Page (or press Ctrl+F), type the text, and click Find Next.

Bookmarking your favorite places

You can personalize your browser by displaying bookmarks to your favorite sites in the Bookmarks listing in the Location toolbar. You can also add your very favorite sites to the Personal toolbar.

Part IV: Doin' Your Own Thing

Use your Windows bookmarks in Linux!

Bookmarks are stored in a Web document, called bookmarks.html, in your personal .netscape folder. Do you have a bunch of Netscape bookmarks in Windows that you want to use in Linux? Create a backup of your bookmarks file and then go to Windows and copy the bookmark.htm file (which is usually in C:\Program Files\Netscape\Users*youname*) over to Linux. Then rename the file you copied to bookmarks.html! (Log in as root and have hidden files showing.)

Adding a bookmark

Suppose you've just landed on the coolest Web page on termite colonies you've ever seen. You know you're going to want to come back to it time and again to see how the termites are progressing. You can either

- Scribble the address down somewhere. Then if you don't lose it, you can type it in again each time you want to visit the site.
- Create a bookmark. Drag the icon that appears to the left of the Location box, as shown in Figure 15-6, to the position you want in the Personal toolbar.

Not much of a contest, is it?

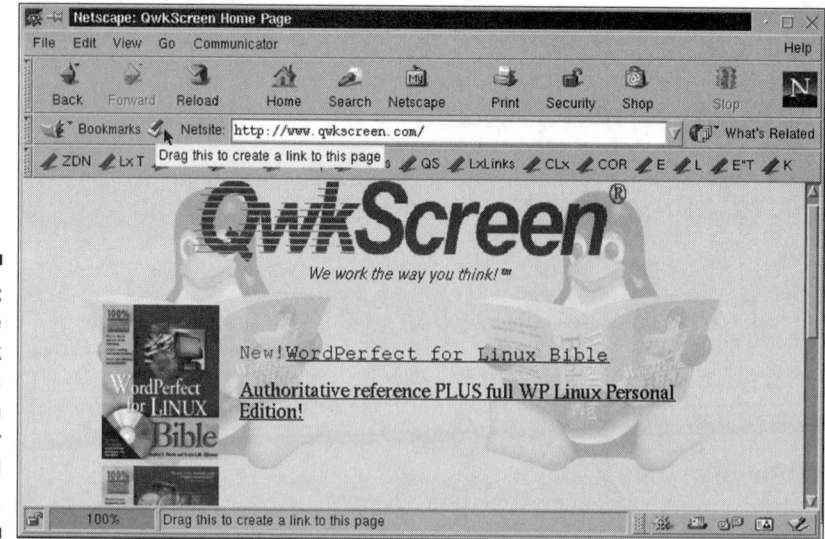

Figure 15-6: Drag the bookmark icon to a place on your Personal toolbar.

Chapter 15: Cruising in Cyberspace 249

You can also choose Bookmarks ➪ Add Bookmark from the toolbar to add a bookmark to your primary bookmark folder (the one that appears when you click the Bookmarks button) or choose Bookmarks ➪ File Bookmark to add a bookmark to a particular folder, as shown in Figure 15-7.

Figure 15-7: Adding a bookmark to a particular folder.

Right-click in the Web page and then click Add Bookmark to add a bookmark to your primary bookmark folder.

Checking Out Corel's Online Services

Corel sees its future out on the Web. To get there, it has to bring you along. That's why you'll find a number of inducements on the Online Services menu. Choose Application Starter ➪ Online Services, as shown in Figure 15-8, and then choose any of the following:

- **Business Community** to read articles and join discussions on business topics
- **Clipart and Photos** to download clipart, photos, graphics, and animations
- **Corel Printing Service** to create the T-shirt or coffee mug of your dreams

Part IV: Doin' Your Own Thing

- **Corel vDrive** to create your own virtual hard drive, and then upload and download files to and from anywhere
- **Current Events** to catch the latest news
- **Designer F/X** to customize your graphics images
- **eFax Services** to send and receive faxes by e-mail
- **Email** to set up an online e-mail account and then send and receive messages from anywhere
- **Graphic Community** to download free goodies and join up with the artistic set
- **JabberIM** to hold text-based person-to-person conversations with other users
- **Linux Community** for information, support, and discussions on Corel Linux and Corel's Linux applications
- **New Online Services** to look for additional goodies
- **Search the Internet** to use the mother of all search engines to search for Web pages, people, or businesses
- **Text F/X** to create graphical text objects using all sorts of special effects

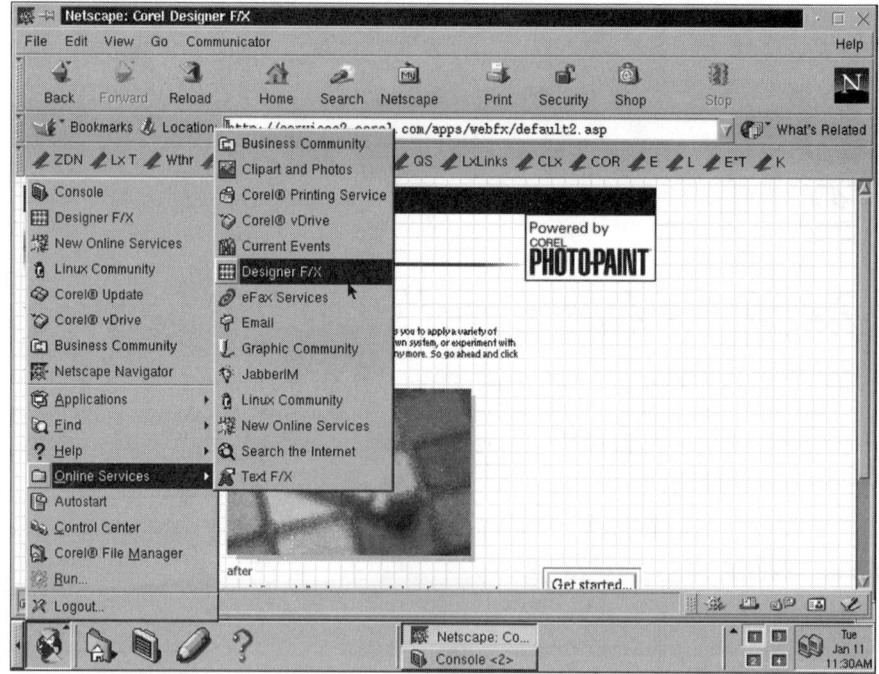

Figure 15-8: Checking out Corel's online services.

Chapter 15: Cruising in Cyberspace *251*

> Use Corel vDrive, eFax Services, and E-mail as your office-on-the-road!

Telling Your Browser Where to Start and How Much to Remember

You can tell Netscape Navigator where to start when you launch it and how many days of history to keep:

1. **Choose Edit ➪ Preferences and then choose Navigator in the tree listing, as shown in Figure 15-9.**

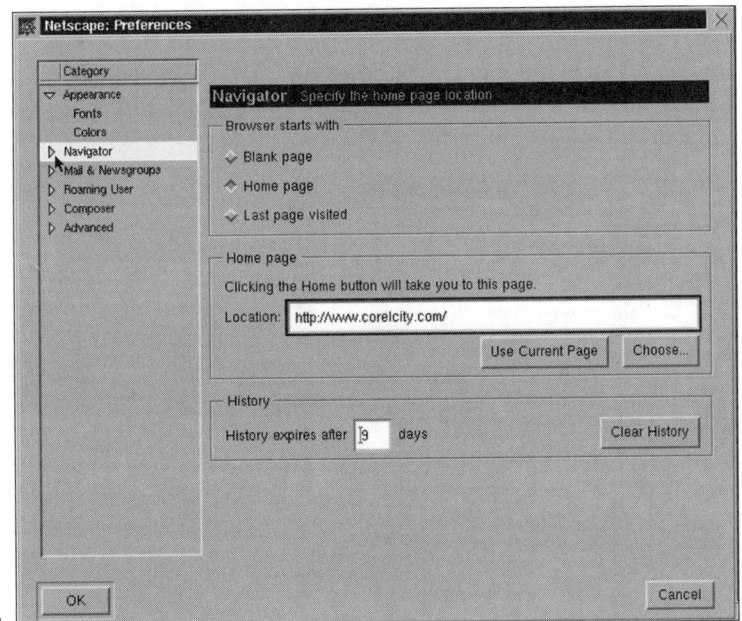

Figure 15-9: Telling your browser where to start and how much history to keep.

2. **Select whether you want Navigator to start with a blank page, the home page (the default), or the last page you visited.**
3. **Specify the home page you want to go to when you launch Navigator or click the Home button:**
    - **Use Current Page,** to use the current page displayed in the browser.
    - **Choose,** to select a Web document on your system.
4. **Specify how many days of history to keep or click Clear History to clear the history immediately.**

The history keeps track of the links you've clicked (showing them in the visited color), and where you've been in the history listing.

TIP

Clearing your history protects your privacy but makes it harder to retrace your steps.

5. **When you've finished making your selections, click OK.**

Getting Your Advanced Navigator's License

To get your advanced Navigation license, choose Help ➪ Help while browsing. The NetHelp facilities appear, with handy contents and an index to locate the information you need.

When using the help contents, click a main heading to display its help topics and then click the topic you want, as shown in Figure 15-10.

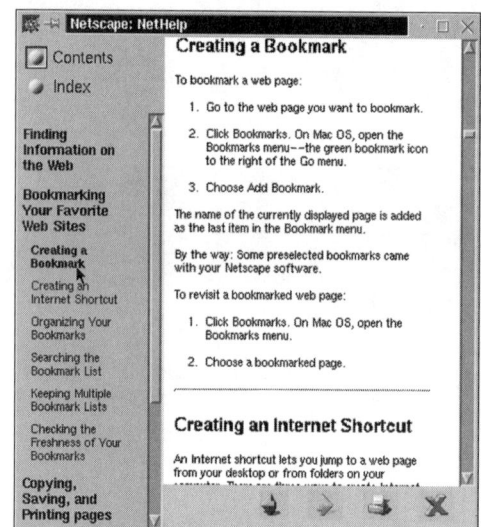

Figure 15-10: Click the headings and topics you want to see.

Taking File Manager for a Cyber-Ride

It's great to be able to pop out to the Web from File Manager whenever you want, without having to launch Netscape. If you're online, simply click the Web button on File Manager's right to go straight to CorelCity, as shown in Figure 15-11.

Chapter 15: Cruising in Cyberspace *253*

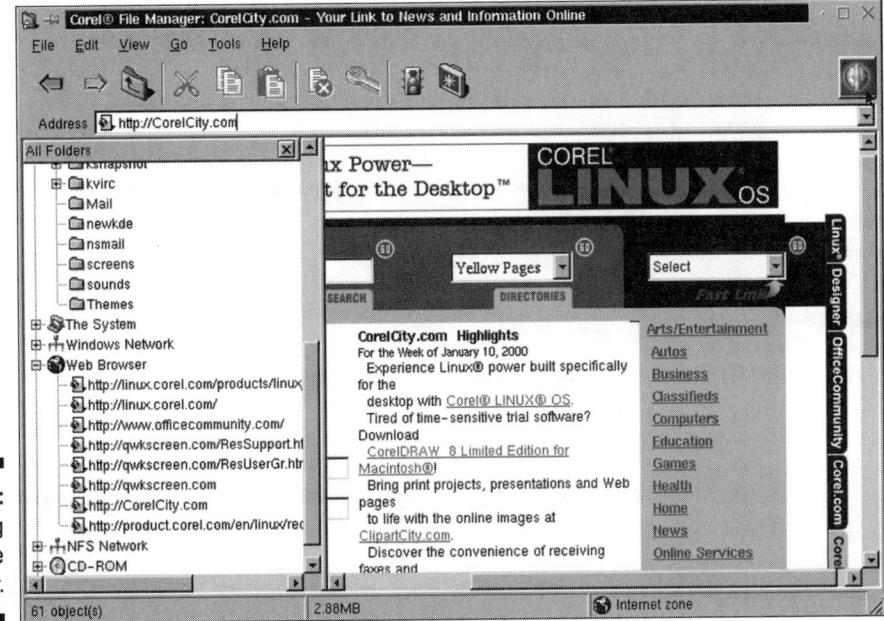

Figure 15-11: Browsing with File Manager.

When browsing with File Manager, try any of these tricks:

- Go to any Web page by entering its URL (Web address).
- Click the Back and Forward arrows to retrace your browsing session.
- Click the Address drop-down list to select any site you visited during the current browsing session.
- Choose View➪Tree to select from the tree the sites you visited.
- Click the Stop button if the Web page doesn't seem to be loading properly.
- Click the Refresh button to make sure you're viewing the latest information.

The beauty of File Manager is that it seamlessly integrates the Web with your local and network files and folders.

Do keep in mind that File Manager is just that — a file manager first and a Web browser second (for now). You won't find bookmarks and other browser features, nor do you get e-mail, newsgroups, and chat integrated in the package.

Part IV: Doin' Your Own Thing

Transferring Files from a Remote Site

When you're online, you can use File Manager to download files from a remote FTP site:

1. **In the Address box, type the address of the FTP site (such as ftp://ftp.corel.com).**

   Make sure to include the initial *ftp://* when entering the address. Otherwise, if you type *ftp.corel.com,* File Manager will think it's a Web site.

2. **Press Enter.**

3. **Locate and select the files you want to transfer.**

4. **Use copy and paste or drag and drop, as shown in Figure 15-12, to download the files to your local folder.**

5. **If the FTP site prompts you for your ID and password, provide them.**

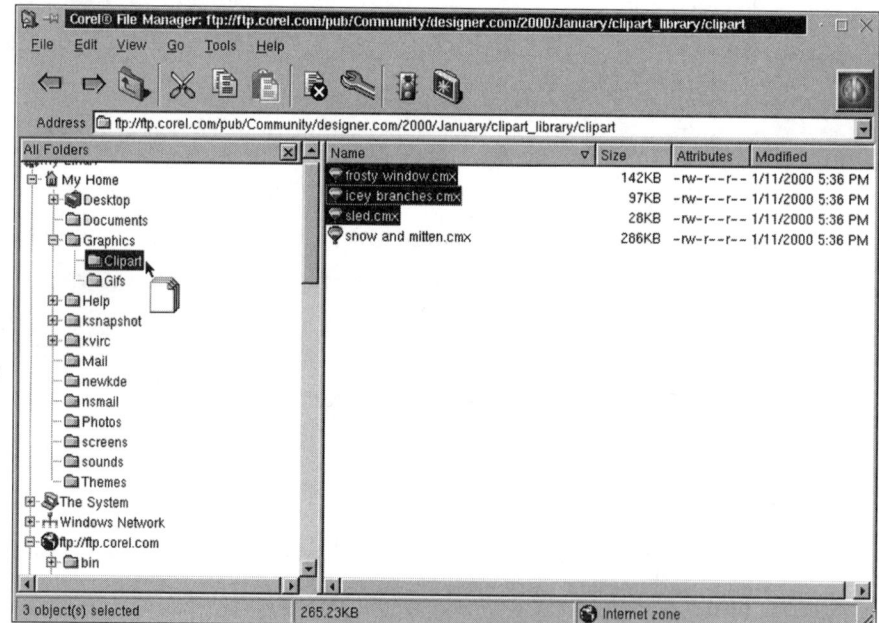

Figure 15-12: Drag and drop files directly from the remote site to your local folder.

That's it. Get up, stretch, and then go make a peanut butter and cauliflower sandwich as your files are being transferred.

Chapter 16

You've Got Mail!

In This Chapter
▶ Finding out what Corel Linux offers for e-mail
▶ Setting up your mailbox
▶ Uncovering how your e-mail is sorted
▶ Getting your e-mail
▶ Customizing the Messenger display
▶ Setting up your address book
▶ Writing and mailing messages
▶ Participating in discussions

E-mail is one of those inventions, like the telephone, radio, and TV, that's fast becoming part of our daily lives and revolutionizing the way we communicate. For example, in putting this book together, my editors and I e-mailed chapters back and forth across continents as fast as you click a mouse. Separation of place and time vanished. Amazing!

I don't know about the telephone and radio, but if I had to choose between e-mail and television, the boob tube would be out the door in a minute.

In this chapter, you look at two uses of e-mail:

✔ To send private messages to others
✔ To add your two cents to public newsgroups, or forums

You're in charge of your personal mail folders. Newsgroup messages are kept on a remote server and managed by someone else. Other than that, mail and newsgroup operations are pretty much the same.

E-Mail Facilities in Corel Linux

Corel Linux comes with a couple of e-mail facilities:

- The Messenger component in Netscape Communicator
- The Kmail utility from KDE

The Messenger facility, which is shown in Figure 16-1, is nicely integrated with the browser. Plus, it's a more mature application than Kmail that handles newsgroups as well, so it's one I use in this chapter. If you decide to use Kmail, the setup procedures and operations are similar.

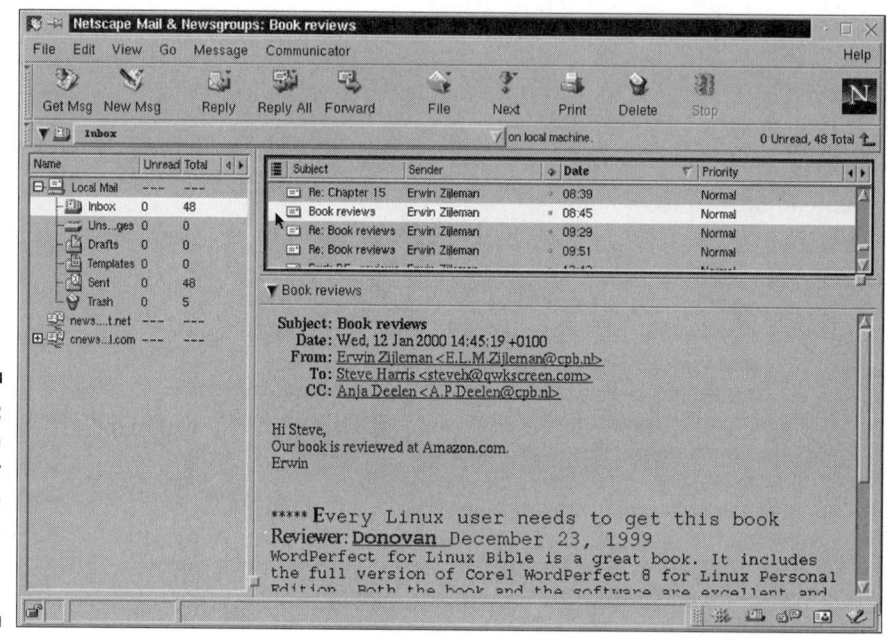

Figure 16-1: Netscape Messenger is a nice e-mail and newsgroup facility.

The download version of Corel Linux comes with only the Netscape browser. The entire Communicator suite, however, is available on your *Corel Linux For Dummies* CD. See Appendix C for installation instructions.

Putting up Your Mailbox

As with browsing the Web, you have to be wired to the Internet to use e-mail. See Chapter 4 for details.

After you set up Web browsing, you can configure Netscape Messenger to send and receive e-mail:

1. **Choose Application Starter ➪ Applications ➪ Netscape Communicator ➪ Netscape Messenger.**

2. **Choose Edit ➪ Preferences.**

3. **Choose your Mail & Newsgroups settings, which are shown in Figure 16-2.**

   TIP: The setting to display plain text messages in a variable-width font gives them a more compact and natural appearance. However, you might find it harder to read some messages, such as those with spaces used to create a table.

4. **Under Mail & Newsgroups, select the Identity category and then fill in any of the following settings, which are also shown in Figure 16-3:**

   - Your name and e-mail address for the From: line of your messages.

     TIP: No matter what the dialog box reads, these entries are for identification only. Your e-mail address is the only required entry.

   - Your reply-to address if that's different from your e-mail address. For example, you could send a message from home and receive the reply at work.

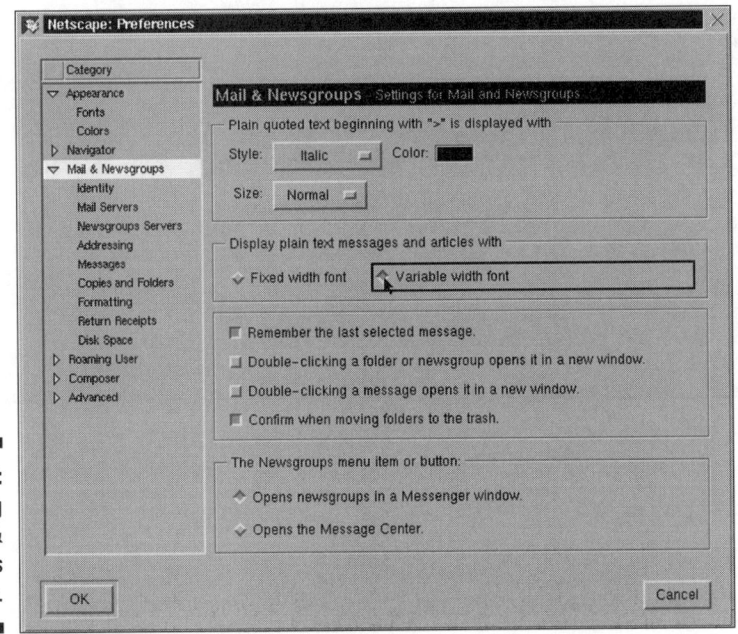

Figure 16-2: Changing your Mail & Newsgroups settings.

- Your organization, if you want that to appear.
- A signature file to attach to the end of your messages. (Create it in the Text Editor.) This is your repeating boilerplate, with such things as your phone number, fax number, address, pearls of wisdom, and a link to your Web page.
- An editable vCard (virtual business card) to attach to the end of your messages. A vCard is more formal and bulkier than a signature file.

  The vCard is sent as a message attachment. Users who don't have a vCard-enabled mail system might not be able to view it.

5. **On the left, choose Mail Servers, as shown in Figure 16-4, and then fill in the following:**

   - Your incoming (POP or IMAP) and outgoing (SMTP) mail servers.
   - Your outgoing mail server user name.
   - The location of your incoming mail folders. (Your network administrator or Internet service provider can give you this information.)

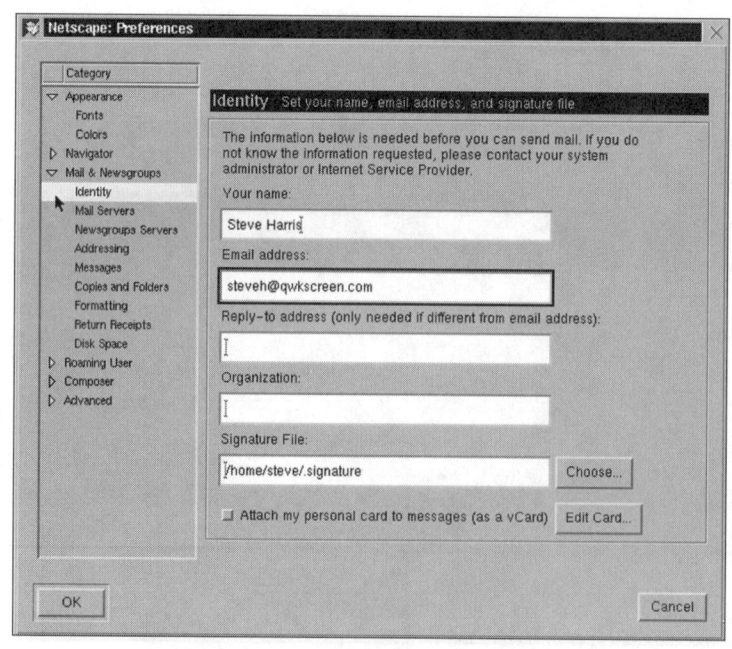

Figure 16-3: Give yourself an e-mail and newsgroup identity.

Chapter 16: You've Got Mail! 259

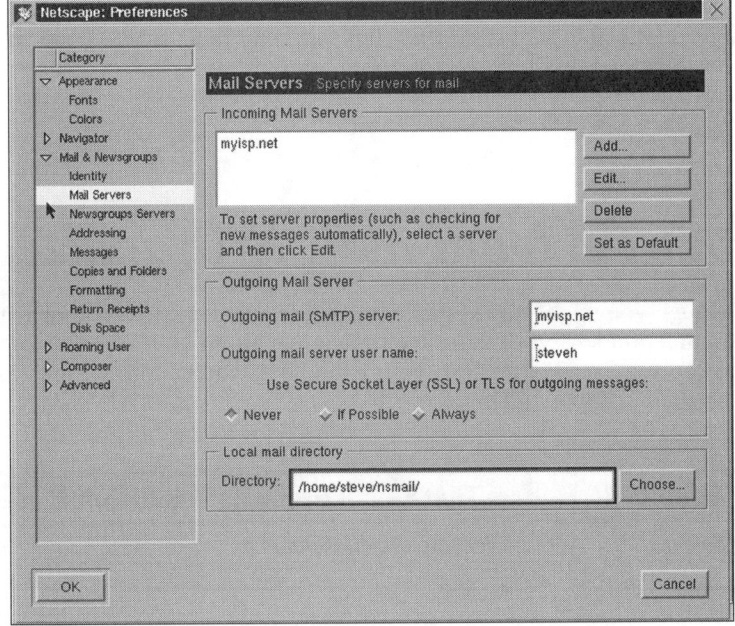

Figure 16-4: Your server's identity is more critical than your own (other than your e-mail address).

6. **At the top of the dialog box, select the incoming mail server and then click the Edit button.**

7. **Edit the incoming mail server with your particulars, as seen in Figure 16-5, and then click OK.**

   You can set how often your mail is automatically checked.

Figure 16-5: Edit the incoming mail server with your configuration.

TIP: Some users of POP mail servers click the POP tab and choose to leave messages on the mail server so that they can read them from two or more locations. Most servers have a size quota, though, so be sure you delete the messages when they're no longer needed. Otherwise, you may find that future incoming messages are bounced!

How Your Personal Mail Is Organized

Although you might never spot them, your e-mail system comes with little gremlins that sort your messages as you go about your e-mail business. As you can see from Figure 16-1, your e-mail gets sorted into various folders, described in Table 16-1.

Table 16-1 Folders That E-mail Gremlins Use to Sort Messages

Folder	What the Gremlins Put in It
Inbox	Messages you got
Unsent messages	Messages completed (usually offline) and waiting to be sent
Drafts	Messages you're still working on
Templates	Standard partial messages that you can fill out and send over and over, such as a weekly report of UFO sightings
Sent	Copies of messages you sent to others
Trash	Deleted messages (until you empty the trash)

As messages relentlessly pile up, you can sort them into subfolders organized by topic. (See "Deleting and organizing messages" later in this chapter.)

Picking up Your E-Mail

Suppose you're all set up and want to see whether the friend you gave your e-mail addresses to has sent you any messages. Ready? Time to go pick up your e-mail:

1. **Activate your network or dial-up access, if necessary.**

    For a dial-up, choose Application Launcher ➪ Applications ➪ Network ➪ Dial-Up.

       Chapter 16: You've Got Mail! **261**

2. **Choose Application Starter ➪ Applications ➪ Netscape Communicator ➪ Netscape Messenger.**

   If you're already browsing the Web with Netscape Navigator, simply click the little Inbox button in the Component bar and skip Steps 1 and 2. You see a little green arrow when you have messages waiting.

3. **Select the message you want to read.**

   Unread messages appear in bold.

Printing and saving messages

Click the Print button (or choose File ➪ Print) if you want to print the current message and show it to a friend. (Just make sure the message doesn't contain last year's jokes.)

To save the current message to disk (outside your mail folder), choose File ➪ Save As ➪ File and then specify the filename and location. You can also choose File ➪ Save As ➪ Template to save the message as a reusable fill-in-the-blanks message in the Templates folder.

Viewing e-mail links and attachments

If a message includes a Web link, you can click the link to view the object of the link in your browser. When a message has an attached file, a paper clip icon appears in the message. Click the paper clip and then click the file, to view it in its associated application or save it to disk.

Picking up new messages

Your incoming mail server is checked every 10 minutes or at whatever interval you specify. If you can't wait, click the Get Msg button.

Configuring Your Messenger Display

You can configure your Messenger display to view your folders, listings, and messages more readily:

Part IV: Doin' Your Own Thing

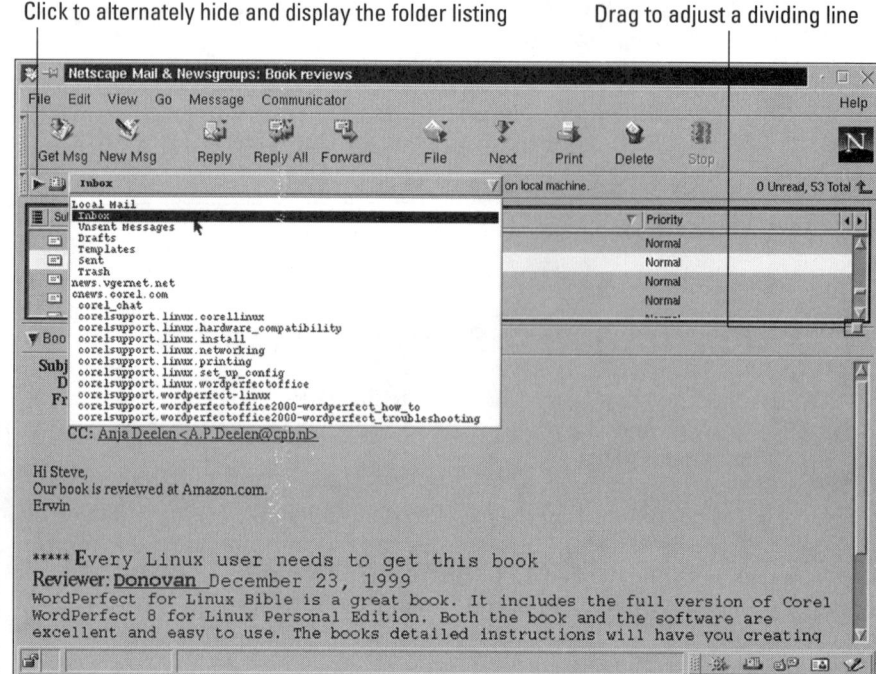

Figure 16-6: Select folders from the Location bar when they're not on display.

- ✓ Click the buttons in the upper right to maximize and minimize your display or drag a side or corner of the display to adjust its size.
- ✓ Drag the little squares to adjust the dividing lines separating the folder listing, message listing, and message display.
- ✓ Click the little triangle to the left of the Location bar to alternately hide and display the folder listing. Note in Figure 16-6 how you can still select folders from the Location bar when they're not displayed.

Addressing Your Needs

It's funny how when you want to contact someone these days, the first thing you look for is not their street address or telephone number but their virtual e-mail address! Of course, the Communicator address book has entries for the physical address too, but it's the virtual one we need for our e-mail. Choose Communicator ⇨ Address Book to display the address book, as shown in Figure 16-7.

Chapter 16: You've Got Mail! *263*

Use your Windows address book in Linux!

Communicator's addresses are stored in the pab.na2 database in your personal .netscape folder. Do you have a Netscape address book in Windows that you want to use in Linux? Copy the pab.na2 file (usually in C:\Program Files\Netscape\Users*yourname*) over to Linux. You can also choose File ➪ Import from the Address Book to add other types of address books to Communicator.

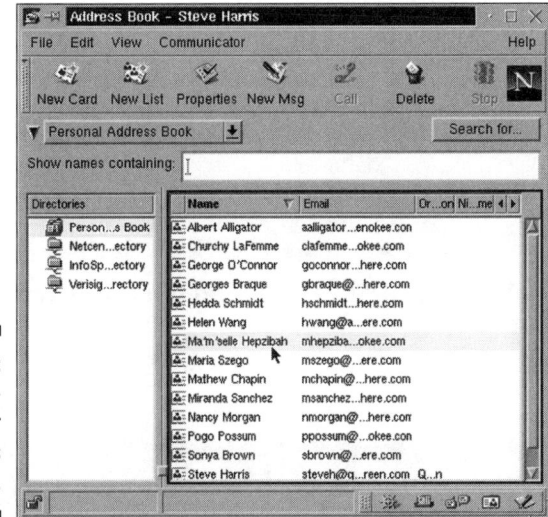

Figure 16-7: Communicator address book.

To add someone to your address book, click the New Card button and fill in the entries.

TIP

Click the **From:** line in a message you received to instantly add the sender's e-mail address to your collection!

Creating and Sending E-Mail

To create and send a new e-mail message from Netscape Messenger:

1. **Click the New Msg button.**

   You can also choose Message ➪ New Message (or press Alt+M).

Part IV: Doin' Your Own Thing

2. **Type the addresses of your recipients. Or click the Address button, double-click the names of your recipients, and then click OK.**

   As you begin typing an address, partial matches on Address Book names appear automatically.

3. **Click the triangle to the left of the To field to choose another recipient type, as seen in Figure 16-8:**

   - **Cc** (carbon copy), to send a copy to someone indirectly affected by the message
   - **Bcc** (blind carbon copy), to send a private copy, unknown to other recipients
   - **Reply-To**, to indicate a reply to a message you've received
   - **Newsgroup**, to post to a newsgroup
   - **Followup-To**, to redirect a newsgroup posting to another newsgroup

4. **Fill in the Subject box and type the body of your message.**

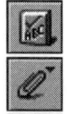

5. **If you want to spell-check your message, click the Spelling button.**

6. **To include a file, Web page (URL), or your Address Book card, click the Attach button.**

7. **Click the Send button to send your message on its way.**

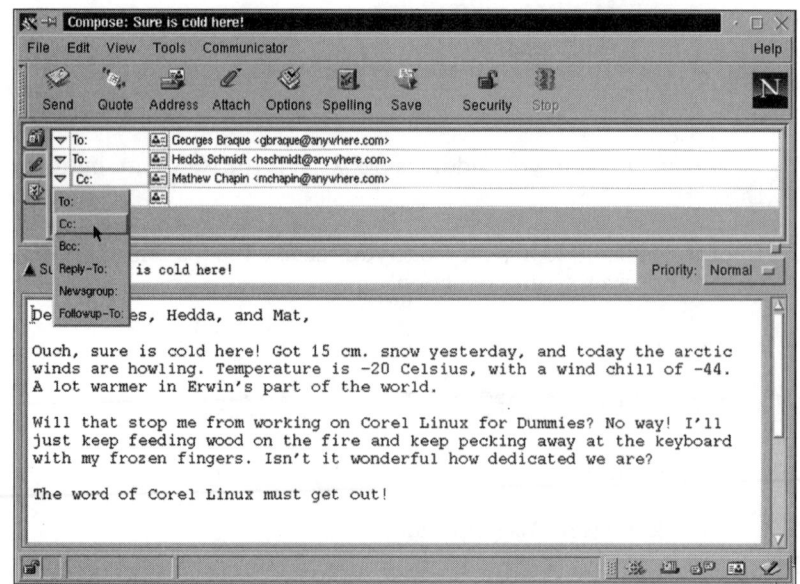

Figure 16-8: Changing the recipient type.

Sending messages later

To compose messages now to send later:

1. **Create each message in the normal manner.**
2. **Choose File ⇨ Send Later.**
3. **When you're ready to send your messages, choose File ⇨ Send Unsent Messages.**

This feature enables you to compose your messages while you're offline, either because you don't have access at the moment or you want to save online charges.

Drafting a message

To draft a message and then complete and send it later:

1. **Create the message in the normal manner.**
2. **Click the Save button and choose As Draft.**
3. **When you're ready to complete the message, display the Drafts folder under Local Mail and double-click the message in the listing.**

Replying to a message

To reply to a message you received:

1. **Click the Reply button (or right-click the message and choose Reply to Sender Only).**

   Click the Reply All button to reply to the sender and all recipients.

2. **Type your reply above, below, or within the quoted message (wherever seems most appropriate).**

   You can also delete superfluous parts of the quoted message to focus your reply.

3. **Click the Send button.**

Forwarding a message

To forward the current message for others to see:

1. **Click the Forward button (or choose Message ⇨ Forward).**

   This automatically changes the subject to "[Fwd: Subject]" to indicate that the message is forwarded.

   To quote the forwarded message within the body of your message, right-click the message and choose Forward Quoted.

2. **Enter the recipients for the forwarded message.**

3. **Preface the message with an explanation, if necessary.**

4. **Click the Send button to forward the message.**

Selecting multiple messages

You can perform a number of operations (such as moving or deleting) on several messages at once. You can hold Ctrl while you click to select multiple messages, or you can hold Shift and click to select a range of messages. Press Alt+A (or choose Edit ⇨ Select ⇨ All) to select the entire listing.

Deleting and organizing messages

If you send and receive a great deal of e-mail (especially if you get spammed with junk mail), your messages will pile up in a hurry. This makes for a messy mailbox and eats up a lot of hard drive space.

To tidy up your mailbox:

1. **Select the messages you want to discard and click the Delete button (or press Alt+D).**

   Your messages are simply moved to the Trash folder rather than deleted, so you aren't warned when deleting. To undelete, press Alt+Z immediately.

2. **To create folders and subfolders for your messages, choose File ⇨ New Subfolder (or right-click a folder and choose New Subfolder).**

   Drag folder icons to rearrange them.

3. **Sort and select messages and then choose Message ⇨ Move Message and specify the folder to move them to.**

Chapter 16: You've Got Mail! *267*

TIP

You can also drag the messages and drop them into a folder.

4. **To remove deleted messages from your trash, choose File ⇨ Empty Trash on Local Mail.**

They'll be gone for good when you do.

When you empty the trash, your mail folders are compressed, so they'll work more efficiently and take up less disk space. You can compress your mail without deleting by choosing File ⇨ Compact All Folders.

Participating in Newsgroup Discussions

To participate in collective newsgroup discussions, you use the Messenger facility, so it's pretty much the same as sending personal e-mail.

Some newsgroups are available only within a company or organization and usually require a password for Internet access. Public newsgroups can be either corporate sponsored or independent. Some groups are moderated to help organize the discussion *threads* (topics) and keep down *flaming* (verbal abuse).

TIP

Newsgroup postings are the main source of e-mail addresses for senders of spam! Some folks like to foil spammers by using a nonexistent e-mail address and then tell others the trick to contacting them in their signature file.

Subscribing to newsgroups

To subscribe to newsgroups from the Messenger facility:

1. **Choose File ⇨ Subscribe.**
2. **Choose Add Server, if necessary, to add a server to the list, as seen in Figure 16-9. Click OK.**

   TIP

   Add cnews.corel.ca for Corel Linux discussions and support.
3. **From the Server listing, select the news server.**
4. **Click to select the groups you want to subscribe to, as seen in Figure 16-10, and then click OK.**

Figure 16-9: Adding a newsgroup server.

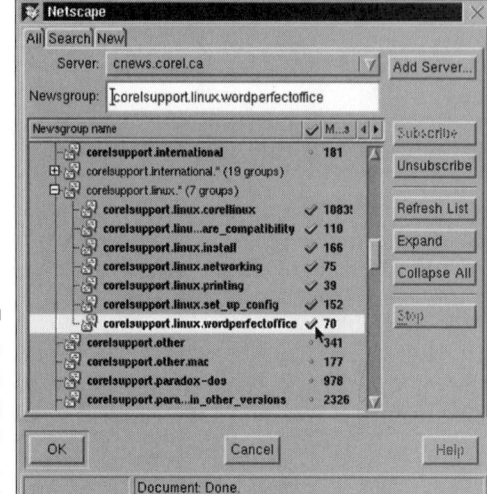

Figure 16-10: Check the newsgroups you want to subscribe to.

When subscribing to discussion groups, you can also do any of the following:

- Uncheck groups you no longer want to subscribe to.
- Click the Unsubscribe button to cancel all subscriptions on that server.
- Click the Expand or Collapse All button to expand or collapse the discussion group hierarchy.
- Click the Stop button to stop the server from loading any more groups.
- Click the Search tab to search for groups.
- Click the New tab to display newsgroups that have been added since the last time you queried the server.

The newsgroups you subscribe to are displayed below the mail folders in Messenger.

Putting in your two cents

Ready to put in your two cents? To join a discussion:

1. **Click the plus (+) box to the left of the server name in the folder listing to display the groups you've subscribed to.**

    Newsgroup servers appear underneath your personal mail folders in the listing.

2. **Select a group to download its message headings.**

3. **If the number of headings exceeds the specified limit, you'll be asked whether you want to download them all, as seen in Figure 16-11.**

    To change the message limit, choose Edit ➪ Preferences and then go to the Newsgroup Server setting under Mail & Newsgroups.

Figure 16-11: Downloading newsgroup message headers.

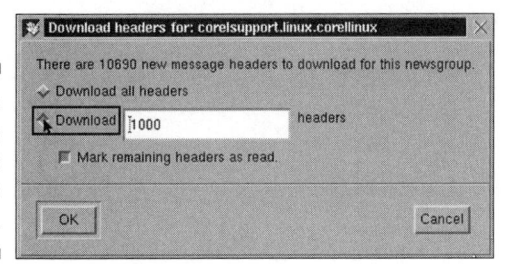

4. **Click the thread you want to read, as seen in Figure 16-12.**

    Any thread with unread messages appears in bold.

    Messages are normally arranged by threads, but you can click the buttons at the top of the listing to sort them by subject, sender, date, and so on. Click a button twice for a reverse sort.

5. **Click the plus (+) box next to the thread to display all its messages, or click the minus (–) box to fold the thread back up.**

6. **Click the Reply button to make your lucid contribution to the discussion.**

    Note that your message is addressed to the newsgroup and appears underneath the current message in the thread.

To reply privately to another poster, right-click the message and choose Reply to Sender Only.

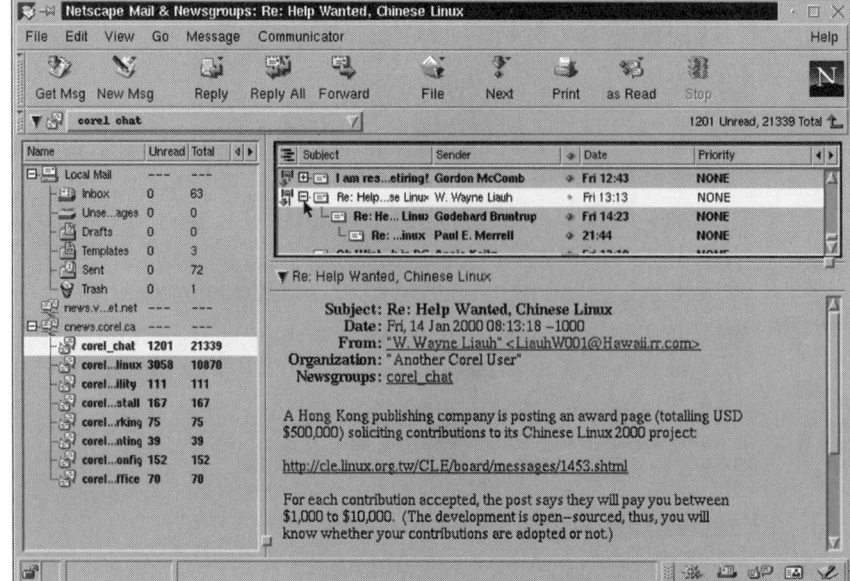

Figure 16-12: Click the thread you want to read.

Starting a new thread

Now that you have the hang of contributing to existing newsgroup threads, perhaps you'd like to start a new thread on a topic of your own. Easy enough — just click the New Msg button, type the heading and body of the message, and then send your posting to the newsgroup.

To quote or not to quote?

Normally when you reply to a newsgroup posting, the previous message is quoted, which might have a quote from the message before that, and so on up the line. This means that even though you might be adding only a few words of wisdom, the reader of your post will have long quotes to wade through, probably for a second or third time.

It's a good idea to select and delete all the old stuff, if your response is perfectly clear without it. You can also selectively quote from the previous message, to make it clear to the next reader exactly what you're responding to.

Marking threads as read

When you're finished viewing the current discussion group, you can click the as Read button and select All Read to mark all the threads as read. That way, you'll feel like you aren't falling hopelessly behind, and you can easily distinguish the new messages the next time you visit the group.

To mark just a particular thread, click the as Read button and select Thread Read. You can select by Date to mark only older messages as read.

Searching for messages on a vital topic

"I know I read a message on this. Where is it?" To search for messages by subject and content:

1. **Choose Edit ⇨ Search Messages.**
2. **Select the e-mail folder to search.**
3. **Construct your query by selecting search fields and conditions and by typing the contents (see Figure 16-13).**

Figure 16-13: Creating a message search query.

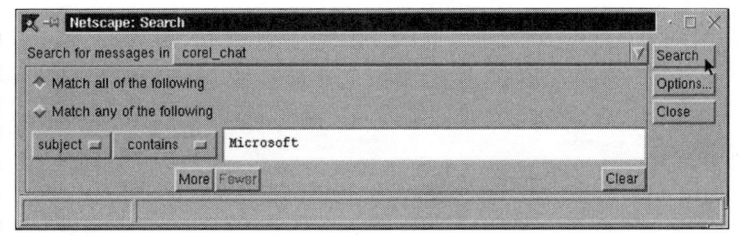

4. **Create more or fewer search criteria, then click Search and choose your message from the search results listing.**

TIP: If your search returns too many hits, click More to add another search criterion. For example, if a search on *Microsoft* returns 400 messages, click More and add *Linux* to your search. Just be sure to choose the Match all of the following option, not the Match any option!

Chapter 17
Upgrade Madness

In This Chapter
- Upgrading and adding software
- Setting up your custom package sources
- Installing Debian packages
- Deleting stuff

*T*o say that Linux changes are coming at a rapid rate borders on understatement. Linux is hot, and its pace of development is torrid! Literally thousands of folks are hard at work on the Linux kernel and its myriad hardware drivers and supporting applications. The contributions of major corporations are accelerating the work of independent hackers. I'm talking about not just the likes of Corel and Red Hat, but also IBM, Sun Microsystems, and other companies too numerous to mention.

Does this mean that your Corel Linux system is obsolete the minute you install it? Certainly not, but it will get better and better. Pretty soon, you'll be able to do everything in Corel Linux that you can in Windows — on a stable, efficient platform. How can you resist checking for the latest stuff?

In addition to upgrading, you might want to add that game or some other application from your *Corel Linux For Dummies* CD that wasn't part of your initial install. Likewise, its simple to remove a program you no longer need.

Updating (Or Adding) with a Smile

Because you're the proud owner of Corel Linux, you're in luck when it comes to upgrades. There are two reasons for this:

- Corel Linux comes in the technically superior Debian modules, or *packages*, which declare any related requirements (*dependencies*) to the installer.
- The Corel Update package manager makes updating your system an incredibly simple and foolproof task.

Interested in updates or additions to your system? Let's go take a look:

1. **Log in as root.**

   Or if you log in as a regular user, be prepared to supply the root password when prompted.

2. **Connect to the Internet if you're updating from a remote site rather than from a CD.**

3. **Choose Application Starter ⇨ Applications ⇨ System ⇨ Corel Update.**

   The Corel Update facility appears, as shown in Figure 17-1.

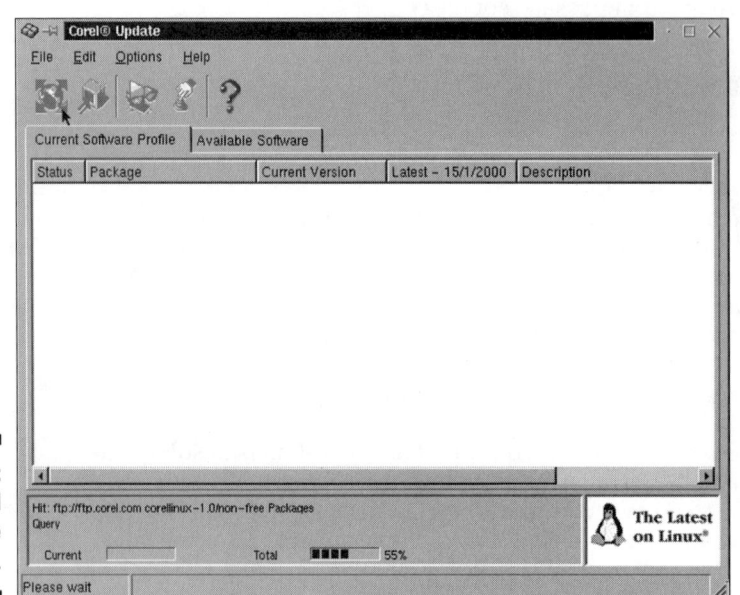

Figure 17-1: Corel Update facility.

4. **Choose Options ⇨ Set file sources to select one or more of the following, as seen in Figure 17-2:**

   - **Corel LINUX CD-ROM,** to use any CD with Debian packages
   - **Distribution Site,** to update from Corel's FTP site
   - **Custom Path(s),** to access other sites with Debian packages (see "Setting Custom Package Sources" later in this chapter)

5. **Click OK and then click the Update Profile button.**

   Corel Update goes to the sources to find what's available, as seen in Figure 17-3.

Chapter 17: Upgrade Madness 275

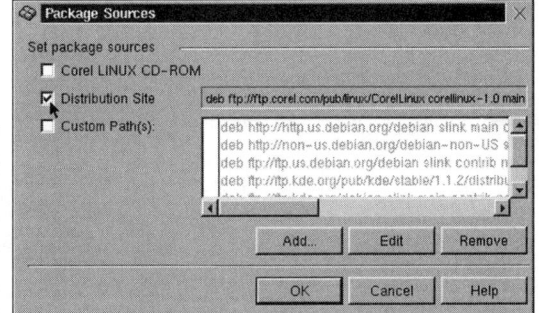

Figure 17-2: Selecting your package sources.

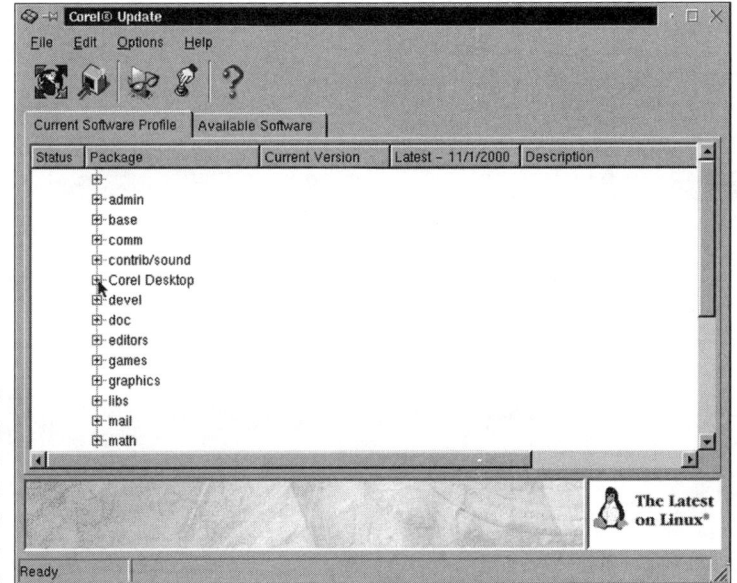

Figure 17-3: Go to the sources to find what's available.

6. **When the information gathering is finished, click the Current Software Profile tab in Corel Update.**

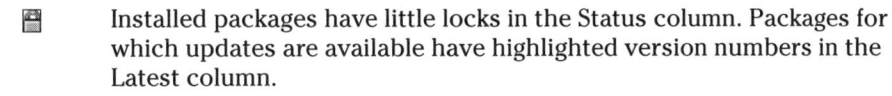

   Installed packages have little locks in the Status column. Packages for which updates are available have highlighted version numbers in the Latest column.

7. **To select packages for update, click the little locks in the Status column to change them to double arrows, as shown in Figure 17-4.**

   Choose Options ➪ View out of date only to show only updated packages.

Part IV: Doin' Your Own Thing

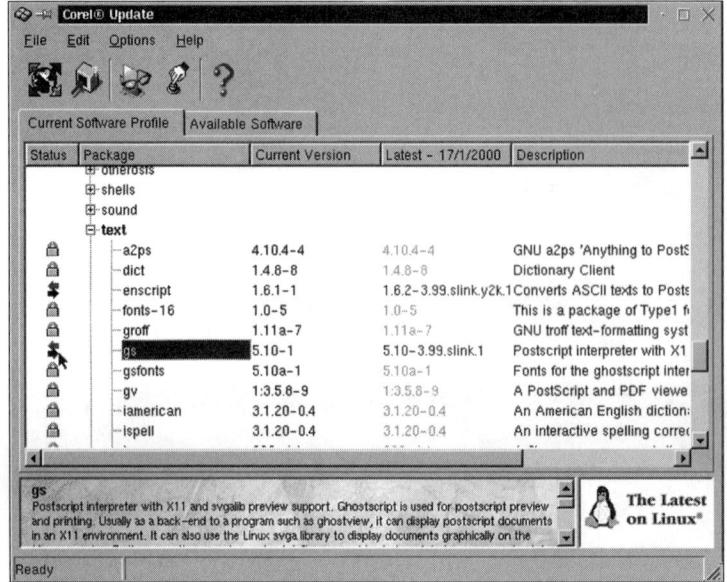

Figure 17-4: Click the little locks to select the updates you want to install.

   8. **Click the Available Software tab and then choose Edit ⇨ Expand All to display all the available stuff that's not on your system, as shown in Figure 17-5.**

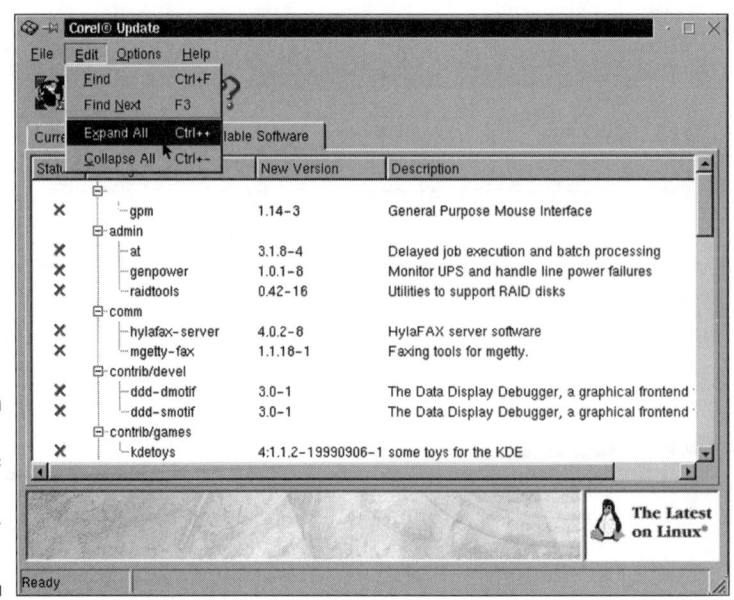

Figure 17-5: All the stuff you can add to your system.

Chapter 17: Upgrade Madness 277

    ⊠   The X icon in the Status column indicates an uninstalled package.

> Press Ctrl+F (or choose Edit ➪ Find) to search package names or descriptions.

9. **Click a package name to view its detailed description at the bottom of the Corel Update dialog box.**

10. **For each package you want to install, click the X in the Status column to change it to a double-arrow, as seen in Figure 17-6.**

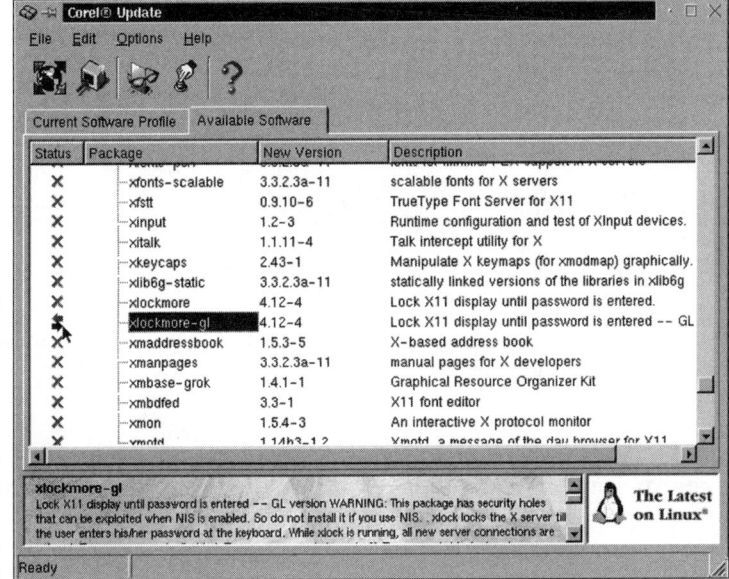

Figure 17-6: Click the X in the Status column for each package you want to install.

11. **Click the Upgrade & Install Packages button to fetch and install the packages you selected.**

12. **When asked whether you want to proceed, click yes.**

Corel Update informs you of its progress and then gives you a cheery "Done!" when it's finished, as shown in Figure 17-7.

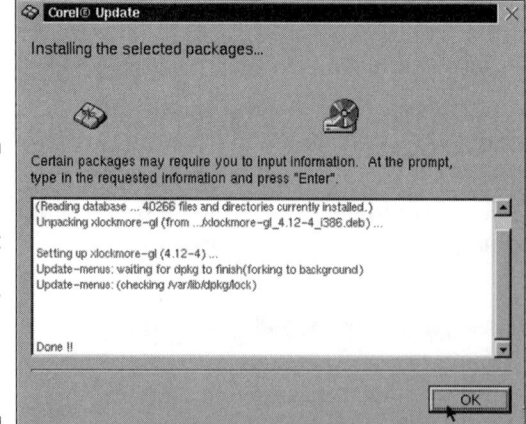

Figure 17-7: Status report showing your successful updates and additions!

Installing Debian Packages from Your Hard Drive

Suppose you already have a Debian package that you got from some other source sitting on your hard drive (or on a network drive). Can you use Corel Update to install it? Yup, sure can! (I love answering my own questions.)

1. **From Corel Update, choose File ➪ Install Deb File and then locate the file, as seen in Figure 17-8.**

Figure 17-8: Select the Debian package you want to install.

2. **Click OK to install the file.**

   It's that simple!

> ### Debian package categories
>
> Debian packages have their own distinctive categories. These are puzzling at first but make perfect sense when you realize that the ultimate goal of the Debian folks is to release a pure version of Linux, unhampered by any commercial licensing restrictions:
>
> - **Main** packages comprise the latest release of the main distribution of Debian. All packages come with full source code and can be freely distributed.
>
> - **Contrib** packages are free themselves but depend on other non-free software. That means they can't be part of a pure, free Debian distribution.
>
> - **Non-Free** packages don't necessarily cost money but have some onerous condition restricting the redistribution of the software.
>
> - **Non-US** packages might be free, but they can't be exported from the United States. (They're mostly encryption software that's dangerous in the hands of Europeans and other known criminals.)

Getting Rid of Stuff You Don't Use

Corel Update is also adept at removing packages you no longer want:

1. **Choose Application Starter ➪ Applications ➪ System ➪ Corel Update.**

2. **For each package you want to remove, click the little lock in the Status column twice to change it to a trash can, as seen in Figure 17-9.**

3. **Click the Upgrade & Install Packages button to remove the packages you selected.**

You can always install the packages again if you want them back. And don't worry that the button says Upgrade & Install. The same process handles deletions too.

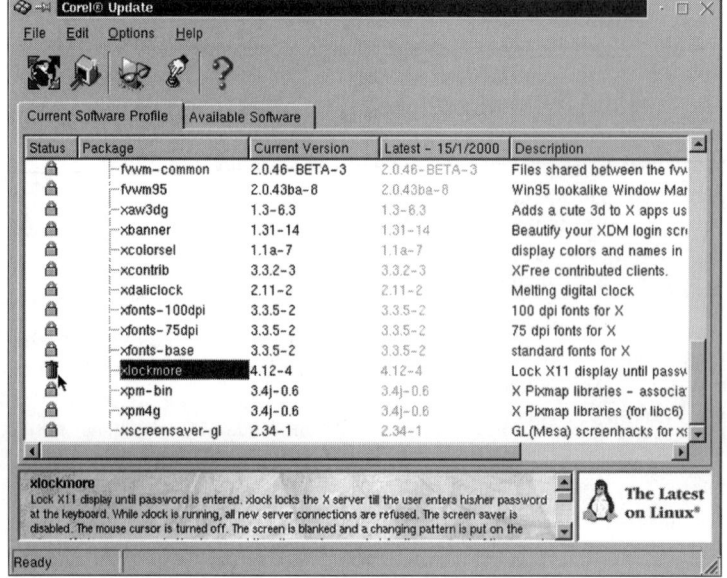

Figure 17-9: Click the little lock twice to send an application to the trash.

Part V
The Part of Tens

The 5th Wave   By Rich Tennant

"It's a ten step word processing program. It comes with a spell-checker, grammar-checker, cliche-checker, whine-checker, passive/aggressive-checker, politically correct-checker, hissy-fit-checker, pretentious pontificating-checker, boring anecdote-checker and a Freudian reference-checker."

In this part . . .

How do I love thee? Let me count the ways. Ten! There's so much good stuff in this book and out there in cyberspace that it's hard to stop at ten. Sometimes, I sneak two or three things under one topic to keep the count down.

Okay, these lists have their decorative side, but a lot of work went into distilling this wisdom for you. The "Ten Places to Get Free Help" list (Chapter 20) is especially vital in times of need.

Chapter 18
Ten Cool Desktop Tricks

In This Chapter
- Autohiding your panel and taskbar
- Moving a window to the top of the pile
- Using multiple desktops
- Using sticky windows
- Dancing around with the Desktop Manager
- Iconifying windows
- Going for the max
- Doing the incredible right-click
- Changing your color scheme
- Adopting a whole new theme

*Y*ou can do so many cool things with the Corel Linux desktop, that it's hard to choose the top ten. Some tricks make you more productive; others are just plain fun! In this chapter, I present ten that you've got to try!

Autohiding Your Panel and Taskbar

The panel is a fabulous tool, but it does take up quite a bit of your screen's real estate. Want to have your cake and eat it too? Then autohide your panel to tuck it discreetly out of view. Then, whenever you need it, just point to where the panel is hidden to pop it back into view.

Right-click a blank spot in the panel, choose Configure, and then click the Options tab. Choose the Auto hide panel option to do just that, as shown in Figure 18-1. You can then drag the sliders to adjust the autohide delay (how long it waits before disappearing) and speed (how fast it disappears).

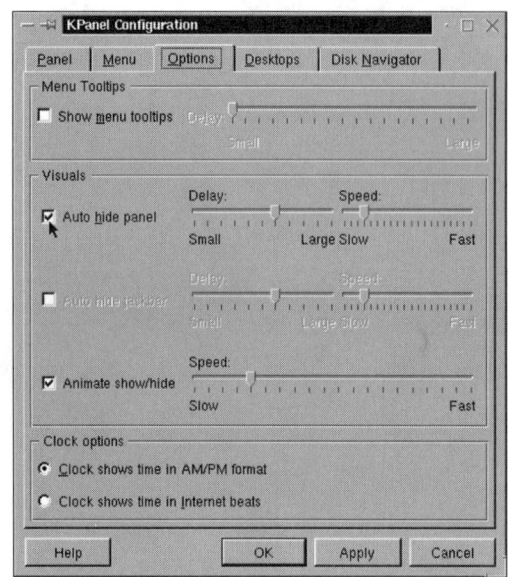

Figure 18-1: My favorite desktop trick is autohiding the panel.

Moving a Window to the Top of the Pile

Suppose that the window you want is buried under a bunch of other windows, with just a little piece sticking out. How can you use it? Easy, just click the little piece, as seen in Figure 18-2, and whoosh! It flies into view.

You'll find a lot more window tricks in Chapter 8.

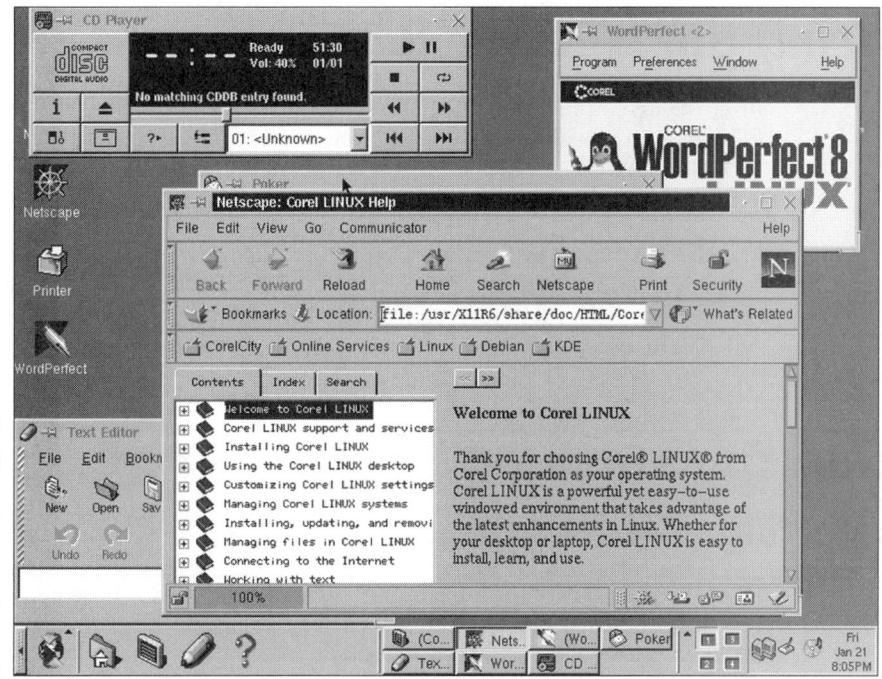

Figure 18-2: Click a piece of any window to move it to the top of the pile.

Using Multiple Desktops

The trick of using multiple desktops is both useful *and* fun, so it isn't even an option. Multiple desktops are a great way to reduce clutter and arrange what you're doing, plus clicking the desktop buttons on the panel to jump from place to place is a blast.

For example, you can tuck your poker game down in the corner on Desktop 4, and then use Desktop 1 for the report you're writing, Desktop 2 for your graphics programs, and Desktop 3 for Internet dial-up, browsing, and e-mail.

Corel Linux gives you four desktops by default, though you can run as many as eight desktops at once. Right-click a blank spot on the panel and choose Configure. Then click the Desktops tab and choose how many desktops you want.

Using Sticky Windows

After the invention of multiple desktops, could sticky windows be far behind? Click that little pushpin at the upper left of any window to stick the window on all your desktops. For example, you might want to make the Text Editor sticky if you're writing something that involves applications in several desktops.

I like to use the sticky (pushpin) button to move a window to another desktop. For example, to move my poker game from Desktop 1 to Desktop 4, I simply click the sticky button, go to Desktop 4, and click the pushpin again to unstick the poker game, so it appears only in Desktop 4.

Dancing around with the Desktop Manager

Click the little button to the left of the desktop buttons on the panel to pop up the graphical Desktop Manager, as seen in Figure 18-3. Now you can drag applications between desktops. Cool!

Figure 18-3: Dragging applications between desktops in Desktop Manager.

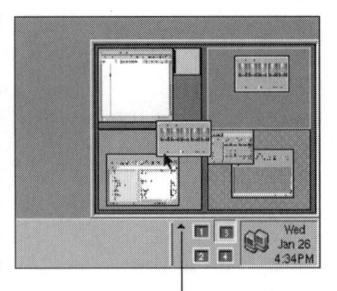

Click here to display Desktop Manager

Iconifying Windows

Even when you're using multiple desktops, they can still get pretty messy. One of the best ways to get rid of window clutter is to iconify the windows you're not using at the moment. This removes the windows from view but leaves their task buttons behind on the panel.

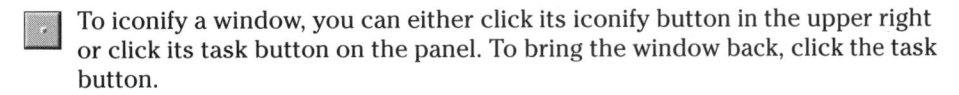

- To iconify a window, you can either click its iconify button in the upper right or click its task button on the panel. To bring the window back, click the task button.

Going for the Max

- For big-time programs such as WordPerfect, you might want to push everything else aside and grab all the screen space you can get. Simple, just click the maximize button (the middle one in the upper right) to plaster your window all over the desktop.

- Notice that when you blow up a window to the max, the maximize button becomes restore. Click the restore button to deflate the window back to its original size.

Doing the Incredible Right-Click

One great thing about a graphical interface is the context-sensitive right-click, which presents you with different options depending on where you are and what you're doing. For example, right-click on the desktop, as in Figure 18-4, to arrange your icons, create a new nickname or desktop folder, or log out of the system.

The incredible right-click works in almost every application. You don't know what to do? Right-click!

Figure 18-4: Doing the incredible right-click.

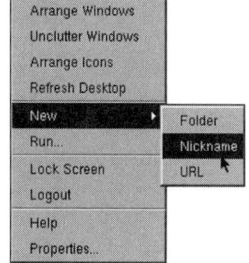

Changing Your Color Scheme

Tired of the same old window colors? You can change the colors of all your window widgets, such as title bars, title text, general background, and window background and text. You can also select coordinated color schemes.

To change your window colors, choose Application Starter ➪ Control Center, double-click Desktop, and then choose Display to open the color settings in Figure 18-5.

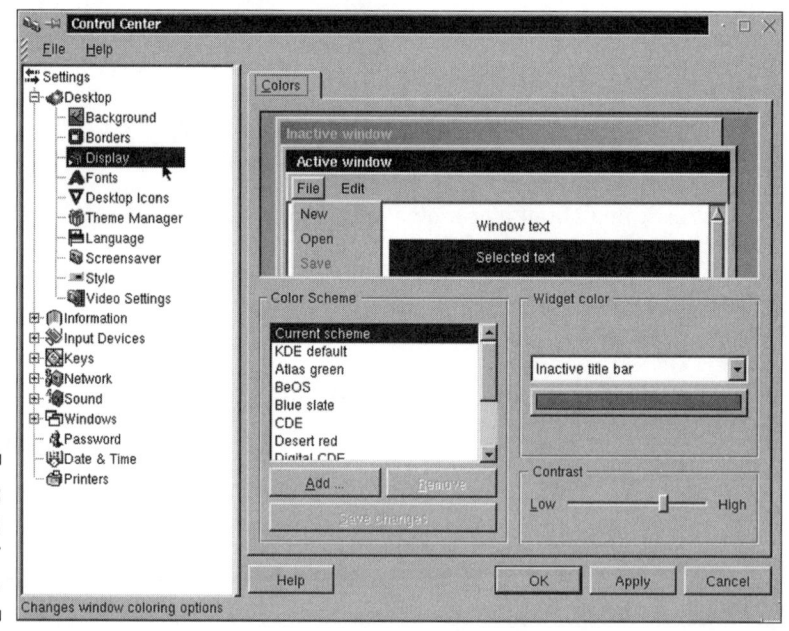

Figure 18-5: Changing your color scheme.

Adopting a New Theme

Changing colors isn't enough? Try adopting a whole new theme! Themes are all-in-one packages with everything from custom colors and wallpapers to borders, icons, sounds, and more. Some theme party outfits are sedate and formal; others are totally wacky and wild!

To adopt a new theme, choose Application Starter ⇨ Control Center. Double-click Desktop and then click Theme Manager. Click on various themes in the list to preview them, as seen in Figure 18-6. Select the one you want and click Apply.

Visit Chapter 10 for lots more on themes.

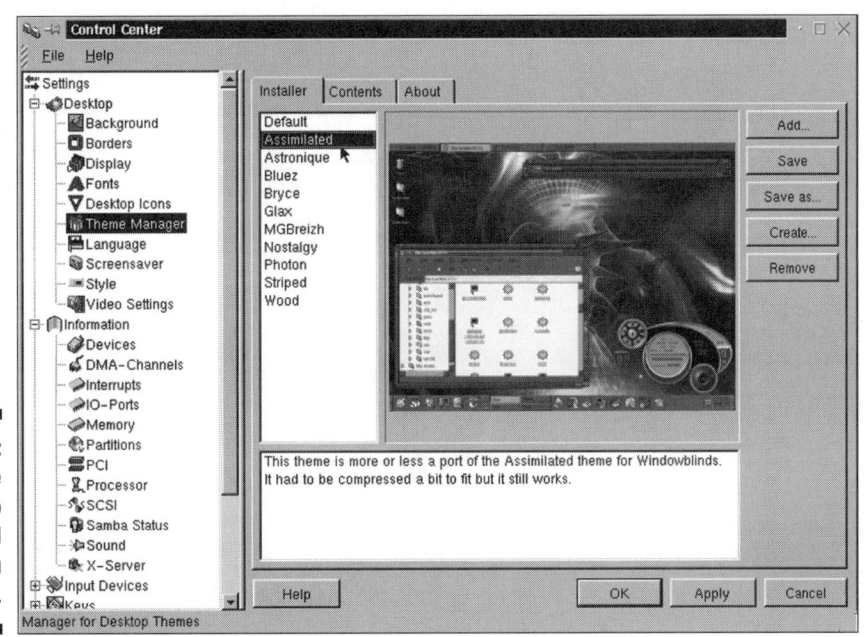

Figure 18-6: Click on the themes to see the wild effects you can apply.

Chapter 19
Ten Things I Circled in the Book

In This Chapter
- Logging in as a regular user
- Changing your boot order
- Creating program shortcuts
- Adding the menu editor to your menus
- Using the find-the-window keyboard trick
- Sounding off
- Putting on the pixels
- Customizing your file manager view
- Moving files with drag-and-drop
- Fishing stuff out of the trash

Do you revere books and hate to dog-ear pages or smear them with marking pens? I understand. This chapter gives you some highlights without dog-earing and smearing.

Logging In as a Regular User

If there's one thing for you to remember, it's to avoid logging in as the root superuser, because this gives you the power to screw up critical system files. Make a habit of logging in under your regular user name instead. When you do need root access to, say, add a new user or install fonts in WordPerfect 8, remember to log out when your root tasks are finished and then log back in under your regular user name.

Often you don't have to log in as root to perform a system task. For example, when using Corel Update as a regular user, the program simply prompts you to enter the root password.

Changing Your Boot Order

Suppose you converted your Windows machine to a dual-boot Linux/Windows system. Normally, you boot up and do all your work, Web browsing, and e-mail in Linux. You only occasionally use Windows programs when there's no close substitute.

But your spouse just hasn't gotten around to changing from the old ways and goes berserk when the machine boots up to Linux. The best way out of trouble, in this case, is to follow the instructions in Chapter 4 to change your Corel Linux Loader (LILO) to boot to Windows by default.

Creating Program Nicknames

Putting program nicknames on your desktop is a great way to launch your favorite applications. For example, if you used Dial-Up a lot, you can put its nickname right on your desktop, so you don't have to hunt in your menus.

Here's the trick for putting a program nickname on your desktop:

1. **Log in as the user for whom you're creating the shortcut.**
2. **Do one of the following:**
    - Open the program for which you're creating the shortcut.
    - Open File Manager and locate the program.
3. **Right-click the title bar of the program's window or the program in the File Manager and then click Create Nickname, as shown in Figure 19-1.**
4. **Type the nickname to appear on the desktop and then specify any command-line options, as shown in Figure 19-2.**

For more on creating nicknames, see Chapter 9.

Chapter 19: Ten Things I Circled in the Book *293*

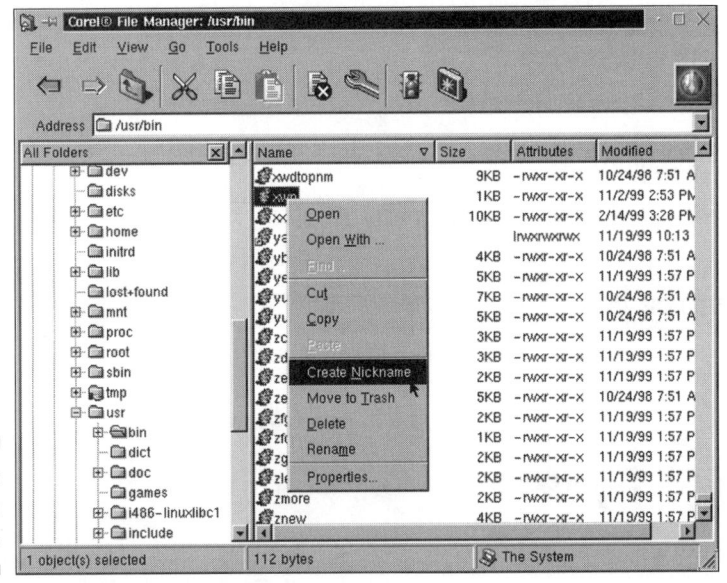

Figure 19-1: Creating a nickname.

Figure 19-2: Enter the nickname to appear on the desktop and specify any command-line options.

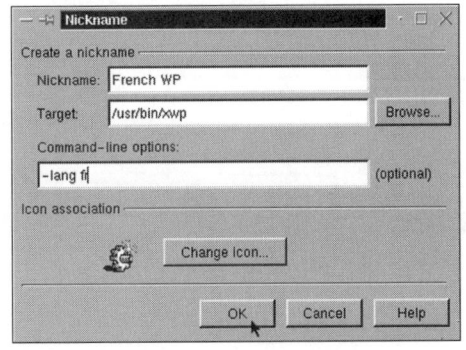

Adding Programs to Your Menus

The best way to spot various program birds in the application forest is to perch them neatly on the branches of your menu tree — ducks here, wrens over there, with a crow or two on top. Here, in a nutshell, is a real easy way to add a program bird, though you have to be logged in as root to do it:

1. **Right-click a submenu, and then choose New ⇨ Nickname.**
2. **Fill in the name.**
3. **Click Browse, select the program, and then click OK.**
4. **If you want to select the program's icon or a close substitute, click Change icon.**
5. **Click OK to add the menu selection.**

Adding a submenu folder is even easier. You'll find this and other menu-editing tricks in Chapter 9.

Using the Find-the-Window Keyboard Trick

You'll find lots of keyboard tricks in Chapter 5, but here's one I especially like. When you lose sight of the window you need, hold down the Alt key and press Tab till you find the window you want, as shown in Figure 19-3. Then let go, and up pops your window!

Figure 19-3: Hold down Alt and press Tab until you come to the window you want.

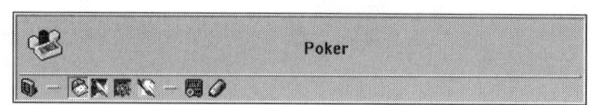

Another trick is to press Ctrl+Esc to display a scrollable list of all the windows on all your desktops.

Sounding Off

If you want to hear what you're doing, try adding a little noise to your computing life:

1. **Choose Application Starter ➪ Control Center, double-click Sound, and then choose System Sounds.**
2. **Choose the enable system sounds option.**
3. **Select an event to which you want to apply a sound, select an associated sound, and then click Apply, as shown in Figure 19-4.**
4. **Repeat Step 3 for additional event/sound associations.**

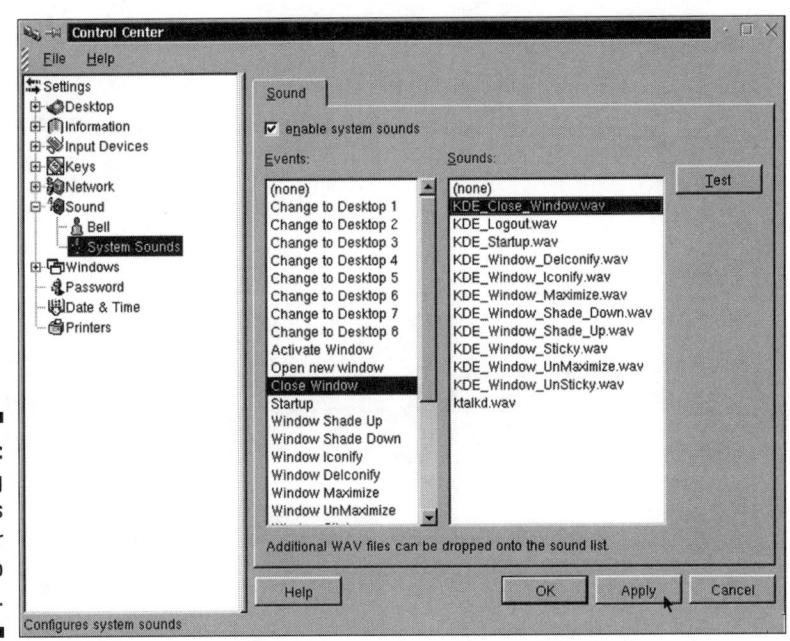

Figure 19-4: Associating sounds with your desktop happenings.

Putting on the Pixels

Perhaps no other setting affects your visual comfort more than the screen resolution you employ. Depending on your graphics card, you can adjust your screen resolution anywhere from the minimal 640 x 480 screen pixels to the 1280 x 1024 pixels (shown in Figure 19-5) or higher.

Chapter 10 gives you step-by-step instructions for changing your screen resolution.

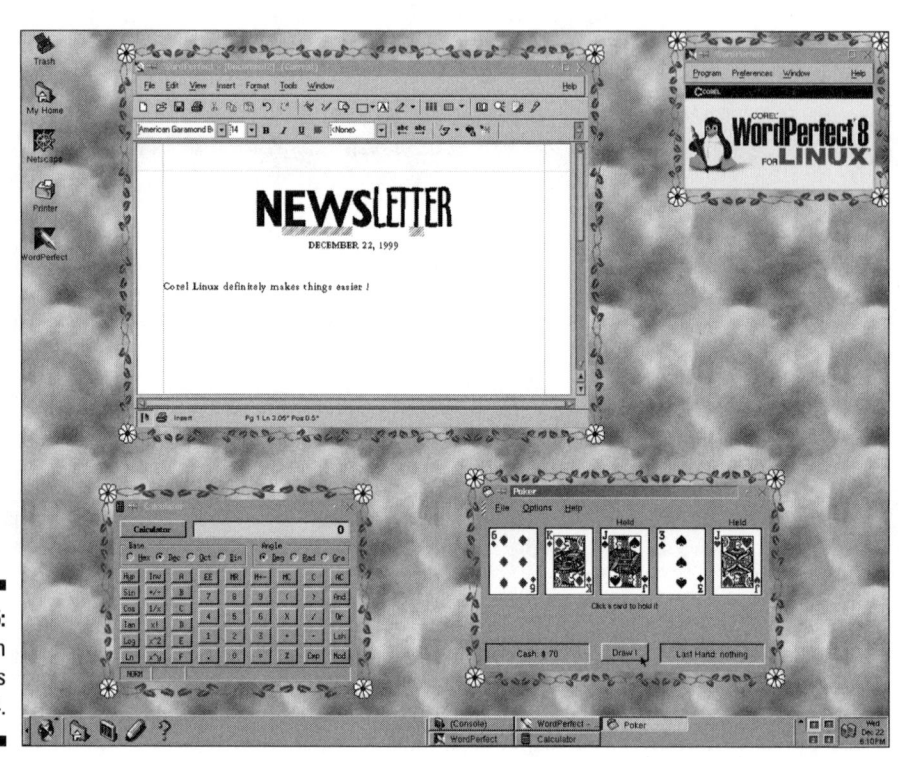

Figure 19-5: This screen resolution is 1280 x 1024.

Chapter 19: Ten Things I Circled in the Book 297

Customizing Your File Manager View

When you're in File Manager, click the View menu to alternately display (with a check mark) or hide various File Manager elements and types of files, as shown in Figure 19-6.

Figure 19-6: Alternately display or hide various File Manager elements and types of files.

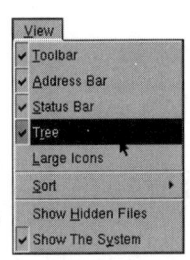

Two important file viewing options are to show hidden files and to show the system, not just your personal folders and files. Figure 19-7 shows what File Manager looks like when you remove the system from view but reveal the hidden files. See Chapter 11 for more File Manager details.

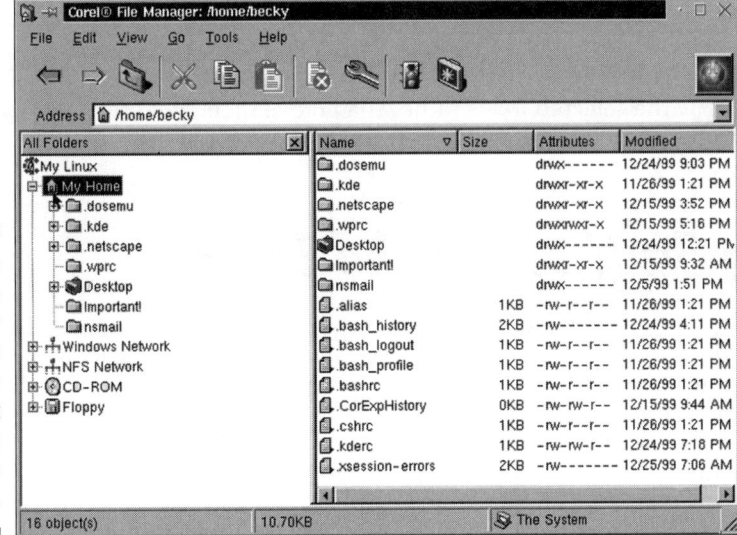

Figure 19-7: File Manager with the system hidden but the hidden files revealed.

Moving Files with Drag and Drop

Another great File Manager trick is to move files with drag and drop. Select the files and folders with your mouse, drag them to the new location, and then drop them into place, as shown in Figure 19-8. (This procedure normally removes the files from the original location. This is not the case, however, in the initial release of Corel Linux, so the files are copied instead.)

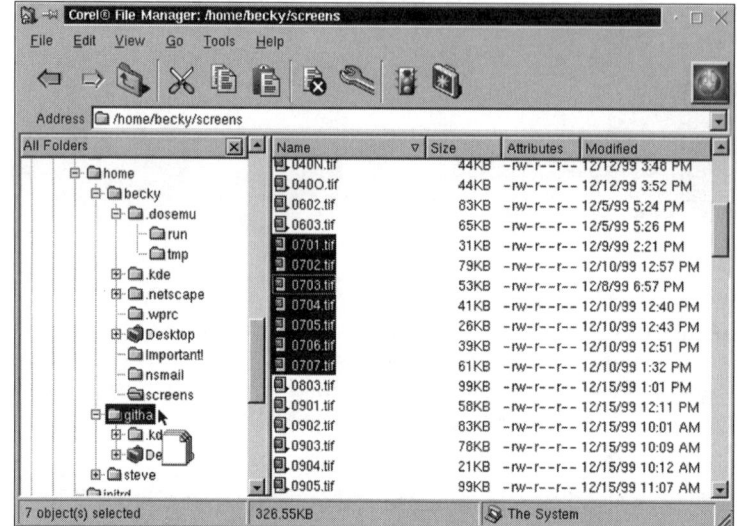

Figure 19-8: To move selected files, drag and drop.

To copy the selected items rather than move them, hold the Ctrl key as you drop them into place. See Chapter 11 for more details.

Fishing Stuff out of the Trash

Have you ever dropped stuff in the trash, only to go back later to fish it out? No need to be embarrassed. Anyway, you can do the same with files you've trashed. Click the Trash icon on your desktop and then select the files or folders you want to retrieve. Choose File ⇨ Restore, or right-click and choose Restore, as shown in Figure 19-9. This sends the files or folders back from whence they came.

TIP

When you're sure there's nothing worthwhile in the trash, right-click the Trash icon to empty the trash can. You'll find more trash tips in Chapter 11.

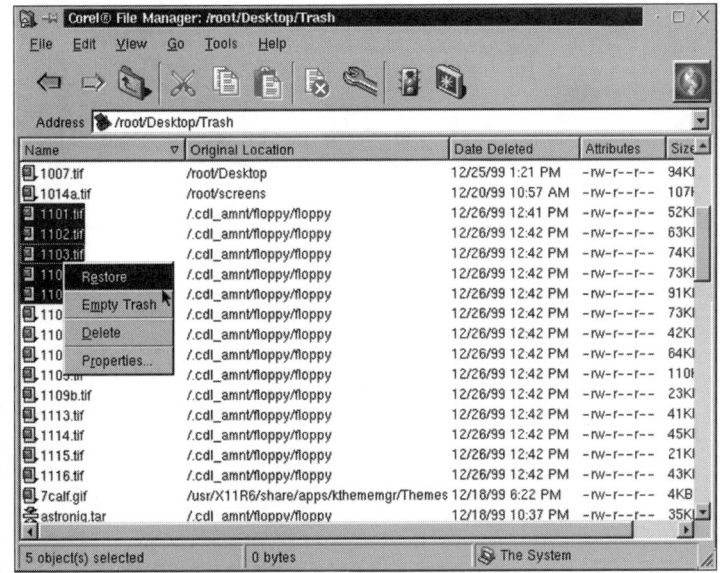

Figure 19-9: Fishing stuff out of the trash.

Chapter 20
Ten Places to Get Free Help

In This Chapter

- Starting from the Corel Community site
- Searching Corel's support knowledge base
- Joining the local Linux user group
- Finding KDE support and documentation
- Getting help at Linux Online
- Looking through the Linux Documentation Project
- Connecting with the Debian support site
- Joining other Linux newsgroups
- Visiting IDG's LinuxWorld
- Browsing online and print magazines

I know you'll find this hard to believe, but not everything about Corel Linux is expounded in this book! In fact, I'm coming out with a weightier tome, the *Corel Linux Bible* (published by IDG Books Worldwide, Inc.), that includes coverage of some advanced features and heavier topics. And for those readers using WordPerfect 8 for Linux, it's hard to resist putting in a plug for *WordPerfect for Linux Bible* (also published by IDG), with its comprehensive coverage of this landmark program.

Aside from our books and the online help mentioned in Chapter 5, where else can you go to solve problems with Corel Linux or pick up clever tips? If you bought a retail package, you get 30 days of installation technical support. What happens if you didn't buy a package or your 30 days are up? Do you have to pay through the nose the minute a problem pops up?

An emphatic no! An immense assemblage of free, community-based help — plus tons of information on all aspects of Linux — is out there.

Subscribe to Support Newsgroups

For the most fabulous and caring support, start your newsreader, add the cnews.corel.ca server to your news reader, and then subscribe to the free Corel Linux support groups on installation, networking, and so on. (See how to do this in Chapter 16.) The corelsupport.linux.corellinux group is the centerpiece of the Corel Linux support groups, with hundreds of messages posted every day.

No matter what your question — from the most basic to the most obscure — you'll get friendly advice from Corel's C_Tech volunteers and other users with similar experiences. More often than not, you'll get two or three alternate solutions!

REMEMBER

We authors love getting e-mail from readers, but we can't handle technical queries. Even if we could, the newsgroups would still be a better bet because you'll find experts there in every imaginable specialized issue.

Start from the Corel Community Web Site

Try the Web site of the Corel Linux community at http://linux.corel.com. This site directs you to important information and support sources, including the growing FAQs (Frequently Asked Questions) list, as shown in Figure 20-1. Click the Technical Support link and then click the Complementary support link to get there.

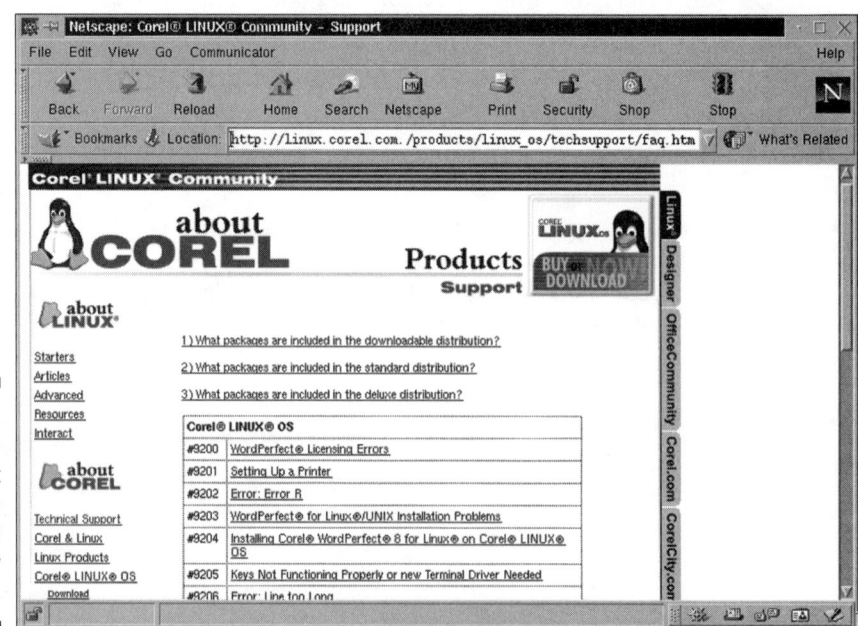

Figure 20-1: Access the FAQ list from the Corel Community site.

Search Corel's Knowledge Base

Corel's technicians pool their knowledge in a searchable knowledge base at http://search.corel.com/kbsearch/. If others have encountered your problem, you're likely to find step-by-step instructions on getting it resolved.

Join Your Local Linux User Group

Linux user groups are sprouting up faster than dandelions. Go to http://www.linux.com/lug/ to locate and join a group near you. You'll even find special interest groups devoted to particular Linux topics.

Find KDE Support and Documentation

Because KDE has a prominent place in Corel Linux OS, the KDE Frequently Asked Questions at http://www.kde.org/documentation/faq/kdefaq.html can be quite helpful to users of Corel Linux as well.

Get Help at Linux Online

Linux Online was one of the first sites focusing on the Linux OS. The Linux Online Help Center, at http://www.linux.org/help/index.html, provides FAQ's, HOWTOs, manuals, and lots of other information, as seen in Figure 20-2.

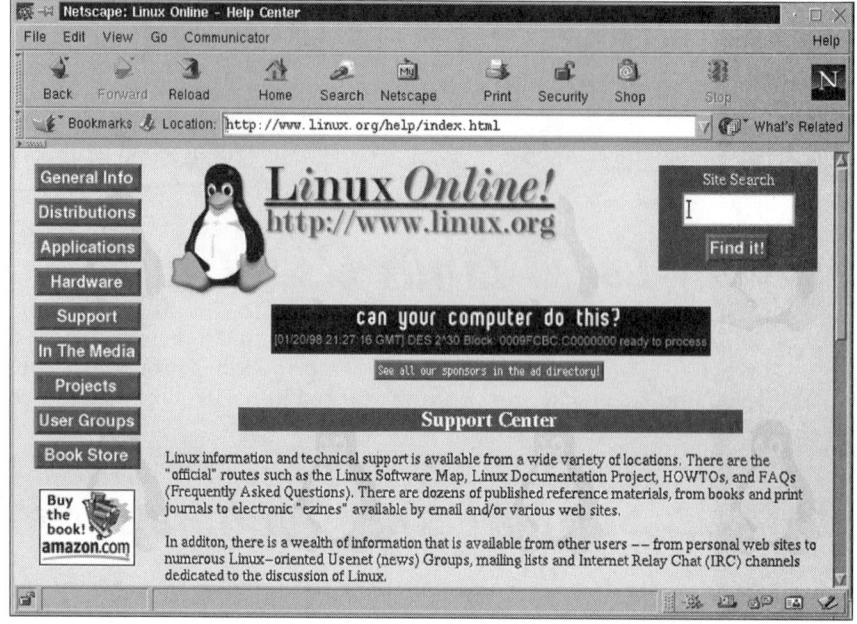

Figure 20-2:
Go to Linux Online for FAQ's, HOWTOs, manuals, and more.

Look through the Linux Documentation Project

The Linux Documentation Project, at http://metalab.unc.edu/mdw/ and shown in Figure 20-3, is dedicated to provide you with free, high-quality documentation for the GNU/Linux operating system.

Browse through the HOWTOs and Linux guides to find assistance with your problem or project. For example, you'll fine the basic System Administrator's Guide, as shown in Figure 20-4.

Chapter 20: Ten Places to Get Free Help *305*

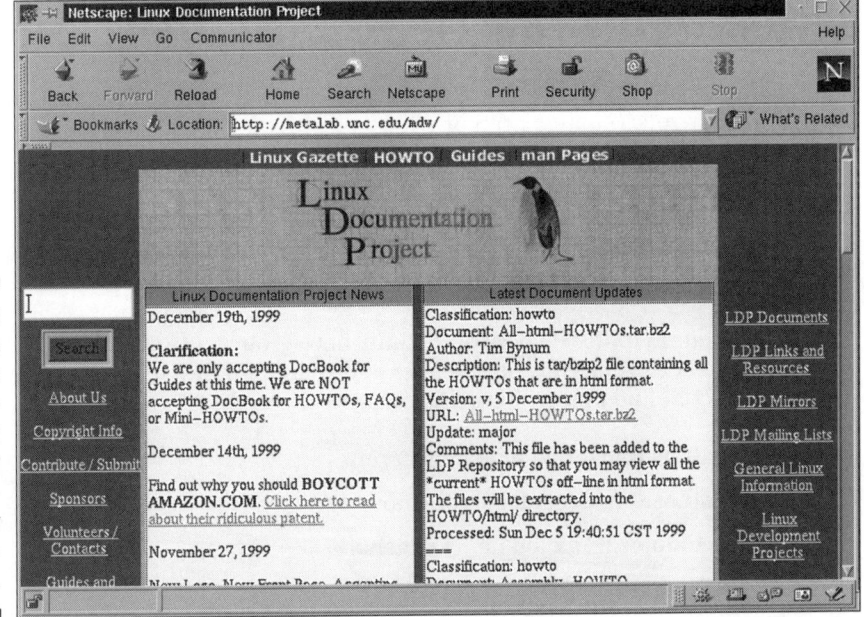

Figure 20-3: Go to the Linux Documentation Project for free, high-quality documentation.

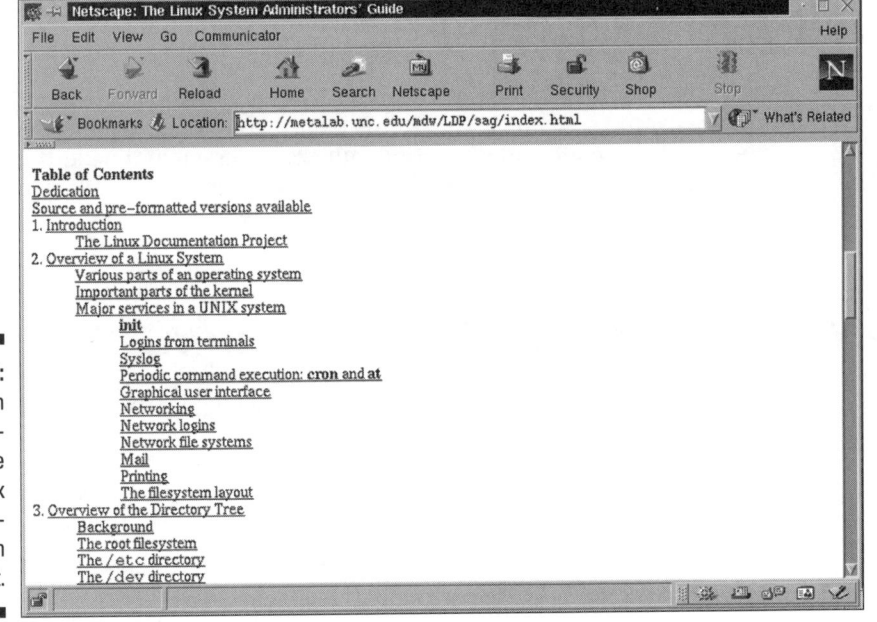

Figure 20-4: System Administrator's Guide at the Linux Documentation Project.

Connect with the Debian Support Site

Corel Linux OS is based on Debian, so the Debian Support site at http://www.debian.org/support can provide you with details on what's under the hood. Go here for interesting clues rather than detailed instructions.

Join Other Linux Newsgroups

In addition to Corel-sponsored Linux newsgroups, others might be of interest. Connect to your ISP's newsreader and search for newsgroups on Linux. Expect to find plenty! Here are four you might like:

- **alt.os.linux**, on Linux in general
- **alt.os.linux.corel**, on you-know-who
- **comp.os.linux**, on Linux in general
- **linux.debian**, on Debian Linux

Visit IDG's LinuxWorld

Walk, bike, fly, drive, train, or swim to IDG's LinuxWorld exposition and conferences at http://www.linuxworldexpo.com/. Meet technicians, check out the latest vendor offerings, and immerse yourself in the Linux culture. Win prizes, buy books, and pick up all kinds of goodies. Hear keynotes by Linux leaders and join the excitement. (Some pretty good parties too!)

Browse Online and Print Magazines

A sure sign of our times is to see several interesting Linux magazines emerge:

- *Linux Today*, at http://linuxtoday.com/index.html, is the place to go to see what's happening. They gather news from many sources, so the articles are a mixed bag in terms of journalistic quality.
- *Linux Magazine* provides excellent background articles and interviews, covering both the business and technical sides of Linux for all levels of users. Check their Web site at http://www.linux-mag.com/ for back issues and subscriptions.

- *Linux Journal*, at `http://www2.linuxjournal.com/`, is another good source of general Linux information.
- *Linux Gazette*, at `http://www.linuxgazette.com/`, is an online publication dedicated to "making Linux just a little more fun and sharing ideas and discoveries."
- *Slashdot* (`http://slashdot.org/`) is a major geek watering hole. It advertises itself as "News for Nerds. Stuff that matters."

You'll also be hearing more and more about Linux on radio, TV, the general press, and around the water cooler, just like Windows is discussed today!

Chapter 21
Ten Places to Get Free Stuff

In This Chapter
- Getting free system updates
- Satisfying your theme hunger
- Getting free updates to Corel's applications
- Setting up a hard drive on the Web
- Subscribing to free e-mail
- Getting fresh apps at Freshmeat
- Finding everything cool at Tucows Linux
- Looking around at Linux Online
- Cruising Cnet for Corel Linux and more
- Installing Corel Linux from this book's CD

*Y*ou don't have to be rich to enjoy the riches of Linux. You get Corel Linux for nothing when you buy this book, plus you'll find a fabulous array of free stuff at the places noted in this chapter.

Getting Free System Updates

Use Corel Update to get free system updates and tons of Debian application packages, as seen in Figure 21-1. Be sure to check out the custom paths to the Debian FTP sites. See Chapter 17 for more on using Corel Update.

Satisfying Your Theme Hunger

Nothing can be more fun than playing with the desktop themes — those all-in-one packages with everything from custom colors and wallpapers to borders, icons, sounds, and more. Some themes are sedate and formal; others are totally wacky and wild!

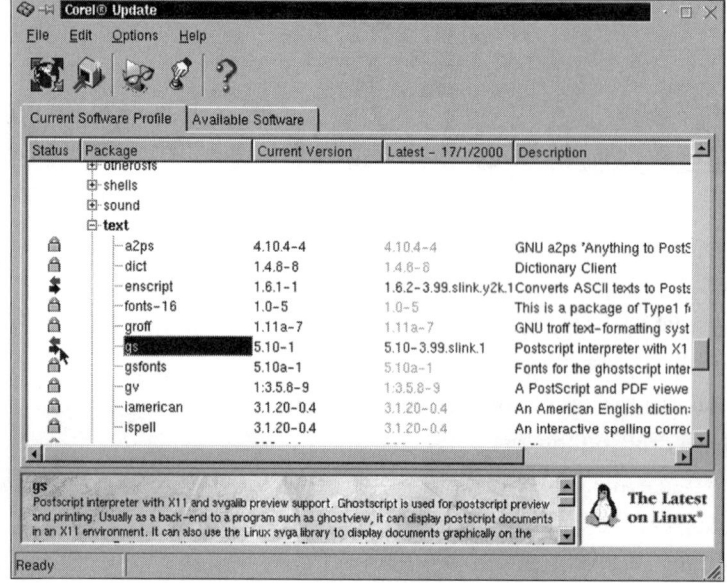

Figure 21-1: Using Corel Update to get free system updates and Debian application packages.

After seeing some of the stupendous effects of some of the themes, you're bound to be hungry for more. To satisfy your visual appetites, head on over to the Web site at kde.themes.org, as shown in Figure 21-2. You can download themes to your heart's content and then add them to your list.

For more on using themes, check out Chapter 10.

Getting Free Updates to Corel's Apps

Corel's FTP site at ftp://ftp.corel.com/ is a valuable source of free stuff. It's the place to look for updates to all Corel office and graphics applications.

Setting Up a Hard Drive on the Web

Use Corel's free vDrive, as shown in Figure 21-3, to create your own virtual hard drive on the Web and then upload and download files to and from anywhere. You won't need a portable PC to take stuff on the road! Great for backups too!

Choose Application Starter ➪ Online Services ➪ Corel vDrive to sign up for your free disk space. Check out Chapter 15 for more Corel online services.

Chapter 21: Ten Places to Get Free Stuff *311*

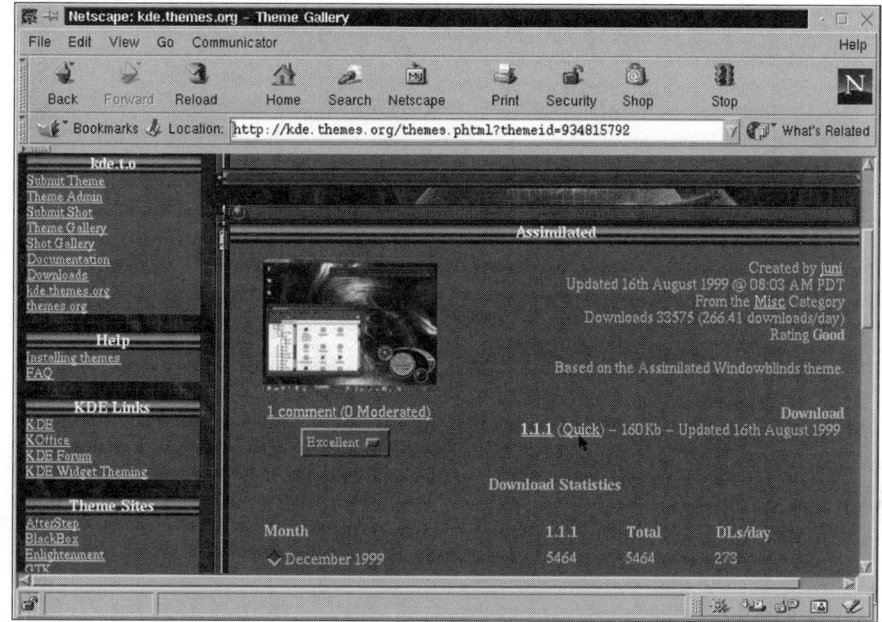

Figure 21-2: Satisfying your theme hunger.

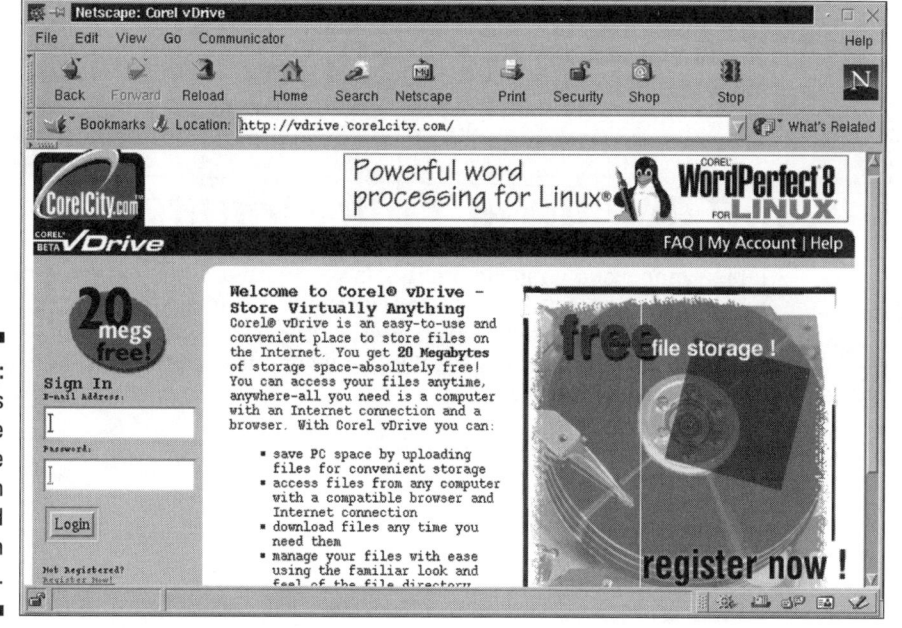

Figure 21-3: Go to Corel's vDrive site to create your own virtual hard drive on the Web.

Subscribing to Free E-Mail

You can set up an online e-mail account to keep the love letters (and business correspondence) flowing while you're on the road. As long as you have Internet access, you'll never be out of touch.

Choose Application Starter ⇨ Online Services ⇨ Email to set up your free online e-mail account, with 3MB of free online storage space for your letters.

Getting Fresh Apps at Freshmeat

Freshmeat at http://www.freshmeat.net/ started back in 1997 as one of the first sources for Linux applications. It still is one of the best places to search for unknown Linux gems.

Finding Everything Cool at Tucows Linux

Tucows Linux, seen in Figure 21-4, is another Linux pioneer that can be reached at http://linux.tucows.com/. It is just as good as its Tucows sibling for Windows software. Looking for some Linux applications? You'll definitely find them here.

Looking around at Linux Online

Linux Online, shown in Figure 21-5, is yet another Linux pioneer that can be reached at http://www.linux.org/apps/. Besides applications, tools, and utilities, you'll find links to Web sites, support, reviews, and other useful information. Looking for something you can't find on their list? Check out their Linux Software Map.

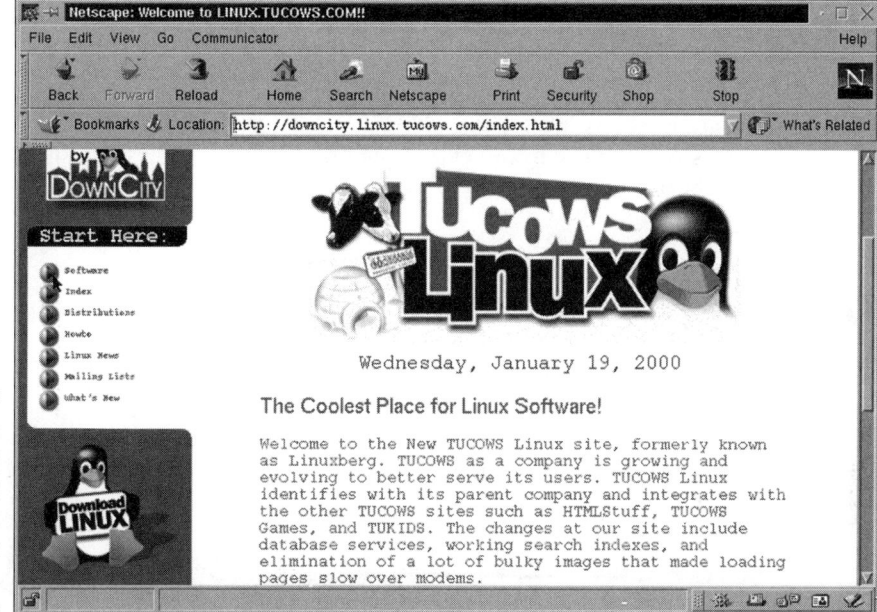

Figure 21-4: Finding everything cool at Tucows Linux.

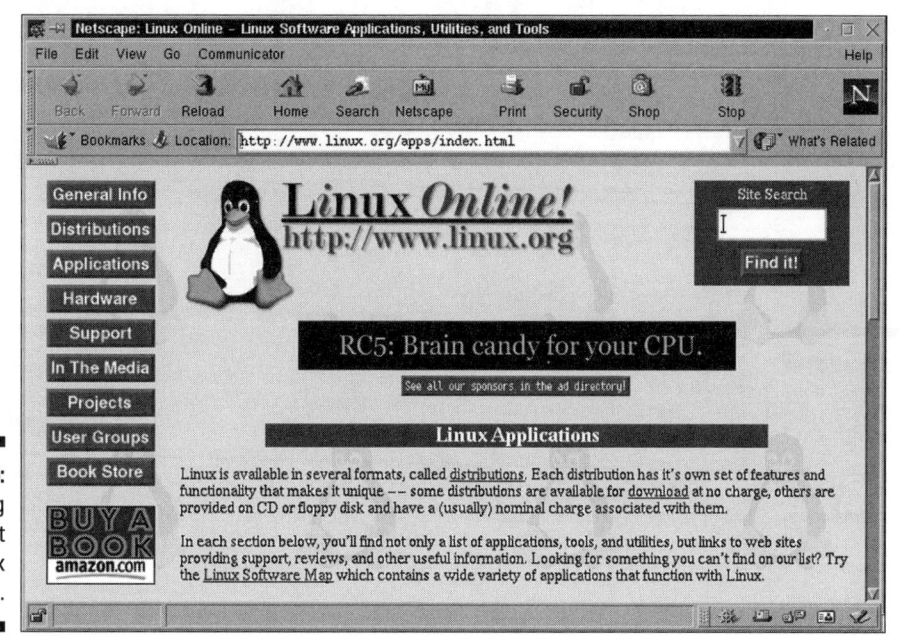

Figure 21-5: Looking around at Linux Online.

Cruising CNET for Corel Linux and More

Probably more folks get Linux from the CNET download site (http://download.cnet.com/downloads/) than anyplace else. They have a lot to offer, and as you can see from Figure 21-6, Corel Linux is their biggest draw and WordPerfect for Linux is number 2!

Installing Corel Linux from This Book's CD

When it comes to free stuff, what could be better than your *Corel Linux For Dummies* CD, with Corel Linux ready to go! See Chapter 2 for installation instructions.

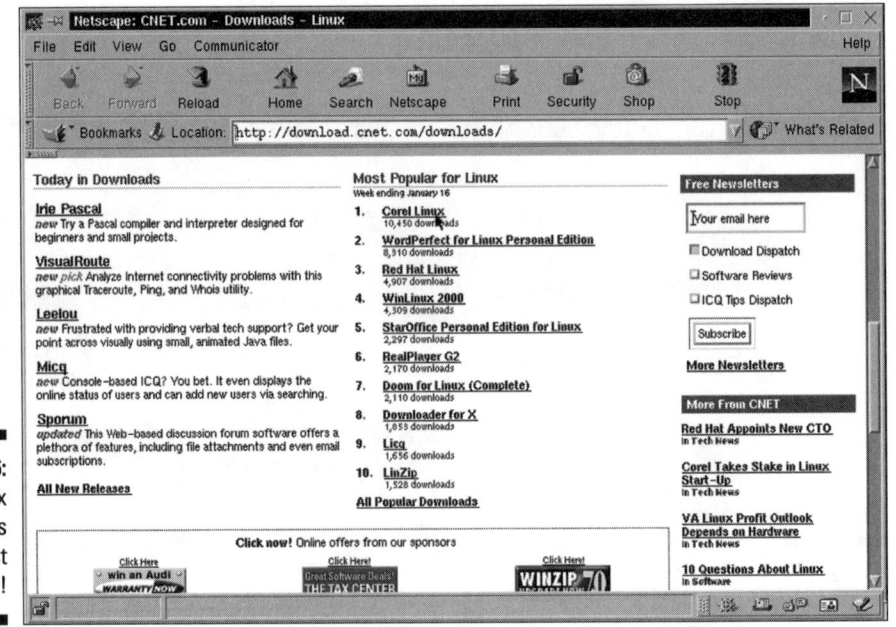

Figure 21-6: Corel Linux is CNET's biggest draw!

Part VI
Appendixes

The 5th Wave   By Rich Tennant

"I couldn't get this 'job skills' program to work on my PC, so I replaced the motherboard, upgraded the BIOS, and wrote a program that links it to my personal database. It told me I wasn't technically inclined and should pursue a career in sales."

In this part . . .

When I was a kid, we had used-car dealers — now these guys are selling not used cars but preowned automobiles, as though they've improved with age by bashing into telephone poles or by grinding piston rings and bearings to dust. They spray that new-car-plastic smell like it was the refined bouquet of a vintage wine.

Well, here are some preowned appendixes that are honestly better for it. You get some true-to-life chronicles in using Linux commands, and I used the glossary in writing this book — honing the definitions as I went. Nothing preowned about the CD, of course — it has spanking new software on a shiny disk.

Appendix A
Commands to the Rescue!

Hey, didn't you tell me that Corel Linux offers a graphical user interface? Why should I use Linux commands? You're right: Corel Linux will probably run in graphical mode all the time. But accidents can happen. What if your graphics fail and Corel Linux boots into command mode? You can

- Wipe out your system and start all over again.
- Try to rescue your files and your configuration.

If Corel Linux starts in command mode, rescuing your files is easy. And with a little outside advice, you might be able to restore your system just by editing a configuration file.

Command Anatomy 101

After you get to know the Linux commands, you'll find that they're nothing to be afraid of. In fact, consider them your friends, waiting to do what they can for you.

Commands can have up to three components:

- The **command** itself, such as ls, cd, or cp
- **Variable information** that you plug into the command, such as a directory name and a path
- **Options** (arguments) that expand or alter what the command does for you

For example, the command

```
ls /home/erwin/work -l
```

lists the files in the /home/erwin/work directory and displays their file size and permissions.

The basic rules for entering commands are simple:

- You must type the command first.
- You may use multiple options at one time, in any order.
- You must separate items in the command line by spaces or tabs.

Each command is normally entered in a single command line. If a command is too long for a single line, press the backslash key (\), followed by the rest of the command. If you want to enter multiple commands in a single line, separate each with a semicolon (;).

Essential Linux Commands

I know it ain't gonna happen to you, but just suppose your graphics go belly-up and you find yourself staring at the Linux command prompt. What to do? For starters, you can type the **ls** command to list files in the current directory.

TIP: In command mode, folders go by their old name of *directories* because you no longer get those cute folder icons to click.

Now suppose that you want to back up some files before you get started. Which commands do you need? How about these:

- The **ls** command to list files in the current directory
- The **cd** command to navigate through directories
- The **cp** command to copy files

These three Linux commands can rescue your files! Suppose that all your Linux data files are in /home/<erwin>/data. You would type this to go to your data directory:

```
cd /home/<erwin>/data
```

Then you'd type the following to make sure all the files are there:

```
ls
```

Finally, you'd type the following to copy all the data files to your data directory in your Windows partition (or copy to a floppy disk, as described later in this chapter, if you don't have or can't access your Windows partition):

```
cp *.* /disks/c/data
```

Sometimes, however, you need more than three commands to get out of a particular scrape. Table A-1 lists the essential ones.

Appendix A: Commands to the Rescue!

Table A-1 — **Essential Linux Commands**

Command	Examples	Results
`ls <file names/directories> <options>`	`ls -l /usr/local`	Lists all files in /usr/local
	`ls *.wpd`	Lists .wpd files in the current directory
	`ls -F /usr/local/data`	Displays the file type
	`ls -lF`	Displays the file size and permissions
`cd <directory>`	`cd /usr/local`	Goes to the /usr/local directory
	`cd ../local/data`	Goes to the parent of /local/data
	`cd ..`	Goes to the parent of the current directory
`cp <options> <file names> <destination> <R>`	`cp *.wpd /usr/local/data`	Copies all files with the wpd extension from the current directory to the /user/local/data directory
	`cp /data/*.* /disks/c/temp`	Copies all files in the data directory to the disks/c/temp directory
	`cp /root/Desktop/X11R6 /usr/X11R6 -R`	Recursively copies all files and subdirectories from /root/Desktop/X11R6 to /usr/X11R6
`mv <file names> <destination>`	`mv *.wpd /usr/local/data`	Moves all files with the wpd extension from the current directory to the /user/local/data directory

(continued)

Table A-1 *(continued)*

Command	Examples	Results
	`mv letter.wpd letter1.wpd`	Renames the letter.wpd file to letter1.wpd
`rm <file names> <options>`	`rm *.*`	Deletes all files from the current directory
	`rm -i /usr/local/*.wpd`	Deletes all files with the wpd extension in the /usr/local directory, but asks for confirmation first
`mkdir <directory>`	`mkdir /usr/local/backup`	Creates the /user/local/backup directory
	`mkdir data`	Creates the data subdirectory in the current directory
`rmdir <directory>`	`rmdir data`	Deletes the data directory located in the current directory
	`rmdir /usr/local/backup`	Deletes the /usr/local/backup directory Note: The directory to be deleted should be empty
`pwd`	`pwd`	Displays the current directory
`cat <file name>`	`cat lilo.conf`	Displays the lilo configuration file, all at once
	`cat /usr/local/config.txt`	Displays the config.txt file in the user/local directory all at once

Command	Examples	Results
`more <file name>`	`more lilo.conf`	Displays the lilo configuration file, one page at a time
	`more /usr/local/config.txt`	Displays the config.txt file in the user/local directory, one page at a time"
`lpr <file name <Pprinter> <#number of copies>`	`lpr --Plp notes.txt`	Prints notes.txt to the lp printer
	`lpr -Plp -#4 meeting.txt`	Prints four copies of meeting.txt
`find -name <pattern>`	`find -name *.wpd`	Finds all files with the wpd extension in the current directory and its subdirectories
	`find -name Letter*.txt`	Finds all file names starting with Letter that have the txt extension
`grep <options> <pattern> <file names>`	`grep -l "Zijleman" *.txt`	Displays the names of all files with a .txt extension that contain Zijleman

Revealing a Command's Secret Powers

Table A-1 shows only some of the options for various commands. To get a quick listing of all options for a particular command, type

```
command --help
```

where you replace *command* with the command you're interested in. To get an in-depth description of the variables and options for a command, type

```
man command
```

This displays the manual pages for the specific command. To show only one page of information at a time, use the -P option:

```
man -P command
```

Rescue Missions

A few real-life examples will illustrate how some simple commands can get you out of major difficulties.

Where did my letters go?

Suppose that you sit down to begin work but Corel Linux starts only in command mode. You don't want to waste time and energy trying to fix things, so you decide to reinstall Corel Linux. However, you want to rescue some letters first. You know that their names all started with *Letter* but you don't remember exactly where you stored them. You also know that you stored important addresses in a text file in the same directory.

You need to do the following:

- Find your letters
- Find your addresses
- Copy your files to a safe place (a folder in the Windows partition or a floppy disk)

At first, without your nice graphical desktop and familiar File Manager, you might feel like you're alone in the wilderness. But as soon as you see how easy it is to find your letters, you'll start to realize that command mode is nothing to be afraid of. To find your files:

1. **Type** cd / **to go to the root level.**
2. **Type** find -name Letter*.wpd **to find your files.**

   Linux searches for the files and displays the names of the files found (including the path:

   ```
   /home/elmz/data/Letter2000_01.wpd
   /home/elmz/data/Letter2000_02.wpd
   /home/elmz/data/Letter2000_03.wpd
   /home/elmz/data/Letter2000_04.wpd
   /home/elmz/data/Letter2000_05.wpd
   ```

Appendix A: Commands to the Rescue! 323

3. **Type** cd /home/elmz/data **to go to the directory where Corel Linux found your letters.**

4. **Find your addresses by searching for a specific string, such as by a name in your addresses list.**

    For instance, if you type

    ```
    grep -l "Zijleman" *.txt
    ```

    Corel Linux displays the name of the file(s) found, such as

    ```
    important.txt
    ```

Now that you've found the files, it's time to copy them to a safe place. You have a choice of copying the files to your Windows partition or to a floppy disk.

To copy the files to your Windows partition, type

```
cp /home/elmz/data/Letter*.wpd /disks/c/data
cp /home/elmz//data/important.txt /disks/c/data
```

If you instead want to copy the files to a floppy disk, you must mount the floppy drive first:

```
mount -t msdos /dev/fd0 /mnt/floppy
```

Then you type

```
cp /home/elmz/data/Letter*.wpd /mnt/floppy
```

That wasn't too hard, was it?

Moving some system files

Here's a real-life example of using command mode that I encountered while writing this book. In demonstrating how you can create a desktop link to your files, I accidentally *copied* my X11R6 graphical system files to the desktop instead of linking to them! My Corel Linux graphical lights immediately went out as I was unceremoniously kicked into black-screened command mode.

The tragedy of moved system files can happen only when you're logged in as root.

After my initial panic, I thought "Wait. This isn't the Windows Blue Screen of Death. I'm still in Linux!" I could use Linux commands to see where my files had gone and then copy them to their original location. Here's how I did it:

1. In command mode, I typed **root** and pressed Enter to log back in as root.

2. I typed my root password. (The password doesn't appear as you type it.)

3. I typed **cd /root/Desktop** to tiptoe over to root's desktop directory.

4. I typed **ls** to see what was on my desktop. (Every icon you place on your desktop has an entry in your Desktop directory.) I saw a bunch of icons, a few folders and files, and sure enough, X11R6!

5. Next, I typed **ls /X11R6** and saw that all my subdirectories were there too.

6. Just to confirm what had happened, I typed **ls /usr**, and saw that X11R6 was no longer in its proper place, in the /usr directory.

7. I typed **cp /root/Desktop/X11R6 /usr/X11R6 -R** to copy everything back from whence it came.

   Note the -R option. That's to *recursively* copy everything in the directory plus all the subdirectories. (Without the -R option, only the directory would have been copied, without its subdirectories.) And note I used an uppercase *R* — options are case sensitive, so -r (reverse, in this case) and -R are different options.

8. When my hard drive stopped making its reassuring whirring and clicking noises, I typed **ls /X11R6** again. Sure enough, the directory and its subdirectories were back where they belonged!

9. I typed **shutdown now -r** and my system restarted in graphical mode!

Editing Configuration Files

Well, rescuing your files wasn't that hard using Linux commands. Now suppose that you have to only edit a few configuration files to get your system back to work. You probably think this will be a snap — just start the editor and make the necessary changes. Unfortunately it's not that easy. You can't use the familiar Text Editor to edit your configuration files. Instead, you have to use a command-line editor such as vi.

Although vi is not the easiest editor to use, most experienced Linux users can't live without it. And after you know how it works, you too might find it fast and powerful. Most Linux distributions offer more than one text editor (such as Emacs or Joe) but vi is the only editor you will always find on any Linux (or UNIX) system.

Appendix A: Commands to the Rescue!

The most confusing thing about vi is that it has three modes of operation:

- Command mode
- Insert mode
- Last-line mode

When you start vi, it's in command mode, which means you have to use commands to edit files and to change to other modes. For example, if you type **x,** you won't see an *x* appear in your file. Instead, vi deletes the character underneath the cursor.

If you want to add or edit existing text, you have to switch to insert mode first. Type **i** from command mode to switch to insert mode. In insert mode, vi more or less works like the editor you're accustomed to. Just don't press the Esc key because you'll be returned to command mode.

Last-line mode is a type of command mode as well but is used for complex vi commands. To switch to last-line mode, you type **:** in command mode. In last-line mode, every command you type is executed after you press Enter. For instance, to save the current file and end your vi session, you would type **wq** and press Enter.

This sounds more complex than it is. Maybe you should just give vi a try:

1. **To start vi, type** vi *filename*.

   For instance, if you type **vi first_try.txt**, you open a new file called first_try.txt in vi, as shown in Figure A-1. Not much to see yet. Maybe you should add some text.

   Don't start typing yet. Remember, you're still in command mode.

2. **Type** i **to switch to insert mode.**

3. **Add text to your file.**

   You can type as many lines of text as you want. Simply press the Enter key to move to the next line.

   Don't try to use the arrow keys to navigate through the text — they won't work, unless you switch to command mode (by pressing Escape) first.

This isn't that hard, is it? Well, vi wouldn't be vi if things weren't a little more complex. Forget about one insert mode — vi has a few. Type

- **i** to insert text at the cursor position
- **a** to insert text after the cursor position
- **o** to begin a new line in insert mode

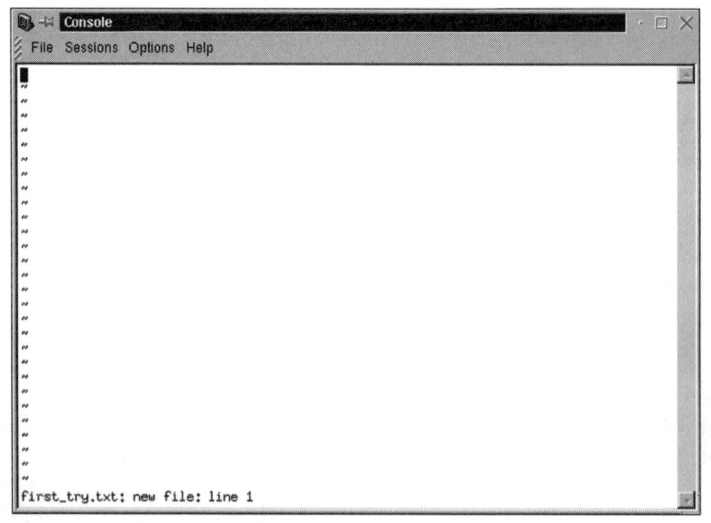

Figure A-1: Opening a new file in vi.

You've added text but how do you delete or edit text? In command mode, type

- **x** to delete the character under the cursor position
- **dd** to delete a complete line of text (first use the arrow keys to go to the line to be deleted)
- **dw** to delete words
- **r** to overwrite existing text

In insert mode (not command mode), you can delete text by pressing the Backspace key.

Now that you know how to add, delete, and edit text, knowing some navigation tricks will help. Apart from using the arrow keys, you can use the commands in Table A-2 to navigate through your text (in command mode).

Table A-2	Handy vi Commands
Command	*Moves the Cursor . . .*
h	Left
l	Right
k	Up
j	Down
w	To the next word

Appendix A: Commands to the Rescue!

Command	Moves the Cursor . . .
b	To the previous word
0 (zero)	To the start of the line
$	To the end of the line
Ctrl+F	One page up
Ctrl+B	One page down
G	To the end of the file
1G	To the top of the file
xG	To line number x

Are you enjoying working with vi? It can do a lot more. Try combining commands. For example, in command mode, typing

```
d$
```

deletes all the text from the cursor to the end of the line.

Well, should you know more? Being able to save a file would be convenient:

1. **Type** : (colon) **to switch to last-line mode.**
2. **Type one of the following:**
    - **w** to save the file
    - **wq** (write and quit) to save the file and exit vi

TIP: If you want to exit without saving, typing **q!** is all you have to do.

To find out more about using vi, type **man vi** to check out its manual pages.

Appendix B
Glossary

Computer terms just keep rolling off the assembly line. This glossary attempts to take care of critical encounters.

.: The current folder (directory) is often indicated by a single period, or dot.

..: The parent of the current folder (directory) is often indicated by two periods.

access rights: Permissions granted or denied by the owner (creator) of a file to allow other users to read, write to, or execute the file.

anchor: Fixing a graphic relative to page margins, text, or another object, so that its relative position remains fixed during editing.

application: A program that performs tasks for the user (for example, Netscape or WordPerfect) as opposed to systems software.

archive: A collection of related files stored as one file in a compressed format.

ASCII: A standard set of characters used in many text files, including Linux configuration files.

autohide: When certain screen features automatically disappear when not needed; this clears the deck for your work. Point to the spot where a feature disappeared to pop it back into view.

binary: A coding or counting system with only two symbols or conditions (off and on, zero and one, mark and space, high and low). The binary system is the basis for storing data in computers.

bit: A binary digit, the fundamental unit of computer data representing either 0 or 1 (off or on).

bitmap: A digital image made up of an assemblage of different colored *pixels*.

boot: To load the *operating system* and other utilities when you start your computer.

boot diskette: A diskette from which you can boot your computer to install or recover programs in some cases. If your computer can boot from a CD-ROM, a Corel Linux boot diskette should not be necessary.

boot sequence: The order in which your computer searches your drives for the *operating system* to load on startup, such as A:, C:, CD-ROM.

byte: An ensemble of eight bits of memory in a computer.

case sensitivity: Names and *command*s are sensitive to case. Thus, a search for myletter.wpd won't turn up MyLetter.wpd. The Linux convention has been to use all lowercase commands and filenames.

CD-ROM (compact disc read-only memory): A non-rewritable CD that commonly stores 650MB of data.

CD-R (compact disk-recordable) drive: Lets you write once to create your own CDs.

CD-RW (compact disk-rewritable) drive: Lets you write to a CD many times, just as you can with a floppy or hard drive.

command: A text instruction to your computer, something you can usually avoid with a *graphical user interface*.

command line: Any place where you can type character commands, such as the *terminal window*, rather than execute commands through graphical selections, such as menus and buttons.

CPU (central processing unit): The processing engine of your computer.

cursor: A blinking line that indicates your text position as you type. Not to be confused with *curser*, who is someone installing new hardware or software.

data: Digital information that is input to, output from, or processed and stored in a computer.

daemon: Not an evil spirit but any background process performing system chores that you don't see on-screen. Daemons load automatically and take care of such things as watching for network connections.

dependency: When one package can't be installed unless another one is.

desktop: A convenient graphical workplace, such as Windows, KDE, or Gnome, set up for a *multitasking* environment.

device: File systems or hardware on your computer mapped to the /dev subdirectory within Linux. For example, /dev/hda1 is the first *partition* on an IDE hard disk, and /dev/ttyS1 is the second serial port to which you might have a modem attached.

digital: A system of storing information as on or off bits for computer manipulation and precise replication.

directory: Same as *folder,* a place for keeping related files.

distribution: A Linux package made up of the Linux kernel, other system software, user applications, and with all major distributions, an installation program. Anyone can put together a Linux distribution, and the operating system can vary widely depending on the kernel version and system software employed.

disc: Optical storage media (CD, DVD, and video disc).

disk: Magnetic storage media (floppy disk or hard disk).

DNS (Domain Name Server): A service that translates alphabetic domain names into unique, numeric *IP addresses*.

domain: A group of computers making up a network or a distinct part of a network with a particular set of privileges. Also refers to Internet ***domain name***.

domain name: The name of the network domain in which your computer resides. Also, the searchable name of an Internet server, such as Corel.com.

DOS equivalent commands: Many Linux *commands* are similar to those used in DOS, even though you type them differently (and they're always lowercase). To change directories, you type CD in DOS and cd in Linux; to list all the files in a directory, you type DIR in DOS and ls -l in Linux; and so on.

DPI (dots per inch): The resolution of a printer, a video monitor, or another device based on dot density. (Camera resolution is the number of pixels.) For example, most laser printers have a resolution of 300 dpi, and most monitors have a resolution of 72 dpi.

drag and drop: Moving (or copying) stuff from one place to another with a mouse. Can be within an application, such as moving a selected paragraph in a word processor or even between two applications, such as dragging a graphic from a drawing program to a word processor.

driver: A program to operate a computer device, such as a hard drive, a keyboard, a mouse, a video card, or a printer.

DVD (digital video disk): A high-capacity replacement for a *CD-ROM,* employing various recording technologies.

Ethernet: A standard way to move packets of data between two or more computers hooked together with cables.

export: Transporting data from one computer, program, format, or device to another.

FAQ (frequently asked questions): A compiled list, especially lists of the most common problems encountered with a program.

file: A collection of information, such as text, data, or images saved on a disk or a hard drive.

file compression: To squish down a file or collection of files for efficient transport. The files are then uncompressed for use after arrival at the new location. Various utilities for this purpose are *gzip and gunzip,* tar, and rpm. Compressed files are identified by the respective filename extensions of .gz, .tgz, and .rpm. (An uncompressed tar archive is .tar.)

file format: A type of program or data file. Some common image file formats include TIFF, PICT, and EPS.

file permissions: See *access rights.*

file server: A computer that serves as the storage component of a local area network and permits users to share its hard disks, storage space, files, and so on.

file system: Formatted space on a drive where directories and files are stored. Several types of file systems are available, such as ext2 for Linux, VFAT for Windows 98, and iso9660 for CD-ROMs. Because file systems don't have drive letters in Linux, you *mount* them to empty Linux directories so that you can access them.

flame: Incendiary newsgroup posting, usually best ignored.

floppy disk: A common removable magnetic computer storage medium, usually a 3.5-inch disk.

folder: Same as a *directory,* a place for keeping related files and folders. Now that Linux has gone graphical, directories look like folders and act like folders, so that's what we call 'em.

format: (1) The particular way a file, such as text or a graphic, is stored, either unique to a program or common to many programs. (2) To prepare a disk to have files written to it, normally wiping out any existing files in the process.

FTP (File Transfer Protocol): Used for sending files over the Internet. An FTP site is a remote location for uploading and downloading files.

gigabyte (GB): A thousand (1024) megabytes of computer memory.

graphical user interface (GUI): A computer screen with picture icons (such as Windows or the KDE desktop) that you can click to do things instead of typing in obscure commands.

group: On a Linux *network,* users can be organized into groups for security purposes, especially for granting *access rights* to various files. A user can belong to more than one group.

gzip and gunzip: Linux utilities to compress files for transport and uncompress them after they're received, respectively. The .gz filename extension is added to compressed files.

hidden files: Linux files that begin with a period and normally aren't displayed. The idea is that if you don't see it, you won't mess with it.

home directory: Each user account in Linux has a home directory (folder), in which the user is free to create and delete files. For example, the user seth will have a /home/seth folder.

HTML (Hypertext Markup Language): The styles behind the richly formatted pages you view in your Web browser.

HTTP (Hypertext Transfer Protocol): Used for formatting and transferring Web pages.

icon: A graphical representation of an object (such as a printer or a file folder) or action (such as saving or pasting) that lets you work intuitively and quickly, without memorizing keystrokes or typing obscure ***commands.***

Internet: A global "network of networks" connecting millions computers and hundreds of millions of users who exchange data, mail, news, and opinions. The operators of each independent host computer decide which Internet services to use and which local services to provide to the global Internet. The terms *Web* and *Internet* are often used interchangeably although the two have technical distinctions.

Internet service provider (ISP): A commercial vendor or organization that hosts Web sites and provides dial-up access to the Internet. They also serve large companies by providing a direct connection from the company's networks to the Internet.

IP address: A unique numeric identifier for a computer or device on a *TCP/IP* network, written as four numbers separated by periods, such as 1.160.10.240.

intranet: An in-house network where members of an organization publish information and interact with each other much as they do on the global *Internet.* Although intranet users can get out to the Internet, access from the Internet to the intranet is usually restricted by a security firewall to prevent unauthorized access.

kernel: The central part of an *operating system* that remains in memory and performs essential services such as managing memory, processes, tasks, and disks.

kilobyte: One thousand (1024) bytes of computer memory or disk space.

LAN (local area network): A network of physically connected computers to exchange files and share peripherals.

LILO (Linux loader): A utility installed in the *Master Boot Record* (or in the boot sector of your Linux partition) that lets you select your operating environment on bootup.

link: (1) A pointer to a file so that you can reference it under another name, without specifying the path. (2) A clickable reference that jumps you to a document or Web page. See also *Web link.*

login: Because Linux is a multiuser system, each user must log in using a valid user name and password.

logout: The exit of a Linux user, so no that no one else can use that account. The Linux system continues to run for other users and processes. See also *shutdown.*

Master Boot Record (MBR): The first sector of your hard disk that contains important stuff used when you boot your computer, including a partition table and a small program to read the table. The program sees which *partition* to boot the operating system from and then transfers program control to the boot sector of that partition.

maximize: To enlarge a window to its maximum size, often the full screen.

megabyte (MB): A million (1,048,576) bytes of computer memory.

mime type: Characteristics attributed to a file based on its filename extension. For example, a file with the .exe extension is identified as an executable program; a .wpd file is a WordPerfect document.

minimize: To shrink a window down to a taskbar icon, to get it out of the way.

modem (modulator/demodulator): A device that converts digital computer data into signals for transmission over telephone lines.

mount: To load a *file system* to an empty Linux directory so you can access its directories and files.

multitasking: Running several programs at once — Linux excels at this. The kernel switches between processes so quickly that they appear to be running simultaneously.

multiuser: You can create multiple user accounts in Linux, each with its own *home directory* and *access rights*. If access is provided via a *modem*, a dumb terminal, or a *network* connection, multiple users can access the system and run programs simultaneously.

network: A group of computers connected to each other, so that they can share information, resources, and peripherals.

newsgroup: An online discussion group or forum, in which you can view and post messages.

open source: Software for which the programming code is freely available to all developers.

operating system (OS): A program, such as Linux or Windows, that controls your computer and manages everything from keyboard and mouse input to monitor, disk, and printer output. It also maintains security and acts as a traffic cop to keep programs from tripping over one another.

package: A compressed bundle of files that make up a specific software component. Various flavors of Linux employ different package formats, such as .deb for Debian (Corel Linux) and .rpm for Red Hat.

panel: The bar at the bottom of the KDE desktop that provides quick access to tools and programs.

parallel port: A high-speed computer connection for printers and other devices.

partition: An isolated portion of a hard disk devoted to a particular system or set of files. Linux programs reside on Ext2 partitions, but Linux can read from and write to DOS and Windows FAT, FAT 32, and NTFS partitions.

path: The address of a file on your machine, made up of a string of folder names separated by slashes, such as /usr/local/wp8/wpbin/xwp.

pixel (picture element): The smallest element of a digitized image. Also, one of the tiny points of light that make up a picture on a computer screen.

Plug and Play (PnP): Computer devices that are automatically installed and configured to keep out of each other's way. Often works better in theory than in practice.

program: Computer instructions to perform a related set of tasks. The Linux *kernel* and WordPerfect *application* are examples of programs.

protocol: Agreed-upon format for transmitting data between two devices, including error checking and any data compression.

proxy server: Intermediate server that intercepts and coordinates the requests of numerous users, often on a single network. Thus, if three users on a network request the same Web page, the proxy server can fetch the page once (a time-consuming operation) and quickly send it to all three users.

RAM (random access memory): The most common type of high-speed computer memory; it's where the CPU stores software, programs, and data currently being used.

ROM (read-only memory): Nonvolatile computer memory, similar to *RAM,* designed for device instructions that remain when the power is off. Can also refer to nonalterable CDs.

root folder: The base of your Linux file tree, indicated by /. Also the /root folder for the *root user*'s files.

root user: The *superuser,* or system administrator, of a Linux installation who can perform any task. The root user can accidentally damage critical files, so even if you have root access, as on a standalone installation, log in as a regular user unless you need to perform system tasks.

rpm: See *file compression.*

serial port: A computer interface connection that transmits data one bit at a time.

shortcut: See *symbolic link.*

shutdown: The process of gracefully closing down your computer during which program settings and files are saved.

SMTP (Simple Mail Transfer Protocol): For sending e-mail messages between servers or from client to server, particularly over the Internet.

spam: Junk e-mail or newsgroup postings. Whatever you do, don't respond to it!

superuser: See *root user.*

swap partition: A separate partition on your hard disk that the Linux kernel uses to store active programs that aren't doing anything at the moment, to make room in system memory for those that are. The space can't be used for normal programs and data.

symbolic link: A pointer that lets you access or execute a file from another location, without actually copying the file. Similar to a Windows shortcut.

tar: Short for the tape archive utility that combines a group of files into a single file with a .tar extension. In most cases *file compression* is used when a file is tarred.

taskbar: The bar at the top of the KDE desktop that lets you switch between active applications.

TCP/IP: Primary networking protocol (transmission format) used by Linux and the Internet. Other protocols such as the Web's *HTTP* and *SMTP* (for e-mail) work under TCP/IP.

terabyte: A thousand (1024) gigabytes.

terminal window: Any place for typing Linux *commands,* often called a terminal emulator in a graphical environment.

thread: A string of related messages, especially in a newsgroup.

TWAIN: The protocol for exchanging information between applications and devices, such as scanners and digital cameras. TWAIN makes it possible for digital cameras and software to "talk" with one another on PCs.

universal serial bus (USB): A replacement for *serial ports* and *parallel ports* that permits high data transfer rates between the computer and multiple peripheral devices, including cameras, monitors, printers, mice, and keyboards.

UNIX: Popular *multiuser, multitasking* operating system developed in the early 1970s, from which much of Linux is derived.

URL (Uniform Resource Locator): The Internet equivalent of a pathname to contact a site or locate a file. Also called a Web address.

USB (universal serial bus): The new, easy way of hooking up scanners, keyboards, mice, speakers, modems, printers, and other devices. Avoids the exasperating hardware conflicts of the old way.

user: Because Linux is a *multiuser* system, each person with system access should have a separate user account and password.

Web: Short for World Wide Web, a collection of documents (called pages) located on computers all over the world.

Web link: Clickable reference attached to highlighted words or an image that contains the URL (address) of a web document. Click the links to jump from page to page on the Internet.

Web pages: Scrollable hypertext documents with *HTML* formatting codes that you see on the Web.

Web site: A collection of related Web pages. Corel's Web site, for example, has many pages attached to it.

Web server: A computer where Web sites reside. One service provider (such as a university) can support many sites on their Web server. You can also set up a Web site on a personal computer.

window: An on-screen box where you work in a program. You can enlarge, shrink, and rearrange multiple windows on your *desktop*.

WINS (Windows Internet Naming Service): A dynamic network database that lets you quickly locate another computer on the network through its current network address.

wizard: A program that leads you through a set of step-by-step instructions, providing help with your selections.

WYSIWYG: Stands for what you see (on the screen) is what you get (as output) and is pronounced "wizzywig."

X Window System: A UNIX/Linux graphical user interface (XFree86 in most distributions) that supports a desktop environment such as KDE or GNOME.

ZIP: A Windows standard form of nondestructive *file compression* used on all types of files for storage and transfer.

Appendix C
About the CD

This appendix describes how to install the bonus stuff on your *Corel Linux For Dummies* CD:

- Adobe Acrobat Reader (12MB installed)
- Netscape Communicator suite (36MB installed, plus room for e-mail and temporary files)
- A bonus collection of more than 100 dazzling desktop themes (40MB)

Please note that you install these bonus items *after* you've installed Corel Linux, as described in Chapter 2.

System Requirements

The minimum system requirements for Corel Linux are

- A Pentium 90 (or equivalent) processor
- 24MB of RAM (64MB recommended)
- 500MB of unpartitioned hard drive space, plus additional space for the bonus stuff on your *Corel Linux For Dummies* CD
- A 2MB VGA PCI graphics card
- A CD-ROM drive
- A 3½-inch floppy disk drive (required if your CD-ROM drive is not bootable)
- A mouse or other pointing device

See Chapter 2 for complete hardware details.

Installing Adobe Acrobat Reader

To install Adobe Acrobat Reader:

1. **Start Corel Linux and log in as root.**
2. **Put your *Corel Linux For Dummies* CD in the CD player.**
3. **Click the File Manager button on the panel.**
4. **In tree view, double-click The System and then double-click the / folder.**
5. **In tree view, double-click your CD-ROM.**
6. **Double-click the extras folder.**
7. **Drag the Acrobat Reader archive linux-ar-405.tar.gz to /tmp, under The System in tree view, as shown in Figure C-1.**
8. **Click the Console button on the panel.**
9. **Type** cd /tmp **and press Enter.**

   Everything you type in the Console is case-sensitive, so please type names exactly as they appear in these instructions.

10. **Type** tar zxf linux-ar-405.tar.gz **and press Enter.**
11. **Type** cd ILINXR.install **and press Enter.**
12. **Type** ./INSTALL **and press Enter (as shown in Figure C-2).**

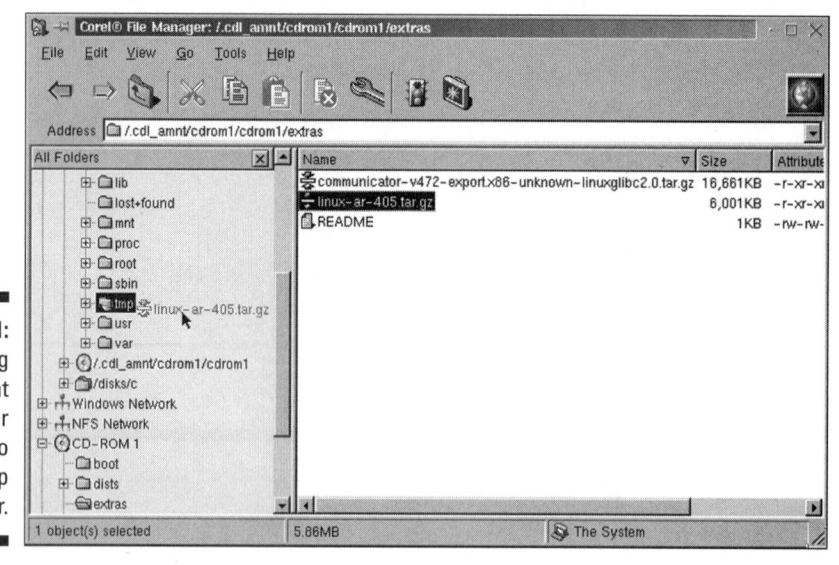

Figure C-1:
Dragging the Acrobat Reader archive to the /tmp folder

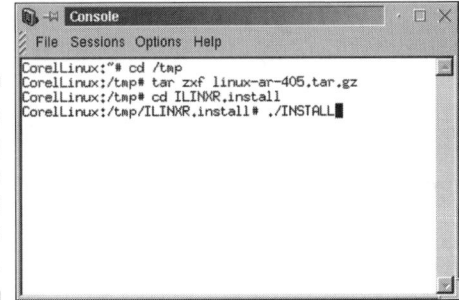

Figure C-2:
Installing Adobe Acrobat from the Console.

```
CorelLinux:~# cd /tmp
CorelLinux:/tmp# tar zxf linux-ar-405.tar.gz
CorelLinux:/tmp# cd ILINXR.install
CorelLinux:/tmp/ILINXR.install# ./INSTALL
```

13. **Read the agreement. When you get to the end, type** accept **and press Enter.**

14. **When you're asked to specify the installation directory, press Enter to accept /usr/local/Acrobat4. Press Enter again to create it.**

    That's it for the Acrobat Reader 4.05 install. Sorry about all the work, but now you can pat yourself on the back for installing from the Console!

Now that you did the hard stuff, change the menu shortcut to find Adobe Acrobat:

1. **Click Application Starter ➪ Applications.**
2. **Right-click Acrobat Reader and then click Properties.**
3. **Click the Execute tab and type** /usr/local/Acrobat4/bin/acroread (**as shown in Figure C-3).**
4. **Click OK.**

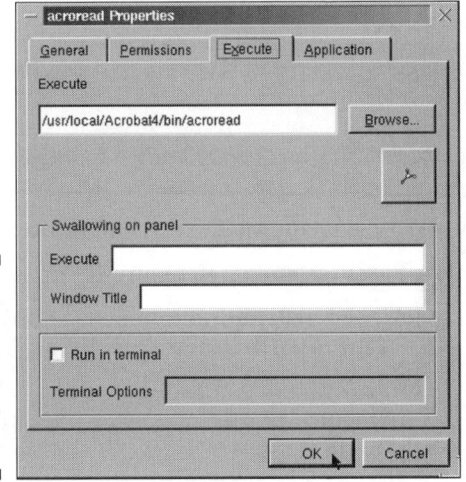

Figure C-3: Changing the menu shortcut to find Adobe Acrobat.

Part VI: Appendixes

Your Acrobat Reader is now ready for use. Click Application Starter ⇨ Applications ⇨ Acrobat Reader and you're on your way. See Chapter 14 for Acrobatic details.

Installing the Netscape Communicator Suite

The download edition of Corel Linux installs *only* the standalone Netscape Navigator browser. By installing the full Netscape Communicator Suite from your *Corel Linux For Dummies* CD, you'll enjoy all the e-mail, newsgroup, and HTML composition facilities described in this book.

To install Netscape Communicator:

1. **Start Corel Linux and log in as root.**
2. **Put your *Corel Linux For Dummies* CD in the CD player.**
3. **Click the File Manager button on the panel.**
4. **Double-click The System in tree view and then double-click the / folder.**
5. **In tree view, double-click your CD-ROM.**
6. **Double-click the extras folder.**
7. **Drag the Communicator archive communicator-v472-export.x86-unknown-linuxglibc2.0.tar.gz to /tmp, under The System in tree view, as shown in Figure C-4.**
8. **Click the Console button on the panel.**
9. **Type** cd /tmp **and press Enter.**

Everything you type is case-sensitive, so please type names exactly as they appear in these instructions.

10. **Type** tar zxf communicator-v472-export.x86-unknown-linuxglibc2.0.tar.gz **and press Enter.**
11. **Type** cd communicator-v472.x86-unknown-linux2.0 **and press Enter.**
12. **Type** ./ns-install **and press Enter (as shown in Figure C-5).**
13. **When you're asked to specify the installation folder, as shown in Figure C-6, press Enter to accept /usr/local/netscape. Press Enter again to create it.**

Lo and behold, Netscape Communicator 4.72 installs on your system! Bet you didn't know it would be so easy.

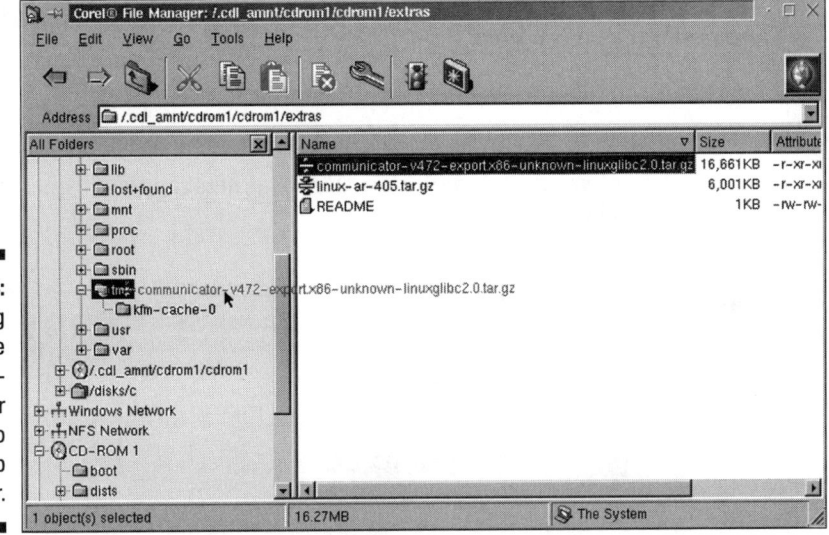

Figure C-4: Dragging the Communicator archive to the /tmp folder.

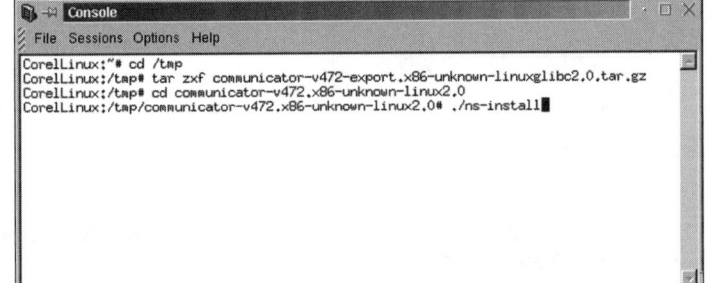

Figure C-5: Installing Communicator from the Console.

Figure C-6: Accepting the default installation folder.

Now that you've installed Communicator, getting it to launch from the menu or a desktop icon is a breeze:

 1. **Click Application Starter ➪ Applications.**
 2. **Right-click Netscape Navigator and then click Properties.**
 3. **Click the Execute tab and type** /usr/local/netscape/netscape %u (**as shown in Figure C-7).**

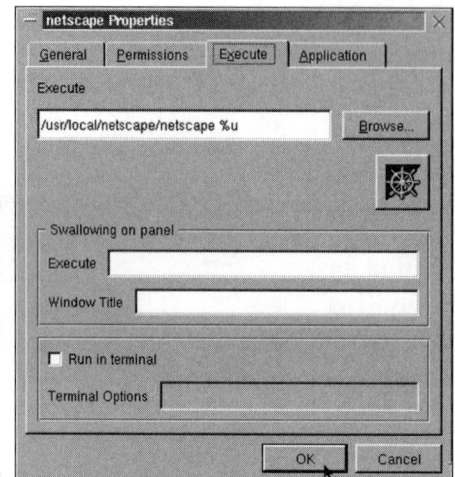

Figure C-7: Changing the menu shortcut to find Netscape Communicator.

 4. **Click the Application tab and change the name from Netscape Navigator to Netscape Communicator.**
 5. **Click OK.**

    That takes care of your menu configuration.

 6. **Right-click the Netscape icon on your desktop, click Properties, and make the same changes as described in Steps 3 through 5.**

    Your Netscape Communicator is now ready for use. Click the Netscape icon on your desktop (or click Application Starter ➪ Applications ➪ Netscape Communicator) and you're on your way.

When you launch Communicator, the browser appears. From here, you can access your e-mail, newsgroups, and composition facilities. See Chapters 15 and 16 for Communicator details.

Want to get really fancy? Create a Communicator submenu with shortcuts to the individual applications, using the following links:

Appendix C: About the CD **345**

- **Collabra:** `/usr/local/netscape/netscape -news`
- **Composer:** `/usr/local/netscape/netscape -edit`
- **Messenger:** `/usr/local/netscape/netscape -mail`

See Chapter 9 for menu editing details.

Installing the Bonus Themes

Your *Corel Linux For Dummies* CD also includes a bonus collection of more than 100 desktop themes. If you copy them to the global Themes folder, they'll be available to all users:

1. **Log in as root to Corel Linux.**
2. **Insert your *Corel Linux For Dummies* CD into your CD-ROM drive.**
3. **Click the File Manager button on the panel.**
4. **In tree view, select your CD-ROM and then double-click the Themes folder.**
5. **Press Ctrl+A to select all the themes and then click the Copy button on the toolbar, as shown in Figure C-8.**

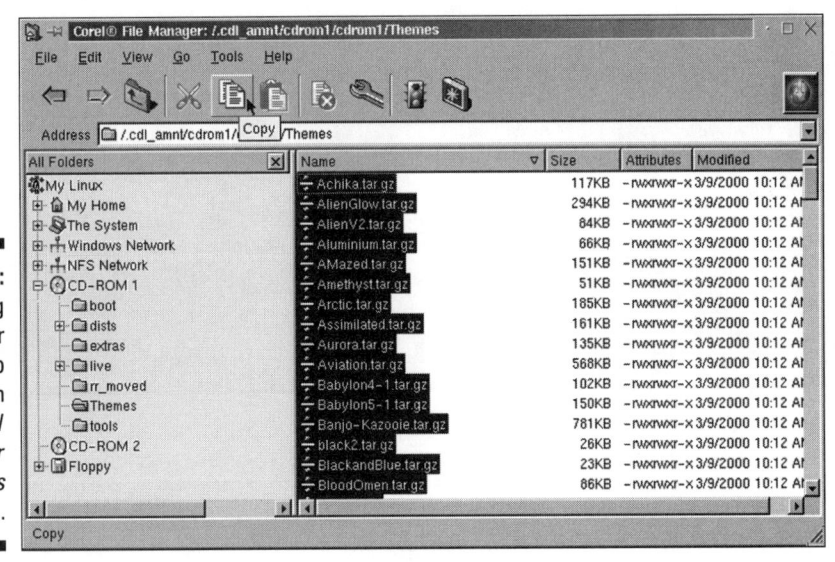

Figure C-8: Copying your desktop themes from your *Corel Linux For Dummies* CD.

6. **Locate and highlight the global themes folder at /usr/X11R6/share/apps/kthememgr/Themes.**

7. **Click the Paste button on the toolbar to copy the themes.**

Then use the Theme Manager described in Chapter 10 to preview and apply your themes. Enjoy!

If You Have Problems of the CD Kind

I tried my best to supply programs that work on most computers that meet the minimum system requirements. Alas, your computer might differ, and some programs might not work properly for some reason. The most likely problem is that you have a Winmodem or some other hardware that is not yet supported by Corel Linux, as described in Chapter 2.

If your machine meets the hardware requirements and you still have trouble installing the items from the CD, please call the IDG Books Worldwide Customer Service phone number at 800-762-2974 (outside the United States, call 317-596-5430).

Index

• A •

acceleration, mouse, 50
access rights, 329
Acrobat Reader option, Applications submenu, 90
active window, 112–113
  keyboard, 113
addresses
  e-mail, 55, 262–263
  IP, 333
Adobe Acrobat Reader, 234
  installing, 340–342
advanced searches, 199–200
alarms for sticky notes, 218
Alt key, 80
anchor, 329
application buttons, panel, 75
Application Starter, 46, 75
  triangles in menu, 76
Application Starter button, 38
applications, 329
  launching, 38–39
  launching from File Manager, 189–190
  menus, 132–134
Applications option, Main menu, 88
Appstart, 87
Archive Administrator, 206
  options, 210
archives, 205–206, 329
  adding to, 199
  creating, 206–207
  editing, 209
  extracting, 208–209
  types, 206
  viewing, 209
  ZIP files, 206

Arrange Icons, 161–162
arranging windows, 114
arrow keys, 80
artist information, audio CDs, 238
ASCII, 329
audio CDs
  artist information, 238
  Internet database, 235
  playing, 235–237
  Sound Mixer and, 237
autohide, 329
  panel, 283–284
  panel and, 142–143
  taskbar, 283–284
Autostart, Main menu, 88

• B •

Back button
  File Manager, 184
  Netscape, 246
backgrounds
  desktop, 154–158
  GIMP, 229–230
  randomly changing, 157
  Web browser and, 230
binary system, 329
bitmaps, 226, 329
bits, 329
blind carbon copies, e-mail, 264
bookmarks
  adding, 248
  Windows, Linux and, 248
bookmarks, Netscape, 247
boot defaults, changing, 68–70
boot disk, 330
boot sequence, 26, 292, 330

booting, 330
  defaults, changing, 68–70
border grabbing mode, windows, 116
borders on sticky notes, 220
brackets in WordPerfect, 215
browsers. *See also* Netscape Navigator
  File Manger and, 185
  protocols, 243
Business Community, Online
    Services, 249
button mapping, mouse, 50
buttons
  panel, 86–87, 137
  windows, 99–100, 150
bytes, 330

• C •

calendar, sticky notes and, 218
carbon copies, e-mail, 264
case sensitivity, 330
CD
  installation, 339–346
  Sound Mixer and, 237
cd command, 318
CD-R, 330
CD-RW, 330
CD-ROM, 330
CD-ROM folder, File Manager, 175
CDs
  audio, 235
  audio, playing, 235–237
  installation, 25–27
chat, Online Services and, 250
check boxes, dialogs, 104
cleaning up the desktop, 113
  arranging windows, 114
  closing windows, 114
  maximizing windows, 117
  multiple desktops, 119
  placement of windows, 117–118
  sizing windows, 116–117

Clipart and Photos, Online
    Services, 249
clipboard
  copying with, 108–109
  moving with, 108–109
close button, 100
closing windows, 97–102
  cleanup and, 114
CNET Web site, 314
color, 288
  desktop, 158–160
  desktop background, 154–156
  GIMP background, 229–230
  sticky notes, 219
  windows, 158–160
COM (communications port), 58
command button, dialogs, 105
command line, 330
  Console, 42
  extras, 94–95
  Midnight Commander, 42
  Shell, 42
command prompt, 41–42
commands, 330
  components, 317
  directories, 318
  essential, 318–321
  options, 321
  searches, 322–323
  system files, 323–324
communications port (COM), 58
Component bar, Netscape, 244
compressed files, 332
configuration
  dial-up connection, 56–60
  keyboard, 49–50
  mouse, 49–50
configuration files, editing, 324–327
connections
  dial-up hardware, 54–55
  Internet, 54–60
console, 42, 87

Index

context sensitivity, 102–103
Control Center, Main menu, 88
copying
  clipboard and, 108–109
  files, 191
  folders, 191
  selected items, 108–109
Corel Community Web site, 302
Corel File Manager option, Main
    menu, 88
Corel Linux
  comparisons to other
    distributions, 12
  flavors, 13–15
  removing from system, 20
Corel Linux Bible, 301
Corel Printing Service, Online
    Services, 249
Corel vDrive, Online Services, 250
Corel WordPerfect option, Applications
    submenu, 89
cost, 11
cp command, 318
CPU (central processing unit), 330
Ctrl key, 80
Current Events, Online Services, 250
cursor, 330
Custom installation, 28

• D •

daemons, 330
data, 330
date and time
  docking station, 75
  setting, 50–51
  sticky notes, 218
Debian Linux, 13
Debian Support Web site, 306
deleting
  files, 194
  folders, 194
  restoring deleted material, 109

dependency, 330
Designer FX, Online Services, 250
desktop, 123, 330
  background, 154–158
  cleaning up, 113–119
  color, 158–160
  color background, 154–156
  fonts, 160–161
  icon arrangement, 161–162
  icons, 86–87
  links, 130–132
  multiple, 77–79, 119, 145, 285
  renaming, 145
  session management, 124
  sound, 167–168
  style, 162–163
  themes, 163–166
  wallpaper, 156–157
desktop button, panel, 75
Desktop installation (minimum), 28
Desktop Manager, 79, 286
DesktopPlus installation (development
    tools, editors), 28
devices, 331
dial-up connection. *See also* Internet
  configuring, 56–60
  hardware, 54–55
Dial-Up dialog box, 56
dialogs, 103–107
digital system, 331
dimmed items, dialogs, 105
directories, 331
  command and, 318
  home directory, 333
disc, 331
disk, 331
disk space, 40
display
  pixels, 168–170
  settings, testing, 170
distribution, 11, 331
DNS (Domain Name Server), 331

Corel Linux For Dummies

DNS servers, 57
docking station, panel, 75
domain, 331
domain name, 331
  ISPs, 55
DOS equivalent commands, 331
DOS/Windows partitions, 29
downloading
  themes, 165
DPI (dots per inch), 331
drafts of e-mail, 265
drag and drop, 108, 331
  files, 298
  files and folders, 192
drivers, 331
  software, 19
drop-down list, dialogs, 104
dual boot, 24
dual boot machines, 15, 23
DVD (digital video disk), 332

• E •

e-mail. *See also* Messenger
  address, 55
  addresses, 262–263
  blind carbon copies, 264
  carbon copies, 264
  checking, 259
  display, 261–262
  drafts, 265
  facilities, 256
  forwarding messages, 266
  free account, 312
  links in, 261
  Messenger, 256–260
  printing messages, 261
  replying to messages, 265
  retrieving, 260–261
  sending messages, 263–265
  servers, 258
  signatures, 258
  sorting, 260
  sticky notes, 221
  vCard, 258
editing
  archives, 209
  configuration files, 324–327
  nicknames, 130
eFax Services, Online Services, 250
Email, Online Services, 250
emptying trash, 193
Esc key, 81
Ethernet, 332
Ethernet cards, 61
  TCP/IP networks, 62
export, 332
external modems, 55
extracting archives, 208–209
extras
  command line, 94–95
  menus, 91–94

• F •

FAQ (frequently asked questions), 332
faxes, Online Services and, 250
file compression, 332
file links, 131
File Manager
  Back button, 184
  CD-ROM folder, 175
  clicking mouse in, 180
  Forward button, 185
  launching from, 189–190
  My Home, 174–175
  organization of, 176–179
  tree view, 175
  view, 185–187, 297
  viewing files, 189–190
  Web and, 252–253
  Web Browser folder, 175
file server, 332
file system, 332

Index

file transfer, web, 254
FileMgr, 87, 297
files
  configuration, editing, 324–327
  copying, 191
  deleting, 194
  drag and drop operations, 192, 298
  Find Files utility, 195–200
  format, 332
  hidden, 187, 333
  moving, 191
  naming, 188
  PDF, 231
  PostScript, 231, 232
  program files, 173
  renaming, 188
  selecting, 190–191
  system files, 173, 174
  trashing, 192
  types, 173–174
  user files, 173
  viewing from File Manager, 189–190
Find Files utility, 195–200. *See also* searches
  basic search, 196–197
  clearing results, 198
  saving results, 199
Find option, Main menu, 88
flames, newsgroups, 267, 332
flavors of Corel Linux, 13–15
floppy disks, 332
  installing from, 25
focus, windows, 284
folder links, 131
folder trees, 176
folders, 332
  copying, 191
  creating with another, 188
  deleting, 194
  drag and drop operations, 192
  files, 196–197
  Find Files utility, 195–200

hyphens in name, 181
  moving, 191
  naming, 188
  NFS Network, 175
  nicknames, 124, 125–126
  organization, 176–179
  permissions, 181–183
  read access, 183
  renaming, 188
  searches, 196–197
  selecting, 190–191
  sorting, 184
  submenus, 132–134
  trashing, 192
  tree view, 175
  Windows Network, 175
  write protection, 183
fonts, desktop, 160–161
foreign languages, 46–49
format, 332
  files, 332
formatting hard drive, 20
Forward button
  File Manager, 185
  Netscape, 246
forwarding e-mail messages, 266
free space, 23
  unpartitioned space, 23
Freshmeat Web site, 312
FTP (File Transfer Protocol), 243, 254, 333
function keys, 80

• G •

Games option, Applications submenu, 89
games, extras, 91
gigabyte (GB), 333
GIMP. *See also* graphics
  background/foreground, 229–230
  bitmaps, 226

GIMP. *See also* graphics *(continued)*
  creating images, 227–228
  features, 224–226
  launching, 226
  marching ants, 229
  selection tools, 229
  toolbox, 226, 228
  tools, 226–228
  Xtns menu, 230
global keyboard shortcuts, 81–82, 137
Graphic Community, Online
   Services, 250
graphics. *See also* GIMP
  creating, 226–228
  extras, 92
  Online Services and, 249, 250
  selecting, 107–108
  vector graphics, 226
Graphics option, Applications
   submenu, 90
grayed out menu selections, 101
groups, networks, 333
GUI (graphical user interface), 333
gunzip utility, 333
gzip utility, 333

• H •

hard drive
  formatting, 20
  V-Drive, 175
hardware
  detection, automatic, 20
  dial-up connections, 54–55
  open source resolutions, 19
  supported, 18–19
  utilities, 19
  Windows only, 18
hardware requirements, 18
Help, 83–84, 87
  extras, 94
Help option, Main menu, 88

hidden files, 187, 333
Home button, Netscape, 246
home directory, 333
HTML (Hypertext Markup
   Language), 333
HTTP (Hypertext Transfer
   Protocol), 333
HTTP sites, 243

• I •

iconify button, 100
iconifying windows, 287
icons, 333
  desktop, 86–87
  desktop arrangement, 161–162
  tips, 75
icons used in book, 5
images, creating, 226–228
indenting text, 214
indents, sticky notes and, 220
installation
  Adobe Acrobat Reader, 340–342
  CD, 339–346
  Custom, 28
  Desktop, 28
  Desktop Plus, 28
  DOS/Windows partitions, 29
  editing partitions, 29
  floppy disk, 25
  hardware requirements, 18
  location, 21, 29
  minimum, 28
  Netscape Communicator Suite,
    342–345
  packages, 28
  partition table, editing, 29
  removing Corel Linux, 20
  reviewing selections, 30
  selecting items to install, 21
  Server, 28
  Take over disk option, 29

Index

themes, bonus, 345–346
types, 27–28
unprotected, 19
installation CD
  boot sequence, 26
  booting, 25–27
internal modems, 55
international keyboards, 48
Internet, 12, 333. *See also* dial-up connection
  addresses, Netscape, 245
  CD artist information, 238
  CD database, 235
  COM port, 58
  connecting to, 60
intranet, 334
IP address, 333
ISDN modems, 55
ISP (Internet Service Provider), 55–56, 333
  connecting to, 60

• J •

JabberIM, Online Services, 250

• K •

KDE
  Kmail, 256
  menu editor, 132–136
kdelnk files, nicknames, 130
kernel, 11, 334
keyboard, 137
  active window, 113
  Alt, 80
  arrow keys, 80
  configuration, 49–50
  Ctrl, 80
  custom scheme, 138–139
  Esc, 81
  function keys, 80
  global shortcuts, 81–82, 137
  international, 48
  languages, 48–49
  menus and, 101
  naming scheme, 138
  numeric keys, 80
  selecting items, 107
  Shift key, 80
  shortcuts, 79, 82–83
  special purpose, 81
  switching scheme, 139
  window controls, 146–147
keyboard shortcuts
  window, locating, 294
kilobyte, 334
Kmail, KDE, 256

• L •

languages, 46–49
  keyboard, 48–49
LANs (local area networks), 60–65, 334. *See also* networks
  hookups, 61
  servers, 61
  TCP/IP, 61
  Windows Workgroups, 61
launching
  GIMP, 226
  Netscape Navigator, 243–244
  programs, 38–39
  WordPerfect, 38–39
launching from File Manager, 189–190
launching programs, panel, 75–76
license agreement, 27
LILO (Linux loader), 24, 334
links, 245, 334
  desktop, 130–132
  e-mail and, 261
  file links, 131
  folder links, 131
  program links, 131
  symbolic, 337
  Web, 337

Linux
  Debian, 13
  history of, 9
  reasons to use, 12
Linux Community, Online Services, 250
Linux Documentation project, 304
LinuxWorld Expo (IDG), 306
Location toolbar, Netscape, 244
login, 35–37, 334
  dial-up connection, 56
  root, 291
login dialog box, 36
logout, 42–43, 334
Logout option, Main menu, 88
ls command, 318

• M •

magazines, 306
Mail & Newsgroups settings, 257–258
mailboxes, sorting mail, 260
main menu, 88
marching ants, 229
maximize button, 100
maximizing windows, 117, 287, 334
MBR (Master Boot Record), 24, 68, 334
megabyte (MB), 334
menu bar, 100–101
menus
  applications, 132–134
  customizing, 136
  extras, 91–94
  grayed out selections, 101
  KDE editor, 134–136
  main menu, 88
  programs adding, 293
  Quick Start items, 143–144
  rearranging, 136
  submenu, 89–90
  submenu folders, 132
Messenger, Netscape, 256.
    See also e-mail
  configuring, 256–260
  deleting messages, 266–267
  display, 261–262
  drafts, 265
  forwarding messages, 266
  new newsgroup threads, 270
  organizing mailbox, 266–267
  posting to newsgroups, 269–270
  replying to messages, 265
  searches, 271
  selecting multiple messages, 266
  sending messages, 263–265
  subscribing to newsgroups, 267–268
Midnight Commander, command line
    and, 42
mime types, 334
minimizing windows, 334
modems, 18, 54–55, 334
  COM port, 58
  external, 55
  internal, 55
  ISDN, 55
  PCMCIA, 55
  Winmodems, 59
mounting, 335
  network share, 202–204
mouse
  button mapping, 50
  click threshold, 50
  configuration, 49–50
  context and, 102–103
  File Manager actions, 180
  menu bar and, 100
  retraining buttons, 147
  right-clicking, 287
  selecting items, 107
  sticky notes and, 218
  windows, 147–149
moving
  clipboard and, 108–109
  nicknames, 134
  selected items, 108–109
  system files, 323–324
Multimedia option, Applications
    submenu, 90

Index

multimedia, extras, 92
multiple selections, text, 215
multitasking, 12, 335
multiuser, 335
My Home, 87, 174–175

• N •

name entry, 27
naming
  files, 188
  folders, 188
Navigation toolbar, Netscape, 244
NetHelp Facilities, Netscape, 252
Netscape, 87
Netscape Communicator
  installing, 342–345
Netscape Communicator option,
    Applications submenu, 90
Netscape Communicator, Messenger,
    256–260
Netscape Navigator, 242
  Back button, 246
  bookmarks, 247
  bookmarks, adding, 248
  Component toolbar, 244
  Forward button, 246
  history, 251–252
  Home button, 246
  Internet addresses, 245
  launching, 243–244
  links, 245
  Location toolbar, 244
  Navigation toolbar, 244
  NetHelp Facilities, 252
  Personal toolbar, 244
  reloading pages, 246
  start page, 251–252
network
  shares, disconnecting, 204
network card, 18
Network option, Applications
    submenu, 90

networking, 12
networks, 335. *See also* LANs
  Ethernet cards, 61
  extras, 92
  groups, 333
  search for computer, 200–201
  share, mounting, 202–204
  TCP/IP, 61
  Windows Workgroups, 61
New Online Services, Online
    Services, 250
newsgroups, 267, 335
  flames, 267
  Linux, 306
  Linux support, 302
  new threads, 270
  posting to, 269–270
  searching, 271
  server, 56
  subscribing to, 267–268
  threads, 267, 269
NFS Network, 175
nicknames
  creating, 128–130
  editing, 130
  folders, 124, 125–126
  kdelnk files, 130
  moving, 134
  program nicknames, 124, 127–128
  programs, 292–293
  removing, 130, 134
  URL nicknames, 124–130
Note utility, 216–221
  appearance of notes, 219–220
  creating notes, 217
  deleting notes, 217
  e-mailing notes, 221
  exiting, 221
  printing notes, 221
  renaming notes, 218
  text manipulation, 218
numeric keys, 80

• O •

On The CD icon, 5
On The Web icon, 5
Online Services, 249–251
Online Services, Main menu, 88
open source, 335
open source operating system, 11
opening PostScript files, 232
opening screen, 26
opening windows, 97–102
operating system, 335
operating systems, 9
 open source, 11
options
 Archive Administrator, 205–206
 commands, 321
ordering windows, 150–151

• P •

packages, 273, 335
 Debian, 13
 installation, 28
 removing, 279
palettes, dialogs, 105
panel, 74–75, 335
 autohiding, 283–284
 buttons, 86–87, 137
 location, 140
 size, 140–142
parallel port, 335
Partition Magic, 20
partitioning tools, 23
partitions, 335
 DOS/Windows, 29
 dual boot machines, 24
 editing at install, 29
 editing partition table, 29
 startup, 37
 swap partition, 24, 336
passwords, 36
 Internet access, 55

paths, 335
PCMCIA modem, 55
PDF (Portable Document Format) files, 231
 printing, 234–235
 viewing, 234–235
Performance Meter, 39
permissions
 folders, 181–183
 root, 184
persistent selections, text, 215
Personal toolbar, Netscape, 244
photographs, Online Services, 249
pixels, 296, 335
 display, 168–170
placement of windows, 117–118
plug and play, 335
POP3 server, 56, 258
ports
 parallel, 335
 serial, 336
posting to newsgroups, 269–270
 new threads, 270
PostScript files, 231
 opening, 232
 printing, 233–234
 viewing, 232
preview area, dialogs, 105
Printer, 87
printers
 setup, 51–54
printing
 e-mail messages, 261
 Online Services and, 249
 PDF files, 234–235
 PostScript files, 233–234
 sticky notes, 221
program files, 173
program keyboard shortcuts, 82–83
program links, 131
program nicknames, 124, 127–128
programming languages, Text Editor and, 213

Index 357

programs, 336
  launching, 75–76
  menus, adding to, 293
  nicknames, 292–293
  switching between, 76–77
property bar, 101
protocols, 336
  browsers, 243
proxy server, 336
PS Viewer (PostScript files), 232

• Q •

Quick Start menu items, 143–144

• R •

radio buttons, dialogs, 104
RAM (random access memory), 336
random desktop background, 157
read access, folders, 183
reloading pages, Netscape, 246
Remember icon, 5
resolution
  settings, 169–170
resources, 301–307
restarting, 42–43
restore button, 100
retrieving e-mail, 260–261
right-clicking mouse, context and, 287
ROM (read-only memory), 336
root, 336
  logging in as, 174, 291
  permissions, 184
  system files and, 174
  terminating users, 39
root folder, 336
Run option, Main menu, 88

• S •

safe mode, 32
scroll bars, 101
Search the Internet, Online
    Services, 250
searches. *See also* Find Files utility
  adding to archive, 199
  advanced, 199–200
  clearing results, 198
  commands, 322–323
  deleting item, 198
  files, 196–197
  folders, 196–197
  network computer, 200–201
  newsgroups, 271
  opening found items, 198
  saving results, 199
  Web, 246–247
selecting items, 107–108
selecting text, 215
selection list, dialogs, 104
sending e-mail messages, 263–265
serial port, 336
  modems, 55
Server installation (Web, file, print,
    Ftp), 28
Server option, Applications
    submenu, 90
servers, 332
  DNS, 57
  e-mail, 258
  extras, 93
  LANs, 61
  newsgroups, 56
  POP3, 56, 258
  proxy, 336
  SMTP, 56, 258
  Webg, 338
session management, 124
settings, Control Center, 45–46
setup, printers, 51–54

share, network
  disconnecting, 204
  mounting, 202–204
Shell, command line and, 42
Shift key, keyboard, 80
shortcuts. *See* nicknames
shortcuts, keyboard, 79, 137
  global, 81–82
  program, 82–83
shutdown, 336
signature files, e-mail, 258
sizing windows, 116–117, 287
sliders, dialogs, 105
SMTP (Simple Mail Transfer
    Protocol), 336
SMTP server, 56, 258
software drivers, 19
sorting folders, 184
sound, 295
  desktop events, 167–168
sound card, 18
Sound Mixer (CDs), 237
spam, 336
spin boxes, dialogs, 104
startup, 35–37
  Windows partition, 37
status bar, 102
sticky notes, 216. *See also* Note utility
  alarms, 218
  appearance, 219–220
  creating, 217
  date, 218
  deleting, 217
  e-mail, 221
  mouse and, 218
  printing, 221
  renaming, 218
  text manipulation, 218
sticky windows, 78, 286
style, desktops, 162–163
subfolders, removing, 134
submenu, 89–90

submenu folders, 132
subscribing to newsgroups, 267–268
support, resources, 301–307
supported hardware, 18–19
swap partition, 24, 336
symbolic links, 337
system extras, 93
system files, 173, 174
  moving, 323–324
system folders
  contents, 178–179
System option, Applications
    submenu, 90
system tasks, managing, 39
system updates, free, 309

• T •

tabs
  text, 214
  WordPerfect, 214
tabs, dialogs, 105
Take over disk option, 29
tar utility, 337
task buttons, panel, 75
taskbar, 337
  autohiding, 283–284
  location, 140–142
  size, 140–142
tasks, terminating, 39
TCP/IP, 61, 337
  connecting to network, 61–63
  Ethernet cards, 62
Technical Stuff icon, 5
terminal window, 337
text. *See also* WordPerfect
  indenting, 214
  Note utility, 218
  selecting, 107–108, 215
  sticky notes, 216, 218
  tabs, 214
  trailing spaces, 214

Index 359

word wrap, 214–215
WordPerfect, 211–212
text box, dialogs, 104
Text Editor, 212–214
  programming languages and, 213
Text F/X, Online Services, 250
TextEd, 87
Theme Manager, 166
themes, 289
themes, desktop, 163–166
  adding/removing, 166
  bonus, installing, 345–346
  downloading, 165
  saving, 166
threads, newsgroups, 267, 269, 337
  starting new, 270
threshold, mouse clicks, 50
time. *See* date and time
Time Display, CD Player, 238
Tip icon, 5
title bar, windows, 99
toolbars, 101
toolbox, GIMP, 226, 228
trailing spaces in text, 214
Trash, 87, 192
  emptying, 193
  removing items, 193
  retrieving items, 298
tree view
  expanding, 176
  folder tree, 176
  folders, 175
Tucows Web site, 312
TWAIN protocol, 337
types of files, 173–174

• U •

Undo button, 109
UNIX, 337
unpartitioned space, 23
Update, 273

updates on Debian packages, 13
upgrades, 273–279
URL (Uniform Resource Locator), 337
URL nicknames, 124, 128–130
USB (universal serial bus), 337
USB ports, modems and, 55
user files, 173
User Manager, 66
User Manual, 83
users, 337
  adding, 66–67
  task management, 39
utilities
  extras, 93
  Find Files utility, 195–200
  Note, 216–221
  tar, 337
Utilities option, Applications submenu, 90

• V •

V-Drive, 175
vCard, e-mail, 258
vector graphics, 226
vertical selections, text, 215
video cards, 19
video settings, 169–170
viewing
  archives, 209
  PDF files, 234–235
  PostScript files, 232
virtual drive, 175

• W •

wallpaper, 156–157
Warning icon, 5
Web, 337
  e-mail links and, 261
  File Manager and, 252–253
  file transfer, 254

Web *(continued)*
  FTP (File Transfer Protocol), 243, 254
  HTTP sites, 243
  Netscape Navigator, 242
  Online Services, 249–251
  overview, 241
  searches, 246–247
Web Browser folder, File Manager, 175
Web browsers. *See* browsers
  GIMP and, 230
Web pages, 338
Web server, 338
Web sites, 338
  CNET, 314
  Corel Community, 302
  Debian Support, 306
  Freshmeat, 312
  Linux Documentation project, 304
  Tucows, 312
windows, 15, 97–102, 338
  active, 112–113
  arranging, 114, 284
  buttons, 99–100, 150
  closing, 97–102, 114
  color, 158–160
  focus, 149, 284
  iconifying, 287
  keyboard controls, 146–147
  maximizing, 117, 287, 334
  menu bar, 100–101
  minimizing, 334
  mouse, 147–149
  opening, 97–102
  ordering, 150–151
  placement, 117–118
  scroll bars, 101
  sizing, 116–117, 287
  status bar, 102
  sticky, 286
  sticky windows, 78
  terminal, 337
  title bar, 99
  toolbars, 101
Windows, 9–10
  bookmarks, 248
  DOS/Windows partitions, 29
  dual boot machine, 15
  starting, 37
Windows Network folder, 175
Windows Workgroups, 61
  connecting to, 64–65
Windows-only hardware, 18
Winmodems, 59
WINS (Windows Internet Naming Service), 338
wizards, 338
word wrap, 214–215
WordPerfect, 87, 211–212
  brackets, 215
  indents, 214
  launching, 38–39
  selecting text, 215
  tabs, 214
  word wrap, 214–215
  wrapping cursor, 215
WordPerfect for Linux Bible, 301
write protection, folders, 183
WYSIWYG (what you *see* is what you get), 338

• X •

X Window System, 338
Xtns menu, GIMP, 230

• Z •

zip, 338
ZIP files, 206

Notes

Notes

Get Certified!

Corel® Certification Program

Certification in one or more of Corel's world-class applications informs current or prospective employers of your proficiency and helps to enhance your marketability in today's competitive business world.

As a Corel-certified candidate, you will enjoy the following benefits:
- official recognition from Corel
- validation of your proficiency in a specific software application
- a certificate stating your credentials
- Corel product discounts
- use of the Corel® Certification Program logo

If your organization uses WordPerfect® or CorelDRAW®, consider certifying your employees in one or more of these suites' applications, including WordPerfect, Quattro® Pro, Corel® Presentations™, CorelDRAW and Corel PHOTO-PAINT®.

Corel has enhanced its certification program by offering application-simulated exams delivered over the Web using the latest technology. This means that, instead of answering multiple choice questions and memorizing menus, you will be tested within the application and assessed on your ability to perform simulated day-to-day tasks. Each exam consists of 40 to 60 questions and has a suggested retail price of $50 US.

And this coupon now makes certification at any level an excellent value!

To receive your $10 instant discount:
- Fill out this form and present it at a participating Corel® Approved Testing Center* prior to taking a Corel® certification exam
- Offer expires Dec. 31, 2000
- Your voucher must be received by your Corel Approved Testing Center by Jan. 31, 2001
- Limit of one (1) voucher per person per test
- This offer is valid only in the United States and Canada
- This promotion is void where prohibited by law
- This offer cannot be combined with any other promotions
- Discount will be issued in the currency in which the exam was paid for
- Valid at participating Testing Centers only

Please visit www.corel.com/learning for a list of Corel Approved Testing Centers, or for details on the Corel® Certification Program.

Warning: Fraudulent submission could result in federal prosecution under mail fraud statutes (Title 18, United States Code, Sections 1341 and 1342). All trademarks or registered trademarks are the property of their respective corporations.

Please print clearly.

Name:

Address:

City: State/Province:

Zip/Postal code: Tel.:

E-mail:

From time to time, we may provide our customers with information about Corel, its products and services. We may also provide our customer lists to third-party companies that have similar products or services. **If you do not wish to receive any information and do not wish to be placed on our customer lists, please check here.** ☐ Please note that if you are a registered Corel product user and you do not wish to be on our customer list, you will not receive e-mail or other notices regarding Corel's special offers, product upgrades, technical support and other updates.

For more information on Corel's privacy policies, please visit our Web site at www.corel.com or contact us at Customer Service, Corel Corporation, 1600 Carling Ave., Ottawa, Ontario, Canada K1Z 8R7, Attention: Privacy. Tel.: 1-613-728-8200, Fax: 1-613-761-9710.

COREL www.corel.com

COREL® CERTIFICATION PROGRAM

Copyright © 1999 Corel Corporation. All rights reserved. Corel, WordPerfect, CorelDRAW, Quattro, Presentations and Corel PHOTO-PAINT are trademarks or registered trademarks of Corel Corporation or Corel Corporation Limited.

Printed in Canada 10/99 JB#44683

SPECIAL OFFER FOR IDG BOOKS READERS

FREE GIFT!

FREE
IDG Books/PC WORLD CD Wallet
and a Sample Issue of
PC WORLD

THE #1 MONTHLY COMPUTER MAGAZINE

How to order your sample issue and FREE CD Wallet:

- ✉ Cut and mail the coupon today!
- ☎ Call us at 1-800-395-5763
  Fax us at 1-415-882-0936
- ☞ Order online at
  www.pcworld.com/subscribe/idgbooks

ORDER TODAY!

FREE GIFT/SAMPLE ISSUE COUPON

Cut coupon and mail to: PC World, 501 Second Street, San Francisco, CA 94107

YES! Please rush my FREE CD wallet and my FREE sample issue of PC WORLD! If I like PC WORLD, I'll honor your invoice and receive 11 more issues (12 in all) for just $19.97—that's 72% off the newsstand rate.

NO COST EXAMINATION GUARANTEE.
If I decide PC WORLD is not for me, I'll write "cancel" on the invoice and owe nothing. The sample issue and CD wallet are mine to keep, no matter what.

Name _____
Company _____
Address _____
City _____ State _____ Zip _____
Email _____

Offer valid in the U.S. only. Mexican orders please send $39.97 USD. Canadian orders send $39.97, plus 7% GST (#R124669680). Other countries send $65.97. Savings based on annual newsstand rate of $71.88.

PC WORLD

SPECIAL OFFER FOR IDG BOOKS READERS

Get the Most from Your PC!

Every issue of PC World is packed with the latest information to help you make the most of your PC.

- Top 100 PC and Product Ratings
- Hot PC News
- How Tos, Tips, & Tricks
- Buyers' Guides
- Consumer Watch
- Hardware and Software Previews
- Internet & Multimedia Special Reports
- Upgrade Guides
- Monthly @Home Section

YOUR FREE GIFT!

As a special bonus with your order, you will receive the IDG Books/PC WORLD CD wallet, perfect for transporting and protecting your CD collection.

SEND TODAY
for your sample issue and FREE IDG Books/PC WORLD CD Wallet!

How to order your sample issue and FREE CD Wallet:

✉ Cut and mail the coupon today!
Mail to: PC World, 501 Second Street, San Francisco, CA 94107

☎ Call us at 1-800-395-5763
Fax us at 1-415-882-0936

☞ Order online at www.pcworld.com/subscribe/idgbooks

PC WORLD

From PCs to Personal Finance, We Make it Fun and Easy!

PCs FOR DUMMIES, 6TH EDITION
ISBN 0-7645-0435-5
$19.99 US/$28.99 CAN
"More than a publishing phenomenon, 'Dummies' is a sign of the times." — The New York Times
#1 Bestselling Computer Book Series
50 MILLION
A Reference for the Rest of Us!
by Dan Gookin
Get the Information You Really Need The Fun and Easy Way
Your First Aid Kit for Fast Relief and Stunning Results
What to Do When Bad Things Happen — Explained in Plain English

PERSONAL FINANCE FOR DUMMIES, 2ND EDITION
ISBN 0-7645-5013-6
$19.99 US/$26.99 CAN
"Eric Tyson is... helping people of all income levels to take control of their own financial future." — James C. Collins, Coauthor of the Bestseller Built to Last
Completely Updated — USA TODAY & National Bestseller!
Expert Advice on How to Spend Less, Save More, and Invest Smart!
A Reference for the Rest of Us!
by Eric Tyson, Financial Counselor, Syndicated Columnist, and National Bestselling Author
The Fun and Easy Way to Manage Your Money
Your First Aid Kit for Dealing with Money — for All Income Levels
What to Watch out for — Explained in Plain English

For more information, or to order, please call 800.762.2974.

www.idgbooks.com
www.dummies.com

IDG BOOKS WORLDWIDE®
FOR DUMMIES BESTSELLING BOOK SERIES™

The IDG Books Worldwide logo is a registered trademark under exclusive license to IDG Books Worldwide, Inc., from International Data Group, Inc. The ...For Dummies logo and Dummies Books are trademarks, and Dummies Man and ...For Dummies are registered trademarks of IDG Books Worldwide, Inc. All other trademarks are the property of their respective owners.

Dummies Books™ Bestsellers on Every Topic!

TECHNOLOGY TITLES

INTERNET

America Online® For Dummies®, 5th Edition	John Kaufeld	0-7645-0502-5	$19.99 US/$26.99 CAN
E-Mail For Dummies®, 2nd Edition	John R. Levine, Carol Baroudi, Margaret Levine Young, & Arnold Reinhold	0-7645-0131-3	$24.99 US/$34.99 CAN
Genealogy Online For Dummies®	Matthew L. Helm & April Leah Helm	0-7645-0377-4	$24.99 US/$35.99 CAN
Internet Directory For Dummies®, 2nd Edition	Brad Hill	0-7645-0436-3	$24.99 US/$35.99 CAN
The Internet For Dummies®, 6th Edition	John R. Levine, Carol Baroudi, & Margaret Levine Young	0-7645-0506-8	$19.99 US/$28.99 CAN
Investing Online For Dummies®, 2nd Edition	Kathleen Sindell, Ph.D.	0-7645-0509-2	$24.99 US/$35.99 CAN
World Wide Web Searching For Dummies®, 2nd Edition	Brad Hill	0-7645-0264-6	$24.99 US/$34.99 CAN

OPERATING SYSTEMS

DOS For Dummies®, 3rd Edition	Dan Gookin	0-7645-0361-8	$19.99 US/$28.99 CAN
LINUX® For Dummies®, 2nd Edition	John Hall, Craig Witherspoon, & Coletta Witherspoon	0-7645-0421-5	$24.99 US/$35.99 CAN
Mac® OS 8 For Dummies®	Bob LeVitus	0-7645-0271-9	$19.99 US/$26.99 CAN
Small Business Windows® 98 For Dummies®	Stephen Nelson	0-7645-0425-8	$24.99 US/$35.99 CAN
UNIX® For Dummies®, 4th Edition	John R. Levine & Margaret Levine Young	0-7645-0419-3	$19.99 US/$28.99 CAN
Windows® 95 For Dummies®, 2nd Edition	Andy Rathbone	0-7645-0180-1	$19.99 US/$26.99 CAN
Windows® 98 For Dummies®	Andy Rathbone	0-7645-0261-1	$19.99 US/$28.99 CAN

PC/GENERAL COMPUTING

Buying a Computer For Dummies®	Dan Gookin	0-7645-0313-8	$19.99 US/$28.99 CAN
Illustrated Computer Dictionary For Dummies®, 3rd Edition	Dan Gookin & Sandra Hardin Gookin	0-7645-0143-7	$19.99 US/$26.99 CAN
Modems For Dummies®, 3rd Edition	Tina Rathbone	0-7645-0069-4	$19.99 US/$26.99 CAN
Small Business Computing For Dummies®	Brian Underdahl	0-7645-0287-5	$24.99 US/$35.99 CAN
Upgrading & Fixing PCs For Dummies®, 4th Edition	Andy Rathbone	0-7645-0418-5	$19.99 US/$28.99CAN

GENERAL INTEREST TITLES

FOOD & BEVERAGE/ENTERTAINING

Entertaining For Dummies®	Suzanne Williamson with Linda Smith	0-7645-5027-6	$19.99 US/$26.99 CAN
Gourmet Cooking For Dummies®	Charlie Trotter	0-7645-5029-2	$19.99 US/$26.99 CAN
Grilling For Dummies®	Marie Rama & John Mariani	0-7645-5076-4	$19.99 US/$26.99 CAN
Italian Cooking For Dummies®	Cesare Casella & Jack Bishop	0-7645-5098-5	$19.99 US/$26.99 CAN
Wine For Dummies®, 2nd Edition	Ed McCarthy & Mary Ewing-Mulligan	0-7645-5114-0	$19.99 US/$26.99 CAN

SPORTS

Baseball For Dummies®	Joe Morgan with Richard Lally	0-7645-5085-3	$19.99 US/$26.99 CAN
Fly Fishing For Dummies®	Peter Kaminsky	0-7645-5073-X	$19.99 US/$26.99 CAN
Football For Dummies®	Howie Long with John Czarnecki	0-7645-5054-3	$19.99 US/$26.99 CAN
Hockey For Dummies®	John Davidson with John Steinbreder	0-7645-5045-4	$19.99 US/$26.99 CAN
Tennis For Dummies®	Patrick McEnroe with Peter Bodo	0-7645-5087-X	$19.99 US/$26.99 CAN

HOME & GARDEN

Decks & Patios For Dummies®	Robert J. Beckstrom & National Gardening Association	0-7645-5075-6	$16.99 US/$24.99 CAN
Flowering Bulbs For Dummies®	Judy Glattstein & National Gardening Association	0-7645-5103-5	$16.99 US/$24.99 CAN
Home Improvement For Dummies®	Gene & Katie Hamilton & the Editors of HouseNet, Inc.	0-7645-5005-5	$19.99 US/$26.99 CAN
Lawn Care For Dummies®	Lance Walheim & National Gardening Association	0-7645-5077-2	$16.99 US/$24.99 CAN

For more information, or to order, call (800)762-2974

IDG BOOKS WORLDWIDE

FOR DUMMIES BESTSELLING BOOK SERIES™

Dummies Books™ Bestsellers on Every Topic!

TECHNOLOGY TITLES

SUITES

Title	Author	ISBN	Price
Microsoft® Office 2000 For Windows® For Dummies®	Wallace Wang & Roger C. Parker	0-7645-0452-5	$19.99 US/$28.99 CAN
Microsoft® Office 2000 For Windows® For Dummies®, Quick Reference	Doug Lowe & Bjoern Hartsfvang	0-7645-0453-3	$12.99 US/$19.99 CAN
Microsoft® Office 4 For Windows® For Dummies®	Roger C. Parker	1-56884-183-3	$19.95 US/$26.95 CAN
Microsoft® Office 97 For Windows® For Dummies®	Wallace Wang & Roger C. Parker	0-7645-0050-3	$19.99 US/$26.99 CAN
Microsoft® Office 97 For Windows® For Dummies®, Quick Reference	Doug Lowe	0-7645-0062-7	$12.99 US/$17.99 CAN
Microsoft® Office 98 For Macs® For Dummies®	Tom Negrino	0-7645-0229-8	$19.99 US/$28.99 CAN

WORD PROCESSING

Title	Author	ISBN	Price
Word 2000 For Windows® For Dummies®, Quick Reference	Peter Weverka	0-7645-0449-5	$12.99 US/$19.99 CAN
Corel® WordPerfect® 8 For Windows® For Dummies®	Margaret Levine Young, David Kay, & Jordan Young	0-7645-0186-0	$19.99 US/$26.99 CAN
Word 2000 For Windows® For Dummies®	Dan Gookin	0-7645-0448-7	$19.99 US/$28.99 CAN
Word For Windows® 95 For Dummies®	Dan Gookin	1-56884-932-X	$19.99 US/$26.99 CAN
Word 97 For Windows® For Dummies®	Dan Gookin	0-7645-0052-X	$19.99 US/$26.99 CAN
WordPerfect® 6.1 For Windows® For Dummies®, Quick Reference, 2nd Edition	Margaret Levine Young & David Kay	1-56884-966-4	$9.99 US/$12.99 CAN
WordPerfect® 7 For Windows® 95 For Dummies®	Margaret Levine Young & David Kay	1-56884-949-4	$19.99 US/$26.99 CAN
Word Pro® for Windows® 95 For Dummies®	Jim Meade	1-56884-232-5	$19.99 US/$26.99 CAN

SPREADSHEET/FINANCE/PROJECT MANAGEMENT

Title	Author	ISBN	Price
Excel For Windows® 95 For Dummies®	Greg Harvey	1-56884-930-3	$19.99 US/$26.99 CAN
Excel 2000 For Windows® For Dummies®	Greg Harvey	0-7645-0446-0	$19.99 US/$28.99 CAN
Excel 2000 For Windows® For Dummies® Quick Reference	John Walkenbach	0-7645-0447-9	$12.99 US/$19.99 CAN
Microsoft® Money 98 For Dummies®	Peter Weverka	0-7645-0295-6	$24.99 US/$34.99 CAN
Microsoft® Money 99 For Dummies®	Peter Weverka	0-7645-0433-9	$19.99 US/$28.99 CAN
Microsoft® Project 98 For Dummies®	Martin Doucette	0-7645-0321-9	$24.99 US/$34.99 CAN
MORE Excel 97 For Windows® For Dummies®	Greg Harvey	0-7645-0138-0	$22.99 US/$32.99 CAN
Quicken® 98 For Windows® For Dummies®	Stephen L. Nelson	0-7645-0243-3	$19.99 US/$26.99 CAN

GENERAL INTEREST TITLES

EDUCATION & TEST PREPARATION

Title	Author	ISBN	Price
The ACT For Dummies®	Suzee Vlk	1-56884-387-9	$14.99 US/$21.99 CAN
College Financial Aid For Dummies®	Dr. Herm Davis & Joyce Lain Kennedy	0-7645-5049-7	$19.99 US/$26.99 CAN
College Planning For Dummies®, 2nd Edition	Pat Ordovensky	0-7645-5048-9	$19.99 US/$26.99 CAN
Everyday Math For Dummies®	Charles Seiter, Ph.D.	1-56884-248-1	$14.99 US/$22.99 CAN
The GMAT® For Dummies®, 3rd Edition	Suzee Vlk	0-7645-5082-9	$16.99 US/$24.99 CAN
The GRE® For Dummies®, 3rd Edition	Suzee Vlk	0-7645-5083-7	$16.99 US/$24.99 CAN
Politics For Dummies®	Ann DeLaney	1-56884-381-X	$19.99 US/$26.99 CAN
The SAT I For Dummies®, 3rd Edition	Suzee Vlk	0-7645-5044-6	$14.99 US/$21.99 CAN

CAREERS

Title	Author	ISBN	Price
Cover Letters For Dummies®	Joyce Lain Kennedy	1-56884-395-X	$12.99 US/$17.99 CAN
Cool Careers For Dummies®	Marty Nemko, Paul Edwards, & Sarah Edwards	0-7645-5095-0	$16.99 US/$24.99 CAN
Job Hunting For Dummies®	Max Messmer	1-56884-388-7	$16.99 US/$24.99 CAN
Job Interviews For Dummies®	Joyce Lain Kennedy	1-56884-859-5	$12.99 US/$17.99 CAN
Resumes For Dummies®, 2nd Edition	Joyce Lain Kennedy	0-7645-5113-2	$12.99 US/$17.99 CAN

For more information, or to order, call (800)762-2974

IDG BOOKS

Dummies Books™ Bestsellers on Every Topic!

TECHNOLOGY TITLES

WEB DESIGN & PUBLISHING

Title	Author	ISBN	Price
Creating Web Pages For Dummies®, 4th Edition	Bud Smith & Arthur Bebak	0-7645-0504-1	$24.99 US/$34.99 CAN
FrontPage® 98 For Dummies®	Asha Dornfest	0-7645-0270-0	$24.99 US/$34.99 CAN
HTML 4 For Dummies®	Ed Tittel & Stephen Nelson James	0-7645-0331-6	$29.99 US/$42.99 CAN
Java™ For Dummies®, 2nd Edition	Aaron E. Walsh	0-7645-0140-2	$24.99 US/$34.99 CAN
PageMill™ 2 For Dummies®	Deke McClelland & John San Filippo	0-7645-0028-7	$24.99 US/$34.99 CAN

DESKTOP PUBLISHING GRAPHICS/MULTIMEDIA

Title	Author	ISBN	Price
CorelDRAW™ 8 For Dummies®	Deke McClelland	0-7645-0317-0	$19.99 US/$26.99 CAN
Desktop Publishing and Design For Dummies®	Roger C. Parker	1-56884-234-1	$19.99 US/$26.99 CAN
Digital Photography For Dummies®, 2nd Edition	Julie Adair King	0-7645-0431-2	$19.99 US/$28.99 CAN
Microsoft® Publisher 97 For Dummies®	Barry Sosinsky, Christopher Benz & Jim McCarter	0-7645-0148-8	$19.99 US/$26.99 CAN
Microsoft® Publisher 98 For Dummies®	Jim McCarter	0-7645-0395-2	$19.99 US/$28.99 CAN

MACINTOSH

Title	Author	ISBN	Price
Macs® For Dummies®, 6th Edition	David Pogue	0-7645-0398-7	$19.99 US/$28.99 CAN
Macs® For Teachers™, 3rd Edition	Michelle Robinette	0-7645-0226-3	$24.99 US/$34.99 CAN
The iMac For Dummies	David Pogue	0-7645-0495-9	$19.99 US/$26.99 CAN

GENERAL INTEREST TITLES

BUSINESS & PERSONAL FINANCE

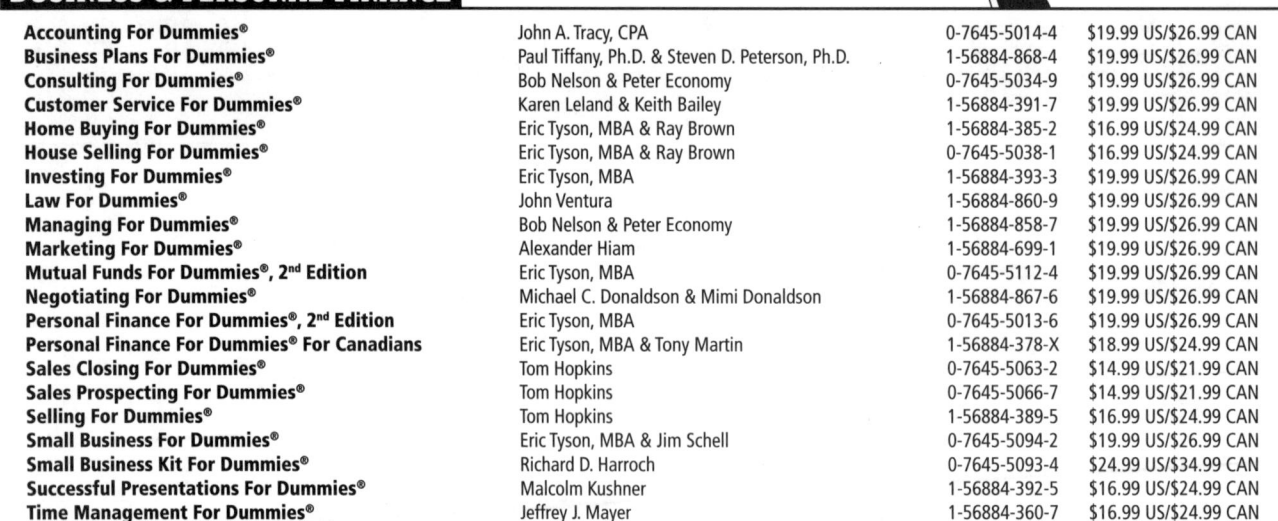

Title	Author	ISBN	Price
Accounting For Dummies®	John A. Tracy, CPA	0-7645-5014-4	$19.99 US/$26.99 CAN
Business Plans For Dummies®	Paul Tiffany, Ph.D. & Steven D. Peterson, Ph.D.	1-56884-868-4	$19.99 US/$26.99 CAN
Consulting For Dummies®	Bob Nelson & Peter Economy	0-7645-5034-9	$19.99 US/$26.99 CAN
Customer Service For Dummies®	Karen Leland & Keith Bailey	1-56884-391-7	$19.99 US/$26.99 CAN
Home Buying For Dummies®	Eric Tyson, MBA & Ray Brown	1-56884-385-2	$16.99 US/$24.99 CAN
House Selling For Dummies®	Eric Tyson, MBA & Ray Brown	0-7645-5038-1	$16.99 US/$24.99 CAN
Investing For Dummies®	Eric Tyson, MBA	1-56884-393-3	$19.99 US/$26.99 CAN
Law For Dummies®	John Ventura	1-56884-860-9	$19.99 US/$26.99 CAN
Managing For Dummies®	Bob Nelson & Peter Economy	1-56884-858-7	$19.99 US/$26.99 CAN
Marketing For Dummies®	Alexander Hiam	1-56884-699-1	$19.99 US/$26.99 CAN
Mutual Funds For Dummies®, 2nd Edition	Eric Tyson, MBA	0-7645-5112-4	$19.99 US/$26.99 CAN
Negotiating For Dummies®	Michael C. Donaldson & Mimi Donaldson	1-56884-867-6	$19.99 US/$26.99 CAN
Personal Finance For Dummies®, 2nd Edition	Eric Tyson, MBA	0-7645-5013-6	$19.99 US/$26.99 CAN
Personal Finance For Dummies® For Canadians	Eric Tyson, MBA & Tony Martin	1-56884-378-X	$18.99 US/$24.99 CAN
Sales Closing For Dummies®	Tom Hopkins	0-7645-5063-2	$14.99 US/$21.99 CAN
Sales Prospecting For Dummies®	Tom Hopkins	0-7645-5066-7	$14.99 US/$21.99 CAN
Selling For Dummies®	Tom Hopkins	1-56884-389-5	$16.99 US/$24.99 CAN
Small Business For Dummies®	Eric Tyson, MBA & Jim Schell	0-7645-5094-2	$19.99 US/$26.99 CAN
Small Business Kit For Dummies®	Richard D. Harroch	0-7645-5093-4	$24.99 US/$34.99 CAN
Successful Presentations For Dummies®	Malcolm Kushner	1-56884-392-5	$16.99 US/$24.99 CAN
Time Management For Dummies®	Jeffrey J. Mayer	1-56884-360-7	$16.99 US/$24.99 CAN

AUTOMOTIVE

Title	Author	ISBN	Price
Auto Repair For Dummies®	Deanna Sclar	0-7645-5089-6	$19.99 US/$26.99 CAN
Buying A Car For Dummies®	Deanna Sclar	0-7645-5091-8	$16.99 US/$24.99 CAN
Car Care For Dummies®: The Glove Compartment Guide	Deanna Sclar	0-7645-5090-X	$9.99 US/$13.99 CAN

For more information, or to order, call (800)762-2974

IDG BOOKS

FOR DUMMIES
BESTSELLING BOOK SERIES

Dummies Books™ Bestsellers on Every Topic!

TECHNOLOGY TITLES

DATABASE

Title	Author	ISBN	Price
Access 2000 For Windows® For Dummies®	John Kaufeld	0-7645-0444-4	$19.99 US/$28.99 CAN
Access 97 For Windows® For Dummies®	John Kaufeld	0-7645-0048-1	$19.99 US/$26.99 CAN
Approach® 97 For Windows® For Dummies®	Deborah S. Ray & Eric J. Ray	0-7645-0001-5	$19.99 US/$26.99 CAN
Crystal Reports 7 For Dummies®	Douglas J. Wolf	0-7645-0548-3	$24.99 US/$34.99 CAN
Data Warehousing For Dummies®	Alan R. Simon	0-7645-0170-4	$24.99 US/$34.99 CAN
FileMaker® Pro 4 For Dummies®	Tom Maremaa	0-7645-0210-7	$19.99 US/$26.99 CAN
Intranet & Web Databases For Dummies®	Paul Litwin	0-7645-0221-2	$29.99 US/$42.99 CAN

NETWORKING

Title	Author	ISBN	Price
Building An Intranet For Dummies®	John Fronckowiak	0-7645-0276-X	$29.99 US/$42.99 CAN
cc: Mail™ For Dummies®	Victor R. Garza	0-7645-0055-4	$19.99 US/$26.99 CAN
Client/Server Computing For Dummies®, 2nd Edition	Doug Lowe	0-7645-0066-X	$24.99 US/$34.99 CAN
Lotus Notes® Release 4 For Dummies®	Stephen Londergan & Pat Freeland	1-56884-934-6	$19.99 US/$26.99 CAN
Networking For Dummies®, 4th Edition	Doug Lowe	0-7645-0498-3	$19.99 US/$28.99 CAN
Upgrading & Fixing Networks For Dummies®	Bill Camarda	0-7645-0347-2	$29.99 US/$42.99 CAN
Windows NT® Networking For Dummies®	Ed Tittel, Mary Madden, & Earl Follis	0-7645-0015-5	$24.99 US/$34.99 CAN

GENERAL INTEREST TITLES

THE ARTS

Title	Author	ISBN	Price
Blues For Dummies®	Lonnie Brooks, Cub Koda, & Wayne Baker Brooks	0-7645-5080-2	$24.99 US/$34.99 CAN
Classical Music For Dummies®	David Pogue & Scott Speck	0-7645-5009-8	$24.99 US/$34.99 CAN
Guitar For Dummies®	Mark Phillips & Jon Chappell of Cherry Lane Music	0-7645-5106-X	$24.99 US/$34.99 CAN
Jazz For Dummies®	Dirk Sutro	0-7645-5081-0	$24.99 US/$34.99 CAN
Opera For Dummies®	David Pogue & Scott Speck	0-7645-5010-1	$24.99 US/$34.99 CAN
Piano For Dummies®	Blake Neely of Cherry Lane Music	0-7645-5105-1	$24.99 US/$34.99 CAN

HEALTH & FITNESS

Title	Author	ISBN	Price
Beauty Secrets For Dummies®	Stephanie Seymour	0-7645-5078-0	$19.99 US/$26.99 CAN
Fitness For Dummies®	Suzanne Schlosberg & Liz Neporent, M.A.	1-56884-866-8	$19.99 US/$26.99 CAN
Nutrition For Dummies®	Carol Ann Rinzler	0-7645-5032-2	$19.99 US/$26.99 CAN
Sex For Dummies®	Dr. Ruth K. Westheimer	1-56884-384-4	$16.99 US/$24.99 CAN
Weight Training For Dummies®	Liz Neporent, M.A. & Suzanne Schlosberg	0-7645-5036-5	$19.99 US/$26.99 CAN

LIFESTYLE/SELF-HELP

Title	Author	ISBN	Price
Dating For Dummies®	Dr. Joy Browne	0-7645-5072-1	$19.99 US/$26.99 CAN
Parenting For Dummies®	Sandra H. Gookin	1-56884-383-6	$16.99 US/$24.99 CAN
Success For Dummies®	Zig Ziglar	0-7645-5061-6	$19.99 US/$26.99 CAN
Weddings For Dummies®	Marcy Blum & Laura Fisher Kaiser	0-7645-5055-1	$19.99 US/$26.99 CAN

For more information, or to order, call (800)762-2974

IDG BOOKS WORLDWIDE

FOR DUMMIES™ BESTSELLING BOOK SERIES

Not all software on the CD is governed by the license; see the CD for more info.

IDG Books Worldwide, Inc., End-User License Agreement

READ THIS. You should carefully read these terms and conditions before opening the software packet(s) included with this book ("Book"). This is a license agreement ("Agreement") between you and IDG Books Worldwide, Inc. ("IDGB"). By opening the accompanying software packet(s), you acknowledge that you have read and accept the following terms and conditions. If you do not agree and do not want to be bound by such terms and conditions, promptly return the Book and the unopened software packet(s) to the place you obtained them for a full refund.

1. **License Grant.** IDGB grants to you (either an individual or entity) a nonexclusive license to use one copy of the enclosed software program(s) (collectively, the "Software") solely for your own personal or business purposes on a single computer (whether a standard computer or a workstation component of a multiuser network). The Software is in use on a computer when it is loaded into temporary memory (RAM) or installed into permanent memory (hard disk, CD-ROM, or other storage device). IDGB reserves all rights not expressly granted herein.

2. **Ownership.** IDGB is the owner of all right, title, and interest, including copyright, in and to the compilation of the Software recorded on the disk(s) or CD-ROM ("Software Media"). Copyright to the individual programs recorded on the Software Media is owned by the author or other authorized copyright owner of each program. Ownership of the Software and all proprietary rights relating thereto remain with IDGB and its licensers.

3. **Restrictions on Use and Transfer.**

    (a) You may only (i) make one copy of the Software for backup or archival purposes, or (ii) transfer the Software to a single hard disk, provided that you keep the original for backup or archival purposes. You may not (i) rent or lease the Software, (ii) copy or reproduce the Software through a LAN or other network system or through any computer subscriber system or bulletin-board system, or (iii) modify, adapt, or create derivative works based on the Software.

    (b) You may not reverse engineer, decompile, or disassemble the Software. You may transfer the Software and user documentation on a permanent basis, provided that the transferee agrees to accept the terms and conditions of this Agreement and you retain no copies. If the Software is an update or has been updated, any transfer must include the most recent update and all prior versions.

4. **Restrictions on Use of Individual Programs.** You must follow the individual requirements and restrictions detailed for each individual program in Appendix C of this Book. These limitations are also contained in the individual license agreements recorded on the Software Media. These limitations may include a requirement that after using the program for a specified period of time, the user must pay a registration fee or discontinue use. By opening the Software packet(s), you will be agreeing to abide by the licenses and restrictions for these individual programs that are detailed in Appendix C and on the Software Media. None of the material on this Software Media or listed in this Book may ever be redistributed, in original or modified form, for commercial purposes.

5. **Limited Warranty.**

    (a) IDGB warrants that the Software and Software Media are free from defects in materials and workmanship under normal use for a period of sixty (60) days from the date of purchase of this Book. If IDGB receives notification within the warranty period of defects in materials or workmanship, IDGB will replace the defective Software Media.

    (b) IDGB AND THE AUTHOR OF THE BOOK DISCLAIM ALL OTHER WARRANTIES, EXPRESS OR IMPLIED, INCLUDING WITHOUT LIMITATION IMPLIED WARRANTIES OF MERCHANTABILITY AND FITNESS FOR A PARTICULAR PURPOSE, WITH RESPECT TO THE SOFTWARE, THE PROGRAMS, THE SOURCE CODE CONTAINED THEREIN, AND/OR THE TECHNIQUES DESCRIBED IN THIS BOOK. IDGB DOES NOT WARRANT THAT THE FUNCTIONS CONTAINED IN THE SOFTWARE WILL MEET YOUR REQUIREMENTS OR THAT THE OPERATION OF THE SOFTWARE WILL BE ERROR FREE.

    (c) This limited warranty gives you specific legal rights, and you may have other rights that vary from jurisdiction to jurisdiction.

6. **Remedies.**

    (a) IDGB's entire liability and your exclusive remedy for defects in materials and workmanship shall be limited to replacement of the Software Media, which may be returned to IDGB with a copy of your receipt at the following address: Software Media Fulfillment Department, Attn.: *Genealogy Online For Dummies,* 2nd Edition, IDG Books Worldwide, Inc., 10475 Crosspoint Boulevard, Indianapolis, IN 46256, or call 800-762-2974. Please allow three to four weeks for delivery. This Limited Warranty is void if failure of the Software Media has resulted from accident, abuse, or misapplication. Any replacement Software Media will be warranted for the remainder of the original warranty period or thirty (30) days, whichever is longer.

    (b) In no event shall IDGB or the author be liable for any damages whatsoever (including without limitation damages for loss of business profits, business interruption, loss of business information, or any other pecuniary loss) arising from the use of or inability to use the Book or the Software, even if IDGB has been advised of the possibility of such damages.

    (c) Because some jurisdictions do not allow the exclusion or limitation of liability for consequential or incidental damages, the above limitation or exclusion may not apply to you.

7. **U.S. Government Restricted Rights.** Use, duplication, or disclosure of the Software by the U.S. Government is subject to restrictions stated in paragraph (c)(1)(ii) of the Rights in Technical Data and Computer Software clause of DFARS 252.227-7013, and in subparagraphs (a) through (d) of the Commercial Computer–Restricted Rights clause at FAR 52.227-19, and in similar clauses in the NASA FAR supplement, when applicable.

8. **General.** This Agreement constitutes the entire understanding of the parties and revokes and supersedes all prior agreements, oral or written, between them and may not be modified or amended except in a writing signed by both parties hereto that specifically refers to this Agreement. This Agreement shall take precedence over any other documents that may be in conflict herewith. If any one or more provisions contained in this Agreement are held by any court or tribunal to be invalid, illegal, or otherwise unenforceable, each and every other provision shall remain in full force and effect.

[more information available at http://www.gnu.org/copyleft/gpl.html]

GNU GENERAL PUBLIC LICENSE

Version 2, June 1991
Copyright © 1989, 1991 Free Software Foundation, Inc.
59 Temple Place - Suite 330, Boston, MA 02111-1307, USA

 Everyone is permitted to copy and distribute verbatim copies of this license document, but changing it is not allowed.

Preamble

The licenses for most software are designed to take away your freedom to share and change it. By contrast, the GNU General Public License is intended to guarantee your freedom to share and change free software—to make sure the software is free for all its users. This General Public License applies to most of the Free Software Foundation's software and to any other program whose authors commit to using it. (Some other Free Software Foundation software is covered by the GNU Library General Public License instead.) You can apply it to your programs, too.

When we speak of free software, we are referring to freedom, not price. Our General Public Licenses are designed to make sure that you have the freedom to distribute copies of free software (and charge for this service if you wish), that you receive source code or can get it if you want it, that you can change the software or use pieces of it in new free programs, and that you know you can do these things.

To protect your rights, we need to make restrictions that forbid anyone to deny you these rights or to ask you to surrender the rights. These restrictions translate to certain responsibilities for you if you distribute copies of the software, or if you modify it.

For example, if you distribute copies of such a program, whether gratis or for a fee, you must give the recipients all the rights that you have. You must make sure that they, too, receive or can get the source code. And you must show them these terms so they know their rights.

We protect your rights with two steps: (1) copyright the software, and (2) offer you this license which gives you legal permission to copy, distribute, and/or modify the software.

Also, for each author's protection and ours, we want to make certain that everyone understands that there is no warranty for this free software. If the software is modified by someone else and passed on, we want its recipients to know that what they have is not the original, so that any problems introduced by others will not reflect on the original authors' reputations.

Finally, any free program is threatened constantly by software patents. We wish to avoid the danger that redistributors of a free program will individually obtain patent licenses, in effect making the program proprietary. To prevent this, we have made it clear that any patent must be licensed for everyone's free use or not licensed at all.

The precise terms and conditions for copying, distribution, and modification follow.

TERMS AND CONDITIONS FOR COPYING, DISTRIBUTION, AND MODIFICATION

0. This License applies to any program or other work which contains a notice placed by the copyright holder saying it may be distributed under the terms of this General Public License. The "Program," below, refers to any such program or work, and a "work based on the Program" means either the Program or any derivative work under copyright law: that is to say, a work containing the Program or a portion of it, either verbatim or with modifications and/or translated into another language. (Hereinafter, translation is included without limitation in the term "modification".) Each licensee is addressed as "you."

Activities other than copying, distribution, and modification are not covered by this License; they are outside its scope. The act of running the Program is not restricted, and the output from the Program is covered only if its contents constitute a work based on the Program (independent of having been made by running the Program). Whether that is true depends on what the Program does.

1. You may copy and distribute verbatim copies of the Program's source code as you receive it, in any medium, provided that you conspicuously and appropriately publish on each copy an appropriate copyright notice and disclaimer of warranty; keep intact all the notices that refer to this License and to the absence of any warranty; and give any other recipients of the Program a copy of this License along with the Program.

You may charge a fee for the physical act of transferring a copy, and you may at your option offer warranty protection in exchange for a fee.

2. You may modify your copy or copies of the Program or any portion of it, thus forming a work based on the Program, and copy and distribute such modifications or work under the terms of Section 1 above, provided that you also meet all of these conditions:

   a) You must cause the modified files to carry prominent notices stating that you changed the files and the date of any change.

   b) You must cause any work that you distribute or publish, that in whole or in part contains or is derived from the Program or any part thereof, to be licensed as a whole at no charge to all third parties under the terms of this License.

   c) If the modified program normally reads commands interactively when run, you must cause it, when started running for such interactive use in the most ordinary way, to print or display an announcement including an appropriate copyright notice and a notice that there is no warranty (or else, saying that you provide a warranty) and that users may redistribute the program under these conditions, and telling the user how to view a copy of this License. (Exception: if the Program itself is interactive but does not normally print such an announcement, your work based on the Program is not required to print an announcement.)

These requirements apply to the modified work as a whole. If identifiable sections of that work are not derived from the Program, and can be reasonably considered independent and separate works in themselves, then this License, and its terms, do not apply to those sections when you distribute them as separate works. But when you distribute the same sections as part of a whole which is a work based on the Program, the distribution of the whole must be on the terms of this License, whose permissions for other licensees extend to the entire whole, and thus to each and every part regardless of who wrote it.

Thus, it is not the intent of this section to claim rights or contest your rights to work written entirely by you; rather, the intent is to exercise the right to control the distribution of derivative or collective works based on the Program. In addition, mere aggregation of another work not based on the Program with the Program (or with a work based on the Program) on a volume of a storage or distribution medium does not bring the other work under the scope of this License.

3. You may copy and distribute the Program (or a work based on it, under Section 2) in object code or executable form under the terms of Sections 1 and 2 above provided that you also do one of the following:

   a) Accompany it with the complete corresponding machine-readable source code, which must be distributed under the terms of Sections 1 and 2 above on a medium customarily used for software interchange; or,

   b) Accompany it with a written offer, valid for at least three years, to give any third party, for a charge no more than your cost of physically performing source distribution, a complete machine-readable copy of the corresponding source code, to be distributed under the terms of Sections 1 and 2 above on a medium customarily used for software interchange; or,

   c) Accompany it with the information you received as to the offer to distribute corresponding source code. (This alternative is allowed only for noncommercial distribution and only if you received the program in object code or executable form with such an offer, in accord with Subsection b above.)

   The source code for a work means the preferred form of the work for making modifications to it. For an executable work, complete source code means all the source code for all modules it contains, plus any associated interface definition files, plus the scripts used to control compilation and installation of the executable. However, as a special exception, the source code distributed need not include anything that is normally distributed (in either source or binary form) with the major components (compiler, kernel, and so on) of the operating system on which the executable runs, unless that component itself accompanies the executable.

   If distribution of executable or object code is made by offering access to copy from a designated place, then offering equivalent access to copy the source code from the same place counts as distribution of the source code, even though third parties are not compelled to copy the source along with the object code.

4. You may not copy, modify, sublicense, or distribute the Program except as expressly provided under this License. Any attempt otherwise to copy, modify, sublicense or distribute the Program is void, and will automatically terminate your rights under this License. However, parties who have received copies, or rights, from you under this License will not have their licenses terminated so long as such parties remain in full compliance.

5. You are not required to accept this License, since you have not signed it. However, nothing else grants you permission to modify or distribute the Program or its derivative works. These actions are prohibited by law if you do not accept this License. Therefore, by modifying or distributing the Program (or any work based on the Program), you indicate your acceptance of this License to do so, and all its terms and conditions for copying, distributing or modifying the Program or works based on it.

6. Each time you redistribute the Program (or any work based on the Program), the recipient automatically receives a license from the original licensor to copy, distribute or modify the Program subject to these terms and conditions. You may not impose any further restrictions on the recipients' exercise of the rights granted herein. You are not responsible for enforcing compliance by third parties to this License.

7. If, as a consequence of a court judgment or allegation of patent infringement or for any other reason (not limited to patent issues), conditions are imposed on you (whether by court order, agreement or otherwise) that contradict the conditions of this License, they do not excuse you from the conditions of this License. If you cannot distribute so as to satisfy simultaneously your obligations under this License and any other pertinent obligations, then as a consequence you may not distribute the Program at all. For example, if a patent license would not permit royalty-free redistribution of the Program by all those who receive copies directly or indirectly through you, then the only way you could satisfy both it and this License would be to refrain entirely from distribution of the Program.

    If any portion of this section is held invalid or unenforceable under any particular circumstance, the balance of the section is intended to apply and the section as a whole is intended to apply in other circumstances.

    It is not the purpose of this section to induce you to infringe any patents or other property right claims or to contest validity of any such claims; this section has the sole purpose of protecting the integrity of the free software distribution system, which is implemented by public license practices. Many people have made generous contributions to the wide range of software distributed through that system in reliance on consistent application of that system; it is up to the author/donor to decide if he or she is willing to distribute software through any other system and a licensee cannot impose that choice.

    This section is intended to make thoroughly clear what is believed to be a consequence of the rest of this License.

8. If the distribution and/or use of the Program is restricted in certain countries either by patents or by copyrighted interfaces, the original copyright holder who places the Program under this License may add an explicit geographical distribution limitation excluding those countries, so that distribution is permitted only in or among countries not thus excluded. In such case, this License incorporates the limitation as if written in the body of this License.

9. The Free Software Foundation may publish revised and/or new versions of the General Public License from time to time. Such new versions will be similar in spirit to the present version, but may differ in detail to address new problems or concerns.

    Each version is given a distinguishing version number. If the Program specifies a version number of this License which applies to it and "any later version", you have the option of following the terms and conditions either of that version or of any later version published by the Free Software Foundation. If the Program does not specify a version number of this License, you may choose any version ever published by the Free Software Foundation.

10. If you wish to incorporate parts of the Program into other free programs whose distribution conditions are different, write to the author to ask for permission. For software that is copyrighted by the Free Software Foundation, write to the Free Software Foundation; we sometimes make exceptions for this. Our decision will be guided by the two goals of preserving the free status of all derivatives of our free software and of promoting the sharing and reuse of software generally.

NO WARRANTY

11. BECAUSE THE PROGRAM IS LICENSED FREE OF CHARGE, THERE IS NO WARRANTY FOR THE PROGRAM, TO THE EXTENT PERMITTED BY APPLICABLE LAW. EXCEPT WHEN OTHERWISE STATED IN WRITING THE COPYRIGHT HOLDERS AND/OR OTHER PARTIES PROVIDE THE PROGRAM "AS IS" WITHOUT WARRANTY OF ANY KIND, EITHER EXPRESSED OR IMPLIED, INCLUDING, BUT NOT LIMITED TO, THE IMPLIED WARRANTIES OF MERCHANTABILITY AND FITNESS FOR A PARTICULAR PURPOSE. THE ENTIRE RISK AS TO THE QUALITY AND PERFORMANCE OF THE PROGRAM IS WITH YOU. SHOULD THE PROGRAM PROVE DEFECTIVE, YOU ASSUME THE COST OF ALL NECESSARY SERVICING, REPAIR OR CORRECTION.

12. IN NO EVENT UNLESS REQUIRED BY APPLICABLE LAW OR AGREED TO IN WRITING WILL ANY COPYRIGHT HOLDER, OR ANY OTHER PARTY WHO MAY MODIFY AND/OR REDISTRIBUTE THE PROGRAM AS PERMITTED ABOVE, BE LIABLE TO YOU FOR DAMAGES, INCLUDING ANY GENERAL, SPECIAL, INCIDENTAL OR CONSEQUENTIAL DAMAGES ARISING OUT OF THE USE OR INABILITY TO USE THE PROGRAM (INCLUDING BUT NOT LIMITED TO LOSS OF DATA OR DATA BEING RENDERED INACCURATE OR LOSSES SUSTAINED BY YOU OR THIRD PARTIES OR A FAILURE OF THE PROGRAM TO OPERATE WITH ANY OTHER PROGRAMS), EVEN IF SUCH HOLDER OR OTHER PARTY HAS BEEN ADVISED OF THE POSSIBILITY OF SUCH DAMAGES.

END OF TERMS AND CONDITIONS

Installation Instructions

Your *Corel Linux For Dummies* CD contains the complete desktop environment described in this book.

First and foremost is the Download Edition of Corel Linux, which includes the following:

- The top-quality, Debian-based operating system
- An enhanced KDE desktop
- Corel Install Express
- Corel File Manager
- Corel Update Package Manager

On top of that, you get:

- Adobe Acrobat Reader
- Netscape Communicator suite
- A bonus collection of more than 100 dazzling desktop themes

Amazing what you get for free these days. Just buy this book and you're all set!

You want the installation instructions promised by the heading? Fooled you! Here's where they are:

- Chapter 2 has detailed instructions on installing Corel Linux.
- Appendix C provides instructions on installing Acrobat, Netscape Communicator, and the bonus desktop themes.

Enjoy the software, and enjoy this book!

WWW.DUMMIES.COM

Discover Dummies Online!

The Dummies Web Site is your fun and friendly online resource for the latest information about *For Dummies*® books and your favorite topics. The Web site is the place to communicate with us, exchange ideas with other *For Dummies* readers, chat with authors, and have fun!

Ten Fun and Useful Things You Can Do at www.dummies.com

1. Win free *For Dummies* books and more!
2. Register your book and be entered in a prize drawing.
3. Meet your favorite authors through the IDG Books Worldwide Author Chat Series.
4. Exchange helpful information with other *For Dummies* readers.
5. Discover other great *For Dummies* books you must have!
6. Purchase Dummieswear® exclusively from our Web site.
7. Buy *For Dummies* books online.
8. Talk to us. Make comments, ask questions, get answers!
9. Download free software.
10. Find additional useful resources from authors.

Link directly to these ten fun and useful things at
http://www.dummies.com/10useful

For other technology titles from IDG Books Worldwide, go to www.idgbooks.com

Not on the Web yet? It's easy to get started with *Dummies 101*®: *The Internet For Windows*® *98* or *The Internet For Dummies*® at local retailers everywhere.

Find other *For Dummies* books on these topics:
Business • Career • Databases • Food & Beverage • Games • Gardening • Graphics • Hardware
Health & Fitness • Internet and the World Wide Web • Networking • Office Suites
Operating Systems • Personal Finance • Pets • Programming • Recreation • Sports
Spreadsheets • Teacher Resources • Test Prep • Word Processing

The IDG Books Worldwide logo is a registered trademark under exclusive license to IDG Books Worldwide, Inc., from International Data Group, Inc. Dummies.com and the ...For Dummies logo are trademarks, and Dummies Man, For Dummies, Dummieswear, and Dummies 101 are registered trademarks of IDG Books Worldwide, Inc. All other trademarks are the property of their respective owners.

IDG BOOKS WORLDWIDE BOOK REGISTRATION

Register This Book and Win!

We want to hear from you!

Visit **http://my2cents.dummies.com** to register this book and tell us how you liked it!

- Get entered in our monthly prize giveaway.
- Give us feedback about this book — tell us what you like best, what you like least, or maybe what you'd like to ask the author and us to change!
- Let us know any other *For Dummies* topics that interest you.

Your feedback helps us determine what books to publish, tells us what coverage to add as we revise our books, and lets us know whether we're meeting your needs as a *For Dummies* reader. You're our most valuable resource, and what you have to say is important to us!

Not on the Web yet? It's easy to get started with *Dummies 101: The Internet For Windows 98* or *The Internet For Dummies* at local retailers everywhere.

Or let us know what you think by sending us a letter at the following address:

For Dummies Book Registration
Dummies Press
10475 Crosspoint Blvd.
Indianapolis, IN 46256

...For Dummies™
BESTSELLING BOOK SERIES

Corel® Linux® For Dummies®

Cheat Sheet

Helpful Hints

- Use multiple desktops to arrange your tasks, putting WordPerfect in Desktop #1, Netscape in Desktop #2, and so on. If you haven't used Linux before, you're going to love this feature!
- Iconify the windows you're not using to clear your desk for the stuff you're working on. Click a window's task button on the panel to make the window disappear or to bring it back.
- Double-click the title bar to alternately shade (roll up) and unshade (unroll) the window.
- Right-click pretty much anywhere to pop up a context-sensitive menu of things to do. If in doubt, right-click!
- Whenever possible, log in under your regular user name, not as root. It's easy for root to mess up system files.
- For a program that you use a lot, right-click its title bar and then choose Create Nickname. After that, you can click the nickname on the desktop whenever you want to launch the program.
- Autohide your panel to tuck it discretely out of view. Right-click a blank spot in the panel, choose Configure, click the Options tab, and then choose Auto hide panel.
- Press Ctrl+Esc to display a scrollable list of all the windows on all your desktops.

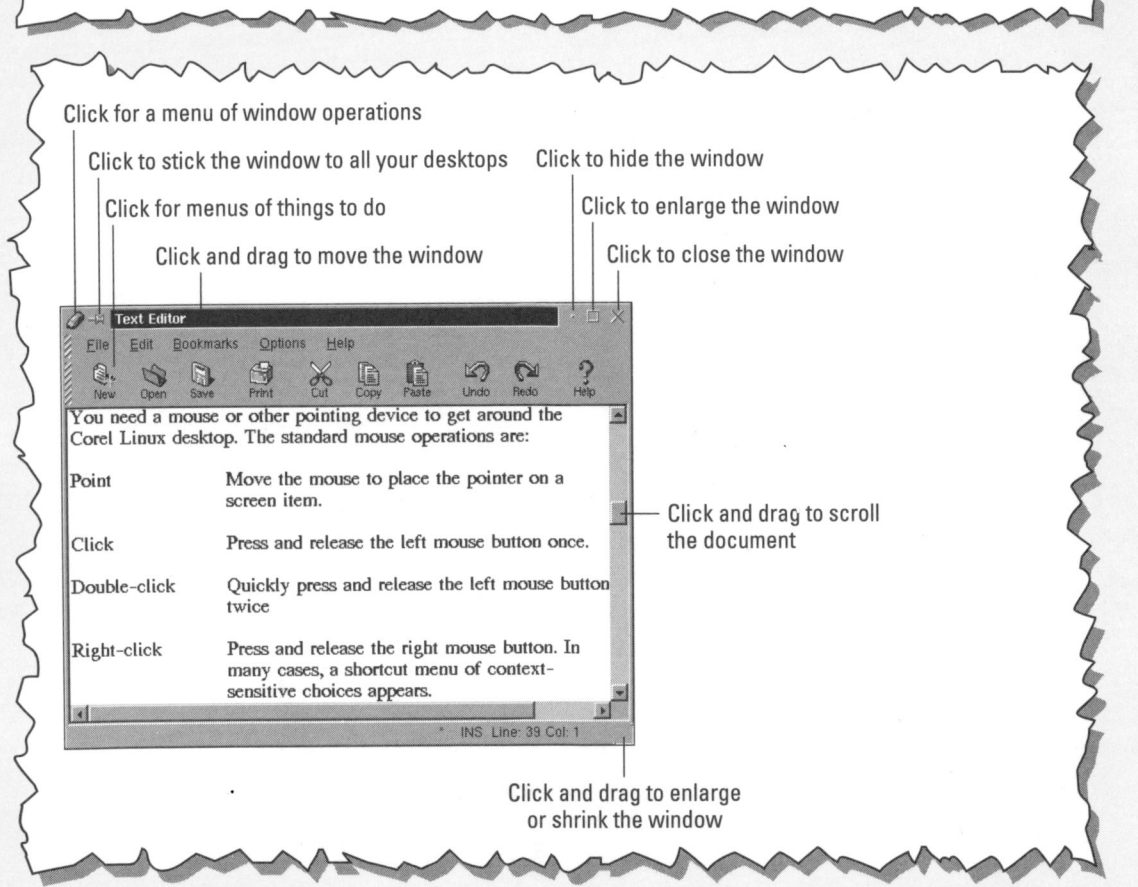

Click for a menu of window operations

Click to stick the window to all your desktops

Click for menus of things to do

Click and drag to move the window

Click to hide the window

Click to enlarge the window

Click to close the window

Click and drag to scroll the document

Click and drag to enlarge or shrink the window

For Dummies®: Bestselling Book Series for Beginners

Corel® Linux® For Dummies®

Cheat Sheet

Handy-Dandy Desktop Keystrokes

Keystroke	Does This Trick
Ctrl+Tab	Switches desktops; hold the Ctrl key and keep pressing Tab until you arrive at the desktop you want
Ctrl+F1–Ctrl+F8	Switches to Desktop #1–Desktop #8
Alt+Tab	Switches between active applications; hold Alt and press Tab until you arrive at the one you want
Alt+F1	Pops up the program menu; you can then search the menus by using the arrow keys and press Enter to run the highlighted program
Alt+F2	Enables you to type a Linux command
Alt+F3	Displays a menu of window operations
Alt+F4	Closes the current window
Alt+F7	Enables you to move the window by using the arrow keys
Alt+F8	Enables you to resize the window by using the arrow keys
Alt+F9	Makes the current window an icon
Alt+F10	Maximizes or restores the current window
Ctrl+Esc	Displays the list of tasks you can switch to
Ctrl+Alt+Esc	Immediately closes the next window you click, without prompting you to save your latest changes

Keystroke Operations in a Window

Keystroke	Operation
Ctrl+W	Close
Ctrl+C	Cut
Ctrl+X	Copy
Ctrl+End	End
Ctrl+F	Find
F1	Help
Ctrl+Home	Home
Ctrl+Insert	Insert
Ctrl+N	New
Page Down	Next
Ctrl+O	Open
Ctrl+V	Paste
Ctrl+P	Print
Page Up	Prior
Ctrl+Q	Quit
Ctrl+R	Replace
Ctrl+S	Save
Ctrl+Z	Undo

Linux Commands to Use in a Pinch

ls	List files	mkdir	Create a directory	more	View a file one screen at a time
cd	Change directories	rmdir	Remove a directory	lpr	Print files
cp	Copy files	pwd	Display the working directory	find	Find files
mv	Move or rename files	cat	View a file	grep	Find text
rm	Delete files				

Copyright © 2000 IDG Books Worldwide, Inc. All rights reserved.
Cheat Sheet $2.95 value. Item 0667-6.
For more information about IDG Books, call 1-800-762-2974.

The IDG Books Worldwide logo is a registered trademark under exclusive license to IDG Books Worldwide, Inc., from International Data Group, Inc. The ...For Dummies logo is a trademark, and For Dummies is a registered trademark of IDG Books Worldwide, Inc. All other trademarks are the property of their respective owners.

For Dummies®: Bestselling Book Series for Beginners